Phantom D

CW01464362

Phantom Democracy

Corporate Interests and Political Power in America

Carl Boggs

palgrave
macmillan

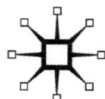

PHANTOM DEMOCRACY
Copyright © Carl Boggs, 2011.
Softcover reprint of the hardcover 1st edition 2011 978-0-230-11574-3
All rights reserved.

First published in 2011 by
PALGRAVE MACMILLAN®
in the United States—a division of St. Martin's Press LLC,
175 Fifth Avenue, New York, NY 10010.

Where this book is distributed in the UK, Europe and the rest of the world,
this is by Palgrave Macmillan, a division of Macmillan Publishers Limited,
registered in England, company number 785998, of Houndmills,
Basingstoke, Hampshire RG21 6XS.

Palgrave Macmillan is the global academic imprint of the above companies
and has companies and representatives throughout the world.

Palgrave® and Macmillan® are registered trademarks in the United States,
the United Kingdom, Europe and other countries.

ISBN 978-1-349-29676-7   ISBN 978-0-230-12010-5 (eBook)
DOI 10.1057/9780230120105

Library of Congress Cataloging-in-Publication Data

Boggs, Carl.
    Phantom democracy : corporate interests and political power in
    America / by Carl E. Boggs.
        p. cm.

        1. Business and politics—United States. 2. Corporate power—
    United States. I. Title.

JK467.B64 2011
322'.30973—dc22   2011005476

A catalogue record of the book is available from the British Library.

Design by Newgen Imaging Systems (P) Ltd., Chennai, India.

First edition: August 2011

Contents

Preface   vii

Introduction   1

1 From Manifest Destiny to Empire   25
   The Founders: Oligarchy and Racism   25
   Conquest and Exterminism   30
   From Warfare to Empire   34
   The Postwar Leviathan   39
   Empire versus Democracy   47

2 The Imperial Labyrinth   57
   The Ideology of Global Domination   58
   Warrior Politics   66
   Subverting Internationalism   71
   Neoconservatism and Liberalism   74
   Iraq and Beyond   78

3 The Power Elite Today   89
   Corporate Rule   91
   The War Economy   102
   National Security State   120
   The Democratic Facade   131

4 The Many Faces of Corporate Power   145
   Media Oligarchy   146
   The Great Lobby Complex   159
   Financial Colossus   170
   The Authoritarian Workplace   178
   The Corporate University   186

5 Medical Tyranny   197
   The Rockefeller Legacy   197
   The Rise of Big Pharma   201

Megacorporations Rule   212
The Cancer-Industrial Complex   216
Institutional Paralysis   220

6 An American Fascism?   **227**
Right-wing Ascendancy   228
The Power Structure Expands   235
Fascism of a New Type?   243

Conclusion   **253**

Postscript: Politics in the Nuclear Age   **257**

Notes   279

Index   295

Preface

Political developments since the early 1980s have fueled a steady rightward ideological trajectory in the United States, beginning with the Ronald Reagan presidency and extending to the Soviet collapse and end of the Cold War, a series of U.S. military interventions in the Middle East, corporate and financial deregulations, 9/11 and its aftermath, intensified globalization, and the growing conservative stranglehold over the mass media. These decades have been marked by the simultaneous growth of American global power in the wake of the "Vietnam Syndrome," much of it justified by the "war on terrorism." Despite social contradictions intrinsic to an increasingly turbulent world system, the power of capital (backed by military force and such transnational institutions as the World Bank and International Monetary Fund) had by the early years of this century achieved new levels of power and legitimacy. In popular terms, these developments could easily lead to an era of futility, disillusionment, and cynicism—a mood fostered virtually nonstop by the corporate media, while for the elite stratum the dominant modus operandi was sure to be continued business-as-usual with a few caveats about terrorism, rogue states, and resource pressures. With the socialist tradition widely discredited as an ideological matrix for oppositional politics, moreover, sources of resistance to concentrated economic, governmental, and military power would be more difficult to locate.

The reality of daunting global challenges—above all ecological challenges—has elicited nothing more than formulaic, regressive discourses masked as populist alternatives to the status quo. As the trend toward freewheeling corporate power intensifies, the rhetoric of free markets, privatization, deregulation, and individual self-sufficiency grows louder, while the dominant centers of power merit elite celebrations of democracy, citizenship, and political rights. The rebirth of nineteenth-century liberalism, having little to do with political actuality, has signaled a profound turn toward ideological escapism rooted in an impressive ensemble of myths, fantasies, and illusions.

This judgment might seem puzzling at a time when political volatility and ideological conflict in the United States appear to be on the upswing, when grassroots insurgencies claim to be fighting "big government," and when many entrenched politicians face heightened opposition. It is no secret that electoral contests are often heated, nasty, and bitterly fought out, that well-funded lobbies are more active than ever, that think tanks and foundations thrive across the political spectrum, or that the mass media is saturated with lively debates over such issues as immigration, gay marriage, health care, taxes, and U.S. interventions in the Middle East. Environmental organizations have proliferated, most nominally dedicated to saving the earth and to some variant of "sustainable development." On the left, a series of mass-based movements has surface since the early 1990s, including the mislabeled antiglobalization protests born in Seattle, scattered immigrant rights mobilizations, and large peace demonstrations preceding the 2003 U.S. invasion of Iraq. Other smaller efforts, mainly on college campuses, have surfaced from time to time. Much of this ferment has extended to rather wide sectors of the population, giving vent to festering anger while offering (however vague) hopes for change. Yet most of what gets processed through established political and media arenas—elections, candidate debates, interest-group lobbying, media engagement, etc.—remains confined to safe ideological parameters, where critical views of corporate, financial, and military power are either ruled off-limits or are restricted to tiny enclaves far removed from legitimate public discourse. No oppositional movement, furthermore, has offered coherent *political* responses to the current predicament based in durable organization, alternative ideologies, and effective institutional strategy. In other words, no movement has been able to generate antisystem potential at a time when fundamental change has become morally imperative. One problem here is that American society has witnessed the solidification of elite power and, with it, increased mass alienation and disempowerment marked by a shrinkage of politics, as citizen participation, public discourse, and social governance continue to atrophy. Sources of this shrinkage are not too difficult to identify: unsurpassed corporate and financial power, bureaucratic expansion, economic globalization, a massive lobby complex, workplace authoritarianism, and a penetrating media apparatus. Since the ancient Greeks, politics has been viewed by philosophers as central to human existence, the very foundation of social governance, community life, citizen participation, and creative statecraft. Theorists as diverse as Aristotle, Rousseau, Machiavelli, Marx, and Gramsci have argued that political activity is indispensable to forging collective identities, public vision, and social change. It was Aristotle who first embraced politics as a medium of social obligation, central to the purpose of human life. Unfortunately, little of this remains in the United States today, despite ritual celebrations of freedom, democracy, and citizenship.

In fact Americans have always believed their nation was truly exceptional, ordained by history or God to bring human progress to a needy and receptive world. The political system, mass media, and educational system remain, to this day, saturated with comforting myths that have become deeply ingrained in the popular folklore. Nothing is more sacred to this messianic outlook than the belief that the United States is a unique and enlightened democracy—for many, the greatest system of governance ever known to mortal beings. Where there is democracy, of course, freedom, human rights, justice, and equality must surely be close behind. Such national exceptionalism is enshrined in civics textbooks, political speeches, official documents, rationales for global behavior, and the bulk of scholarly works on American politics.

Among fanciful myths of American public discourse, surely none is more disconnected from everyday political life than the notion of an actually-thriving democracy. Any careful reading of history, however, shows that the United States has, to varying degrees, always been closer to an oligarchy ruled by a narrow stratum of wealthy elites—a power structure today increasingly dominated by gigantic corporate interests in partnership with big government and big military, consistent with C. Wright Mills's thesis formulated more than a half-century ago in his seminal *The Power Elite.* That so many Americans believe with great certitude that their country is a model democracy—and that its international role is similarly exemplary—is a tribute to either first-rate media propaganda or, more likely, the broader workings of ideological hegemony across the entire public terrain. If democracy rests upon deep and sustained citizen participation where ordinary people can make shared decisions on matters central to their lives, then a society dominated by corporate interests, a war economy, and national security-state—and legitimated by a corporate mass media—cannot possibly meet that standard. Indeed it falls considerably short of most "actually-existing" European democracies, notably postwar Scandinavian social democracy—the concrete yardstick used throughout this book. A venerable constitution, hallowed body of laws, separation of powers, open elections, party system—none of this, crucial as it might be, guarantees a thriving, living democracy, or indeed anything beyond elite rule. My argument in the following chapters is that American society today is best understood as a "phantom democracy," a species of militarized state capitalism where public access, collective governance, institutional accountability, and free communications scarcely define the political system or shape arenas of daily life such as the workplace, media, education, and local communities. For one thing, corporate lobbies have achieved growing power over elections, government agencies, legislative decisions, and to some degree even scientific research. The January 2010 Supreme Court ruling (in *Citizens United vs. FEC*), giving corporations virtually unlimited license to purchase electoral outcomes, simply enlarges this plutocratic legacy. The parochial, self-serving ideology of U.S. exceptionalism, historical foundation of such imperial strategems as Manifest Destiny and The American Century, turns into a cruel hoax in an era when American domestic and global power more closely resembles oligarchical rule than democracy.

The early twenty-first century finds the United States in a steady downward trajectory of social decay and political authoritarianism that some argue could lead to fascism or its equivalent. While structural and legal features of liberal democracy remain firmly in place—constitutional rights, elections, two-party system, rule of law—from an *ideological* standpoint elements of historical fascism are indeed on the ascendancy: superpatriotism, corporatism, militarism, ethnocentrism, a resurgence of "traditional values." Enclaves of local democratic activity, already weak and marginalized, have come under increasing attack by restive elites striving for maximum control of both domestic and global realms. The political culture has shifted so far rightward that even "liberalism" is today widely demonized as subversive, treasonous, or "un-American." President Obama, by all accounts a moderate "centrist," has been vigorously attacked as a "communist" or "Marxist" totally unfit for office. With Republicans and Democrats converging around shared corporate and imperial priorities, and with liberalism in crisis, significant reform prospects seem more distant than ever, virtually guaranteeing a fragmented, alienated, depoliticized mass public detached from the main levers of power. As oligarchical rule becomes more entrenched and popular inputs diminished, the social infrastructure erodes, the gulf between rich and poor widens, and joblessness increases while military

Should I surrender?

expenditures rise to the level of all other nations combined. In a society boasting of literally thousands of billionaires, the United States (in 2010) had 50 million people living in poverty, tens of millions unemployed, more tens of millions losing homes, thousands dying or wounded in distant wars, and 500,000 perishing yearly from cancer. It was a society, moreover, living on the edge of ecological disaster—its growth-obsessed economy more unsustainable with each passing year. The richest and most powerful country in history had become home to dark undercurrents of runaway greed, violence, corruption, and militarism. As elites, their media representatives, and rightwing populists resist even moderate change, the loudest "protest" voices emanate from Tea Party militants directed not against uncontrolled Wall Street, corporate, and military power but against "big government" regulations and social programs. Here, in a twist of historical irony, we see American exceptionalism turning back on itself, pushing the society further down the road of crisis, turbulence, and potential catastrophe.

To speak of "oligarchy," meaning rule of the few, runs completely against the grain of American historical fictions centered around not only democracy but "free markets," a fantasy derived from the supposedly golden age of competitive capitalism. The reality of an integrated corporate-state system appears difficult for the vast majority of Americans to grasp. Mainstream academic work in the social sciences studiously ignores the issue of corporate power as if it were taboo. A close look at the economic landscape, however, reveals that just a handful of gigantic business enterprises—most of them transnational—control virtually every sector of market activity. A few corporations dominate energy (ExxonMobil, BP, Shell, Chevron, etc.), food production (ConAgra, Tyson, McDonalds, etc.), insurance (Aetna, Prudential, UnitedHealth, etc.), military contracts (Raytheon, TRW, Lockheed-Martin, Northrop-Grumman, etc.), the media (Disney, TimeWarner, NewsCorp, Sony, etc.), technology (Microsoft, Hewlett-Packard, Google, etc.), pharmaceuticals (Pfizer, Abbott, AstraZeneca, BristolMeyersSquibb, etc.), and so on across the economic terrain. This relatively small number of behemoths not only control the flow of profits and wealth but also wield enormous power over markets, assisted by government subsidies and myriad other supports. They maintain imposing bureaucracies, determine investments, manage labor relations, perpetuate massive income gaps, help shape popular culture, and colonize much of the political process not only through their control of the media but the intervention of business-funded lobbies, political action committees (PACs), think tanks, foundations, corporate-backed R&D, and public relations enterprises. Such leverage enables big business to fight and weaken government regulations while taking over the work of such public agencies as the Environmental Protection Agency (EPA), Food and Drug Agency (FDA), Tennessee Valley Authority (TVA), Federal Communications Commission (FCC), and National Institutes of Health (NIH). Their capacity to globalize—to shift their base of operations anywhere in the world—endows them with sufficient flexibility to evade the counterforce of organized labor, consumers, local communities, and even governments. The trend toward oligarchy, reinforced by globalization and empire, has only intensified over the past two or three decades. To maintain the fantasy of "free markets" under these conditions is to indulge in sheer denial.

The American grand historical narrative has always been fixated on democracy, even at times when slavery, destruction of Native populations, colonial oppression, and extreme oligarchic rule were at their height. Imperial presidents of the past—Jackson, Polk, McKinley, Theodore Roosevelt, Wilson—all believed they were bringing democracy to an unruly and backward world, and all were quick to rely on military force. Their chauvinistic rationale merely assumed that American behavior was "democratic," that existing practices amounted to forms of self-governance bequeathed by wise and progressive Founders of the Republic. President Wilson, during and after World War I, said the task of U.S. foreign policy was to "make the world safe for democracy"—a rhetorical gesture inherited by subsequent American leaders and taken seriously ever since by establishment politicians, media figures, and academics. Surely John F. Kennedy and his circle of Ivy League liberals were convinced the United States was valiantly promoting democracy in Vietnam as it fought tyrannical communism, a trope followed to the letter by Presidents Johnson and Nixon. The George W. Bush administration, staffed with an influential group of militaristic neocons, righteously believed the U.S. military invasion and occupation of Iraq was urgently needed to advance democracy, or so it was offered for public consumption. The Iraq debacle, going back to the early 1990s, speaks loudly and persuasively to this outlandish fiction. The actual legacy of "shock-and-awe" combined with "democracy-promotion" is more than a million Iraqi deaths, nearly five million displaced, a ruined infrastructure, economic calamity, shattered families, and a puppet government that, until at least 2010, was mainly controlled from Washington. And Iraq was hardly an aberration: the same destructive and authoritarian logic applied to U.S. interventions in Korea, Vietnam, Chile, Central America, Indonesia, and Turkey among others. That political, media, and academic elites shamelessly perpetuate the fiction of American democracy-promotion only magnifies the shame.

The power elite that Mills so boldly analyzed has only further consolidated its hold over American society in recent decades. The Obama presidency was widely expected to bring change and democratization to a society broken by eight years of Bush's warmaking, Wall Street profligacy, corporate deregulation, and economic ruin. The promise, however, never gained much traction, nor, in practical reality, could it have. Obama was restrained by, and beholden to, the same institutional and ideological forces that held previous White House occupants captive: corporate and financial interests, the lobby complex, permanent war economy, national security state, and a U.S. imperial presence in every corner of the globe. For genuine change or democratization to occur, the entire system of production and consumption would have to be extensively transformed. Fiscal policy, national debt, military spending, global bases and interventions, investment priorities—all these are established within set parameters, largely outside the realm of political debate or public input. Thus the 2008 presidential debates, in the tradition of earlier corporate-sponsored spectacles, were never likely to confront pressing issues beyond the usual bromides and platitudes. Upon election, Obama was expected to assume his rightful place within the Washington establishment, which of course he did—as quickly revealed by his mostly conservative appointments. Within a year of taking office, he presided over massive Wall Street bailouts, yielded to the insurance and pharmaceutical companies on health care, extended Bush-era rendition and surveillance practices, escalated the war in Afghanistan, seemed ready to keep U.S. troops in Iraq indefinitely, upheld the same destructive (and doomed) pro-Israel policies, pushed for record Pentagon spending, retreated on aggressive Wall Street legislation, and moved timidly on global warming at Copenhagen. Obama's domestic and international policies, in other words, generally fell in line with the much-castigated and unpopular Bush-Cheney agenda. Meanwhile, American society was slipping further into the recesses of economic crisis, social decay, and authoritarian rule.

The eclipse of what little remains of American democracy coincides with the steady expansion of corporate and imperial power, reflected in the growth of military spending that approached a staggering $1 trillion in 2010. Pentagon contractors were able to amass huge profits at a time when budget deficits and fiscal crisis weaken every municipal and state government in the United States—and when the federal government is hobbled by its own escalating deficits and shortfalls. The insatiable demands of empire clash at every turn with requirements for a sustainable economy, viable social programs, and political democracy, yet the war machine moves full-speed ahead, its momentum hardly dented. Some critics mistakenly conclude that Washington can no longer "afford" its empire and that its global power—symbolic of U.S. exceptionalism—is finally coming to an end. While this argument is seductive, as it points toward a more peaceful future, no evidence can be marshaled to support it: the Pentagon in 2010 had more resources at its disposal, in the world, and in American society, than any time in the past, and like other swollen bureaucracies, its managers will never voluntarily relinquish their hold over power and privilege. In the tradition of previous empires, American power is far more likely to collapse from its own internal contradictions than from calculated decisions made at the summits of power. As always, large-scale institutional controls follow a self-perpetuating logic, especially in the case of military power, which easily can employ patriotic appeals and national security threats to legitimate its bureaucratic domain. Meanwhile, the costs of empire are sustained overwhelmingly by ordinary American taxpayers.

The ruling interests in fact pursue U.S. world hegemony without ever taking into account the stupendous costs and risks of blowback endemic to the imperial project. Neoconservative ideology (explored in chapter 2) remains very much alive in a world that Washington elites believe is riddled with anarchic disorder and diabolical enemies. Writing in a *Los Angeles Times* op-ed column, leading neocon Max Boot exulted over the capacity of U.S. power to bring security and progress to others in the world fortunate enough to have a benevolent American patron and protector. "The very fact that the entire world is divided into American military commands is significant," he notes. "There is no French, Indian, or Brazilian equivalent—not yet even a Chinese counterpart. It is simply assumed without need for comment that American soldiers will be central players in the affairs of the entire world. It is also taken for granted that a vast network of U.S. bases will stretch from Germany to Japan—more than 700 in all...They constitute a virtual American empire of Wall-Mart style PXs, fast-food restaurants, and gyms." Such brazen imperial hubris, if exhibited elsewhere in the world, would be viewed as a sign of demented fascism, but in the United States it is standard thinking among the upper crust, as the moral and political guidepost of U.S. global behavior is now unapologetically chauvinistic. This seems eminently reasonable since, as Boot argues, "American power is the world's best guarantor of freedom and prosperity," adding that, "…countries that dismiss the prospects for continuing American leadership do so at their peril." Such ominous warnings will appear to most of the world as real threats that Washington is prepared to back by some combination of economic, political, and military power.

Boot's arrogant celebration of empire has deep origins in U.S. history, a motif explored at length in chapter 1. Its democratic pretenses have served as ideological cover for oligarchical power, domestically and internationally, as I discuss in the following chapters. The pretense of an indispensable nation, taking on the burdens of spreading democracy, building global order, and shaping history, was always destined to produce an aggressive but ultimately self-defeating, imperial ethos. Superpower profligacy was bound, sooner or later, to invade the homefront, as the corporate-imperial behemoth takes precedence over virtually every domestic priority. Neocon ideologues like Boot are so infatuated with U.S. global power that they cannot grasp how that power can so easily turn on itself, devouring economic, political, and social resources within domestic society. In the face of mounting crisis, therefore, inhabitants of the American and global commons may have no alternative but outright rebellion—first, to recapture the public sphere, and second, to dismantle the war machine and lay the groundwork for sustainable development and a peaceful world. From this standpoint, any penetrating critique of American politics must extend far beyond the usual focus on stolen elections, corruption, bad leaders, "mistaken" policies, and presumed violations of the Constitution. Oligarchical tendencies run much deeper across history. The critical perspective adopted in this book revolves, instead, around long-term historical factors, that is, pervasive structural and ideological trends going back to origins of the Republic.

One problem is that public space in American society for such democratization has been generally limited, partial, and uneven. Yet to argue that the system has been governed by an oligarchic elite, as I do in this book, by no means suggests that spheres of citizen participation and local democratic governance have been entirely absent. In fact U.S. history is replete with democratic experience: popular insurgencies, town meetings, social movements, third-party formations, community organizations, municipal populism, and the like. Although often episodic and short-lived, such democratic energies have made noteworthy inroads into the political culture, set restraints on elite rule, created pressures for social reforms, paved the way toward new legal codes, and broadened participatory space. U.S. history would be something altogether different were it not for the enduring legacy of labor, feminist, civil rights, community, antiwar, and environmental struggles, made possible by the dedication and sacrifice of millions of Americans who in myriad ways carried on the fight against established power. Scattered zones of democratic space today owe everything to these popular incursions and upsurges. It might be argued that the era of 1960s new-left radicalism and its aftermath, new social movements, represents a pinnacle of civic participation and popular rebellion in which millions of people were strongly engaged, able to set new priorities, and influence the course of events. Social advances helped expand citizenship, enlarge the public sphere, and revitalize local governance in opposition to the dictates of oligarchic power. Still, despite such forward progress, the national power structure remained largely intact, controlled by the same elite stratum that would boast even more ambitious global objectives. If multiple, though primarily local, zones of democratic participation retain a foothold across the public landscape, these areas never expanded to the point they could undermine, much less overthrow, an oligarchic power structure that confounds virtually every familiar illusion of American political mythology. Any far-reaching democratization of American society will inevitably face the task of confronting—and transforming—that power structure.

Like any book, this one is strongly influenced by the seminal work of others—in this case, by C. Wright Mills (*The Power Elite*, 1956), Fred Cook, (*The Warfare State*, 1962), Herbert Marcuse (*One-Dimensional Man*, 1964), and Seymour Melman (*The Permanent War Economy*, 1974). I also owe an intellectual debt to more recent works that critically deconstruct class and power relations in American society: Michael Parenti (*Democracy for the Few*, 1983), Robert McChesney (*Rich Media, Poor Democracy*, 1999), G. William Domhoff (*Who Rules America?*, 2006), Chalmers Johnson (*Nemesis*, 2006), Sheldon Wolin (*Democracy, Inc.*, 2008), and James Petras (*Rulers and Ruled in the United States*, 2008) among others. The legacy of Mills, visible throughout this study, remains especially pervasive, as he uniquely explored the confluence of corporate, government, and military interests in forging elite power. Later critics have taken up Mills's agenda, if only partially and unevenly, often fixated on just one part of the integrated power structure. Many, unfortunately, have carried forward deep assumptions embedded in American democratic mythology. The approach chosen here builds upon Mills while extending critical analysis into other terrains—for example, the media, workplace, higher education, community life, and the all-important medical sector. Oligarchy, in other words, is not confined to corporate rule or governmental processes alone, but enters into and transforms every realm of public life. It is especially reinforced by the workings of imperial and military power—a centerpiece of this book.

The author wishes to especially thank four colleagues—Peter McLaren, Tom Pollard, Ray Pratt, and John Sanbonmatsu—for the ideas they have shared through many conversations and communications as this project was unfolding. He is deeply indebted to Laurie Nalepa for her constant intellectual presence and emotional support.

CARL BOGGS
Los Angeles, February 2011

Introduction

The idea of democracy as popular sovereignty or consent of the governed—that is, some form of self-rule—goes back at least as far as the ancient Greeks, but as modern zeitgeist with universal meaning it dates to the French and American revolutions of the late eighteenth century. The struggle for democratic governance entailed not only overthrow of the *ancien regime* (monarchy, aristocracy, state-church, colonialism) but promised an epic transformation of politics, the economy, culture, and social life. Across the succeeding two centuries and more the ideal of democracy, whether articulated within liberal, Marxist, anarchist, or populist traditions, gained hegemony as global discourse, to the extent that even dictatorships sought to legitimate their domination as in some fashion "democratic." Lenin and the Bolsheviks, for example, claimed that Soviet bureaucratic centralism, or "dictatorship of the proletariat," was a thousand times more democratic than liberal-capitalist tyranny since it was grounded in the collective will of a victorious proletariat. Democracy as a guiding motif of public life passed through multiple agencies: great philosophers, movements, parties, revolutions, states. Democratic energies fueled struggles for national independence, social justice, human rights, and freedom from tyrannical rule. In its most radical expressions, democracy was a force associated with enlightenment rationality, social progress, and opposition to concentrated power of every sort—in government, the economy, church, military, bureaucracy. Such opposition was usually routed through local forms of authority (town assemblies, rural and urban councils, grassroots citizens groups, popular legislative bodies, etc.), the assumption being that power was to be *transformed,* made broadly accessible, rather than simply ameliorated or even abolished.

As the democratic zeitgeist spread geographically and ideologically, so too did multiple counterforces: corporate power, big government, the military, imperialism, and that most pervasive of hierarchical forms, bureaucracy. Such counterforces gained strength with the

⌐odernity, a phenomenon theorized by such diverse observ-
⌐Karl Marx, Max Weber, Joseph Schumpeter, and the "elite
⌐⌐orists" Gaetano Mosca, Vilfredo Pareto, and Robert Michels,
whose famous "iron law of oligarchy" was applied to authority
relations within all large-scale organizations. Marxists argued that
beneath the noble democratic pretenses of liberal-capitalism could be
located a deeper authoritarian substructure rooted in class domination. It turns out that counterforces to democratic rule were notably strong in the American experience, where a particularly ruthless
form of capitalism—giving rise to a concentrated system of economic
power—achieved unique success even though popular sovereignty was
ritually taken for granted. If strong populist impulses of thinkers like
Thomas Paine and Thomas Jefferson retained ideological currency
across U.S. history, the actuality of oligarchic governance was hard
to ignore despite the spread of citizenship rights to new groups. Over
time, the historic convergence of corporate, political, and military
power would become a defining feature of American public life, even
if never recognized as such by the celebrants of American exceptionalism. The stubborn problem here revolves around the ultimate fate
of democracy in societies, like the United States, where the prevailing
zeitgeist remains so deeply entrenched in the political culture and yet
is so detached from the historical reality.

For American society, the legacy of oligarchic rule has deep origins
in the founding practices and early history, when a small nucleus of
wealthy European elites gained ascendancy and charted a new political
course during the struggle for national independence. The plantation
slave economy survived until the Civil War, while colonialism solidified its hold throughout the nineteenth century with the frontier push
westward. A well-developed corporate system gained ascendancy by
the 1890s, with a powerful military establishment taking shape at the
time of World War II. War mobilization, military Keynesianism, and
national security state—all closely bound up with corporate interests—
remain to this day the heritage of the Good War and its aftermath, to
the detriment of popular institutions. An elitist outlook compatible with
domination, exploitation, warfare, and wealthy privilege, hardly alien
to the Founders, would become entrenched within the American landscape. In this context, Sheldon Wolin points out that, since "democracy
is about participating in self-government, its first requirement is a supportive culture, a complex of beliefs, values, and practices that nurture
equality, cooperation, and freedom."[1] The problem is that corporate
and imperial hegemony work incessantly against the sustainability of

such a political culture. In his book *Democracy, Inc.*, Wolin refers to "a profound transformation of politics effected by the imperium of superpower. Exit the citizen, enter the corporate actor. Politics comes to replicate the structure and culture of corporate capitalism: it is rationalized, capitalized, elite-dominated, viciously competitive, and technologically dependent. Instead of an expressive politics that encourages the voicing of concerns, grievances, and proposals, we have a controlled politics that tolerates dissent but is unresponsive to protests and proposals from below."[2] A more conservative observer, Kevin Phillips in *Wealth and Democracy*, concedes that "...by 2000 the United States could be said to have a plutocracy when back in 1990 the resemblance to the previous plutocracy of the Golden Age had not fully matured," adding that "the essence of plutocracy, fulfilled by 2000, has been the determination and ability of wealth to reach beyond its own realm of money and control politics and government as well."[3] C. Wright Mills, in his classic *The Power Elite*, made essentially the same argument roughly a half-century ago.

Still, after more than two centuries of grossly unequal class and power relations, democracy remains the central narrative of American politics. In fact "democracy" long ago segued into a popular mythology impervious to rational critique, a mythology with special ideological force in a world of threatening change, ambiguity, and uncertainty. The undemocratic power structure described by Wolin and Phillips, and earlier by Mills, has resonated little within both elite and popular consciousness, except at times of populist insurgencies; the very essence of popular mythology is that it blindly resists ideological dissent and political opposition. Such mythology was nurtured from the outset by an arrogant, resilient national exceptionalism, endowing Americans with a special historical mission. This meant that for Americans infatuated with this popular mythology, "democracy" would always be identical to actually existing institutions and practices, however authoritarian, bureaucratic, or coercive, and however much the mythology conflicted with historical facts.

This arguments set forth in this book are shaped by the conviction that, while still a matter of common wisdom, American democracy at the start of the twenty-first century is an increasingly problematic concept, lacking in both historical and empirical substance. Against the realities of an entrenched state-capitalist system, with its concentrated corporate, government, and military power, references to "democracy" have often degenerated into a ritualized language that tells us relatively little about the character of living social and authority relations.

Precious little attention is nowadays devoted to the constituent elements
of a thriving democratic system, whether among politicians, the media,
and even supposedly objective academics normally reluctant to take
political labels at face value. Even harsh critics of American politics
often seem willing to accept, with apparently few second thoughts, the
familiar existing signposts of democracy taken from civics textbooks
discourse—consent of the governed, will of the people, popular sovereignty, self-governance—that, when closely examined, end up woe-
fully thin on actual content. A guiding thesis of this study is that such
facile renditions have grown mostly stale and useless. The same holds
for long-standing equations of democratic politics with a constitution,
open elections, "pluralism," a capitalist economy, and certain legally
protected rights and freedoms. None of these conditions, however salu-
tary, is sufficient to reproduce a vital system of democratic governance
while at least one of them (capitalism) arguably works against it.

The concept of "phantom democracy" suggests that, behind a
legacy of constitutional rights and electoral politics, American
governance has always been to varying degrees oligarchic, shaped
by commercial interests and ideologies that dominated the thinking of the Founders. This analysis owes a great debt to the seminal
work of Mills, who in the 1950s argued that corporate, government, and military interests merged to form an expanding power
structure relegating party competition, elections, and legislative
activity to something of a commodified spectacle detached from
actual decision-making processes.[4] More than a half-century later,
Mills's arguments seem even more plausible, especially at a time
when the permanent war economy and national security-state dwarf
the scope they achieved during the Eisenhower era. Mills saw that
various myths and illusions of American democracy, endemic to the
needs for political legitimation, had deep roots in U.S. history, thus
calling into question a familiar impulse to glorify the past or view
authoritarian trends as a recent departure from that romanticized
past. Alexis de Tocqueville's classic *Democracy in America* remains
a nearly sacred text for politicians, scholars, and others looking to
retain celebratory narratives rooted in an imagined golden age of
popular sovereignty and self-governance. To be sure, significant
moments of local participation have surfaced across U.S. history,
but the larger, more durable tradition explored here winds up closer
to the oligarchic dimensions of Mills's power elite, reinforced by
the postwar growth of empire and corporate globalization. Viewed
thusly, the main thesis extends well beyond such familiar and

more immediate concerns as stolen elections, political corruption, "big government," ruthless politicians, growth of ultraright ideology, or "hijacking" of the U.S. Constitution by the second George Bush administration.[5] These issues are surely worrisome enough and will be explored in the following chapters, yet they scarcely exhaust what is meant here by "phantom democracy," which turns on broader structural and ideological forces at work throughout the long expanse of U.S. history.

If we accept even a relatively modest—yet nonetheless concrete— view of democracy, as I do in this book, then the United States dismally fails even this minimal test. While it might be tempting to invoke more radical notions of democracy as a basis for judging American institutions—notions drawn from such traditions as anarchism, syndicalism, progressive social movements, and recent Green tendencies—the path chosen here is to frame American politics against the experience of "actually existing" democracies in such regions as postwar Scandinavia. This approach turns out to be more historical than strictly theoretical. In other words, one can find useful measures of democratic politics in lessons derived from advanced industrial societies not markedly different from the United States, not only in the realm of government but throughout the public terrain where questions of economic power, work structures, race relations, the media, and global behavior can be taken into account. To be a functioning system, democracy requires certain minimum conditions: universal and open suffrage, constitutional rights and freedoms, popular access to economic and political institutions, free party competition offering genuine alternatives, local governance, and developed norms of citizen participation. It cannot survive, moreover, in the absence of popular involvement based on readily accessible and diverse sources of information. Any ideal of democracy confined to formal procedures or governmental processes alone is ultimately flawed since economic and social life, integral to the commons, must be subject to roughly the same criteria of access and participation. In present-day American society such indices, except for constitutional rights and universal suffrage, bear little relationship to living political experience. Glaring examples of oligarchical rule, such as President George W. Bush's decision to invade and occupy Iraq, constitute an historical pattern rather than isolated cases, to be detailed at some length in the following chapters.

Any close historical study of governing structures and practices in American society will reveal that elite power has generally trumped democratic governance and that corporate interests have routinely prevailed over public access to information, open debate, and collective decision-making. In the realm of all-important economic and foreign policy, history demonstrates that public influence has been minimal to nonexistent—a reality aggravated by deregulation of corporate and financial power, intensified globalization, and expansion of the war economy. Elite rule is the logical outgrowth of a militarized state-capitalism that steadily diminishes the power of workers, consumers, and local communities. As the power structure first systematically charted by Mills gains new reach and durability with each passing year, the old narrative about the happy marriage of democracy and capitalism reveals anew its complete bankruptcy.

This progressive weakening of the public domain extends throughout American society. While the impoverishment of democratic norms and practices has deep historical origins, it was greatly accelerated following the upsurge of social movements and governmental reforms during the 1960s and 1970s. The following chapters explore an American political trajectory quite at odds with exceptionalist discourses celebrating democratic virtues of a nation bringing freedom, self-government, affluence, and progress to its own people and others, of a government "making the world safe for democracy." Such fanciful pretenses are called into question by a lengthy tradition of colonial expansion, economic rapacity, racism, and militarism.[6] Not only do powerful corporate and imperial agendas clash with the requisites of democratic politics, so too does authoritarian rule at the workplace, ubiquitous bureaucratic power, extreme social inequalities, a political system resting on skewed representation, and solidification of a war economy and security state required for U.S. global supremacy—all undergirded by a mass media owned and managed by a tiny handful of business elites. In contrast to well-known accounts recalling something of a golden age of American democracy, the perspective argued here is that the route to corporate and military domination, to oligarchy and imperialism, was always compatible with the Constitution and reigning political ideology of the Founders.

It is worth mentioning here how celebrated renditions of the American political experience—for example, in the work of Alexis de Tocqueville—have been at odds with the historical record. Visiting the United States in the 1830s, Tocqueville, a French aristocrat, saw democracy as the central American narrative rooted in popular beliefs and "habits of the heart" that distinguished the United States from the European experience. Throughout *Democracy in America*, Tocqueville wrote glowingly of a political system taking root on fertile terrain

unsullied by encrustations of the *ancien regime,* his occasional criticisms usually overlooked by cheerleading historians and commentators
inclined toward the bloated excesses of praise. Tocqueville observed
that "the social state of the Americans is eminently democratic. It has
been like that ever since the birth of the colonies but is even more so
now [in the 1830s]."[7] A few pages later, he added that "...in America
the sovereignty of the people is neither hidden nor sterile as with some
other nations; mores recognize it, and the laws proclaim it; it spreads
with freedom and attains unimpeded its ultimate consequences."[8] He
continued: "In the United States in our day the principle of the sovereignty of the people has been adopted in practice in every way that
imagination could suggest."[9] Later, Tocqueville asked on the basis of
his travels: "How is it that the United States, where the inhabitants
arrived but yesterday in the land they occupy...that each man is as
interested in the affairs of his township, of his canton, and of the whole
state as he is in his own affairs? It is because each man in his sphere
takes an active part in the government of society."[10] Reflecting on an
imputed "respect for law," he wrote that "...in America the people
obey the law not only because it is their work but also because they can
change it if by any chance it does injure them."[11]

Generalizations of this sort, scattered across hundreds of pages of
Democracy in America, gave rise to a cottage industry among scholars trumpeting the virtues of a unique American "democracy" that
fed into myths of U.S. exceptionalism. For most of these interpreters,
Tocqueville's own remarkable genius resided in his keen recognition
of the political brilliance of the Founders. Tocqueville's visit, after
all, came at the height of "Jacksonian democracy," seen as an axis
of enlightened, progressive, freedom-loving impulses vital to a population seeking novel political forms. The ethos of self-governance
reigned supreme, energized by the never-ending Western frontier.
Astonishingly, Tocqueville's simplistic conclusions—and others' later
uncritical embellishments of them—came in the midst of one of the
harshest slavery systems ever created, not to mention the genocidal
destruction of Indian tribes orchestrated in part by that great architect of "radical democracy," Andrew Jackson. They came at a time
when voting rights were mostly limited to white-male property owners, with roughly 90 percent of Americans considered unworthy of
citizenship. They also notably came at a time when American law-
breaking was legendary, whether in the forceful seizure of others'
lands or violations of treaties signed with Indians, a pattern later to
become a routine feature of U.S. foreign policy. And they came at a

time when Jackson had just erected an imperial presidency, enabling the White House from that time forward to run roughshod over Congress and the public on matters of war and peace, an elite arrogance soon embraced by President James K. Polk as he set out to conquer Mexican lands through preemptive war. Even more astonishingly, Tocqueville and his later admirers had the audacity to affix the "democratic" label to such a manifestly undemocratic, perhaps more accurately oligarchic and barbaric, political conditions.

In actuality the new republic bore little resemblance to democracy, more closely approximating an oligarchical system with restricted suffrage and dominated by elites *fearful* of mass participation and broad forms of representation. The founding documents were assembled by a small assemblage of rich European men. A few, like Thomas Jefferson, spoke of a populist kind of democracy, but the actuality of concentrated power quickly overwhelmed such visionary sentiments; the radicalism of Paine and Jefferson inevitably vanished in the midst of harsher plutocratic realities. The anti-English rebellion (and the Constitution it produced) was driven more by conflict between rival commercial interests than by insurgency from below as colonial propaganda would have it, though moments of popular upsurge did contribute to the outcome.[12] At the time Tocqueville visited the United States the country was actually divided into four discrete regions: the commercial Northeast, Southern plantation economy, agrarian middle section, and a rapidly expanding Western frontier. The North was dominated by rising industrial, banking, and trade interests; the South was a fiefdom of slaveholders; and the West was being madly colonized by growing numbers of white settlers aided by the federal government and military. Little mass participation (or "popular sovereignty") marked the politics of these regions. Only in the middle part of the country, home of the fabled small farmer of Jacksonian lore, was local "democracy" even made into a pretense—and this would be a small percentage of the total American population before the Civil War. Even here, however, the yeoman of liberal mythology was largely disenfranchised, swept up by larger market forces centered in the Northeast and elsewhere. Moreover, even the pitifully little access small farmers and others might have had to the machinery of government was checkmated by the far greater leverage of powerful commercial interests, including banks. For this and other reasons, "Jacksonian democracy" turned out to be yet another historical fiction.

The cherished liberal tradition itself was largely bereft of democratic impulses. From the outset the American Republic coexisted easily with harsh class divisions, a hierarchical market economy, plutocratic domination, deep social inequalities, racism, and a fierce social Darwinism, most of which seemed to escape the probing eye of Tocqueville and his followers. Everything revolved around a self-interested individualism according to which people (read: affluent white men) were inexorably driven by the struggle for power, wealth, and social advantage. Much of the nineteenth-century American landscape was anything but hardly lawful, taking on Hobbesian features of untrammeled aggression and savagery. C.B. Macpherson generously referred to the political system as "protective democracy for market man," noting that early liberalism was "neither inspiring nor inspired" as an ostensible model of democracy.[13] Based on a self-centered ethos of possessive individualism, the system was geared to maximizing economic self-interest, compatible with a society of atomized individuals hardly fit for participatory democracy of the sort Paine and Jefferson presumably had in mind. To be sure, grassroots forms like town meetings and local assemblies did exist here and there, only to be eventually devoured or marginalized by rising manufacturing, financial, and other business interests. The American developmental pattern, in Macpherson's terms, was characterized by a later shift from "protective" to "equilibrium" democracy congruent with the corporate/elitist model that would prevail from late nineteenth century onward. Government, as theorists like Max Weber and Joseph Schumpeter would later emphasize, followed a largely bureaucratic and *procedural* structure: voters would choose among competing elites within a pluralistic state-capitalist system, all based on elite power, institutional cohesion, and regulation of class conflict.[14] Liberalism thus set out to supplant older forms of tyranny (aristocracy, monarchy, state church) only to replace these with newer and often more pervasive forms (corporations, state, military).

The problem, however, goes deeper than the familiar limits of liberalism or oligarchic tendencies within the Republican system. Any honest reflection on the American political legacy must face up to the dark history of imperialism, militarism, and indeed genocide this legacy encouraged, or at least tolerated. Such darkness, where recognized at all, is usually interpreted as an aberration from the norm, a departure from American "core values," but that is a profoundly false reading of the history. In a far more accurate rendering of U.S. history, Ron Takaki, in *A Different Mirror*, observes that American expansionism had always been rife with violent aggression and racism, part of an "errand into the wilderness" that came with frenetic pursuit of individual (and collective) wealth and power. Speaking of the real Andrew Jackson, who openly bragged of the mass murder of Indians by army troops he led into battle before winning the presidency, Takaki notes that Jackson looked to the (forced) disappearance of Indian tribes as both moral and inevitable, a tribute to the superiority of white civilization. For Jackson, like other U.S. war heroes of the frontier, bloodshed visited on inferiors was a sign of historical progress.[15] This history was no melting pot: if Americans were indeed the most virtuous (and democratic) of all peoples, then those who stood outside or were opposed to this virtuous juggernaut would have to be either converted or destroyed. Only the most "worthy part of mankind" would be admitted to citizenship, a worthiness that in any event guaranteed little in the exercise of democratic rights. Nonwhite groups, then as later, would be targets of an insatiable colonial machine, the engine not of progress but of what Takaki calls "the racialization of savagery."[16] Barbarism on the frontier and against Mexico would be repeated in the Philippines, Central America, Japan, Korea, Vietnam, and other Asian societies.

In contrast to a purported democratic and peaceful American innocence, a trope echoed by Tocqueville and others, Michael Rogin calls attention to the fierce self-consciousness Americans possessed as they went about conquering and destroying along the path Westward. More than that, violent conquest and expansion would define what it meant to be American, what both patriotism and the liberal project historically signified. It was a matter of progress versus savagery since "in the white scheme civilization, no less than death, meant the disappearance of Indians."[17] If particular Indian tribes or individuals did not behave like savages, they would eventually be forced to do so: "Whites turned Indians into wanderers by killing their game, by destroying their crops and burning their villages, and by moving a tribe from one location after another as whites wanted the land."[18] For Indians who remained on their land, of course, nothing less than oppression and eventual death was their fate. This was the kernel of Jacksonian removal policy carried out, in different ways, until the final massacre at Wounded Knee in 1890. Rogin astutely comments that such "large-scale transfer of native populations, in the name of security and modernization, has continued to appeal to American statesmen. Indian removal bears resemblance to 'force-draft urbanization' in Vietnam..."[19] At the time Tocqueville wrote his book, Indians were being systematically "removed" for white expansion that would ultimately extend from the Appalachians to the Pacific

Ocean, with its new "civilized" towns and cities, railroads, military forts, and commercialized agriculture.

The continuing American pretense of democratic and peaceful virtue in an historical context of virulent colonialism, militarism, and racism—in fact genocidal destruction—remains a great intellectual paradox. Millions died in the name of progress with millions of others displaced or forced into slavery, yet American folklore persists within a fraudulent democratic narrative comprised of untold myths, distortions, and fictions. Reflecting on the Indian catastrophe, Ward Churchill writes: "The American holocaust was and remains unparalleled both in terms of its magnitude and the degree to which the goals were met, and in terms of the extent to which its ferocity was sustained over time by not one but several participating groups. The ideological matrix of its denial is also among the most well developed of any genocide—or, more accurately, series of genocides—for which a significant amount of information is readily available."[20] Of course where this history is not actually denied or repressed it is justified and even celebrated, as in hundreds of Hollywood Westerns that managed to transform Indian victims into demons, or an educational system that glorifies an imagined democratic past while overlooking its legions of victims. Referring to the period romanticized by Tocqueville, Howard Zinn writes: "If you look through high-school textbooks and elementary school textbooks in American history you will find [President] Jackson the frontiersman, soldier, democrat, man of the people—not Jackson the slaveholder, land speculator, executioner of dissident soldiers, exterminator of Indians."[21] Churchill is right in observing, moreover, that such ideological mystification has always extended across the American political spectrum.[22]

Little needs to be added here regarding the long history of American slavery, a tyrannical plantation system enforced by laws, courts, prisons, and terror and legitimated by an ideology presenting master-slave relations as the "natural" condition of humanity. By 1860, on the eve of the Civil War, some 4 million blacks were subjugated to this barbarism. The system was built on a racial hierarchy that would have lasting repercussions for American society, overthrown not through popular outrage or democratic upheavals but as the outcome of a bloody Civil War whose protagonists (including President Lincoln) never favored abolition until it was essentially a fait accompli. As Zinn points out, "The American government had set out to fight the slave states in 1861, not to end slavery, but to retain the enormous national territory and markets and resources."[23] Barrington Moore notes that Northern leaders were intent, above all, on forging the *economic* integration of North and South, with moral issues scarcely entering the picture.[24] The ar of course did bring an end to slavery, but gave rise to a Reconstruction order nearly as oppressive and violent: by 1900, all Southern states had written into law the disenfranchise-ment and segregation of black populations as part of the Jim-Crow system. There would be no "sovereignty" for blacks—indeed for any nonwhite groups—although that would scarcely have been possible within an oligarchic corporate-liberal system, which had become more entrenched with each passing year.

The French philosopher Jean-Jacques Rousseau identified several requisites for a vibrant democracy, including roughly equal access to decision-making, peaceful social and foreign relations, community rooted in trust and reciprocity, and an egalitarian social structure. "Community" for Rousseau meant not only submergence of individu-alism within a larger collectivity but a solidifying concept of the public good. Following Aristotle and prefiguring Marx, Rousseau was con-vinced democracy could never survive much less flourish where deep social divisions, marked by extremes of wealth and poverty, continued over time. Democracy required a framework of social cooperation and mutual aid, perhaps even (as Marx and later socialists would affirm) a state of classlessness in which the social division of labor was finally transcended. Founders of the American Republic, in contrast, were des-perately *fearful* of democracy precisely because it upset their firm belief that power should rest in the hands of wealthy elites, that is, "the more capable set of men", in the words of James Madison. Those who owned no property, according to Framers of the Constitution, were not quali-fied for full citizenship much less political leadership. Rights accrued to the minority of (white-male) property owners, with all others dis-enfranchised. The crucial task of governance, for Madison and his peers, was to protect existing wealth and power arrangements within a system, allowing for some modicum of freedom from the old feudal restraints. The later trajectory of American politics, as we have seen, followed the broad precepts and agendas established by the Founders, generally consistent with the outlook of classical liberalism.

During the roughly two centuries after birth of the Republic, an epi-sodic history of popular struggles did expand the scope of participation and rights, although constituent elements of a democratic society like those outlined by Rousseau grew more remote as corporate, govern-ment, and military power expanded. Of course, Rousseauian tenets are viewed today as just another exercise in utopian dreaming, useless for conducting business in the real world. Instead we find perpetuation of an oligarchic elite that naturally coexists with mass political alienation reflected in low voter turnouts, feeble knowledge of public affairs, declining sense of political efficacy, and generalized cynicism toward politicians and government. While certain formal rights and freedoms have expanded across the decades, by late twentieth century the American electorate was subordinated to a power structure driven by empire, corporate globalization, and oligarchic domestic interests. If American society today looks radically different from its historical origins, there is little doubt that fundamental class and power relations exhibit a strong historical continuity; present-day militarized state-capitalism rests on both old and new foundations. Just as Madison and other leading Founders had hoped, business and wealth remain firmly in control not only of government but of the entire domestic society.

The transition from Manifest Destiny to frontier expansion to global imperialism follows a definite historical logic: elite domination in the name of special American virtues, entitlements, and destiny. World War II brought the United States into full-blown superpower status, marked by a war economy, security state, and imperial hegemony. The clashing demands of empire and democracy, already visible in the nineteenth century, would be more starkly evident in the postwar era. Mills illuminated perhaps better than anyone the tight connection between rising military power and corrosion of domestic politics, a view carried forward and refined by Seymour Melman and such other critics as Fred Cook, William Appleman Williams, and Paul Sweezy. President Eisenhower, in his famous 1961 farewell address, spoke compellingly of the same linkage. More recently, Chalmers Johnson, reflecting on "the last days of the American Republic," restated a motif largely ignored by mainstream scholars and journalists typically worshipful of pluralist democracy, observing that "the histories of Rome and Britain suggest that imperialism and militarism are the deadly enemies of democracy." Over time, empire reproduces the impulse toward domination, violence, and warfare, which sooner over later gives rise to domestic authoritarianism. Thus: "imperialism and militarism will ultimately breach the separation of powers created to prevent tyranny and defend liberty. The United States today, like the Roman Republic in the first century B.C., is threatened by an out-of-control military-industrial complex and a huge secret government controlled exclusively by the president."[25] That such an imperial behemoth could be in the business of "promoting democracy abroad"—a self-righteous pretense of American foreign policy since at least Woodrow Wilson—is rather laughable.

The shadow of empire hovers tenaciously over the entire American landscape. Politics, government, the economy, social life, culture—all this is mediated through the prism of U.S. foreign and military policy that today is still driven by an ideology of national exceptionalism. In the early twenty-first century, with the American presence extended across the globe, the United States had an economy increasingly dependent on its military. It had several hundred military bases scattered across more than 100 countries, remained the world's dominant nuclear power, had pushed the NATO alliance eastward, was setting out to "remap" the Middle East, was on the verge of space militarization, and was engaged in two protracted, costly wars. Washington had the most powerful war machine ever, built strong enough to repel any challenge from within the fortress itself. Such military force would be amassed at an exorbitant price, in lives, resources, and a legacy of social ruin, while the old rhetoric about the United States bringing democracy, human rights, and free markets to a needy world had grown increasingly hollow. Following World War II, this system demanded a tight corporate-government-military partnership, oriented to geopolitical leverage by means of warfare, global surveillance, intelligence operations, private contracting, counterinsurgency, covert actions, and a lucrative arms trade. Superpower ambitions conflict with democratic possibilities at every turn: support for dictatorial client-states, proxy wars, abrogation of international rules and norms, overthrow of foreign governments, and neoliberal economic policies on behalf of corporate interests. A security state was erected on vast and secretive executive powers, expanded surveillance and law enforcement, a sprawling military-industrial lobby, and an imperial presidency with diminished restraints. The war economy has for decades devoured valuable material, technological, and human resources better used to revitalize the American urban infrastructure, social services, and workforce.

While the United States remains world champion in the sphere of military force—as in corporate investments, banking operations, and energy consumption—its manufacturing base has eroded, its public transportation lags well behind many lesser-developed nations, its overall health care indicators rank at the lower tier of industrialized societies, its public schools are in perpetual crisis, and its poverty rate has reached more than 20 percent of the population. One dynamic American growth industry is prisons, which in 2010 housed 2.3 million inmates—one consequence of the largest, most costly law enforcement apparatus in the world. High levels of crime, gang warfare, domestic violence, drug and alcohol addictions, suicide, and family breakdown reflect a decaying, fragmented social order endemic to chronic lopsided priorities. American deaths from chronic diseases—cancer, heart disease, diabetes, long-term infections—rank among the world's highest, as does consumption of pharmaceuticals (roughly $350 billion worth yearly). Even with the Obama reforms, affordable health care remains elusive for tens of millions of Americans. Social inequality widens by the year: in 2010, the top one percent of Americans possessed as much wealth as the bottom ninety percent, the lowest 20 percent left to share a paltry 3.4 percent. High-level business executives received on average 450 times the income of ordinary workers, while union membership dropped to 13 percent of the workforce, with benefits suffering accordingly. Congress and other governing institutions remain white-male-dominated, with conditions at major corporations even worse: more than 95 percent of CEOs in 2010 were white men. The cycle of lopsided power and wealth accumulation has continued across the decades, reproduced by a seemingly irresistible force of nature. The United States today represents a truly "exceptional" nation, though nowhere near the beacon of equality, democracy, and progress imagined by earlier celebrants of Manifest Destiny and the American Century.

Taking this deplorable state of affairs into account, a critical observer is led to ponder, in the tradition of Aristotle, Rousseau, and Marx, whether a viable democratic politics is even imaginable in contemporary America. Could either of the major parties offer meaningful policy alternatives to voters? Could vigorous and open debates be given space within the media and political establishments? Could citizens hope to collectively exert influence on the conduct of government, corporations, and military? Could a popularly elected Congress, riddled with corporate lobbies, be entrusted to carry out far-reaching significant reforms? Recent history is informative: with its failure to enact strong health care legislation in 2009–10, the U.S. Congress had not passed a major piece of social legislation for nearly a half-century, since enactment of Medicare and the Voting Rights Act of 1965. The overall postwar record has been equally depressing. Badly needed social initiatives (on health care, transportation, child care, the environment)—not to mention financial regulations—have been nullified or watered down by the influence of corporations, their lobbies, and the underwriting of military priorities. The role of wealth in politics, as outright corporate largesse, campaign funding, Political Action Committees (PACs), lobbies, and personal riches, has no equivalence among popular groups and communities. The January 2010 Supreme Court ruling stripped away those few barriers remaining in the way of unlimited corporate influence-peddling.

A political system steeped in archaic practices—single-member constituencies, electoral college, private campaign funding, an encrusted seniority system, unwieldy legislative procedures, lopsided rural representation—had grown more dormant, out of touch with pressing global and domestic challenges. Legislative bills addressing rampant greed that helped trigger the worst U.S. economic calamity since the Depression were half-hearted, despite the leverage of a Democratic president backed by strong congressional majorities. Equally muted were efforts to arrest growing levels of unemployment, massive home foreclosures, and global warming.

In the end, entrenched oligarchical rule diminishes citizenship as it heightens political alienation. Despite unprecedented access of Americans to information through universities, bookstores, publishing houses, the popular media, and online sites, the population remained largely ignorant when it comes to political knowledge, a condition Rick Shenkman refers to the "age of ignorance."[26] Information of most sorts is readily available, though not often embellished with social or historical context. A strikingly large number of Americans do not read newspapers, magazines, or books regularly. Knowledge about political candidates and their stand on crucial issues is sadly lacking.[27] Even college-educated Americans are found to have surprisingly little awareness of basic historical and political facts—unable, for example, to identify such countries as Russia, China, and Iraq on a world map, or to date events like the Vietnam War and World War II. Even after Obama's uplifting 2008 presidential campaign, moreover, American citizens typically remained mistrustful of elected officials and their parties. Cynicism and pessimism about the future were widespread, intelligible enough in a society where economic fears and anxieties were so widespread. Many felt resentful over excessive taxation and spending, "big government," false promises, and the remoteness of politicians. Millions of Americans responded to Tea Party appeals for small government and free markets during the 2010 midterm elections, seemingly oblivious to the hypocrisy involved in a movement supporting gigantic corporate and military power while parading as libertarian. Hopes placed in the democratic potential of informational technology, moreover, have run aground at a time when social problems seem impervious to far-reaching change, whether through more accessible information or electoral choices. Susan Jacoby, in *The Age of American Unreason,* observes that "the greater accessibility of information through computers and the Internet serves to foster the illusion that the ability to retrieve words and numbers with click of a mouse also confers the capacity to judge whether those words and numbers represent truth, lies, or something in between."[28] It could be that the new technology has actually reinforced political alienation insofar as it offers false hopes for renewed community and democratic participation.

Could the power elite in America somehow be dethroned by popular insurgency or other forms of political opposition? In more immediate terms, could older visions of democracy be given new life in a system where citizen participation has been increasingly partial, uneven, and alienated? Could time-honored dreams of liberals and progressives come to fruition at a time when the matrix of dominant corporate, government, and military interests is so entrenched, so impervious challenge much less overthrow? Optimism would surely be the preferred outlook, yet there can be no return to a clean slate, as if more than two centuries of oligarchic and imperial history had never left its imprint on American political culture and institutions. Empire, the war economy, security-state, corporate power, globalization, the bureaucratization of public life—these stubborn conditions of life remain deeply embedded in the landscape, likely to persist into the indefinite future. Democratization would require a thorough restructuring of this pervasively authoritarian order, far beyond any normal strategy of reforms and regulations. Elite rule will be all the more difficult to penetrate in a Hobbesian world rife with popular fears, political insecurity, and social atomization. The power structure nurtures a passive, frightened, loyal citizenry, crucial to the legitimation process. The media dwells on the surface partisanship of American politics, but the elites in both parties converge around larger priorities of class privilege, power arrangements, and U.S. global ambitions.

Many progressives take inspiration from a long history of popular upheavals, uprisings, and struggles for change waged by Americans to secure a better life, what Wolin identifies as "demotic moments."[29] These are sporadic but often repeated expressions of civic engagement, typically collective and sometimes spontaneous outbursts of democratic energy—protests over felt grievances, direct action, and social reform struggles that broaden public space for citizen participation. Demotic moments capture the visionary ideals of Paine, Jefferson, Thoreau, Frederick Douglas, Emma Goldman, and their heirs across U.S. history, a powerful and optimistic legacy running counter to (and frequently offering alternatives to) the dominant oligarchy.

A pressing question remains, however, as to the historical impact of such demotic moments. Gains have in fact been considerable—the

securing of better wages and working conditions for labor, the right to
vote for women and others, sweeping reforms won by popular movements of the 1960s and 1970s, environmental legislation, and perhaps
an earlier end to the Vietnam War forced by the antiwar and GI movements. Demotic moments have expanded the realm of civic engagement, inspired new collective identities, softened class and institutional
oppression, and given electoral politics strong impulses toward reform.
Voices of dissent and opposition among workers, minorities, women,
and local activists across the decades live on as sources of inspiration for
new generations.[30] This legacy has, from time to time, indeed presented
a challenge to oligarchical power, a counterforce often working *outside*
the established institutional matrix. Whether demotic moments can
morph into transformative politics across time, or convert local energies
into more durable struggles for change, would be yet another matter.
The problem is that demotic moments are often episodic, immediate,
restive, and lacking in durability. Many have been crushed by coercive
state or military power. Others have lacked ideological coherence or
structural unity and quickly vanished from the scene. Still others have
disappeared, or at least receded, once concrete reforms were achieved.
Yet others have disintegrated out of their own spontaneity-driven
chaos. It could be argued that, for the most part, demotic moments
lacked modern political content: effective organization, a developed
ideology, strategic focus on state power, and institutional continuity.
In cases where local upsurges or movements did intersect with electoral
politics, as with the postwar labor and civil rights movements, their
trajectory was usually toward structural absorption and ideological
deradicalization. Salient as the demotic legacy has been, therefore, it
has rarely moved to the level of challenging dominant class and power
relations; oligarchic rule prevailed, despite periodic crises, threats, and
challenges.

In the end, democratization will require far-reaching structural and
cultural transformations; ingrained popular attitudes, beliefs, habits,
and biases will have to be drastically altered. Short of genuinely radical
changes, smaller and more immediate steps toward democratization
are surely possible, against predictable elite resistance. Compelling
models of social democracy, however limited and flawed, do exist in
the real world. If, as Wolin argues, "democracy is about the conditions that make it possible for ordinary people to better their lives by
becoming political beings and by making power responsive to their
hopes and needs," then clearly new stages along this journey are conceivable.[31] Classical revolutionary theory often disparages the notion

of stages, but such theory nowadays is less than helpful, for immediate moves toward broad social change are not beyond reach. This could mean, as Wolin suggests, initial efforts at "renewing the meaning and substance of 'representative democracy' by affirming the primacy of Congress, curbing the growth of presidential power, disentangling the stranglehold of lobbyists, democratizing the party system by eliminating the barrier to third parties, and enforcing an austere system of campaign finance."[32] It would further demand strong initiatives toward dismantling the war economy and security state—no easy task, to be sure, but eminently feasible if future "demotic moments" can be sustained and broadened through grassroots efforts in enough communities and workplaces.

Mainstream rejoinders to the argument that American politics is oligarchic rather than democratic follow predictable lines of thought: flawed as the system might be, it is the best that human beings have invented for an imperfect world. After all, it requires no great intellectual courage or vision to invoke quasi-utopian democratic theories borrowed from the Greeks, Rousseau, the anarchists, and others, but in the messy world of everyday politics it is imperative to compromise with harsher practicalities. "Realists" typically point to the geographical size, economic maturation, and social complexity of American society, the implication being that earlier "models" of democracy were relevant only to preindustrial societies, thereby recycling the myth of U.S. "exceptionalism." Some call attention to demanding international "burdens" inherited by the United States, forcing concessions on the economy, social programs, foreign policy, and political democracy. In the universe of "actually-existing democracies," therefore, the American system—for all its weaknesses—is probably the best mortal human beings can hope to achieve under conditions of modernity, a system still worthy of being promoted around the globe. Such rejoinders, self-serving as they are, correctly insist that normative judgments be grounded in historical experience and viable comparisons rather than utopian visions of what democracy might be under optimum conditions. An embrace of the Greeks or Rousseau, while inspiring, hardly constitutes a guidepost for critical understanding of present-day American politics, as the times are so radically different. For this reason, I have chosen for comparison a living example from within "actually-existing democracies" of the twentieth century: Sweden, at the height of its postwar achievements.

Radical democracy, to be sure, sets forth ideals worth incorporating into a framework of ultimate goals that, while perhaps never fully reachable, can advance both discursive and practical elements of democratic participation. It is surely appropriate to those "demotic moments," which, from time to time, challenge or overturn everyday routines. Such modern theorists as Cornelius Castoriadis, Murray Bookchin, Paul Goodman, Takis Fotopoulos, and Michael Albert have arrived at versions of radical democracy drawn from anarchism, utopian socialism, syndicalism, council communism, and more recent popular movements such as feminism and ecology.[33] These theorists share a number of emancipatory precepts: collective participation, extension of democracy beyond government into other arenas of public life, egalitarian social and authority relations, local forms of popular activity such as community assemblies and workers' councils, socialization of the economy. Following the anarchist Prince Kropotkin and others, Castoriadis refers to the "permanent self-institution of society," while Fotopoulos argues for an "inclusive democracy" extending across the entire social terrain. Bookchin goes further, insisting on the abolition of all forms of hierarchy leading to the complete transformation of society and "reharmonization of human life with nature."[34] Anticipating a final break with concentrated power and the social division of labor, radical democrats, usually on the fringes of broader movements, follow Rousseau, Marx, and the anarchists in their contempt for a liberal tradition that falsely upholds the ideal of "freedom" within a system of concentrated economic power and political oligarchy. For Douglas Lummis, the sine qua non of radical democracy is a renovated political culture in which all citizens, finally, can participate in every realm of social and political life.[35] However laudable these visions might be, they hardly suffice as a concrete historical model against which to critically analyze American politics, especially as no political system or society has ever measured up to these emancipatory yardsticks.

European social-democracy, on the other hand, has a visible history going back to the late nineteenth century, when mass-based parties built around electoral politics began to flourish in such countries as Germany, Italy, France, England, Belgium, Holland, and Sweden, all eventually joining the Second International. Their goal was an egalitarian society to be achieved by peaceful, evolutionary methods—winning votes, building trade unions, extending social reforms, creating local cooperatives, and other grassroots forms. Success would depend on the parties' capacity to whittle away at the leverage of private capital through widening social investments linked to democratized governance and planning. This would later be understood as the "third road" between global capitalism and communism of the Third International, both rejected for their embrace of concentrated economic and political power. Democratization beyond liberalism was at the core of this strategy, which looked to the socialization of public life against the extreme privatism, consumerism, hierarchy, and fragmentation of market society. This model, with Sweden often in the vanguard, took hold across Europe by the 1930s, fueled by political responses to the global economic crisis and a search for left alternatives to Soviet bureaucratic centralism. Scandinavian social-democratic parties won elections, expanded their institutional base in unions, coops, workers' councils, and local townships, and governed more or less continuously for several decades. In Sweden, perhaps more than elsewhere, they broadened their mass support and loosened the hold of big capital, implementing social and political reforms that would be the envy of other nations— all without overthrowing market relations, corporate power, or liberal-democratic governance. A broadened social contract and expanded public sector were built on strong dedication to universal rights and entitlements applicable to all spheres of public life.

Despite recurrent crises, challenges, and setbacks, the leading social-democratic nations (misleadingly called "welfare states") have largely if often tenuously held to this principle of universalism through social governance. Whatever their problems and defeats, they have been shining beacons of democracy when compared to the United States and its client-states. In 2010 the Swedish political system remained probably the most democratized in the world. The Riksdag, or parliament, shares power with an elaborate network of local assemblies and councils, rendering legislative work more open and accessible, more embedded in communities, than elsewhere. Municipal and county governments supplement and reinforce these national arrangements. Elections are publicly financed, held every four years (for the Riksdag), mercifully last only a few weeks, and allow for multiparty representation based on a four-percent rule (threshold for a party being seated). According to the 1971 Swedish Constitution, national elections are held to select delegates for a single legislative chamber from party lists in the 28 regional districts. About one-fourth of all Swedes belong to parties, with voter turnout consistently above 85 percent. Mass participation is actually solicited within communities, workplaces, schools, and unions, with labor, women, and youth liberally represented in electoral politics, where barriers of wealth and social status are minuscule compared to the American experience. Women's representation in the Riksdag has ranged from 35 to 50 percent throughout the postwar years (in contrast to roughly 15 percent today in the U.S. Congress). For the September

2006 parliamentary elections, six parties were seated, resulting in a "Red-Green" government comprised of Social Democrats, Greens, and the smaller Left Party. In terms of the big picture, writes Henry Milner, "The electoral system facilitates and encourages coordinated, organized participation both within and among the parties."[36]

After gaining a foothold in Sweden during the 1930s, the Social Democrats steadily broadened the public sector at the expense of corporate power—a partial but still meaningful triumph of politics over markets—without, as mentioned, dismantling the business structure altogether. Most reforms were extended and institutionalized consistent with a broadened social contract upheld across the political spectrum. Social classes remain, but their consequences for daily life have drastically narrowed owing to the secular impact of governmental policies. From time to time, especially during economic downturns, the "Swedish model"—reliant on high levels of taxation and a large, active public sector—has come under fire, leading to a decline of Socialist popularity, austerity programs, and capital flight, but the "model" has survived. Since the early 1980s public investment has remained at roughly 70 percent of GDP, with the military sector (at $5.7 billion in 2008) accounting for only 1.5 percent of total government spending. While global market pressures obviously tend to constrict government options, the Swedes have tenaciously held to ambitious public agendas. For their part, the Social Democrats, even at times of retreat, have managed to retain a multiclass base (labor, elements of the middle strata and professionals, etc.). The economy, meanwhile, has sustained relatively high levels of growth over time, hovering at roughly three percent in the decade after 2000.

Social democratic policies have generated the most comprehensive social programs in the world—a complex network of services, activities, and human relations the public has come to regard as non-negotiable. The Swedish national health care system—free, accessible, highly-efficient, human-centered—is without parallel in the world, administered mostly through municipalities. A wide range of public services is generously available to all citizens regardless of economic or social status: child care, extended parental leave, counseling services, sick leave, treatment for occupational injuries, and many others. Good, affordable housing is available to the general population, as is public transportation in all parts of the country. Unemployment compensation is paid for at least one year, at close to full income. Retirement pensions are among the most stable and well-subsidized in the world, eliminating old-age nightmares. Environmental regulations at the workplace and in communities are strict and fully enforced. Far more than a "welfare state," the Swedish system is driven by an elaborate planning network routed through a system of regional and municipal bodies. Dedicated from its inception to providing social services as basic rights—while reducing inequality, eliminating poverty, and empowering citizens—this system, despite inevitable ebbs and flows, has achieved remarkable success.[37] Roughly the size of California with a population of 10 million, Sweden in 2008 had a literacy rate of 99 percent and the best general health indicators in the world, with life expectancy at 85 for women and 81 for men. Its per capita income was $43,000 yearly, with relatively modest gaps in wealth and a poverty rate at less than three percent. Wages remained high, with unionization at 85 percent of the workforce (compared to 13 percent in the United States). There were no billionaires, and just a few millionaires. Violent crime was extremely rare, with little public funding needed for the jail, prison, and court systems. Universal child care ensured a place for all children in public day care between ages two and six. Education through college was widely accessible and relatively inexpensive for all Swedes. As of 2010, all social programs mentioned above remained completely intact, despite sporadic grumblings about high taxes and difficulties created by the global economic downturn.

Though hardly flawless, the legacy of *political* democracy in Sweden has generally stood the test of time, crisis, and challenge. Elections furnish multiple alternatives, are relatively brief and inexpensive, focus mainly on issues rather than personalities, engage the public through meetings rather than TV and advertising, and allow for surprisingly open entry into politics and government. Public meetings are held regularly in communities and at workplaces. Municipalities remain lively centers of civic participation, especially since they play a vital role in the implementation and oversight of social programs.[38] Official Swedish government literature states "it is important to remember that democracy exists not just on a political level but also permeates the whole society." What so emphatically distinguishes Sweden from the United States is not only the existence of a thriving multiparty system, proportional representation, public campaign financing, open access, and gender balance but those other necessary conditions of citizen democracy: extension of mass participation beyond government, universal public services, a dynamic infrastructure, and a relatively egalitarian social structure. This ongoing and creative dialectic between government and society, between political and civil realms, endows the Swedish system with a vitality lacking in most other countries, though generic forms of social democracy do exist in other parts of the world.

At a time when the global economic crisis has driven the American developmental model rightward—dramatized by the Tea Party insurgency, Republican victories in 2010, and vigorous defense of "free markets"—the Europeans, beyond Scandinavia, have fought to retain strong elements of social democracy. While an unstable, profit-driven, and inequitable Wall Street paradigm holds sway in the United States, nations of the European Union still look to broadened economic and political democracy marked by generous social investments, emphasis on public infrastructure, and participatory forms (coops, works councils, powerful unions, etc.). In this context, the ethos of democratization located in community and municipal empowerment is far more deeply embraced across Europe than in the United States, trumpeted by its elites as the best of all democracies. While the American system becomes more authoritarian with each passing year, with mounting extremes of wealth and poverty, the Europeans have held fast to those social priorities mentioned above: universal health care, accessible higher education, cheap and efficient public transportation, abundant low-cost housing, and a more protective safety net for those harmed by the crisis. As quality-of-life indicators remain comparatively high, moreover, leading European countries have managed to sustain relatively high levels of growth and productivity while turning increasingly to green technology. Sweden, Holland, Germany, Denmark, and Finland rank among the top ten competitive economies in the world, as EU nations combined were able to generate a much higher domestic product than the United States and China combined. Despite fanciful rhetoric of "free markets" in the United States, public spending remains as high as for most European societies, the difference being that more than half of all American tax revenues go to the military, warfare, intelligence operations, law enforcement, and the prison complex.

As for the Swedes, they long ago realized that a living democracy would be unthinkable in a society dominated by vast corporate power, a huge military, institutional oligarchy, and extreme differences between rich and poor. While the Social Democrats have inevitably made their share of compromises over the years, their undoubted achievements constitute (at their peak) a model of "actually-existing democracy" for the real world.

From Manifest Destiny to Empire

American political culture has been shaped by a long history of national exceptionalism rooted in claims of a unique democratic politics, a messianic patriotism, and special normative entitlements underpinning the U.S. role in world politics. While righteously upholding the ideals of freedom, human rights, and rule of law, however, U.S. leaders have routinely subordinated those ideals to overriding economic and geopolitical interests. Reflecting on this legacy, Howard Zinn writes that "aggressive expansion was a constant of national ideology and policy,"[1] reflected in genocidal wars against Native Americans, slavery, and theft of Mexican and Spanish lands followed by the post–World War I invasion of Russia, and a succession of bloody military interventions in Mexico, Central America, Korea, Indochina, the Caribbean, Persian Gulf, and Balkans—not to mention countless proxy wars, covert actions, and related ventures leading to the post-9/11 "war on terror," marked by ongoing wars in Afghanistan and Iraq. U.S. foreign policy was traditionally cloaked in the veneer of Enlightenment rationality, material prosperity, and liberal-democratic values, all driven by advances in science and technology. Beneath this profoundly "civilized" dedication to a new rational order, however, was always the quick readiness to use armed force as an instrument of national power. Great European ideals coexisted with an opportunistic realpolitik that was destined to clash with democratic priorities in a world where pressing corporate and colonial interests were always at stake.

The Founders: Oligarchy and Racism

In the overly generous view that most observers hold of early American history, the original colonists were dedicated apostles of freedom, democracy, limited government, political rights, and social equality. A closer reading of U.S. history, however, illustrates an altogether different picture: the 55 white European men who drew up the Constitution embraced such ideals, if at all, in only their most truncated and cosmetic form. Men of great wealth and property, most of whom owned slaves, wanted a strong federal government, and thought suffrage should be limited to white-male property owners in order to contain popular impulses. Their most urgent desire was to protect their accumulated wealth and power after independence from Britain was secured by the Revolutionary War. Zinn notes, correctly, that "the Constitution was a compromise between slaveholding interests in the South and moneyed interests in the North," hardly the recipe for a vibrant democratic politics.[2] With few exceptions, the colonial settlers looked to centralized power as a means of keeping order, destroying Indian resistance, maintaining slavery, conducting warfare, and (later) facilitating conquest of the Western frontier. The merger of government, large commercial interests, and military power had already taken shape, albeit in embryonic form, by the early nineteenth century. Those sacred American "principles" celebrated by most historians and embellished in civics textbooks thus fall into the category of self-serving mythology.

In his detailed study of the U.S. Constitution, Robert Dahl starts by asking, "Why should we feel bound today by a document produced more than two centuries ago by a group of fifty-five mortal men, actually signed by thirty-nine, a fair number of whom were slaveholders, and adopted only by thirteen states, by votes of fewer than two thousand men, all of whom are long since dead and mainly forgotten?" To what extent should Americans feel reverence, Dahl adds, for a small circle of Framers whose views (patriarchal, racist, and colonial) were so morally and politically repugnant, so unworthy of later emulation?[3] A sensible response might be "not at all," but we know the Framers remain at the center of a romantic ideology uncritically carried forward by an intellectual culture historically aligned with illusory discourses. As Dahl points out, the subsequent trajectory of the Constitution has been anything but democratic; far-reaching changes were driven largely by social movements and historical events that *challenged* the formative documents, and slavery was abolished only after a long and bloody civil war. Further, nothing in the Constitution prohibited or even discouraged such oppressive traditions as racism, sexism, and imperialism, not to mention drastically unequal wealth, power, and share of other resources. No wonder this system, provincially upheld as a beacon of enlightened values within the doctrine of American exceptionalism, has rarely served as an inspiration for other nations, as Dahl stresses. (Some might respond, correctly, that the Constitution was simply a product of its time—but that merely begs the question of why such an outmoded document remains the object of contemporary worship.) For those cheerleaders of "American values" who believe a thriving legacy of democracy was simply, and for reasons never made clear, derailed later by individual leaders like Richard Nixon or George W. Bush, a deeper, more critical historical perspective might be worth consulting.

Contrary to received wisdom, the U.S. Constitution laid the groundwork for centralized government and elite rule, not surprising for a document that actually evokes contempt for the democratic capacities of ordinary people. It was the artifact of a predemocratic era in which all forms of domination, later contested, were mostly taken for granted. While it is true that participation in limited forms (mainly voting) has steadily broadened over time—and with it the codification of many basic rights—elite power has continued to define American society into the present. This should hardly seem astounding, for, as Sheldon Wolin puts it, the American political system was "born with a bias against democracy."[4] It was a system, in other words, fully compatible with concentrated forms of corporate, government, and military power: Congress, the presidency, the court system, parties, workplaces, schools, and universities—all these arenas of public life have been hierarchical and bureaucratic, with modest degrees of popular involvement at best. While power had grown more authoritarian across the landscape, few people (earlier or later) paused to question the "democratic" label so ritually affixed to American social and political life; the flattering label was taken for granted. Power became even further elitist and bureaucratic during the twentieth century with the growth of an imperial system linked to a domestic security state. As Wolin notes, "Virtually from the beginning of the nation the making of the American citizen was influenced, even shaped by, the making of an American imperium."[5]

The Founders erected a power structure that was essentially *hostile* to democracy, attached to an ideology that understood human nature as innately violent, aggressive, and driven by material self-interest, a "human nature" needing to be pacified by government power and the greater wisdom of privileged elites. Without such imposed limits, the masses—consumed by extreme passions—would threaten a social order tied to private property. Richard Hofstadter wrote several decades ago that "it is ironical that the Constitution, which Americans venerate so deeply, is based upon a political theory that at one crucial point stands in direct antithesis to the mainstream democratic faith."[6] Those without property, it was widely felt, lacked the skills, outlook, and experience required for democratic governance. Laissez-faire ideology was fine but would have to be subordinated to the imperatives of oligarchical power, fully at odds with the notion of popular self-activity so fundamental to democratic norms. Despite the ideal of citizen sovereignty enshrined in the Declaration of Independence and Jeffersonian populism, therefore, oligarchical power ultimately held sway through the late nineteenth and early twentieth centuries despite challenges from a series of social movements: labor, women's suffrage, populism, anarchism, Progressivism, and socialism. These challenges did soften harsh inequalities and injustice, but made little dent in overall class and power relations. A profoundly elitist system of governance persisted, even after a series of Constitutional amendments granted suffrage to new groups after decades of intense popular struggles.

The Constitutional framework was in fact thoroughly compatible with plutocratic governance that was fostered by what is best described as extreme capitalism, where private property, accumulation of money and wealth, and material interests took precedence over competing values. Later development was anything but egalitarian and democratic as frontier life encouraged a strong Darwinian ethos. Those capitalist institutions that mattered most—banks, trading, manufacturing, mining, landed property—were only marginally affected by political activity limited to the sphere of parties, elections, and lobbying that was itself dominated by capitalist interests. While the political franchise expanded throughout the nineteenth and early twentieth centuries, it was pegged to an activity (voting) overwhelmed by rapidly expanding corporate power and wealth that took off after the Civil War and accelerated during the 1880s and 1890s. The fanciful notion of a simple agrarian and small-town America could not emerge from the reality of a modernizing, urban, industrial, and financial oligarchy committed to high levels of economic growth; a freewheeling, libertarian paradise governed by ordinary citizens was illusory from the outset. While the "first new nation" possessed no aristocracy, monarchy, or state church, it did have an elitist power structure rooted in newer structures of domination. Great fortunes were to be made in the urban centers of New England, New York, Philadelphia, Boston, Chicago, and across the Western frontier to California. The spread of unfettered capitalism meant drastic social inequality, contradicting promises of an agrarian community championed by such ideologues as Jefferson and Jackson. In New York, for example, by 1828 the top 1 percent of the population controlled roughly 30 percent of the wealth, which grew to a staggering 40 percent by 1845, a trend characteristic of other major cities.[7] The myth of American egalitarianism was shattered by expanding gulfs between the rich and the poor, between corporations and the rest that, as is well known, inevitably were in conflict with conditions vital to democratic participation. Even leaving aside the ugly persistence of slavery (which gave way to harsh Jim Crow laws) and genocidal policies on the frontier, plutocracy was hardly an arrangement conducive to broad-based political engagement, decision-making, and governance.

The Civil War ushered in a new era of uneven development with a massive realignment of income and wealth from South to North, from agrarian to urban areas, coinciding with an expanded government, military, and Eastern financial aristocracy, along with the rise of corporate moguls little interested in anything resembling democratic politics: Rockefeller, Carnegie, Field, Gould, et al. By the end of the century, the fortunes of the ten leading corporate owners had increased almost threefold from 1873.[8] Wealth was generated through huge combines, trusts, financial schemes, and corporations strong enough to take over most realms of public life. By the 1890s virtually half of all wealth was controlled by less than one percent of American families. As for Congress, it had evolved into a citadel of privileged interests, the Senate famously being condemned as the "House of Industrial Lords." Indeed, for many decades the Senate was not actually chosen by voters, but rather by state legislatures. As one populist observed in 1880, reflecting a widely held view, "The great common people of this country are slaves, and monopoly [capital] is the master."[9] Although populism had grown into a force to be taken seriously in the Midwest and West by the 1880s, it failed to significantly tip the balance of power away from the ruling elites, having gained little foothold in the political system or economy. Between 1880 and World War I the nation witnessed the rise of broad social movements—not only populism but Progressivism, organized labor, socialism, feminism, and anarchism—all seeking to somehow democratize the power structure, pave the way toward social equality, and (in some instances) fight imperialism by working mostly outside the party duopoly—but these forces ultimately failed to transform a top-heavy power structure that World War I would eventually serve to consolidate.

Contrary to the fiction of a laissez-faire economy giving shape to nineteenth-century American society, several forces—Westward migration, industrial development, and conquest of new lands—combined to sharply increase state intervention across the social landscape. The federal government was crucial to Western expansion in many ways: military operations, railroad construction, mail and communications, land exploration and surveying, the Indian agencies, building of local infrastructures, and, of course, law enforcement. The U.S. government also routinely intervened to neutralize threats to settlements, provide key social supports (such as health care and education), subsidize "free" enterprise, enter into (mostly phony) treaties with Indians, and operate federal reservations. There was scant evidence of a much-celebrated "free market," then or later, nor was "rugged individualism" widespread even across the frontier given the extensive role of government. Heroic self-reliance among white settlers, popularized in dozens of Hollywood movies, was just another seductive fiction. Neither economic nor political life was organized along principles of laissez-faire economics, limited government, or democratic politics.

The argument that early U.S. history followed an oligarchical trajectory conflicts with the conventional wisdom that views the Founders as architects of a new democratic order. The Declaration of Independence did, of course, locate sovereignty in the individual citizen who possessed rights to "life, liberty, and the pursuit of happiness," a noble Jeffersonian principle that enshrines "the people" as the central agency of governance. This "democratizing" side of early American politics gave special meaning to the Bill of Rights, enacted to protect citizens from government tyranny. Jeffersonian populism seemed most compatible with fashionable laissez-faire ideology and minimalist government that, in theory at least, permeated nineteenth-century American public life. The legacy of a strong central state, at first associated with Alexander Hamilton and the Federalists, was always more consistent with elite power, an approach that on the surface appeared to lose resonance during the "age of democratic revolution." The problem, however, was that Jeffersonian ideals, though lofty, were always more illusion than reality when viewed in the context of actual, living American history.

Conquest and Exterminism

The tradition of U.S. exceptionalism is nowhere more visible than in the centuries-long destruction of Native peoples, a tradition that has shaped American foreign and military policy up to the present. European settlers and their heirs left a trail of conquest, slavery, warfare, and destruction, legitimated by a complex mixture of "whiteman's burden," Christianity, Enlightenment ideology, material prosperity, and other residual vestiges of European culture. This ideological amalgam underpinned the Indian Wars, slave economy, conquest of Mexican lands, and later U.S. expansion into Central America and Asia. An Indian population estimated as high as 15 million when Columbus arrived in the Western hemisphere was reduced to less than 300,000 by 1900, the result of colonists' insatiable demand for land, resources, power, and religious hegemony. With slavery and frontier expansion, the settlers had by the mid–nineteenth century erected a massive network of exploitation held intact by economic and military power. The idea of Manifest Destiny originated in the prerevolutionary period when the Puritans looked to conquer new frontiers they saw as inhabited by savages lacking the capacity to develop land they had occupied for centuries. Celebrating a nascent "empire of liberty," the Puritans set themselves up as harbingers of a liberal revolution that would sweep away obstacles to human progress—"progress," unfortunately, often requiring maximum use of armed force. Integral to a special national and religious community with a messianic zeal, expansionism came with few limits or apologies. Familiar romantic images of early settler populations as inward-looking and isolationist, and respectful of other cultures, were always a fiction.

The historic forging of a new republic deepened this sense of uniqueness and entitlement, formally endowing the European colonists with a civilized virtue and national destiny grounded in deep convictions of racial superiority. As Zinn observes, "There is not a country in world history in which racism has been more important, for so long a time, as the United States."[10] Those backward peoples obstructing U.S. Westward expansion were brushed aside as subhuman, savage, godless, and fit for extermination. This outlook was destined to spread beyond continental frontiers, justified by such diktats as the Monroe Doctrine (1823), which proclaimed that Latin America would henceforth be subject to U.S. domination, accompanied by an implicit warning that Washington had the right to intervene anywhere in the Western hemisphere to ensure its hegemony. During the nineteenth century the U.S. militarily intervened in several Latin American nations more than 100 times—a prelude to later ventures in Central America and the Caribbean—after wresting away Mexican territory in the 1840s. Elected president in 1844, James K. Polk affirmed U.S. entitlement to Mexican lands it had long coveted. Provoking war on the basis of contrived imminent threats to American security, Polk simply annexed vast regions of present-day

Texas, California, New Mexico, Arizona, and Montana by means of what nowadays would be called "preemptive war." With full contempt for Mexican sovereignty, Polk argued the United States was free to attack a foreign country so long as its (self-proclaimed) national interests were at stake. The war against Mexico was the first one supported by mass patriotic frenzy extending across the ideological spectrum, anticipating an even more virulent jingoism at the time of the war against Spain a half-century later. Like Indians and blacks, Mexicans were demonized as backward, ignorant, and undemocratic, unworthy proprietors of the land they inhabited.

American conquest of new frontiers was understood as a necessary step in sweeping away archaic barriers to liberal ideals of material growth and prosperity. President Jackson's infamous Indian removal policies of 1830 were widely seen as making possible the transition from savagery to civilization, from backwardness to modernity. As Michael Rogin observed, the Westward push was based on the dual premise that Native peoples were simultaneously children in need of harsh parental authority and fearsome warriors.[11] Bereft of "civilized" virtues, the Indians were deemed unable to negotiate contracts or properly exploit land, and also feared as the menacing out-of-control terrorists of the period, as innately violent killers lacking restraint. Indians exhibited a particularly barbaric culture congruent with a Hobbesian state of nature, a culture that would have to be pacified or eradicated. It was not enough for the federal government to get rid of indigenous tribes or herd them into remote confinement; the whole of Native American culture and historical memory would have to be destroyed. As the United States signed numerous treaties with those few remaining Indians that had been forced into reservations, it routinely and unilaterally broke such agreements, especially where the land was found to contain important natural resources. At one point, Jackson himself posed the question: "And is it to be supposed that the wandering savage has a stronger attachment to his home than the settled, civilized Christians?"[12] Contrary to any imaginable democratic ethic, native peoples were denied humanity and thus any genuine claim to political rights, much less citizenship, even as the governing circles continued to celebrate liberal principles. Federal negotiators signed treaties as essentially a tactical ploy, to be violated or broken at the slightest whim, as in the case of Cherokees and Crees whose villages were demolished in the wake of Jackson's Removal Act. This was basically a dictatorship in which contracts and laws related to Indian life could be overridden by political decree or military force. Given whites' entrenched attitudes of racial supremacy and national exceptionalism, it would be no difficult matter—in the nineteenth century or later—to ignore or dissolve supposedly binding agreements.

By 1890, with the U.S. massacre of Sioux civilians at Wounded Knee, the conquest of Indian lands had come to a merciless end just as Westward expansion had run its course, leaving in its wake an authoritarian system reinforced by the consolidation of financial and industrial power. Expansionism was now fully embedded in the political culture, a taken-for-granted reality by the upper echelon of politicians, business leaders, military establishment, and Christian churches. As frontier champions like Theodore Roosevelt were quick to recognize, by the turn of the century, the United States was prepared to carry forward its Manifest Destiny to other parts of the world. Roosevelt, among others, believed the legacy of Indian conquests had cleared the terrain for a modernizing, enlightened, civilizing project superior to anything the world had ever seen. An ideology of national exceptionalism would be passed along to succeeding generations of Americans. For such unabashed colonialism to be fully inculcated into the popular consciousness, however, the dark side of U.S. history was best submerged within high-sounding discourses about freedom and democracy. Over time, in fact, that terrible past would be roundly *celebrated* as in yearly Columbus Day rituals, the worshipful treatment given such leaders as Jackson and Roosevelt, and proliferation of Hollywood "Western" movies romanticizing the genocidal past.[13] Not only did criminal deeds vanish from collective memory through elaborate modes of political and cultural erasure, but the dominant image of American pubic life that emerged from the period was turned into a revitalizing mythology of rights, equality, and citizen participation, surely one of the most impressive propaganda achievements ever.

The racist dimension of early (and later) American politics deserves special attention, as it remains organically connected to broad areas of social life as well as global behavior. It reveals, perhaps more lucidly than any other discourse, how the rhetoric of democracy has been so detached from actual political behavior. Ronald Takaki, a historian for whom racism is central to understanding the American past, argues that "race...has been a social construction that has historically set apart racial minorities from European immigrant groups."[14] Nonwhite groups, the victims of dispossession, slavery, exploitation, and extermination, were denigrated as unworthy of civilized treatment. Not only Native Americans and blacks but others—Mexicans, Irish, Asians, Jews, etc.—were dehumanized by harsh stereotypes. Those with different skin color, religions, or culture were scorned and oppressed at the very time Westward migration was said to be about "progress" and "democracy." A predatory and violent frontier ethos departed little from earlier U.S. history, but did articulate what had become, in significant part, a white-supremacist agenda. Both Jefferson and Jackson, lauded in history texts as champions of the ordinary person, not only owned slaves but viewed Indians as barbaric impediments to progress. Thus Enlightenment rationality, like the Constitution itself, could evolve alongside such practices as slavery, segregation, and Jim Crow laws at a time when everyday "American values" revolved around land theft, maximum wealth accumulation, and social domination.

In 1814 Jackson could write: "I must destroy those deluded victims [Indians] doomed to destruction by their own restless and savage conduct."[15] For Jackson, apparently, extermination was a product of the Indians' own supposed primitivism. At the Battle of Horseshoe Bend in 1818, Jackson and his troops surrounded 800 Creek Indians and slaughtered them all, including women and children, Jackson saying afterward that the massacre was a forward step on the march toward civilization. Author of forced migration, Jackson continues to be treated as a national hero, a genius of the Indian Wars, and one of the greatest U.S. presidents. In Washington, Jackson famously asked: "What good man would prefer a country covered with forests and ranged by a few thousand savages to our extensive Republic, studded with cities, towns, and prosperous farms...and filled with the blessings of liberty, civilization, and religion?"[16] It was upon this ruthless foundation that the American Dream was constructed and carried forward. Rights and freedoms? Those privileges, however truncated, scarcely extended beyond the realm of white-settler culture and Eastern capitalist society. The atavistic outlook embraced by Jefferson, Jackson, and other early leaders of the republic would be forever embedded in the logic of American development on its twisted journey toward Manifest Destiny.

From Warfare to Empire

By 1900, with Indian conquests finished and the British Empire in decline, some U.S. leaders were now relishing dreams of their nation becoming the greatest power on earth. This was naturally conceived as a benevolent mission, endorsed by an American-loving deity, but its motivations fit the pattern of long European colonial experience: geopolitical advantage, new markets, natural resources, and extension of military power. References to a Christian-ordained destiny, visible even in statements by such later presidents as Ronald Reagan and George W. Bush, have a righteous lineage going back to Jackson, McKinley, and Theodore Roosevelt, for whom God was an unswerving American partisan. It seemed logical, therefore, for Protestant messianism to take U.S. expansion far beyond continental shores. As World War I approached, the United States was moving rapidly toward industrial and technological—if not yet military—global predominance that infused American patriotism with a distinct fervor. In this period, of course, U.S. advances were yet to be translated into anything close to global hegemony.

The ascendancy of U.S. international power gained impetus from the frontier experience, Monroe Doctrine, and events surrounding the Spanish-American War. That contrived military venture enabled Washington to annex lands occupied by Spain, including Puerto Rico, Guam, Cuba, and the Philippines. When the United States moved to occupy the Philippines in 1898, fed by jingoistic media frenzy, President McKinley was known to have prayed to Almighty God for counsel, saying "that we could not leave them [Filipinos] to themselves—they were unfit for self-government—for they would soon have anarchy and misrule over there worse than Spain's wars, and there is nothing left for us to do but take them all and educate the Filipino, and by God's grace do the very best we could by them...And then I went to bed and slept soundly."[17] But Philippine insurgents never received that message, instead fighting back against ruthless American efforts to pacify the country and establish the first U.S. beachhead in Asia. It took U.S. military forces nearly three years to crush the insurgency at a cost of hundreds of thousands of civilian lives in a war that conceded few limits to barbarism and concluded with Senator Albert Beverage proclaiming that "the Philippines are ours forever."[18] In the wake of exterminism directed against the Indians, Washington was quite ready to initiate another war of attrition during which American forces killed and destroyed as a badge of national honor: mass murder would be a vehicle of U.S. imperial designs sold to the public as a crusade for democracy.

If during the years preceding World War I U.S. military strength remained undeveloped relative to later decades, the political impulse toward expansion abroad remained very much alive. In 1917 President Woodrow Wilson sent tens of thousands of troops to the European theater, for a "war to end all wars," a campaign that would "make the world safe for democracy." The political and media systems cranked out full-scale propaganda to generate patriotic fanaticism behind a war that would leave more than 10 million dead on the battlefield and another 20 million dead from diseases and casualties related to combat. Although Wilson is still revered as something of an "idealist" dedicated to international democracy, U.S. military operations during the period had little to do with democracy in Europe or at home where, in 1917, the president got Congress to pass the infamous Espionage Act, allowing government to incarcerate antiwar dissidents for up to twenty years. In late 1917 federal agents set out to smash the radical Industrial Workers of the World, raiding some 48 Industrial Workers of the World (IWW) meeting halls across the country, arresting dozens of movement leaders, and seizing information used (successfully) as courtroom evidence to destroy the leadership. Wilson then set in motion the notorious Palmer Raids targeting thousands of leftists, a prelude to anticommunist hysteria and witch hunts of the late 1940s and 1950s. An expert at democratic rhetoric, Wilson oversaw an authoritarian government that paid little heed to citizen rights and fought defiantly (though unsuccessfully) against women's suffrage. Jailed for his opposition to the war, the socialist Eugene Debs said: "They tell us that we live in a great free republic, that our institutions are democratic, that we are a free and self-governing people. That is too much even for a joke...Wars throughout history have been waged for conquest and plunder."[19]

The notion of a progressive, democratic, peace-loving Wilson turns out to be another great myth of U.S. history. Aside from his contributions to the carnage of World War I, Wilson intervened militarily in Mexico (1914), Haiti (1915), the Dominican Republic (1916), Nicaragua (1916), Mexico again (1916), and Panama (1918), all to secure U.S. economic and military interests in alignment with the Monroe Doctrine. None of these countries, it should be emphasized, were bequeathed democratic institutions; on the contrary, the Wilsonian legacy was one mostly of brutal dictatorships like that of the tyrannical Anastasia Somoza in Nicaragua. In the summer of 1918, the United States set up a naval blockade of the Soviet Union and sent expeditionary forces to Murmansk, Archangel, and Vladivostok, hoping to overthrow the nascent government, an often forgotten imperial episode driven by overwrought fears of worldwide communist victory.

General Smedley Butler, a Marine Corps leader during World War I, had witnessed in close quarters U.S. military interventions in the Philippines, Mexico, Central America, and Haiti, concluding after painful reflection that such operations had nothing to do with democracy—never a factor in these regions—and everything to do with superprofits for huge military businesses. He admitted that his own role was that of a "gangster for capitalism," since war was just another corporate racket, but one where the costs were all-too-often tallied in the millions of lives. In Butler's view, those continuous U.S. wars should never have been fought, as the only beneficiaries turned out to be a tiny stratum of fortune-seekers. As for U.S. national agendas, noble ideals were nothing more than legitimating symbols to mobilize Americans around blind patriotism. Like earlier U.S. military conflicts, the Great War made a mockery of such ideals. He wrote: "So vicious was this war propaganda that even God was brought into it. With few exceptions our clergymen joined in the clamor to kill, kill, kill. To kill Germans. God is on our side...it is His will that the Germans be killed...Beautiful ideals were painted for our boys who were sent out to die. This was the 'war to end all wars'. This was the 'war to make the world safe for democracy.' No one told them that dollars and cents were the real reason. No one mentioned to them, as they marched away, that their going and their dying would mean huge war profits."[20]

Throughout the twentieth century the United States waged large-scale military action against six Asian nations, leading to millions of casualties in Japan, Korea, Vietnam, Laos, and Cambodia as well as the Philippines. World War II, described in American historical lore as the quintessential "good war," proved only a slight departure from earlier patterns as the war, especially in the Pacific, turned into what John Dower called a "war without mercy" that took military combat to new levels of bloodshed. The Japanese attack on Pearl Harbor had multiple origins, all stemming from a buildup of U.S.-Japan rivalry over imperial domination of the Pacific, that is, access to raw materials, trade, spheres of political influence, and military control. By 1941 the rivalry had become fierce, marked by ideological rigidity and political (mixed with racial) arrogance on both sides, aggravated by new U.S. military deployments in the Philippines, Guam, Wake Island, and Hawaii, then further heightened by the Washington oil embargo on Japan. The U.S. insistence that Japan withdraw from China and Indochina was summarily and understandably rejected. Admiral Harold Stack, chief of Naval Operations, had in early 1941 decided to make permanent the stationing of a reinforced Pacific Fleet in Hawaii, a move the Japanese viewed as hugely provocative. Scores of U.S. ships based at Pearl Harbor were used to monitor, harass, and test the Japanese navy while also disrupting trade routes.[21] By late 1941 Japanese leaders felt they had no option but to respond militarily, a shift in attitude well-known to American leaders who had anticipated such likelihood.[22]

Warfare between the United States and Japan contained an explosive racial as well as imperial dimension from Pearl Harbor onward. As Dower writes, the Pacific theater quickly turned into a "spellbinding spectacle of brutality and death," marked by sheer hatred on both sides.[23] It appeared that no U.S. military enemy was ever so detested as the Japanese, who became objects of racial caricatures, reflecting attitudes long predating Pearl Harbor. Stereotypes used to degrade the Japanese replicated those used against Native Americans, Asian immigrants, and Filipinos. The Japanese were depicted in American political and popular culture as innately primitive and barbaric, so backward that U.S. leaders doubted their capacity to carry out successful military campaigns; they were deemed clueless as to how to manufacture first-rate ships and planes or adequately train crews. One military official in the field was quoted as saying "we can lick the Japanese in 24 hours." Even when U.S. officials came to possess information about a likely Japanese attack it was met with contemptuous disbelief—a myopia that turned to indignant shock on the morning of December 7. The rapid conversion of American hubris into a mood of terrifying amazement could well have emerged as a central motif of Pearl Harbor, more compelling than the racist narrative of unspeakable treachery by architects of a "sneak attack"—as if military campaigns were supposed to be telegraphed to the enemy in advance. What Dower aptly refers to as "exterminist rhetoric" continued throughout the war, making possible the later fire bombings of some 65 Japanese cities (with overwhelming civilian casualties) followed by the atomic incineration of Hiroshima and Nagasaki in August 1945, at a point when the war was all but formally over, killing as many as 400,000 civilians.[24] Dower adds: "In the case of the Japanese enemy...the [racist] obsession extended to men and women far removed from the place of battle, and came to embrace not just the enemy's armed forces but the Japanese as a race and culture."[25] At one point the fanatically militaristic Admiral Bull Halsey threatened to kill off "the entire Japanese race," a sentiment echoed by other U.S. military leaders, typically with little sense of irony.

Abundant evidence shows, moreover, that the Roosevelt administration was not only fully aware of the Japanese buildup to war but had developed its foreign and military policy in a manner intended to provoke a (desired) hostile response. According to historian Robert Stinnett and others, Franklin D. Roosevelt (FDR) was anxious to enter World War II but needed Japan to fire the first salvo in order to force an isolationist Congress (and nation) to join the battle. From this standpoint, the United States was hardly an innocent sleeping giant and Hawaii (a military fortress) was no quaint, peaceful island paradise, nor were decision-makers caught totally off-guard by the Pearl Harbor attack—though reports indicate that Washington officials failed to pass along timely messages to the armed forces command in Hawaii. After reviewing some 200,000 documents, Stinnett writes: "By provoking the attack, Roosevelt accepted the terrible truth that America's military forces—including the Pacific Fleet and the civilian populations in the Pacific—would sit squarely in harm's way, exposed to enormous risks."[26] By means of well-planned covert and overt actions, the United States had implemented an eight-point scheme to incite the Japanese to war, including the embargo, military support for the Chinese nationalist regime, expansion of the Pacific Fleet, and dispatch of naval task groups into Japanese waters (a violation of international law), while summarily dismissing all Japanese protests.

It is further worth noting that the military repercussions of the Pearl Harbor attack have been drastically overblown: while tactically audacious, the bombing did little to immobilize U.S. capabilities in the Pacific, or even in Hawaii itself. The aging battleship fleet, hit hard on December 7, was already in decline as an instrument of naval warfare, but more significantly the ground facilities received little damage, including the huge submarine base, oil depots, supply warehouses, dry docks, and repair shops so vital to restoring U.S. naval power in the Pacific. Even the overall casualty count from the raids was not extremely high when compared with later Pacific theater engagements and U.S. aerial bombardments in Japan that killed at least a million civilians in 1945: at Pearl Harbor there were 2,403 dead and 1,178 wounded, with a civilian toll of 63. But with the attack FDR had achieved his goal— U.S. entry into World War II, leading to full-scale war footing and patriotic mobilization. Pearl Harbor and its protracted aftermath not only united the country behind a lengthy war campaign but gave rise to the sprawling military-industrial system that remains a durable feature of American society today. The war of attrition in the Pacific, with its epic fusion of imperialism, racism, and militarism—eventually leading to a massive shift of U.S. armed forces into Asia—followed a long trajectory of colonial expansion rooted in Manifest Destiny.

The Postwar Leviathan

The Allied battlefield victory in 1945 paved the way toward an institutionalized military-industrial system in the United States, with sustained high levels of Pentagon spending, a powerful nuclear strike capability, growth of the National Security State (NSS), new opportunities for military ventures, and reinforced commitment to armed forces power across the postwar years. The Cold War framing of new global demons (Communists) brought an obsession with "national security" far beyond U.S. borders—the only nation so preoccupied, as the Soviet Union was still focused on rebuilding its war-torn society and protecting its own borders. The postwar system extended the familiar pattern of U.S. military vigilance tied to standard ideological claims of modernity, progress, freedom, and democracy. While expanded global power was understood as a natural American mandate for international supremacy, it was a mandate that gave Washington license to support right-wing dictators as in South Korea, the Philippines, Indonesia, Pakistan, and Greece, always in the name of promoting "democracy," although no public debate about whether the United States should have become a full-fledged imperial power ever took place, nor would it ever.

U.S. strategic bombing at the end of World War II, elevated to new levels of barbarism at Hiroshima and Nagasaki, set the contours for postwar American thinking about global power. The Truman Doctrine, invoked in the late 1940s to "save" countries like South Korea, Iran, Greece, and Turkey from communist subversion, established the new paradigm by affirming U.S. entitlement to intervene militarily anywhere it chose. The self-chosen heir to Pax Britannica, Washington took on the role of global Leviathan prepared to rid the world of threats—or at least perceived threats—to its power aspirations. At the peak years of the Cold War (1947 to 1975), the United States took virtually every move to escalate the arms race, creating in the process the most far-flung military presence the world had ever seen. The Pentagon and NSS grew steadily, with some dips, underwritten by a "bipartisan" consensus of Republicans and Democrats that approved bloated military budgets and new global deployments with little congressional debate or public input. The political system, media, and academia became integral to the NSS behemoth that, as President Dwight Eisenhower warned in 1961, was destined to threaten the very firmament of democratic governance. Postwar interventions in Greece and Turkey, the rise of McCarthyism, the Korean War, erection of a nuclear first-strike capability, President John F. Kennedy's ambitious global liberalism, and the Vietnam War all reflected this postwar shift. The Cold War marked a new phase of aggressive U.S. behavior, consistent with familiar elite claims of a special American mission in the world.

In 1950 Korea emerged as the main Cold War battleground, five years after U.S. troops entered the peninsula and prepared for an indefinite stay following partition of the country that was never endorsed by any legal arrangement. When civil war erupted the United States (with UN complicity) turned the conflict into the first major global confrontation between communism and the West, pitting "democracy" against "tyranny" even while South Korea was ruled by iron-fisted dictator Syngman Rhee. Truman's decision to invade North Korea grew out of an aggressive rollback scheme to "liberate" the North using massive armed force, but hopes of rapid victory were dashed once the Chinese entered the war. A long, bloody stalemate ensued, but instead of proposing a negotiated settlement that could have saved millions of lives, the United States persisted in a war of attrition that General Douglas MacArthur ordered be brought to a vulnerable civilian population. MacArthur wanted to target every installation, factory, village, and means of communication—a scorched-earth campaign bearing all the features of World War II operations. U.S. military planners held that total destruction of both military and civilian targets was a legitimate war aim, a stratagem that would produce up to three million avoidable deaths. For Truman the stakes were indeed high—the United States could not afford to "lose" Korea after having already "lost" China in 1949. God, democracy, and even Western civilization were fully on the line in this epic Cold War clash. Political elites and the media dwelled on the menace of "superhuman red hordes" taking over vast expanses of Asia, a region now more than ever regarded as an indispensable outpost of U.S. global power.

The Korean War, like the Spanish-American War, was fueled by moral certitude linked to a sense of military superiority backed by relentless saturation bombing.[27] At the time of the stalemate General Matthew Ridgeway would intone: "It is not a question of this or that Korean town or village. Real estate here is incidental... The real issues are whether the power of Western civilization, as God has permitted it to exist in our beloved lands, shall defy and defeat Communism, whether we are to survive with God's hand to guide and lead us, or to perish in the dead existence of a Godless world."[28] Such genocidal attitudes naturally coincided with ruthless warfare in which civilians were to suffer terribly—little different from the frontier, the Philippines, or Japan—but of course such attitudes inevitably contradicted democratic pretenses as massacred people could hardly enjoy any form of participation. Truman, moreover, appeared ready to use nuclear weapons to break the Korean stalemate, having already employed biological weapons that, however, proved largely futile and counterproductive.[29] A deepening American culture of militarism, fueled by an ever-present racism, gave apocalyptic thinking a veneer of rationality within the prevailing ideological climate. Horrific crimes against a godless tyranny could be made more palatable. Decades later, Washington still possessed a sprawling network of military bases on the Korean peninsula, its troops armed with tactical nuclear weapons targeted on a diabolical enemy that itself had become nuclearized—an enemy President George W. Bush would include in his post-9/11 "axis of evil."

As with previous wars, the Korean intervention was broadly endorsed by the American public, which was convinced that new Communist demons had to be fought. As with others Koreans were doubly objectified: dismissed as racially inferior, they were at the same time an imminent threat to U.S. national security. Here and later the Cold War provided a convenient ideological backdrop for such Manicheistic narratives in which a benevolent, peace-loving democracy finds itself under siege from a Red tyranny out for world domination. Despite much anticommunist saber rattling, however, the Eisenhower years amounted to something of an interregnum in this overwrought historical drama. Then, for nearly 15 years, Vietnam served as the gruesome battleground between the East and the West, with over 3 million Vietnamese killed (along with 58,000 Americans). As with Korea, those resisting U.S. power were attacked as backward and vile, as worthless "Gooks," while being feared as skilled fighters, part of a new "yellow horde." Relying on the supremacy of technowar that in Vietnam included almost daily saturation bombing runs, the United States was able to destroy most of the country but failed to win the war against a determined insurgency. Referred to as "Injun country" by many GIs, Vietnam was the locale of a good many fantasies, myths, and illusions consistent with Manifest Destiny. It was a cauldron of imperial ambitions, dressed as usual in democratic garb, now gone terribly sour amidst unspeakable carnage.

Technocratic war managers in Washington and Saigon unveiled everything short of nuclear weapons: aerial bombardments, a massive fleet of helicopter gunships, tiger cages for captives, chemical defoliation of jungles and crops, wanton destruction of entire villages and hamlets, extensive use of incendiary weapons, and warfare extended to neighboring countries (Laos, Cambodia) as well as to North Vietnam. Such military aggression and criminality could never have occurred without the systematic dehumanization of the Vietnamese as a people, including wholesale denigration of their culture and history. U.S.

leaders waged combat as if people's lives—by the hundreds, thousands, even millions—were disposable within a larger geopolitical calculus. For Americans, the entire war experience and its aftermath—defeat and humiliation for the invading military power—was met then, as now, with collective denial. As Bruce Franklin writes, "The various forms of denial of the Vietnam War and of the people, history, and culture, and even the very nation of Vietnam have spread wide and deep in American politics, psychology, and culture."[30] Three decades after the war, no U.S. leader has ever acknowledged the criminal horrors their military brought to an undeveloped third world country nor have any apologies or reparations been offered. To imagine democratic prospects in such a nightmarish setting, in the midst of untold death and destruction, would be Strangelovian in the extreme.

The failed U.S. crusade in Vietnam is often explained by mainstream political and media figures as miscalculation by well-meaning strategists, a worthwhile project run aground on the shoals of military timidity, political weakness, and media treachery—self-serving fictions that would resurface in the 1980s *Rambo* episodes, Hollywood's vain attempt to convert Vietnam into another "good war." The reality was altogether different: U.S. militarism recognized few limits in waging a total war as part of all-out counterinsurgency operations initiated by Kennedy and fellow Cold Warriors in the early 1960s. The Indochina fiasco gave rise to recriminations at the top only after U.S. battlefield and political costs became intolerable. As William Gibson observes, years of horrors in Vietnam mattered little to Pentagon officials obsessed with the achievements of technowar; terrible Vietnamese casualties ("body counts") scarcely entered into cold bureaucratic calculations.[31] War managers were afflicted with a case of national hubris, bad outcomes being simply a matter of good guys doing their best in pursuit of noble ends. If the Vietnamese themselves somehow failed to recognize the Americans were bearers of enlightened ideals, then such flawed understanding would be corrected once "hearts and minds" were won over with more effective messages. If the war was viewed by Americans then and later as something of a "quagmire" or "morass," suggesting hopeless tragedy instead of criminal deeds, then wiser decision-making could be the difference, turning humiliating defeat into dramatic victory. That was in fact the message of former secretary of defense Robert McNamara's 1995 memoirs as well as Errol Morris's film on McNamara, *Fog of War*.[32] The Vietnam catastrophe, however, reflected the very bankruptcy of technowar ideology joined to the larger myth of U.S. exceptionalism.[33]

The Vietnam debacle was made possible by a Cold War ideology favored by JFK liberals, an outlook marketed for public consumption as the renewed struggle for global democracy. Kennedy believed a militant anticommunism was needed to counter Soviet designs in the third world. By 1961, Indochina stood out as a decisive test for renovated counterinsurgency warfare. The New Frontier eagerly took up military challenges sure to heighten global tensions, even raising the specter of all-out war with the USSR (as over Cuba) that JFK seemed willing to risk. This warrior mentality coincided with U.S. military buildup presented to Americans as an obligation to face urgent new world challenges. According to JFK, "Other countries look to their own interests. Only the United States has obligations which stretch 10,000 miles across the Pacific, 3000 or 4000 miles across the Atlantic, and thousands of miles to the South. Only the United States...bears that kind of burden."[34]

JFK's celebrated legacy has only concealed his disastrous policies, as in Cuba and Indochina. The energetic Cold War agenda was framed as a "democratic revolution" that, however, would demand renewed faith in military power, a bold counterinsurgency strategy, and close ties to third-world oligarchical interests, anticipating the rise of neoconservative ideology a few decades later. During Kennedy's brief reign, as Bruce Miroff points out, "Global interventionism was sanctioned for America by its historical destiny; Americans sent to foreign nations became by definition the safeguards of freedom."[35] It is often forgotten that Vietnam was really JFK's war, inherited by later presidents—a war viewed in emphatically *ideological* and global terms. The military intervention in Vietnam emerged as an epic clash between good and evil, democracy and totalitarianism, with non-negotiable "American values" at stake. JFK took the Cold War to new heights just after Eisenhower's historic warning about the dangers of a military-industrial complex, and his presidency bears ample responsibility for the carnage the United States brought to three Asian countries.

The Vietnam War not only brought catastrophe to Indochina but left U.S. foreign policy temporarily weakened from military humiliation at the hands of a far weaker foe. It would take perhaps another two decades for Washington to resolve the "Vietnam syndrome," and then only partially. Meanwhile, the 1970s and 1980s witnessed a period of half-hearted, though costly, interventions in Central America and the Caribbean (El Salvador, Nicaragua, Grenada, and Panama) to crush oppositional movements and defend U.S. interests. A crucial turning point was collapse of Soviet power in the late

1980s and early 1990s, allowing the United States to achieve lone superpower status. The end of the Cold War signaled a unipolar world dominated by American power, a hegemonic U.S. presence in the Middle East ushered in by the 1991 Gulf War, and shift toward a more overt strategy of world supremacy. The Gulf War also marked a new phase of technowar built around more sophisticated communications and surveillance networks. The U.S. obsession with Iraq served as a launching pad for broadened geopolitical aims that were blunted during the Cold War nuclear standoff with the USSR. The Middle East had earlier been identified as a key arena of resource competition, as Washington sought greater control of energy sources while angling to limit access of others (notably China, Russia, and Japan). For the United States, democratization of the Middle East was always a smokescreen to cover underlying imperial motives. After all, the United States had supported authoritarian regimes in Iran (the Shah), Iraq (Saddam Hussein), Saudi Arabia, Egypt, and Kuwait among others.

The U.S./NATO military attack on Yugoslavia in the spring of 1999 came at the end of a decade-long bloody civil war among several rival forces where, coinciding with Western interests in the Balkans, Serbs alone were demonized and targeted. Serbs leaders were eventually charged (by Western prosecutors) with "ethnic cleansing" and "genocide" at the Hague Tribunal, even as thorough investigation showed that large-scale atrocities had been the work of all parties (Croatians, Bosnian Muslims, and Kosovo Liberation Army as well as Serbs), the difference being that these other groups were allied with NATO forces. The Clinton administration was so anxious for military action that UN Security Council approval was never sought, much less given. The bombings hit densely populated Serb areas with a variety of high-tech weapons including antipersonnel bombs, incendiary devices, and shells armed with depleted uranium. Proclaiming an era of new internationalism, mainstream American political, media, and academic circles heralded the arrival of an era of "humanitarian intervention," labeled President Clinton's "new humanism" doctrine, according to which the national sovereignty of targeted countries could be violated for sufficient cause (determined by authors of the doctrine). Leaving aside silly descriptions of Serbs as modern-day Nazis and Slobodan Milosevic as the new Hitler, the claim of a humanitarian, altruistic U.S. military intervention could hardly pass scrutiny. Deeper questions had to be posed: What was the role of U.S./NATO geopolitical motives in the region? What international body or agreement ever sanctioned armed

attacks violating the sovereignty of a country legally protected by the
UN Charter? What empowered the United States, with its long tradition of military aggression and outlawry, to appoint itself global arbiter
and savior? Why was *one* party to the civil war—the only party, as it
happened, resistant to U.S. hegemony—singled out for attack? Why
indeed was military action necessary in any case?

Answers to such questions reveal fatal defects in the Clinton
Doctrine while also pointing to the extraordinary hubris of U.S.
global pretenses. The new global humanism was nothing more
than fancy justification for NATO's long-expected eastward thrust
designed to eradicate the last bastion of independent power in Eastern
Europe. In fact, earlier presidents (Jackson, Polk, McKinley, Theodore
Roosevelt, Wilson, and both Bushes among them) resorted to nearly
identical rhetoric, selling U.S. military aggression as an instrument of
civilization, progress, and democracy—although in the Balkans this
propaganda took on a decidedly more "liberal" veneer, rendering it
palatable to those who might otherwise have dissented from such an
operation. Just the opposite of democracy promotion, "humanitarian
intervention" was clearly a cynical move by the most powerful states
to justify military attack on weak, vulnerable targets.

The Balkans venture turned into something of a dress rehearsal
for the 2003 invasion of Iraq, helping legitimate supposedly new rules
of global behavior and clearing the way for "preemptive war" leading to "regime change" that became the cornerstone of Bush's grand
strategy. Flaunting the UN Charter and world opinion, the United
States eagerly initiated its notorious "shock and awe" campaign as
another spectacle of awesome American might. This intervention
had its origins in the 1991 Gulf War, followed by years of brutal
sanctions, sporadic bombing raids, and myriad covert actions preceding the invasion. It had been endorsed by the 1998 Iraq Freedom
Act passed overwhelmingly by Congress at a time when weapons
of mass destruction (WMD) and fighting Hussein's tyranny were
scarcely mentioned. It was given ideological cache by Bush's 2002
National Security Strategy document, stressing heightened U.S. military posture, broader global objectives, and reinvigorated efforts to
block international rivals. Global laws and treaties, as throughout
history, were treated as obstacles to U.S. power and maneuverability.
Outright imperial arrogance prompted Americans, including many
liberals and progressives, to think "victory" and "liberation" would
arrive quickly and smoothly in Iraq. When a widespread Iraqi insurgency quickly surfaced, it was met with national disbelief: escalating

chaos and violence was explained as a matter of Iraqi backwardness regarding Washington's enlightened motives, or as simply the Arab proclivity for sectarianism and violence. After 9/11, moreover, the expanding U.S. imperium was understood in mainstream ideology as a truly positive development, as qualitatively superior to all previous empires given its identification with human rights, freedom, and democracy. Regime change, preemptive war, shock-and-awe militarism, even violations of international law, all this would serve benevolent purposes when carried out by the noble superpower.

Empire versus Democracy

By the early twenty-first century it had become fashionable to argue that the long era of U.S. exceptionalism was over—that more than two centuries of American history was now superseded by a new reality, the inexorable "limits of power." Washington was said to have morphed into a weakened giant incapable of imposing its will on an unruly world, its resources too limited for such a daunting task. This was Andrew Bacevich's conclusion in *The Limits of Power,* subtitled "The End of American Exceptionalism."[36] While U.S. global power was of course never inexhaustible, there is little evidence to suggest the main features of U.S. exceptionalism—imperialism, militarism, superpatriotism, racism, extreme capitalism—have somehow vanished, or even diminished. In fact trends of the past few decades illustrate just the opposite: an expanding global power armed with unprecedented levels of military force, an expanded world presence, and proven willingness to intervene to advance its own geopolitical interests. There is no actual proof of any declining U.S. imperial scope or capacity, as reflected in its hundreds of military bases scattered around the world, its full-spectrum domination of the air, seas, and land, its massive high-tech surveillance capabilities spanning the globe, its preparation for a monopoly on space-based military deployments, and its continued large-scale armed presence in Iraq and Afghanistan. As of late 2009, this imperial labyrinth had evolved into the most far-reaching, costly, and sophisticated military behemoth in history, with no signs of retreat.

Contrary to the myth of a special American "pragmatism" open to diverse currents of opinion—with an implied readiness to take on sharply reduced global status—the postwar system has been shaped by a strong corporate liberalism intertwined with maximum superpower agendas, embraced with few reservations across the mainstream ideological spectrum. This is of course hardly a novel development.

Alexis de Tocqueville observed in the mid-nineteenth century that American society was already rooted in a pervasive liberal consensus wedded to a deep-seated Christianity. The settling of new frontiers injected a populist spirit of regeneration, mastery of nature, rugged individualism, warrior mentality, and devaluing of rival ideologies— tendencies increasingly visible as the United States achieved super- power status. A peculiar messianic nationalism gained impetus from an explosive mixture of ideological and religious traditions that have not abated over time. As President Bush once remarked about his decision to launch warfare against Iraq and Afghanistan, God stands on the side of American patriots as they go about the challenge of ridding the world of evil monsters. Throughout the postwar years Americans remained among the most patriotic (and religious) peo- ple in the world.[37] As Washington set its sights on pursuit of global supremacy, it inevitably affirmed the special efficacy of military power in world politics. The arrival of full-fledged empire gave rise to a privileged set of rules, laws, and normative guideposts embed- ded in national exceptionalism—fully at odds with requirements for international peace and cooperation, not to mention democracy. The U.S. defense of imperial power eventually conflicted with statutes of the UN Charter, Geneva Accords, independent tribunals, and inter- national treaties the United States chose to ignore or reject where they were deemed to interfere with national dictates. Washington has long abided by only those arrangements it finds congruent with its own agendas promoted by such institutions as the World Bank, International Monetary Fund, World Trade Organization, and ad hoc war-crimes tribunals it finances and controls. For decades the leading practitioner of military violence in the world, the United States has only capriciously adhered to the rule of law it so righteously champi- ons. While the United States presents itself as indispensable bastion of legality in a world of chaos and violence, its behavior often feeds into and replicates that very lawlessness. Hostile to the elementary prin- ciple of universality, the United States routinely adopts a duplicitous modus operandi, condemning others for behavior (torture, human rights abuses, possessing weapons of mass destruction, violating rules of battlefield engagement) it considers necessary, or at least tolerable, for itself. Special rules are enforced by superior economic, diplomatic, and military clout, as at the ad hoc tribunals where designated ene- mies are tried for war crimes while similar or worse offenders (includ- ing the United States itself) are usually immunized from such charges. Washington has rejected the International Criminal Court, refused

World Court jurisdiction, and disregarded such global pacts as the Kyoto Accords, Torture Convention, Outer Space Treaty, and Nuclear Non-Proliferation Treaty when opportune.

U.S. leaders have long believed their resources to be rather infinite, an arrogance born in part of a high-tech military supremacy that gives the Pentagon an aura of invulnerability. Technowar as ideology, like technological rationality in general, imbues superpower ambitions with special legitimacy, lending credibility to "God's master plan," as Bob Woodward referred to Bush's rationale for Washington's intervention in the Middle East.[38] Since World War II, if not earlier, supremacy in the realm of high-tech weaponry has been a pillar of U.S. global power.[39] The United States today arrogates to itself the right to produce, deploy, and use nuclear weapons at a level far beyond that of any other nation, its WMD arsenal (including chemical and biological potential) larger than that of all other nations combined. It reportedly has plans for nuclearizing outer space, is building new cycles of "mini-nukes," laid out four options for atomic warfare in the 2002 Nuclear Posture Review, provided nuclear assistance to India and others, routinely blocks moves toward arms control, retains first-use strategy, and possesses chemical weapons in violation of international conventions. And the United States remains the only nation to have *used* nuclear (Japan), chemical (Vietnam), and biological (Korea) weaponry. After 9/11, moreover, readiness to use devastating firepower ("shock-and-awe") converged with the avenging mood of a nation engaged in a global war on terror. Elevated moral and political status drawing on technowar conveys the fiction that American weapons qualitatively differ from those used by other states—instruments of peace rather than aggression, democracy rather than militarism. Being exemplary in its democratic politics, economic wealth, and moral goodness, the United States was destined to face envious challengers—primitive Indians, insurgent peasants, communists, terrorists, popular movements, drug traffickers, intellectual dissidents, ordinary gangsters—demanding perpetual vigilance. Constraints on power readily vanish in the midst of ongoing struggles for virtuous order, as "peace" and "democracy" can never be secured without an armed, "full-spectrum" Leviathan. Given present-day levels of U.S. global power—and blowback that such power generates—the Leviathan (read: Pentagon) takes on an increasingly authoritarian, militaristic role in a brutal, anarchic state of nature.

As the Leviathan forcibly repulses challengers to imperial hegemony, pretenses of a unique American democratic mission will be harder to sustain. Aside from its well-documented record of military interventions around the world, the United States has supported a litany of dictator-ships, sponsored proxy wars, backed death squads, and orchestrated dozens of covert operations while having *overthrown* several popularly elected governments. Whether as Jeffersonian or Jacksonian popu-lism, Wilsonian idealism, JFK's global liberalism, or the more recent neocon doctrine of spreading "American values" to a hostile world, the democratic myth retains a life of its own even as long historical experience contradicts it. This rhetorical charade is joined by the ritual claim that Washington occupies the vanguard of global human rights, as shown by its "humanitarian interventions," but the historical legacy speaks quite differently: the United States is a champion violator of human rights and international law, predictable enough in cases of out-right military aggression. U.S. aerial terrorism against such nations as Japan, Korea, Vietnam, Laos, and Cambodia rank among the worst criminal deeds since 1945, matching kindred atrocities and abuses on the ground (wanton attacks on civilians, torture, forced dislocations, use of inhumane weapons, etc.). Washington has long assisted states (Israel, Turkey, Indonesia, Colombia, and others) responsible for hor-rendous violations of the UN Charter, Geneva Conventions, Torture Convention, and Universal Declaration of Human Rights.

A supposed repository of democracy and freedom in a Hobbesian world of tyrants, rogue states, and terrorists, the United States has erected a massive permanent war economy and security state that inexorably reproduces authoritarian institutions and practices. For decades, this system has endowed an imperial presidency with wide leverage at the expense of Congress and other (potential) spheres of citizen participation. This has meant a steadily narrowed public dis-course and weakened local governance. The marked decline of ide-ological pluralism, historically weak in the United States, signals a growing and dramatic contradiction between empire and democracy, global power, and popular governance at a time when the two major parties are merging into a single corporate entity; as the Iraq war has shown, even moderate dissent is rendered impotent. What Fred Cook wrote in 1962 seems more relevant today, especially after decades of foreign policy consensus: "Not only has Congress largely lost the means of control; it has lost the will."[40] The continuous growth of intelligence, law enforcement, and surveillance, endemic to the security state, reinforces centralizing and bureaucratic forces daily bolstered by empire and militarism. The U.S. imperial presidency vigorously, and most often successfully, resists limits to its power, a tendency reinforced by the corporate media. Theory has traditionally implied Constitutional limits to authoritarian power, but such limits have been transcended in the age of empire.

Returning to the global arena, accounts of U.S. hostility to and subversion of democracy are both exhaustive and well-documented: Washington has supported, often unconditionally, dictatorial regimes in South Korea, the Philippines, Indonesia, Chile, Brazil, Guatemala, Cuba, Iran, Saudi Arabia, Kuwait, Vietnam, Greece, Colombia, El Salvador, Nicaragua, and many other nations. What these regimes shared in common was a deeply authoritarian politics and an egregious record of human rights offenses. To win support for U.S. imperial agendas, Washington has used a creative variety of instruments: global economic bodies like the International Monetary Fund, transnational corporations, CIA operations, the State Department, global surveillance, and military intervention. In some postwar instances, the United States has manipulated free elections or *overthrown* popularly elected governments (as in Iran, Guatemala, Greece, Chile, Brazil, and the Dominican Republic), deploying its ample resources to infiltrate local civic organizations, trade unions, student and professional groups, media outlets, and political parties. In none of these cases was democracy anything more than a propagandistic ploy, as both methods and goals were cynically and thoroughly *antidemocratic*. Two noteworthy cases of postwar U.S. outlawry—alliances with South Africa and Israel—involved decades-long economic, political, and military backing of regimes guilty of massive, ongoing human rights abuses and military atrocities. The only remotely credible instance of American democracy promotion, the Marshall Plan to revive postwar European economies, must be dismissed since the main recipients of largesse (France, Germany, Italy, etc.) had possessed multiparty systems and open elections before the war. Further, the plan was designed overwhelmingly to stabilize the same corporate capitalism that had prevailed for decades across Europe. Here it is worth mentioning that American corporations like Ford, General Motors, and IBM maintained significant business connections with such fascist systems as Germany, Spain, and Italy *during* World War II ("trading with the enemy") while the U.S. political establishment welcomed Nazi scientists, experts, and other elites who could serve the U.S. postwar economy. As for U.S.-occupied Japan and Korea, these nations were essentially governed by martial law well into the 1950s, after which mostly single-party authoritarian regimes prevailed.

After World War II, the United States moved to establish close ties with Francisco Franco's Spain, the most dictatorial system in

Europe, but one eager to join the anti Communist crusade then fueling American politics. By 1950 Washington had recognized the fascist regime, exchanging ambassadors, which allowed U.S. deployment of four military bases in the country. President Dwight Eisenhower later visited Franco in Madrid as ties between the two nations strengthened. This was the same government that for years had been brutally crushing political opposition, banning all competing parties and trade unions, blocked any media and cultural life not directly sanctioned by the regime, and enforced Catholicism as the official Spanish religion. According to Franco, for whom the army (along with the Church) was the dominant institution of Spanish society, "our regime is based on bayonets and blood, not on hypocritical elections." Though liberalized somewhat after the later 1950, this authoritarian system remained intact until Franco's death in 1975, with the unwavering support of Washington in its holy war against Communism.

In the period 1947–49, with enunciation of the Truman Doctrine, the United States gave full support to a fledgling Greek military dictatorship—leaders of which had sided with the Nazis during World War II—to defeat a coalition of popular forces Washington denounced as "Communist." With Greece fully integrated into the NATO alliance as an American client-state, many years of repressive, corrupt government followed. Later, in 1967, CIA covert operations helped empower another Greek junta to head off popular elections expected to favor the left, namely, the Socialist party of George Papandreou, elected prime minister in 1964 but ousted thanks to U.S. economic, political, and military pressure. The Colonels' brutal regime led to a wave of arrests, torture, and mass killings of people opposed to neofascist rule in Greece. For the United States, establishing space for NATO in the southeastern Mediterranean trumped any concerns about democracy.

At the end of World War II, the United States took over South Korea, an entity artificially detached from the North, installing and financing the brutal Sygmun Rhee dictatorship that, reinforced by American military occupation, moved to crush all political opposition in the Cold War crusade to protect "democracy" against Communist "totalitarianism." While restricted elections were held in the South during the postwar years, the regime was nothing more than a puppet of U.S. geopolitical interests, dominated by an ensemble of U.S. military power, local and multinational corporations, and centralized government. During the 1950–53 war, U.S. armed forces reduced large regions of both North and South to rubble while killing at least three million Koreans—people who could never enjoy the blessings of self-government even if such a system had been created. Following the

Korean debacle, the United States turned its gaze toward the Middle East, again using CIA subversion to overthrow the popularly elected Mossadegh government in Iran, substituting the corporate-friendly but tyrannical Shah regime that unleashed 25 years of terror on the Iranian population. Iran remained a staunch U.S. ally and pivotal Cold War outpost in the region, essential to a rollback of Soviet power but irrelevant to any democracy promotion. The Shah welcomed American investments and military bases at a time when thousands opposed to the dictatorship were arrested, tortured, and executed by Iranian security forces trained and backed by Washington. This episode in U.S. geopolitical skullduggery has become too well-known to require further elaboration.

In Guatemala less than a year later, the United States revisited this Cold War scenario in a region long regarded as an American fiefdom, overthrowing the popularly elected Jacobo Arbenz government and installing a client regime based in domestic oligarchical rule and American military power, setting in motion decades of brutal dictatorship, grinding poverty, atrocities against indigenous peoples, and free reign to scattered CIA-sponsored death squads. Guatemala remained a bastion of U.S. counterinsurgency activities orchestrated by the State Department, Pentagon, and CIA well into the 1990s. Opposition to the dictatorship, as in neighboring El Salvador, was mercilessly and systematically crushed, with tens of thousands killed and "disappeared." Democracy? Human rights? Only the most twisted Orwellian imagination could arrive at such a conclusion in the midst of these unspeakable horrors.

Turning to Indonesia—fifth most populous nation in the world— the record shows that Washington engineered a military coup against the popular nationalist leader Sukarno in 1965 to set up a U.S.-friendly Suharto regime in alliance with Indonesia military. As in Greece, Iran, and Guatemala, U.S. intervention opened the gates to many years of state terror, with Suharto massacring more than 500,000 "communists" during the 1960s, followed (from mid-1970s onward) by even worse mass killings of secessionists in East Timor. As elsewhere, the coup was preceded by lengthy CIA involvement, part of a general U.S. strategy to destroy mass-based nonruling communist parties going back to the late 1940s. (By the mid-1960s the Indonesian Party was in fact the largest communist organization outside the Soviet Union and China.)

The 1973 U.S. overthrow of popularly elected Salvador Allende in Chile followed roughly the same pattern: a Washington-backed military coup, led by neofascist Augusto Pinochet, set up a dictatorship in place of Allende's broad leftist coalition elected through free and open voting—a coalition, however, that failed to meet the approval of the Nixon-Kissinger White House. When covert actions failed to undermine Allende, the United States pursued a more coercive alternative that, in the end, brought more than two decades of state terror to Chileans, along with a "free market" open to American corporate interests to a degree the Allende government had never been. Less than a month before the coup Secretary of State Kissinger had remarked: "I don't see why we need to stand by and watch a country go Communist because of the irresponsibility of its own people." One can only surmise the State Department and CIA had better grasp of local interests than the Chilean people. In any event, Kissinger's bold remark captured perfectly the spirit and essence of postwar U.S. foreign policy underwritten by strong bipartisan consensus.

Nowhere perhaps have democratic illusions run deeper than in the long U.S. crusade to build a generation of potent Islamic fundamentalist insurgencies to defeat Soviet power, Communism, and the secular left—first in Afghanistan during the 1980s and then across the globe. The rightwing Mujahedeen, Taliban, and al Qaeda gained ascendancy in large measure through American financial largesse, military aid, and political backing that served U.S. interests in the Middle East and Central Asia, leaving behind a violent theocratic politics unmatched in the modern world. Initially confined mostly to Afghanistan, these jihadic organizations—called "freedom fighters" in the American political and media establishments—quickly spread to North Africa, Indonesia, the Philippines, Pakistan, the Balkans, and throughout the Middle East and Central Asia, some eventually turning against Washington. Jihadic forces rejected modernity and democracy from the outset, but this never bothered U.S. policy-makers intent on destroying the secular left. While American opinion leaders still maintain that global terrorism has roots and sponsorship in Iran, the more embarrassing truth is that modern *Islamic* terrorism was born and nourished during the Afghan wars of the 1980s, a product of the largest CIA covert program (with funding of $5 billion) during the Cold War years. The United States hoped militant jihadic groups could defeat leftist movements and governments in Central Asia, the Middle East, the Pacific, and the Balkans.[41] Thousands of jihadic fighters were trained, armed, and given logical assistance to fight the "evil empire" and secular opposition to Western interests as in Yugoslavia.

The Bosnian situation, grossly distorted in the Western media, deserves special attention. Thousands of jihadists were recruited, organized, and financed by Washington throughout the 1990s to join secessionist movements against former Yugoslavia, targeting the secular-leftist Serb government (one duly elected). Fighters came to Bosnia from several countries, many of them veterans of the Afghan wars, to support the theocratic Muslim government of neofascist Alija Izetbegovic. While Bosnia had large Croatian and Serb populations, Christians as well as Muslims, Izetbegovic's unwavering goal—fully endorsed by the United States—was a Muslim dictatorship as bulwark against Serb power, friendly to Western interests. Bosnian secessionists took up a holy war against Serbs, pursuing "rebirth" of a region having strong ties to Saudi Arabia and Pakistan, which used its secret intelligence agencies to help build the Taliban and kindred organizations.[42] In just a few years the Izetbegovic regime, like the Taliban in Afghanistan, had deteriorated into a government of corruption, tyranny, violence, and intolerance, all the while receiving Washington's aid and blessings. This sorry pattern extended to Kosovo secessionists of the Kosovo Liberation Army (KLA), another terrorist group financed and armed by the United States to destabilize Serbia. The 1999 U.S./NATO military attacks on Yugoslavia signaled a broader Western strategy, laying the groundwork for the sprawling U.S. Camp Bondsteel, a symbol of long-planned American presence in the Balkans. These interventions are still depicted in the U.S. public sphere as a wonderful triumph of democracy against dictatorship, though the reality has been just the opposite: jihadic terrorism and dictatorship operated as cynical tools of Western power in a geopolitically vital region, directed *against* democratic hopes, paving the way toward a NATO push eastward and solidification of American imperial designs in southeastern Europe. The Balkans episode, as with the Iraq and Afghanistan ventures, did give expression to a familiar American model of "democracy"—one firmly rooted in globalized corporate and military domination reinforced by authoritarian state rule.

* * *

U.S. exceptionalism carries forward elements of continuity and change, established patterns and recent departures, consistent with a project of imperial expansion and, more recently, pursuit of global hegemony. Prospects for democratic governance were checkmated from the very beginning of colonial rule, stymied by a plutocratic order resting on wealth, privilege, and strong federal government. The ideal of popular governance entered the prevailing discourse, to the limited extent it did, as useful legitimating myth. Charting U.S. development across the nineteenth century and beyond, a developmental pattern becomes apparent in which popular governance was stifled in virtually every region of public life. The Constitution, as we have seen, was always compatible with oligarchical rule and authoritarian power. The economic system, falsely defined as "free enterprise," opened the door to boundless corporate power, dysfunctional industrial growth, a vast gulf between rich and poor, the destruction of nature, and workplace environments best described as tyrannical. This was a history too of virulent racism manifest in slavery, exterminism, Jim Crow laws, harsh oppression of minorities, and a chauvinistic imperialism. Women were until 1920 denied basic rights, including suffrage. The nineteenth century witnessed a steady expansion of state, corporate, bureaucratic, and military power endemic to uneven industrialization and colonial expansion, trends that accelerated across the twentieth century. The two-party system was thoroughly entangled with privileged interests and extreme wealth from its very inception. And U.S. foreign policy was shaped by colonial ambitions, conquest, militarism, and support of any dictator willing to facilitate these agendas. Trends institutionalized by the late nineteenth century and popularly resisted with only marginal (but nonetheless crucial) successes here and there, nurtured a pervasive antidemocratic social and political life present to this day.

Early U.S. history demonstrates that neither ideological nor structural conditions for even a minimalist democracy existed, much less flourished; dominated by a narrow privileged stratum, the system could never generate an informed, engaged citizenry required for even limited self-governance. Parties and elections were dominated by capitalist wealth, voters (for the most part a tiny percentage of the American public) reduced to passive consumers in a political marketplace where "politics" rarely went beyond personalities, contrived dramas, and trivialized debates. "Public opinion" turned out to be little more than manipulated consent—beliefs, attitudes, and preferences manipulated by elite interests and discourses. American government was always confined to the orbit of big capital, its institutional branches and agencies colonized by private interests consistent with the formation of state capitalism. What the Founders set in motion has indeed survived, through recurrent peaks and valleys—an institutionalized network of power kept fully intact through two centuries of history despite expansion of popular suffrage, cyclical upheavals, the achievements of social movements, and perpetual crises.

2

The Imperial Labyrinth

The previous chapter explored the historical origins and overall trajectory of Manifest Destiny as it evolved into a durable part of American political culture. U.S. exceptionalism took on new features from one period to another, one presidency to another, one military engagement to another, yet was grounded in a unique sense of historical destiny that has remained intact up to the present. In this chapter, we explore in greater relief the *ideological* content of that exceptionalism, centered on what might be called the "neoconservative turn" in U.S. foreign and military policy since the end of the Cold War and, more emphatically, since the events of 9/11. As before, attention focuses on interwoven elements of change and continuity. We shall see that this ideological "turn" constitutes no radical departure from past imperial thought and behavior, as its main components are readily identifiable with reference to U.S. history.

As we have seen, the post-9/11 milieu gave new impetus, and probably new legitimacy, to the U.S. pursuit of world supremacy. Elite acknowledgment of empire, previously kept sotto voce had by the early twenty-first century come to the surface, with fanfare. The actuality of imperial expansion, long denied or repressed, was now unabashedly celebrated within the political establishment, corporate media, and academia. The terrorist attacks generated worldwide sympathy for the United States, assisted by the global power of a media that privileges distinctly American experiences of suffering and victimhood. The attacks helped validate U.S. geostrategic moves to consolidate U.S. domination of the world system. As at the end of World War II, the United States could now widely be perceived as an "indispensable nation" dedicated to universal ideals of democracy, peace, human rights, and lawful behavior among nations. But such a perception was highly misleading, as would be reflected in the brazen 2003 U.S. invasion and occupation of Iraq. The 9/11 events performed yet another function, reinforcing the idea—already held at the summits of power—of a Hobbesian world rife with threatening evil, a nightmarish arena demanding maximum vigilance by the imperial Leviathan. The leading superpower now had a more pronounced burden of imposing and preserving world order. Any challenges to that order, any attacks on the hallowed rights and entitlements of the exceptional nation and its spheres of power, would be countered by American economic, political, and military force, part of an epic struggle of good against evil, of democracy against an assemblage of sinister terrorists, rogue states, and tyrants opposed to American hegemony. Of course, *this* particular empire was understood to be qualitatively superior to all preceding ones, a benevolent and freedom-loving power differing from the predatory, militaristic Roman, British, Spanish, Japanese, and Soviet empires.

The Ideology of Global Domination

It is often argued that the neoconservative turn in American politics was the work of a small "cabal" of right-wing "defense intellectuals" who gained control of the Pentagon and pressured President Bush to follow a hyperaggressive line: preemptive warfare, unilaterialism, contempt for the United Nations, Pentagon buildup, reconfiguring the Middle East, and so forth. While this view contains a small kernel of truth, a more accurate rendering of neocon ideology locates it squarely within American political traditions, an extension of familiar national motifs that take on new meaning in the post–Cold War setting.

As discussed in chapter 1, after the final conquest of Indian lands and closure of the frontier, imperial expansion turned outward, energized by a renewed culture of national exceptionalism. Theodore Roosevelt intoned on the eve of the Spanish-American War that U.S. military ventures ought to be welcomed, even celebrated, for benefit of the American character, blessed with a civilizing mission to uplift supposedly inferior peoples around the world. A U.S. penchant for military ventures would build upon the Revolutionary War success, the Monroe Doctrine, conquest of Mexican territory, and protracted warfare against Indian tribes. Brute force was not to be avoided but rather embellished as an instrument of progress and democracy, a refrain heard repeatedly to the present day. By 1900 the United

States had already built the firmaments of an imperial system, with Americans having grown accustomed to foreign policy conducted at the barrel of a gun, as part of the national birthright. U.S. intervention in World War I, an endless pit of death and destruction that President Wilson idealized as a battle for global democracy, broadened the national quest for economic and geopolitical advantage. Long dominant in much of Latin America, the United States set out to consolidate a foothold in Mexico, the Caribbean, Central America, Asia, and the Pacific islands in the years leading to World War II.

A racist framing of military combat during the familiar "good war" denigrated the Japanese as both primitive children and threatening madmen needing to be taught stern lessons—a reprise of the Indian stereotypes. The idea of foreign demons had become deeply etched in the national psyche, consistent with the Pacific Theater "war without mercy" and domestic internment camps for Japanese-Americans. For the American public World War II brought fuller attention to ideological themes that would be later associated with neocon politics: grand imperial ambitions, glorification of military power, elevated national hubris, cynical views of international law, pretense of a democratic, peace-loving foreign policy. The U.S. decision to drop atomic bombs on Japan—defended on the pretext of avoiding a bloody invasion when in fact the end of hostilities was imminent—was itself a moment of national exceptionalism, intended to convey a message to the world (mainly the Soviet Union) of Washington's heightened global ambitions. Nuclear supremacy would soon enough set the contours of postwar U.S. foreign and military policy, a vital element—we know now—of the Cold War dialectic. The Truman Doctrine, invoked in 1947 as a response to large Communist gains in such countries as Greece, Yugoslavia, Turkey, Italy, and France, announced that the United States was ready to forcibly intervene anywhere U.S. interests might be threatened. A crucible of Cold War ideology, this doctrine was embraced as vital to preservation of the "free world," a recycling of what later would be called "preemptive warfare." Building on exaggerated fear of Communist takeovers, the United States moved quickly to expand its already far-reaching global presence. The first major opportunity for the Truman Doctrine came in Korea, the site in 1950 of total warfare conducted under UN auspices, as Washington sought to "roll back" Communism while solidifying its geopolitical foothold in Asia. Delaying any political settlement as long as Truman remained in office, the United States visited a scorched-earth campaign on Korea, seemingly ready to use atomic weapons to break the long military stalemate. The Korean War served to legitimate escalating levels of Pentagon spending and further buildup of U.S. global power, including far-reaching covert-action operations and counter-insurgency programs.[1]

Roughly a decade later, as the military-industrial complex evolved into an institutionalized fixture of American life, the JFK presidency revitalized these Cold War priorities as it pressed for a deepening worldwide liberal "revolution" that, in the tradition of Wilsonian "idealism," would allow the United States to remake the world on the basis of its own geopolitical agendas. As with Democrats Wilson and Truman, JFK's own brand of idealism assumed a scenario of confrontation with threatening enemies—in this case, of course, worldwide Communism. The presumption that U.S. military force ought to be projected globally was increasingly seen as a natural right that would be carried into later presidencies, long before neocons would adopt and refine these same policies in the name of democracy and human rights.

Neocon ideology took shape in the late 1970s, in large part a reaction against the 1960s new-left insurgency, the counterculture, Vietnam defeat, and growth of new social movements galvanized mainly by feminism and ecology. The driving force was a visceral hatred of leftwing politics that for many extended to mainstream liberalism and its strong manifestation in the 1972 McGovern presidential campaign. Dubbed by some as a "party of intellectuals," the neocons sought to expand their presence through the media, universities, and think tanks, taking inspiration from earlier liberalism, especially its expansionary, global side championed by presidents Wilson, FDR, Truman, and JFK. Despite a pretense of "outsider" status, neocon political and intellectual ambitions would enjoy remarkable success within mainstream political culture from the early 1980s onward. The messianic strain of liberalism embraced by neocons was rooted in deep-seated opposition to movements for social change. Gary Dorrien referred to "an intellectual movement originated by former leftists that promotes militant anti-Communism, capitalist economics, a minimal welfare state, the rule of traditional elites, and a return to traditional cultural values."[2] With passage of time could be added a fierce patriotism, an aggressive military posture, and preoccupation with U.S. (also Israeli) geopolitical leverage in the Middle East. While the role of former leftists like Irving Kristol was noteworthy in the neocon ascendancy, its significance has no doubt dwindled over time since, regardless of origins, the ideology revolved largely around global priorities. Thus a debilitating flaw in American political culture was a certain weakness of will, an inclination toward compromise, indecisiveness, and a tendency toward "appeasement" in global affairs. Many neocons—Irving and William Kristol, Norman Podhoretz, Paul Wolfowitz, Charles Krauthammer, and Joshua Muravchik among them—adopted something of a Hobbesian outlook dwelling on international chaos and imminent threat of sinister enemies, leading to their support of virtually any policy to elevate U.S. international power, including support of oligarchical interests abroad and expanded government at home. Some took a cue from Machiavelli's concept of elite manipulation in defense of noble objectives—in this case focused on democracy.[3] The resort to authoritarian power and military force was taken as a political imperative, to secure worldwide peace and democracy.

A leading architect of neoconservatism, the late Irving Kristol called the movement one of disaffected ex-liberals who, having flirted with left politics, had suddenly been "mugged by reality," referring mainly but not exclusively to the "realities" of global conflict. He founded and edited the magazines *Encounter* and *Public Interest* while becoming deeply involved in AEI and similar right-wing think tanks. According to Republican strategist Karl Rove, Kristol, through his prolific writing, editing, and speaking, "made it a moral imperative to rouse conservatism from mainstream Chamber of Commerce boosterism to deep immersion in ideas."[4] Such ideological renewal was trained overwhelmingly on issues related to foreign and military policy. Working with such kindred academics as Norman Podhoretz, Richard Pipes, Nathan Glazer, and Daniel P. Moynihan, Kristol helped create a vital synthesis of Cold War Democrats and Reagan antiCommunist hawks that took root in the early 1980s, driven by hatred of the liberalism that looked perhaps a little too skeptically at corporate power and a militarized foreign policy.

In a universe of imminent threats, the neocons wanted maximum freedom and maneuverability for the United States in world affairs. If the Vietnam syndrome had epitomized defeat and humiliation, it was now time for shrewd leaders to revitalize U.S. imperial agendas while making their peace with big government needed to advance those agendas. A troublesome liberal frailty, dramatized in Hollywood by the 1980s *Rambo* episodes, had to be countered. Moral qualms about warfare, about flexing U.S. military power, had to be overcome, as would arcane obstacles imposed by international law. As Muravchik wrote in 1987, "the West knows little about ideological war. But the

place to start is with the assertion that democracy is our creed, that
we believe all human beings are entitled to its blessings, and that we
are prepared to do what we can to help others achieve it."[5] Muravchik
and other neocons insisted the United States must be in the vanguard of fighting tyranny and threats to global order wherever they
appeared. By the early 1990s, with the Cold War over and the Soviet
system a matter of history, the United States would have a freer hand
to fulfill its historically appointed mission of reshaping the planet to
meet requisites of the New World Order.

At first peripheral to the centers of power, by the late 1990s neocon
intellectuals grew more emboldened, pushing for aggressive military
ventures without fear of being dismissed as extremists, their ideas
now resonating within the political and media establishments, as (in
Dorrien's words): "America's struggle for the world was [becoming] a
crusade to fulfill the destiny of America itself."[6] Self-evident was the
fact the United States stood for fundamental rights everywhere, just
as Wilson, Truman, and JFK had maintained during their time. Not
surprisingly, in order to advance these "fundamental rights" U.S. foreign policy would now and then have to sidestep bothersome international laws and conventions, and be prepared to opt for machtpolitik
(capitalized?) resting on military force. The concept of national sovereignty (for others) was revisited with a view toward its obsolescence.
Certain treaties might have to be taken less literally. Approached in
hindsight, the 1991 Gulf War could be appreciated as a "unipolar
moment" when the United States was able to achieve quick military
victory in the absence of serious global opposition. As Krauthammer
said at the time, "American strength and will [means] the strength
and will to lead a unipolar world, unashamedly laying down the rules
of world order and being prepared to enforce them."[7] The Gulf War
helped revitalize American patriotism and militarism while ostensibly
eradicating the Vietnam syndrome at the same time. Rapid and easy
triumph over the evil Saddam Hussein was received across the political spectrum as a cathartic national release, a breakthrough giving
the neocons enhanced political credibility as they began to agitate for
the ouster of the still-ruling Hussein.

Neocon influence in the corridors of American officialdom rose
dramatically toward the end of the century, sped along by the rightward ideological shift within media outlets like Fox TV, the peri-
odicals *Commentary* and *Weekly Standard,* and think tanks like the
American Enterprise Institute, Hoover Institute, Heritage Foundation,
and Manhattan Institute. For all their supposed hostility to the

Beltway, neocons had become quite comfortable within mainstream political culture. If their growing presence was often explained as the work of small cliques scheming backstage, the actuality was rather different: their ascension was a product of the combined influence of think tanks, books, journals, and websites as well as manifestoes laid out by groups like the Project for a New American Century (PNAC). Some observers thought the neocons had no coherent ideology, but that too was fallacious given their rather uniformly dogmatic views on foreign policy. Still others argued that rising neocon influence after 9/11 prefigured a "sea change" in U.S. global behavior, departing from American traditions resting on the rule of law, multilateralism, and preference for diplomacy over armed force, but this likewise scarcely held up to close scrutiny. Central neocon motifs in fact have deep roots in American history, tied to outlooks and policies earlier advanced by such presidents as Polk, McKinley, Theodore Roosevelt, Wilson, Truman, JFK, and Reagan, all celebrating some variant of U.S. exceptionalism (including "preemptive warfare"). As mentioned above, a cavalier attitude toward international rules and treaties has long defined the conduct of U.S. foreign policy. And the premise of national exceptionalism—that superior U.S. "values" have universal relevance, worthy of being exported abroad—is hardly a novel development, as we have seen.

Neocon influence relied on skill and persistence at setting political agendas with aggressive clarity and patriotic zeal. Their approach deviated from standard conservatism in a willingness to embrace big government, with its permanent war economy and national security apparatus, even accepting huge tax increases and fiscal deficits. Like Theodore Roosevelt, they believed the United States should be responsible not only for its own fate but for "the destiny of mankind," the very substance of public statements by PNAC such as its well-known 2000 manifesto "Rebuilding America's Defenses", which argued that the United States was entitled to rule the world and could no longer tolerate challenges to its hegemony. Washington would manage the world system according to its own moral precepts and political agendas, no apologies needed. The 9/11 attacks and the "war on terror" helped legitimate a foreign policy geared to perpetual military vigilance. Threats emanating from elsewhere now seemed menacingly real. Patriotic appeals were more saleable to the American public, giving the imperial executive freedom to pursue a neocon agenda that looked to armed intervention in Afghanistan, Iraq, and perhaps beyond. Leading White House and Pentagon figures openly identified with neocon ideas—Vice President Richard Cheney, Secretary of Defense Donald Rumsfeld, and upper-echelon military officials Paul Wolfowitz, Richard Perle, William Libby, and Douglas Feith among them.

It is commonly assumed that neocon ideology is heavily indebted to the work of Francis Fukuyama and Samuel Huntington, whose influence during the 1980s and 1990s helped shape U.S. foreign policy, but their influence has been exaggerated. Fukuyama, in his influential *The End of History,* did insist that "Western" (namely American) values grounded in liberal democracy were superior to all rivals and had achieved a natural (perhaps irreversible) ascendancy in the world arena. As the "end-point of ideological evolution," liberalism had by virtue of its compelling universality superseded all competitors: monarchy, fascism, communism, dictatorship in its myriad forms. This was Fukuyama's famous "end of history" that, despite residues of backwardness and resistance, would bring prosperity and freedom across the globe, superior to anything known throughout history A liberal politics of freedom and abundance would render identities and conflicts bound up with religion, nationalism, and localism obsolete, spelling an end to tyranny and large-scale warfare. We can see now that Fukuyama was hopelessly utopian about the end of history: in fact, the very identities and conflicts he thought would disappear over time—for example, religion and nationalism—have actually intensified since he began writing. He also failed to recognize the disruptive consequences of mounting economic and ecological crises, not to mention intensifying blowback against U.S. global power. Fukuyama's premise of triumphant liberal democracy was in any case anchored to the thesis of gradual ideological ascendancy, or Hegelian surge, rather than outright military encounters of the sort anticipated by neocons.

Huntington's familiar "clash of civilizations" thesis, on the other hand, did anticipate global encounters between the West and rival centers of power such as Islam and China, between the U.S. imperium and assorted challenges to it. Like Fukuyama, he emphasized the superiority of "Western" ideals over potential competitors and foresaw intense conflict between agents of modernization and their opponents, but departed from Fukuyama's facile assumption that the West, or liberal democracy, has emerged (or will soon emerge) as universally hegemonic. Huntington in fact questioned the view that the Western model, even loosely defined, is destined to prevail over all rivals.[8] On the contrary, he saw world politics as a complex field of diversity and chaos, with some older identities remaining intact or even gaining strength. He did argue that the United States must act decisively to defend liberal democracy under siege, yet nowhere did he maintain that the United States must promote global liberalism through armed force, arguing instead that (a) future conflicts will be largely ideological and cultural rather than military, and (b) efforts to spread political beliefs by force will run aground given the immense resistance they encounter.[9] Huntington's perspective, therefore, stands at odds with the neocon agenda in terms of both goals and methods.

The neocon ascendancy owes much of its momentum to the rightward shift in American media culture and the capacity of that culture to bring what was previously thought to be extreme views into the mainstream public sphere. The gulf between this "new" conservatism and established opinion, notably on foreign policy, had shrunk considerably after the early 1990s, a trend strengthened by the Bush-Cheney presidency and the events of 9/11. Neocon ideology had gained a strong foothold in the corporate media, including network and cable TV, radio, op-ed pages, book publishing, and the Internet, facilitated by big-business generosity that funneled billions of dollars into neocon-friendly projects at universities, think tanks, lobbies, and media outlets. Before Obama's breakthrough victory, the previous three decades had been marked by a conservative takeover in Washington fueled by deregulation, eclipse of the Fairness Doctrine, and growing concentration of media power. This resulted from a well-orchestrated campaign to shape public consciousness, its success easily measured on the terrain of U.S. foreign policy where neocon ideas gained new credibility and influence. Large sectors of media culture were essentially transformed into propaganda vehicles bolstered by the growing popularity of the Fox TV network and kindred outlets.

In its take-no-prisoners approach to ideological combat, the right adopted a pugnacious style exemplified by Rush Limbaugh and Glenn Beck on talk radio, Bill O'Reilly and Sean Hannity at Fox TV news, and dozens of Limbaugh clones across the country. Theirs is a stark good-versus-evil world in which the United States stands for everything noble against a proliferation of spineless liberals, traitors, terrorists, and rogue tyrants. Once corporate-funded foundations and institutes began to flourish in the 1980s, conservatives were able to gain added leverage within the media system, their discourses infused with a savage partisanship branding "liberals" and "the left" as unpatriotic, weak, appeasing, and worse. As David Brock observed in his seminal *The Republican Noise Machine*, this ideological "guerrilla strategy" allowed the right to better dictate the contours of the

political debate, instill public readiness to celebrate U.S. military ventures, and inspire an upswing in patriotism reinforced, to be sure, by
the events of 9/11.[10] It was this very shift in the political culture that
helped legitimate Bush's decision to invade Iraq.

Warrior Politics

The neocons have long had a love affair with military power, translated into support for high levels of Pentagon spending, sophisticated
weapons systems, and interventions abroad. They remain fixated on
extending U.S. global hegemony, by force where deemed necessary.
Like the American frontier settlers, many neocons came to embrace
something akin to warrior politics, not only in policy choices but as
a way of life.

An influential text in neocon literature was Robert Kagan's *Of
Paradise and Power* (2003), which dealt with a widening gulf between
the United States and Europe in approaches to world politics.[11] Kagan
saw the world as beset with anarchy in which the United States,
owing to its legacy of democracy and human rights, would be forced
to assume leadership heavily reliant on "policies of coercion," at a
time when international laws and treaties were less useful as guideposts of behavior. Chaos dictates a preference for unilateralism and
military force at a time when European nations, softened by aversion
to conflict and warfare, look to diplomacy, compromise, and lawful
behavior.[12] Such differences in political culture stem from an obvious
power chasm: with its sprawling empire and widely dispersed military
forces, the United States is naturally more inclined to use force, to
act from preponderance of armed strength, than Europeans whose
public spending for many decades favored the welfare state and social
priorities. In Kagan's words, "Those with great military power are
more likely to consider force as a useful tool of international relations
than those who have less military power."[13] What the United States
seeks above all is *hegemony,* while Europeans—less infatuated with
nationalism after two disastrous world wars—prefer less ambitious,
more cooperative foreign policies. It follows that Washington "naturally seeks a certain freedom of action to deal with the strategic dangers that it alone has the means and sometimes the will to address."[14]
Kagan recognized that imperial ambitions resonate across U.S. history and that such ambitions shape present-day impulses on the world
stage, helping extend the "empire of liberty."[15] Rather than shrinking
from this legacy, American leaders should firmly and happily embrace

it, a path far easier to traverse in the wake of the Soviet collapse. The United States now occupies an exceptional place in world politics, unthinkable without the resolve to act militarily and adopt the "language of military power."[16] Kagan recognized that the "logic of force" has shaped U.S. behavior at least since World War II, especially after decision-makers learned the lessons of Munich ("appeasement") and Pearl Harbor (surprise enemy attack), but 9/11 pushed Washington further along the path of warrior politics. Facing crisis, the United States should be willing to stand alone, ready to confront menacing evil with punishing violence, much like the isolated sheriff Gary Cooper in the 1952 film *High Noon*. Americans ought to be proud of their awesome military power, ignoring European restlessness over the cowboy, or warrior, mentality that came to permeate Washington during the Bush years.

This Hobbesian ethos was taken to new lengths in the work of Robert Kaplan, who, like Kagan, saw a world of mounting anarchy that only American power could overcome. His effusive praise of U.S. imperialism captured enduring features of the national experience—adventure, heroism, self-interest, brute strength, and superpatriotism. Taking inspiration from Machiavelli, Kaplan focused on the creativity of political elites skilled at manipulation, deceit, and secrecy in the service of enlightened virtues. "Good" leaders might be forced to do "bad" things for desired political outcomes since, in the end, the "morality of results" trumps everything. Dynamic governance requires detaching ethics from politics, whether in the conduct of warfare, the struggle against anarchy and mob rule, or efforts to create a new order.[17] Thus, "as Machiavelli cruelly but accurately put it, progress comes from hurting others."[18] Hardly original with the neocons, this marriage of Hobbes and Machiavelli resonates deeply across U.S. history, from the Founders to the present.

Kaplan argued that political violence is inescapable to the extent coercion, rapacity, and aggression are intrinsic to human nature, just as conflict is endemic to international relations. These conditions demand a Leviathan to preserve order and stability—the very authoritarian edifice the United States can easily provide insofar as "the military could play the role of Leviathan more successfully than the democratically-elected civilians."[19] In this conflicted and fearsome world, an all-powerful nation will rarely play by the rules since in a state of nature most *everyone* is driven by naked self-interest, and nobody can be trusted. Like other neocons, Kaplan stressed the failure of international law to furnish a matrix of peace and order, suggesting it is time to jettison old-fashioned beliefs in the efficacy of national sovereignty.[20] A warrior politics naturally favors power over legality, national interest over internationalism, military force over diplomacy. Warfare itself—an unfortunate but essential preoccupation of imperial leaders—inescapably violates global rules since these rules protect the weak from the strong. In an anarchic world, therefore, the leading superpower is entitled to pursue its objectives with abandon, with just two provisos: keep (its own) casualties low the stock market high.[21] Kaplan casually noted that "our prize for winning the Cold War is not merely the opportunity to expand NATO, or to hold democratic elections in places that never had them, but something far broader: We and nobody else will write the terms for international society."[22] It thus falls upon benevolent American power to be the "Romans of the modern world," as it aims to enforce imperial order on a disorderly and threatening planet. It would be difficult to find a bolder formulation of antidemocratic politics grounded in national exceptionalism than Kaplan's discourse here.

Kaplan takes warrior ideology to new levels in a later book, *Imperial Grunts* (2005), based on first-hand experience with frontline soldiers as protectors of U.S. imperialism. In an introduction aptly titled "Injun Country," Kaplan described American military outposts as a new version of nineteenth-century U.S. cavalry operations against Indian tribes, since in each instance the real national heroes are ordinary soldiers in the field, and not elites working comfortably at the summits of power. Today, of course, the challenges stiffen insofar as "by the turn of the twenty-first century the United States military had already appropriated the entire earth, and was ready to flood the most obscure areas of it with troops at a moment's notice."[23] Modern-day grunts are true protagonists of empire—dedicated, willing to risk everything, adventurous, anxious to tame new frontiers. In Kaplan's view, since aerial campaigns and other forms of technowar usually fall short of their promise, the burden falls on small marine units, Spec-Ops troops, and scattered battlefield personnel deployed to harsh locales such as Iraq and Afghanistan. Thus: ".... while the entire planet was a battle space for the American military, I would learn that the fewer troops that policed it the better. Small light and lethal units of soldiers and marines, skilled in guerrilla warfare and attuned to the local environment... could accomplish more than dinosauric, industrial age infantry divisions."[24]

In Kaplan's view, the legacy of war against Indians was destined to live on as U. S. imperial power came face-to-face with new Hobbesian threats. As in the past, moreover, the modern warrior is best advised to adopt the battlefield ethos and skills of the "Indian" enemy, starting with bravery and tenacity. Here Kaplan recognized an enduring contradiction of empire: it generates multiple forms of resistance, or blowback. Armed encounters give rise to a "war culture," the result of a "morally enlightened state" doing what needs to be done.[25] At the core of this culture, Kaplan identifies everyday soldiers whose "willingness to die was also the product of their working-class origins. The working classes had always been accustomed to rough unfair lives... [with] less of an articulated and narcissistic sense of self than the elites [and who] could subsume their egos more easily inside a prideful unit identity... "[26] Grunts nowadays face a third-world environment similar to the Old West, as military action brings predictable "collateral damage" to civilian populations and infrastructures.[27] The lowly grunts facing the horrors of warfare sacrifice valiantly on behalf of their nation's geopolitical interests—exactly what Smedley Butler argued, from a more harshly critical perspective, in *War is a Racket* many decades ago.[28] For Kaplan, of course, these risks and sacrifices are both necessary and redemptive, vital to perpetuation of American greatness.

The warrior ethos is grounded in elite assumptions about power and warfare going back to the Founders, whose meek liberalism was always mediated by the omnipresent figure of Hobbes. Indeed the early colonists—and most of their heirs—were far less concerned with democracy than with laying the foundations of liberty that extended beyond the individual to freewheeling enterprise mixed with the frontier spirit. The Founders came face-to-face with a chaotic state of nature represented by myriad threats: British tyrants and their soldiers, Indians, a harsh frontier terrain, and so forth. Methods for overcoming such turbulence and ensuring conditions of freedom (above all *economic* freedom) inevitably pushed the colonists and settlers in the direction of protective authoritarian power, the Leviathan, based in a predictable system of rules, laws, and procedures. Never a democrat, Hobbes had argued that personal liberty was ultimately independent of a specific governmental form; in other words, freedom can flourish without any semblance of democratic participation. A mighty sovereign power can guarantee liberty of movement, expression, interaction, and contractual activity, uncompromised by external hindrance, obstacles, or predation, indicating that submission to such power functions, ironically, to *augment* freedoms while naturally undermining prospects for self-government. This Hobbesian view of social life and governance permeated not only the U.S. Constitution and Federalist Papers but the later manifestations of "minimalist" American liberalism that remained fully compatible with unbridled corporate power and a huge military machine. It was precisely this liberal tradition that entered in neocon ideology of the late 1970s and beyond. Especially when combined with Machiavellian impulses (the reverse side of Hobbesian thinking), this view of politics turned into a convenient ideology for elites obsessed with security, law enforcement, military power, and corporate autonomy, at the same time fearful of local democratic impulses. It provides the ideal framework for preserving a savage capitalism within a system of authoritarian state power, a lesson neocons immediately took to heart. Revealed in this ideological matrix are the twin grand fictions of American public life: free markets and democracy.

Other neocons have taken the fashionable Hobbes-Machiavelli nexus to yet another level. Michael Ledeen, author of a book on Machiavelli and whose *The War Against the Terror Masters* is filled with references to the Italian theorist, elevates warrior discourse beyond even Kaplan's fantasies. A lesser-known but established figure in neocon circles, Ledeen has worked at the Pentagon, State Department, and National Security Council as well as the American Enterprise Institute. In the 1980s he was a behind-the-scenes facilitator of the illegal Iran-Contra conspiracy. He was described by some as a mover behind the U.S. war against Iraq and remained a vehement partisan of armed intervention in Iran, helping set up the Center for Democracy in Iran (CDI) dedicated to "regime change" by force if necessary. In Ledeen's world, as described in *Terror Masters,* the United States faces myriad enemies of Western democratic values, masterminded largely from Tehran. That the United States faces epic battles against Islamic opponents has nothing to do with its own global behavior and everything to do with the deep hatred and envy Islam harbors toward the innocent, democratic, peace-loving superpower. At this point Ledeen's view of U.S. history descends into the kind of propaganda served up by Fox TV News and Radio Free Europe, referring, for example, to a "bloodthirsty Islam" with its fanatical desire to destroy the West (without discernible political motives), as Iran hovers backstage, the "mother of modern Islamic terror".[29] In the years before 9/11 Ledeen and his cohorts at AEI were pushing for a "counter-jihad" against terrorists and their patrons in Tehran, Baghdad, and Damascus, hoping to refashion the Middle East to fit U.S. and Israeli interests—again by force if needed, tolerating and even relishing the resulting chaos.

While the United States has a long record of installing and working closely with dictatorial regimes, Ledeen was somehow able to justify this mission as part of a "national tradition of fighting tyranny,"[30] one of several necon myths. The goal was to bring "rules of a free society" to nations where such traditions did not exist, without mention of U.S. economic or geopolitical objectives. The notion that "politically backward" cultures can be (and ought to be) transformed from outside, possibly by armed might, has of course furnished the ideological veneer for aggressive militarism throughout history.

Ledeen claimed to have arrived at these insights from Machiavelli, famous for recognizing that politics ultimately revolves around naked power and manipulation. Machiavelli, in Ledeen's account, is said to have taught that *virtu* must be imposed on a brutish world through state power, including military force, and that "if we win, everyone will judge our methods to be appropriate."[31] No doubt the Bush administration took such neocon "Machiavellian" injunctions to heart when it decided to invade and occupy Iraq. Ledeen's version of Machiavelli, however, is distorted to justify self-serving neocon view of U.S. imperial ambitions that, under conditions of increasing blowback, could easily backfire—precisely the outcome in Iraq. Machiavelli did argue that violence and warfare are inescapable elements of the political equation. Yet in *The Prince* and other writings he further addressed the problem of how to *minimize* coercive excesses be erecting state power on a matrix of laws, social practices, and habits of civility. Machiavelli grasped what would later become a truism—that popular consent is necessary for broad legitimacy and stable governance, which, used wisely by strong leaders, would eventually *reduce* dependency on violence. Indeed he opposed brute imposition of political rule, favoring some type of republic. Ledeen's own warrior outlook combined with neocon imperial hubris actually requires another ideological source, more akin to the ruthless systems of domination that defenders of the British and French empires in their bloody heyday, and architects of U.S. Manifest Destiny, had in mind.

Subverting Internationalism

Neocons pretend to be strong internationalists dedicated to U.S. global benevolence and peaceful relations among nations, yet their emphasis on warrior politics leads inexorably to just the opposite: a jaundiced and one-sided view of international rules, laws, agreements, and discourses. Their worldview favors compromise except where American interests are at stake, in which case the preference is for machtpolitik as an instrument of national leverage. As noted above, neocon ideologues, such as Robert Kagan, Richard Perle, and Robert Kaplan, are contemptuous of global laws, treaties, and organizations seen as conflicting with U.S. interests, with Kaplan arguing that international law is "fundamentally utopian" since everyone knows that powerful states always subordinate the weaker ones.[32] Warriors are bound to resist contractual agreements tied to mutual cooperation and equal relations to the extent it limits their power and flexibility. Today, with the ascent of global terrorism and dispersed resistance to superpower domination, the United States insists upon maximum freedom to respond quickly and forcefully to new crises.

Exceptionalist discourse gained new credibility after 9/11, not only within the mass media and political system but also in academia, while American criticism of the UN became more virulent. Some established law professors—John Yoo at University of California at Berkeley, Alan Dershowitz at Harvard, and Eric Posner at Chicago, for example—argued that crucial tenets of international law (including Geneva Convention statutes on treatment of prisoners) had become unworkable and obsolete. Some have laid out the case that practices generally regarded as torture could now be legitimate interrogation methods.[33] Following superpower logic, these and other legal experts suggest that "civilized nations" are entitled to use "uncivilized means," even if that means violation of international treaties and precedents. This is hardly novel, as the historical evidence is clear: U.S. leaders have long felt justified in violating or jettisoning international agreements such as the Kyoto Protocols, Nuclear Nonproliferation Treaty, ban on space militarization, torture convention, International Criminal Court, the UN Charter, Geneva Conventions, World Court, and certain rules of military engagement where it suits American dictates. Well before 9/11 and rise of the "Bush doctrine," the U.S. often blithely followed its own dictates as it lectured other nations about adhering to universal standards. Over time, American political and intellectual culture has fully absorbed this exceptionalist outlook. As Philippe Sands wrote in *Lawless World,* the idea of International Criminal Court jurisdiction is one that normally reduces U.S. politicians, the media, and normally tepid academic gatherings to fits of hysteria.[34] Washington views the ICC, the first truly independent juridical body, as illegitimate, preferring its own financed and controlled tribunals (as at The Hague and Baghdad) for trying designated enemies.

Posner and coauthor Jack Goldsmith, in *The Limits of International Law*, claim the relevance of international law has been "grossly exaggerated," since everyone knows the distribution of global power is what *really* dictates national behavior. Most agreements, they insist, wind up as nothing more than "legal rhetoric."[35] World politics is driven overwhelmingly by competing national interests, with laws and treaties only masking or rationalizing those interests. Government leaders prioritize the twin goals of national security and economic advantage over competing moral or legal concerns, which are denounced the moment they interfere with self-interest. Such contempt for international law makes perfectly good sense within a neocon framework postulating a Hobbesian state of nature and "Machiavellian" solutions for overcoming it. As noted, the right-wing assault on internationalism has been particularly visible in its uncompromising hostility to the UN and other nominally independent bodies. For much of its history, the UN has actually operated in sync with American preferences, while U.S. veto power in the Security Council has been available to block unfriendly decisions—yet neocons nowadays protest vehemently when the U.N. deviates even slightly from Washington designs. Many conservatives paint the UN as an out-of-control monster dominated by third world countries, infused with a fanatical "anti-Americanism," and hostile to U.S. military ventures. Some urge the United States to withhold some or all of its financial contributions to various UN social and educational agencies. Others believe the UN is exerting a stranglehold on American sovereignty, as shown by Security Council refusal to sanction the U.S. invasion of Iraq. In *An End to Evil* (2003), David Frum and Richard Perle ask: "When did the United States require the Security Council's permission to defend itself?"[36] In response, they argue that whenever the United States does not prevail in UN deliberations, it should "unashamedly and explicitly reject the jurisdiction of these rules."[37] After all, it is common knowledge that the United States is "fighting on behalf of the civilized world."[38]

A few neocon ideologues pursued this line of thinking even further. Thus, in *Neoconservatism* (2006), Douglas Murray wrote that the UN ought to be denied legitimacy, repudiating the international body as a "false contract,"[39] puzzling given the crucial role Western powers played in setting up the organization after World War II. Murray contended that "the U.N. has no spiritual authority, no legal authority, and not even a very impressive track record in getting things right."[40] What he found most troubling was that so few member governments are "free and democratic," although a good number of these "undemocratic" states actually remain clients of the United States. A leading neocon, John Bolton, was named acting U.S. Ambassador to the UN in 2005 and immediately gave expression to what was called a "politics of bellicosity," relentlessly working to turn the organization into an even more pliant tool of American interests. He merely laughed at proposed diplomatic solutions to a variety of Middle East conflicts, tried to block resolutions aiding poor countries, expressed deep pessimism over arms control, threatened to cut off U.S. funding if Washington-friendly "reforms" were not approved, and vetoed Security Council resolutions condemning Israeli military attacks on Lebanon in summer 2006. His repeated tirades invited a far higher level of worldwide antagonism to Washington than was the case during the Clinton presidency.[41] Of course Bolton's antics were fully congruent with neocon thinking, indeed with the broader legacy of U.S. exceptionalism outlined in chapter 1.

Neoconservatism and Liberalism

The "neocon turn" is generally understood as a radical departure from American political traditions, especially in its embrace of unilateralism, preemptive war, and global supremacy, but this is greatly exaggerated. In fact neocon ideology conforms to established patterns going back to the nineteenth century, in at least two ways. First, as neocon influence within elite circles expanded—more visibly after 9/11—the society has witnessed a broadening common ground between liberals and conservatives, Democrats and Republicans as revealed by the former's support of Bush's war on terror, the Patriot Act, and the Iraq war, seeming to weaken only when public opinion surveys indicated (by late 2006) growing public impatience with war and occupation. The reality is that conventional liberalism has rarely offered much alternative to "bipartisan" U.S. foreign policy, especially in the postwar era. Second, as we have seen, Democratic leaders across the past century—Wilson, FDR, Truman, JFK, Johnson, Clinton—were all committed in varying degrees to an aggressive military stance, basic elements of which intersect with contemporary neocon thinking. JFK's brand of Cold War liberalism emerges as crucial precursor to Bush's post-9/11 militarized foreign policy, just as parallels between Vietnam and Iraq had become more glaring over time. For the bulk of its history American politics took shape within a liberal consensus defined by market priorities, corporate power, and foreign expansion.

Opposition to this consensus was ritually attacked as "un-American," "unpatriotic," even in tune with the demonic threat of the moment, with intellectual dissent and political opposition easily marginalized. The national mythology of American greatness and entitlement has long prevailed across the liberal-conservative divide, with "politics" essentially vanishing on issues of war and peace.

Neoconservatism first appeared as an outgrowth of liberalism gone sour, its proponents increasingly frustrated with Democratic Party failure to sustain a hawkish enough anticommunist foreign policy. Neocons wanted to counter a debilitating "anti-Americanism" that grew out of the Vietnam defeat and a 1960s radicalism that morphed into the new social movements of the 1970s. They were drawn to the classical liberalism of Wilson, Truman, and JFK supposedly jettisoned by later Democratic politicians grown soft on Communism.[42] Many were outraged by "capitulation" in Vietnam and failed efforts to overthrow the Castro regime in Cuba, united in their demand for a strengthened military to fight any threat to U.S. power. Theirs was a revitalized crusade for American global hegemony even as aspirations toward empire were meekly disavowed at the time. President Reagan provided a national forum for advancing such views, that is, political space to better confront the "evil empire," but in fact the main (foreign policy) themes of both neocon and Reaganite ideology departed only stylistically from earlier liberal views. The Clinton presidency, while a target of visceral right-wing hatred, upheld international goals closely aligned with those of the neocons, including strong antiterrorist legislation, a bolder Star Wars program, uncompromising support for Israel, sanctions against Iraq, and unprovoked military action in the Balkans. Indeed the 1998 Iraq Freedom Act was passed by Congress and approved by the White House during Clinton's tenure. No less than Reagan and the two Bushes, Clinton was convinced that world supremacy was a matter of American historical destiny.

By the late 1990s, a growing stratum of liberal intellectuals and politicians was sharing neocon ideas, fixated on heightened and dispersed U.S. military power to fight a new cycle of enemies: Arab/Muslim extremists, terrorists, and rogue states plus remnants of the Communist left. With advancing economic globalization, moreover, American interests were becoming far more *international* in scope as resource struggles and kindred interests settled on the Middle East, especially after 9/11. Liberals no less than neocons identified the Pentagon as key instrument in the worldwide struggle of democracy against Islamic jihadism, the new "totalitarianism." Just as the

United States stood for "humanitarian intervention" against "ethnic cleansing" and "genocide" in the Balkans, it would now constitute an indispensable bastion of enlightenment and modernity against barbarism—a moral imperative neocons and liberals readily shared in common. In the Balkans, of course, a war launched by the Democrat Clinton made liberal support virtually automatic. Clinton would be remembered as a partisan of "liberal internationalism," a doctrine intimately bound up with the requirements of U.S. global power, in the tradition of Wilson, Truman, and JFK.

When the United States and NATO carried out the 1999 bombing campaign in Yugoslavia, prominent liberal intellectuals like Paul Berman, David Rieff, Michael Walzer, and Christopher Hitchens surfaced as hawkish backers of the Pentagon, their opinions barely distinguishable from those of the neocons—celebration of American global power, unconditional defense of Israel, hopes of "remapping" the Middle East, a quick readiness to intervene militarily. These same liberals would enthusiastically support Bush's invasion and occupation of Iraq as linchpin of the war on terrorism. The possibility of limits to American hegemony did not enter their narrow calculus—nor apparently did concern for blowback, that is, the likelihood U.S. militarism would generate resentment and opposition worldwide.[43] Such liberals, moreover, accepted at face value standard Washington claims to be spreading democracy and human rights without so much as acknowledging economic and geopolitical aims at stake. During and after buildup to the Iraq war, their righteous anger was directed not at Bush—architect of an illegal, bloody, and costly war—but at the popular antiwar movement, limiting any criticisms to secondary matters of tactics, timing, and efficiency. In their view, protesters were simply oblivious to the monstrous evils of the Hussein regime. In the end, leading congressional Democrats went along with the devious Bush/Cheney warmaking agenda, endorsing all the false pretexts, appropriating tens of billions of dollars, voting for executive war powers, endorsing the Patriot Act without serious debate, and closing ranks around a beleaguered president until public opposition made that untenable. Even as war and occupation turned into a bloody and costly disaster, even as many liberals finally urged a vague "change of course" in 2006, few Democratic politicians seemed ready to argue for rapid U.S. troop withdrawal to end the seemingly bottomless Iraq disaster.

By the end of the second Bush's reign, neoconservatism had infused American political culture with a right-wing ideological zeal that owed considerable debt to the Reagan years. This zeal sometimes took on quasireligious features—visible mostly in foreign policy but also in the style of political behavior epitomized by the grassroots Tea Party outbursts over health care reform starting in summer 2009. As Neal Gabler observed, a populist strain of conservatism was being transformed into something akin to a political religion fueled by dogmatic certitude and self-righteous anger.[44] Gabler noted that this frenzied style went beyond strict policy concerns, morphing into a fundamentalism where "belief in one's own rightness [is] so unshakeable that it is not subject to political caveats." Normal political discourse grounded in debate and compromise was anathema to these energized conservatives, typified by the tirades of hundreds of talk radio hosts (mostly white males) around the country. In this supercharged milieu, opponents of unbridled corporate and military power (including the most tepid liberals) were denounced as treasonous, evil, and anti-American. Fear mongering and wildly emotional outbursts became the stock in trade. In the spring and especially summer of 2009 Tea Party activists held gatherings at which Obama was scorned as, alternatively, fascist and socialist, Hitlerite and Stalinist, a president who was turning the country into a totalitarian system. Protesters against even the mildest health care reform screamed about "death panels," "Communist medicine," and leftist conspiracies to rob ordinary people of medical choices, and imminent dictatorship. Added Gabler, "Having opted out of political discourse, they are not susceptible to any suasion. Rationality won't work because their arguments are faith-based rather than evidence-based."[45] Here it would seem the warrior culture characteristic of neocon ideology had begun to permeate both domestic and global realms at high-temperature levels. While on the surface populist in form, this new conservatism moved steadily, indeed self-consciously, away from discursive processes essential to even a minimalist democratic culture.

Despite such threatening virulence, this fundamentalism amounts to much less a break with the past—with some romanticized notion of democratic politics—than is commonly assumed. The neocons, as we have seen, championed superpatriotism, militarism, and imperial grand designs that brooked little debate or opposition insofar as these values were consistent with the legacy of national exceptionalism and Manifest Destiny. In both instances we have a form of religious orthodoxy typical of extreme political dogmatism. Gabler argued that "the fundamentalist political fanatics will always be more zealous than mainstream conservatives or liberals. They will always be louder, more adamant, more aggrieved, more threatened, more will to do anything to win. Losing is inconceivable. For them, every battle is a crusade—or a jihad—a matter of good and evil."[46] The Obama presidency apparently gave rise to a convergence of elite and populist strains in the "new" conservatism, fueled by nearly hysterical defense of corporate and imperial power at a time when that power looked as if it could be weakened—possibly a reprise of that very historical fascism the tea-baggers, anti-health-care reform fanatics, and right-wing talk show hosts projected onto Obama and mainstream liberals.

Iraq and Beyond

The post-9/11 world was ideally suited to neocon beliefs and agendas that the Bush administration seemed perfectly happy to advance. In an uncertain and challenging world, familiar neocon discourses appeared likely to gain currency—clash of civilizations, jihadic threats, centrality of military force, endless warfare. A warrior modus operandi—preemptive war, willingness to skirt international law, schemes for regime change, diminished rules of engagement—gathered broad acceptance as U.S. leaders invoked rights, entitlements, and privileges available exclusively to them. The necocons' genius was a capacity to tap into strains of elite thinking at the far end of establishment ideology, rendering it "mainstream." Their concept of power depended on a moral absolutism and national exceptionalism equating political vitality with military force.

Bush's Iraq venture—brazen, illegal, and planned well in advance—had unmistakeable roots in neocon thinking well before 9/11 and even the 2000 election, outlined in 1997 and 2000 PNAC documents calling for the overthrow of Hussein (frustrated in 1991) and remaking the Middle East to suit American and Israeli designs. Neither terrorism nor weapons of mass destruction entered the strategic picture, then or later—nor did democracy. As is well known, the Bush presidency brought leading neocons into foreign policy-making, including Cheney, Rumsfeld, and such high-level Pentagon officials as Wolfowitz, Perle, and Douglas Feith, with the neocon Bolton named acting U.S. ambassador to the UN. These proponents of regime change in Iraq, with crucial help from ambitious public relations campaigns, were euphoric about war, totally convinced of its righteousness and blind to any pitfalls. After six months of difficult and bloody military occupation, Perle and coauthor David Frum, in *An End to Evil*, could write: "We liberated an entire nation, opening the way to a humane, decent civil society in Iraq... "[47], adding, "The brilliant performance of our troops in Iraq hinted at what technology and a bold operational plan, superbly executed, can do."[48] Scarcely troubled by the unlawful, duplicitous, savage, and unpopular character of the invasion, Perle and Frum scoffed at the UN, insisting that the United States required no Security Council permission to initiate military action.[49] The immediate postinvasion period was filled with wildly utopian assessments both within and outside Bush circles.

In *A Long Short War* (2003), Hitchens, erstwhile liberal turned neocon, could barely restrain his enthusiasm for the Iraq war. After toasting Wolfowitz for being correct about the need for regime change in Iraq long before others, Hitchens complimented Bush for his patient, rational leadership throughout the buildup to war. Moving across Iraq in the company of U.S. and British troops, he wrote triumphantly of rapid military victories and strong welcome "liberated" Iraqis gave to advancing soldiers with cries of "Boosh, Boosh!" supposedly coming from young children—hardly, as it turns out, a prelude to the later horrors of occupation. Hitchens referred to the warmhearted presence of "big, happy, friendly, gullible Western officers,"[50] taking a page from Hollywood's World War II propaganda movies. Those soldiers had every reason to be happy: they were on the road to uplifting success, disposing of thieves, rapists, murderers, and other threats lurking about Iraq, ready to uncover vast hidden arsenals of WMD. (Already spelled out earlier) Sprawling U.S. military convoys were to ally with brave Kurds engaged in "fighting a battle for all of us."[51] Hitchens sagely observed that the invasion not only liberated Iraq, but saved precious oil reserves from Saddam Hussein's clutches "with scarcely a drop [of blood] spilled."[52] Even at this early juncture reports counted hundreds, perhaps thousands of Iraqi deaths, but this hardly registered on Hitchens' otherwise sensitive moral radar screen. His book contains wild attacks on the antiwar movement that in late 2002 and early 2003 attracted millions into the streets in the United States, Europe, and around the world. Hitchens was not impressed, stating (without evidence) that the movement was organized by leaders who thought Hussein was a good guy and supported by "blithering ex-flower children" along with "ranting neo-Stalinists in the streets."[53] If the "potluck peaceniks" had their way, he wrote, the world would be overrun by tyrants like Milosevic and Hussein while misguided activists are obsessed with fighting *American* power, their ill-fated antiwar protests based

on nothing but "hysterical predictions." Every single Hitchens con-
tention was so far removed from reality as to scarcely require critical
response.

The aforementioned Douglas Murray's *Neoconservatism* was written mainly to furnish a rationale for the Iraq war. Murray believed
neocon ideology had saved the day against both outmoded conservatism and dangerous liberalism, thanks to Bush's courageous policies, writing, "President Bush has reminded people that America's
concerns are the world's concerns, and that the world's concerns are
the natural concerns of America,"[54] adding, "If America was to stay
free, then it had to work to make other people free."[55] The United
States, we are told, represents the chief surviving model of human
progress, its leaders obligated to conquer tyranny, lawlessness, and
evil wherever it surfaces. Neocons brought to foreign policy a moral
dedication to fight opponents of the West, starting with that tyrant
of all tyrants, Saddam Hussein. In Murray's words, "The outrages
of 9/11 demonstrated the need for a shakeup in the world… [begin-
ning with] the overthrow of another threatening tyranny.[56] Iraq was
the most imminent threat, said to harbor both terrorists and arsenals of WMD—although of course such claims were never proven
and Murray himself made no effort to do so. Echoing Kagan and
Hitchens, Murray denounced France and Germany as "appeasers,"
stating: "In Europe especially, a popular determination to confront
a present and growing threat was, at best, lacking."[57] Antiwar critics were themselves wicked enemies of the United States, filled with
self-hatred and sympathy for jihadists and terrorists.[58] Were any neocon contentions revised or junked following years of military occupation that brought untold death and destruction to a nation the United
States was ostensibly liberating? Consistent with the fundamentalism
outlined above, neocon views remained firm: a "democratic Iraq" was
on the rise, furnishing a model of freedom for others in the Middle
East and elsewhere—a seismic moment in a people's history.[59] The
idea that war and occupation might be related to the U.S. quest for
resources was dismissed as "stupid," the product of critics' nihilistic
hatred of a democratic society in which they are fortunate enough to
live. Murray was still convinced an Iraqi democracy had been fully
realized, destined to spread across the region.[60] Such contentions will-
fully ignore a basic reality: the Iraq puppet government never had
control over such vital decision-making areas as foreign policy, trade,
commerce, investments, education, and the media—quite a truncated
notion of democracy.

After years of chaos and violence in Iraq, however, neocon fantasies persisted, a testimony not only to the force of political illusion but to cold indifference to human suffering on a vast scale. A team of U.S. and Iraqi epidemiologists found, as early as October 2006, that the civilian death toll after the invasion had reached a staggering 650,000, as reported by the Johns Hopkins School of Public Health and published in the British journal *Lancet*.[61] In early 2009 the London NGO Iraq Body Count reported total Iraqi deaths attributable to military intervention at between 800,000 and 1.3 million, along with 1 million war widows and more than 3 million displaced, many of whom had to resettle in tent cities or in neighboring countries like Syria and Jordan. Unemployment consistently hovered at nearly 50 percent, with the public infrastructure in shambles. From 2003 until at least 2009, the Iraqi population was victimized by arbitrary detentions, torture, routine military abuses, and random violence—a "land of horrors," according to one UN report, all traceable to the invading and occupying power that bears full legal and political responsibility according to the Nuremberg precedent. Meanwhile, U.S. apologists continue to uphold this exercise in savagery as a wonderful triumph of civilized virtues, an epic moment of liberation and democracy, as the neocons concede few limits to their imperial fantasies of remaking the Middle East. Sadly, each catastrophe that followed the invasion—perpetual disorder, horrendous casualties, terrorism, ecological destruction— had been anticipated at the outset, not only by antiwar critics but by many policy experts at the Pentagon, CIA, and State Department. The U.S. invasion of Iraq violated basic international moral and legal standards, starting with failure to win UN Security Council support. Regime change involved abrogation of international legality that, unfortunately, was rubber-stamped by a pliant Congress, the courts, and the media. Warmaking could not have proceeded without systematic deceit, media manipulation, public relations crusades, and deliberate misuse of intelligence data—all on the pretext of fighting a nonexistent threat. War crimes inevitably followed: wanton attacks on civilians as in Fallouja and Hadditha, illegal detentions, torture, used of banned weaponry, local atrocities, and prohibited colonization of a nation's institutions and resources, among others. Meanwhile, the Bush clique managed to enlarge the American imperial presidency and security state, symptomatic of an already severely deteriorating political culture.

And the Bush/neocon partisans of "preemptive warfare" were fully (no underlining here) prepared to go beyond Iraq: despite catastrophes in Afghanistan and Iraq, some neocons were by spring 2007 loudly agitating for regime change in Iran. The pretext? Virtually identical to what preceded Iraq—to fight terrorism, stop WMD proliferation, and promote democracy—even if disaster seemed built into yet another manifestation of brazen imperial hubris. Tactical possibilities for eliminating the great Iranian threat were many, including air strikes, economic sanctions, commando raids, aid to "democratic opposition" groups, covert action, perhaps even invasion. Here again the neocon project merged with the mainstream consensus, as reflected in passage of the 2007 Iran Freedom Support Act giving the president freedom to intervene against a sovereign nation—one said to be a fearsome threat to the West even as it was entirely surrounded by U.S. military forces. The claim that Iran represented a grave menace while exercising its Non-Proliferation Treaty (NPT) right to develop peaceful nuclear energy in fact echoes what neocons at the AEI and *Weekly Standard* had been arguing for months, even years. The Iran Act, urging sanctions and "democratic transformation" with implicit threat of military action, was passed overwhelmingly, with opposition from only 21 representatives and none of the senators voting against.

The 2008 Obama presidential victory, a remarkable historical event, raised hopes among many Americans of new departures from the Bush/neocon years, especially in U.S. global behavior. Obama did hold out prospects for a new course and a politics of hope, moving away from outlooks and policies that had made the United States an international pariah. There were indeed suggestions of change: closing down Guantanamo, abandoning torture, curtailing surveillance, exiting Iraq, securing peace between Israel and the Palestinians, a new opening to Islam. The problem was not so much Obama's uplifting discourse but rather that he remained trapped in the old ideological paradigm owing to his instinctive centrist liberalism, a huge debt to corporate lobbies, financial largesse provided by Wall Street, and deep commitment to the Israel Lobby. In fact, Obama set new records for campaign fundraising, tapping the support of banks, telecommunications, pharmaceuticals, insurance, and military-industrial enterprises. While Obama in his run to the White House did rely on a populist campaign tied to the Internet, he had no choice but to accommodate privileged interests in setting the agendas of his presidency. His appointments spoke volumes: the conservative, staunchly pro-Israel Rahm Emmanuel as Chief of Staff, the former general Robert Jones as hawkish military adviser, and such Wall Street veterans as Timothy Geithner, Larry Summers, and Robert Rubin to his economic team. It would be business-as-usual at the White House, with such huge donors as J.P. Morgan Chase, Citigroup, and Goldman Sachs expecting precisely that. Though he ran as something of a "people's candidate," Obama would have enormous difficulties straying far from elite priorities, whether on the Middle East, Pentagon spending, largesse to failing banks and corporations, or domestic policies like health care. Within a year of his breakthrough election, Obama was reneging, capitulating, or simply dragging his feet on such promises as withdrawal from Iraq, closing of Guantanamo, and full-scale overhaul of the health care system. In some respects, Obama seemed to be following the trajectory of Bush, as even many Democrats came to reluctantly concede.

As for the long and unforgiving war in Afghanistan, Obama, taking a page from Bush, remarked in a speech to the Veterans of Foreign Wars that "We must never forget. This is not a war of choice. This is a war of necessity. Those who attacked America on 9/11 are plotting to do so again. If left unchecked, the Taliban insurgency will mean an even larger safe haven from which al Qaeda would plot to kill more Americans."[62] The "safe haven" Obama referred to is actually located in Pakistan. In any event, whether the Taliban—a home-grown popular force—could be evicted by armed force, whether it actually poses a threat to the United States, or indeed whether such a "war" is winnable given the harsh terrain, mounting blowback, growing material costs, and shrinking public support for a seemingly endless drain on human lives and resources, was never addressed by Obama. Nor were the daunting political and military dangers posed by expansion of military conflict into Pakistan, where the U.S. unmanned drones had carried out dozens of missions. Meanwhile, even as the Taliban "threat" appears remote by any rational calculus, U.S. intervention escalated under Obama as both military and CIA "surges" were ordered. As of late 2009, reports indicated a rapidly growing CIA Afghan deployment, with more than 700 operatives in the field working to fight off an increasingly popular and sophisticated insurgency.[63] The spies were being used for myriad purposes—linking up with Spec-Ops forces, collaboration with other intelligence units like the National Security Agency, funneling money to warlords, pursing "high-value targets," conducting surveillance, and tracking Afghan public opinion that had turned drastically against the American presence. The CIA also escalated its Predator drone program in both Afghanistan and Pakistan, leading to hundreds of civilian dead and wounded. As of early 2011 Congress was still giving the president essentially a blank check for the Afghan operations, in the absence of serious public debate. If there was ever a noteworthy difference between Obama and his Bush/neocon predecessors on the crucial matter or war and peace, it appeared to have vanished within two years of Obama's election to the White House.

Regarding Iran, tensions between Washington and Tehran mounted significantly after 2003, ostensibly around Iranian nuclear ambitions, but it is no secret that Israel and its powerful American lobby long favored aggressive moves to neutralize a tenacious Middle East adversary. Iran, after all, was a patron of Hezbollah, a militant group with close ties to Palestinians and an extensive presence in Lebanon. U.S. threats to Iran have risen with talk of punishing economic sanctions, diplomatic maneuvers to isolate the country, and not-so-veiled warnings of possible military action since 2003. A focus of mainstream U.S. political and media obsession, Iran soon enough permeated American public consciousness as a major "threat" without, however, any logical or factual basis of the fears. After "discovery" of an Iranian nuclear site in September 2009 (actually long known to U.S. intelligence), the media frenzy heightened, typified by a front-page *Los Angeles Times* headline warning: "Time for talk may be over."[64] It was said to be well-understood that Iran had been deceiving the world about its nuclear weapons ambitions. The *Times* reported that "Tehran was threatening the stability and security of the world"—by now a standard rhetoric for mainstream political and media venues, inherited from the neocon ideological arsenal.

Left unsaid here is that Iran, desperately in need of nonpetroleum sources of domestic energy, has always been fully within its rights spelled out by the NPT, to which the Iranians subscribe. The facilities in question are rather ordinary and well known to international observers, in any event several years removed from any significant weapons potential. While the Iranians are depicted in the United States and Israel as global outlaws, the reality is that the only two nuclear powers in the region—massive and concealed—are the United States and Israel. Further, in producing new cycles of nuclear weapons, the United States stands outside the NPT while Israel, with its stockpile of at least 200 atomic warheads, rejects both the treaty and global inspections regimes. The very demands made of Iran are arrogantly refused by the real nuclear outlaws of the Middle East. (In 2007 Iran proposed a Middle Eastern nuclear-free zone, summarily rejected by both Washington and Tel Aviv.) Meanwhile, the Iranians—never having invaded or threatened neighboring countries—remain surrounded by massive American armed force deployed in Iraq, Kuwait, Afghanistan, throughout Central Asia, and the Persian Gulf. Referring to possible military action against Iran, Secretary of Defense Robert Gates repeated in September 2009 that "we obviously don't take any options off the table," a lightly veiled military threat in direct violation of the UN Charter prohibiting such declarations. The Israelis have routinely made similar warnings at a time when Iranian leaders have made no such threats. In an op-ed commentary, neocon John Hannah of the Washington Institute for Near Eastern Policy, a key mouthpiece of Israeli agendas, suggested that it might be necessary to "cripple Iran to save it," arguing the time had arrived for crippling sanctions or even military intervention.[65] U.S. and Israeli eagerness to carry out regime change in Iran demonstrates the stubborn persistence of neocon thinking into the Obama era.

By late 2008, the media was celebrating the great U.S. military "surge" triumph in Iraq that, following Bush's deployment of additional tens of thousands of troops to the field, appeared to have consolidated American occupation while reducing the count of dead and wounded on both sides. Disaster had seemingly been transformed into miraculous victory, turning the Middle East into smoother sailing for U.S. geopolitical strategy. At the heart of this supposed reversal of fortune was a revived counterinsurgency program recycled from U.S. experiences in Vietnam, Central America, and elsewhere. If military force remained vital to this approach, its success was attributed mainly to an ideological and cultural offensive borrowed from the infamous "winning of hearts and minds" campaign in Indochina, designed to win local populations over to foreign rule. Championed by General David Petraeus, then commander of U.S. forces in the Middle East, this "new" counterinsurgency (COIN) strategy is viewed in leading government, military, and academic circles as a model to be extended to Afghanistan and beyond, a clear sign that Washington is gearing up for other military occupations to "fight terrorism" well into the future. Presented as an alternative to brutal warfare, COIN would presumably give rise to a more balanced, refined U.S. modus operandi for the twenty-first century, superseding "shock and awe." By 2009 COIN had become a full-blown doctrine widely endorsed across the political spectrum and cheerfully inherited by the Obama presidency.

While this strategy has rarely worked in the past, a more crucial problem is that it augurs long-term Washington efforts to wage counterinsurgency warfare around the world, largely in the context of pursuing geopolitical advantage in the Middle East and elsewhere. The COIN program is sure to be extremely costly as it mobilizes a combination of political, cultural, technological, and military resources to legitimate old-fashioned imperial ventures. Designed to counter blowback, the strategy in fact is likely to ensure more of the same as U.S. occupation—always backed and reinforced by military power—persists over time. (As of this writing, the U.S. had occupied Iraq for more than eight years and Afghanistan for nine years, with local resistance and political violence a daily reality into the year 2011.) Counterinsurgency is, by definition, protracted, difficult, violent, and destined to fail as foreign efforts to "reconstruct" alien societies inevitably generate insurgency in some form. While ostensibly open-ended, socially constructive, and humanitarian, the COIN program—much like the ruthless "strategic hamlet" project in Vietnam—is innately totalitarian as it sets out to indoctrinate entire populations against their national experience and interests. Imperial hubris is such, however, that Washington elites are prepared to move full-speed ahead with their plans to dominate and transform other societies without casting a critically reflective eye on historical failures.

In this context, it is highly misleading to claim anything akin to a "surge" victory in Iraq. Social disorder, infrastructure collapse, civic violence, and insurgency remain durable features of life in both occupied Iraq and Afghanistan, with no signs of reversal even as the Pentagon agitates for another "surge" in Afghanistan. While violent resistance in Iraq at least temporarily declined with the addition of new American forces, the reality for Iraqis continues to be massive displacements, roundups, detentions, home break-ins, surveillance, and of course ongoing pitched battles between insurgents and the occupying military. At the same time, U.S. efforts to atomize, fragment, and pacify Iraqi society worked to some extent, pushing the country further along the path of psychological despair, local conflict, and hopeless tribalism so earnestly favored by the occupiers whose overriding goal has been to destroy any vestige of national unity or social cohesion. The sole unifying force remains the U.S. military. As Tom Hayden writes, echoing a familiar motif of American history: "The goal of COIN is to replace Arab nationalism with a subdued, fragmented culture of subservient informants split along tribal and sectarian lines, like the mercenary Ute manhunters against the Navajo." That indeed is very much the lesson—and the outcome—of the "surge" in Iraq. Hayden adds: "The effect of the 'gated communities' and Kit Carson Scouts—indeed, the effect of much of the U.S.

occupation after 2003—has been to grind native populations into a state of anarchic fragmentation, with the vacuum often filled by sectarian militias."⁶⁶ Whether such creative imperial schemes can work over the long run is another matter, but what seems obvious is that U.S. planners have nothing in mind remotely resembling democracy for the Iraqi or Afghan people. Meanwhile, the dark consequences of American foreign policy unfold in the shadows, outside the purview of Congress, the media, and the court of public opinion.

*   *   *

The depth of U.S. imperialist culture, with its longstanding, taken-for-granted claims of global entitlement, was on graphic display in the well-received documentary *No End in Sight* (2007), a reputed "antiwar" film produced by Charles Ferguson. To be sure, Ferguson's work explores mostly the dark side of the American Iraq venture—the terrible casualties, mass exodus of refugees, social chaos, and economic breakdown—setting forth scant optimism about long-term U.S. involvement in the region. The problem is that the film depicts the disaster as a tragic "quagmire," that is, Washington policy failures that undercut (ostensibly noble) U.S. objectives. These failures, related in interviews with a parade of mainstream commentators including former government and military officials, are traced to the inability of American occupiers to control and stabilize a country descending into chaos. We are also told that massive destabilizing forces were at work among the Iraqi people. *No End in Sight* identifies a major problem in *lack of planning* at the White House and Pentagon for a well-run, stable occupation, a lapse resulting from Bush administration insistence that military success would be a cakewalk as Iraqis eagerly welcomed their Western liberators. A major villain of the drama turned out to be Secretary of Defense Rumsfeld, whose unwavering faith in technowar nourished unrealistic possibilities—for example, the belief that victory could be pulled off with relatively few troops and little preparation. According to the "expert" consensus in *No End in Sight,* better Pentagon foresight would have meant larger troop deployments and superior equipment in the field. U.S. failure to pacify a volatile society was guaranteed by lack of efficient organization utilizing planners, managers, linguists, and security personnel who could put an end to the lawlessness, violence, and turbulence. A familiar complaint was need for additional occupying personnel knowledgeable about Iraqi history, politics, culture, and language (a different kind of "surge").

In a word, disaster could have been avoided with more sophisticated leadership in Washington.

Equally culpable was the Iraq population itself: totally unprepared for the "democracy" that Americans so generously tried to export, the majority of Iraqis appear in the documentary as thankless hoodlums and terrorists, caught up in sectarian hatred and violence that pushed the society out of control. Insurgency was portrayed as the work of rogue extremists, pockets of crazed gangsters, scruffy militias, and ruthless terrorists irrationally hostile to the benevolent foreign presence, unschooled in the ways of self-government. The conundrum, according to *No End in Sight,* was that the morass had deepened to such an extent that U.S. control of the entire region was being thrown into question; with Iraqis unprepared for democracy, strategic goals might have to be abandoned.

During this expertly made two-hour documentary we find no mention of the U.S. invasion and occupation of a sovereign nation being fundamentally wrong from its inception—an act of political, legal, and moral outlawry. We find no reference to the long list of shameless lies used by the Bush administration to justify war, nor was there so much as a glimpse into the well-known geopolitical ambitions motivating Washington. Such omissions were to be expected given that the film was infatuated with the myth of an enlightened superpower bringing democracy and freedom to a country mired in backwardness. Neither the filmmakers nor their many commentators seemed aware of fatal contradictions endemic to an imperial power using its military force to take over a distant, sovereign country. We are told the Iraq venture has been nothing but a well-intentioned failure of good people ineptly pursuing noble objectives; a more efficient and less costly military occupation—on distinctly American terms—was the preferred result. And the Iraq "quagmire"? Unfortunately, the Iraqis—unschooled in the ways of modern politics—allowed their country to descend into lawless violence and social breakdown, after having long supported a brutal dictator. Could years of military horrors and political domination visited upon Iraq by the largest war machine in history have contributed anything to this state of affairs? Logic and common sense would dictate an affirmative response, but *No End in Sight*—saturated from beginning to end with unreflective imperialist sensibilities—demonstrated no interest in exploring this larger historical picture.

3

The Power Elite Today

The postwar age of organized state capitalism has meant, for the United States above all, the steady expansion of corporate, government, and military power—the most concentrated and far-reaching system of rule in history. Although many theorists—Karl Marx, Max Weber, Joseph Schumpeter, and Franz Neumann among them—foresaw the oligopolistic, bureaucratic, and rationalizing tendencies of modern capitalism, certainly none could have foreseen the enormous scope of domination American ruling elites would forge well before the twentieth century drew to a close. If none of these theorists were likely to have been seduced by proclamations of democratic governance among those same elites, neither could they have envisioned a behemoth penetrating every corner of the globe, legitimated by an ideology of special national entitlement and enforced by the largest war machine the world has ever seen. While Frankfurt School thinkers like Max Horkheimer, Theodor Adorno, and Herbert Marcuse did expect advanced capitalist societies to evolve into "totally-administered" systems, even their staunch pessimism could hardly measure up to the awesome sweep of a rogue superpower like the United States. This chapter looks at the structure and ideology of an American power elite first systematically explored by C. Wright Mills nearly a half-century earlier, focused on corporate expansion, the war economy, security state, and broad authoritarian trends within a nominally democratic political order.

A pressing question immediately arises: if American society is indeed ruled by a narrow, oligopolistic stratum of privileged elites, could those classical democratic ideals associated with the Greeks, Locke, Rousseau, Jefferson, and other nineteenth-century liberals have much relevance for present-day American politics? Could the ideological cornerstone of the political system be little more than curious fantasy, a grand illusion fit only for civics textbooks and campaign rituals? The old myths and illusions always die hard—even, or perhaps especially, among the most educated strata, while great myths surrounding democracy remain probably the most difficult for Americans to question, whatever the evidence at hand. Take, for example, the liberal Andrew Bacevich's statement, in *The Limits of Power* (2008), that "Today, no less than in 1776, a passion for life, liberty, and the pursuit of happiness remains at the center of America's civic theology. The Jeffersonian trinity summarizes our common inheritance, defines our aspirations, and provides a touchstone for our influence abroad."[1] Or another, from political scientist Jean Bethke Elshstain, who calls for renewed appreciation of a "good" American imperialism that, through its benign exercise of global power, can help restore democracy, human rights, and rule of law in a Hobbesian world overrun by terrorists, thugs, and ethnic cleansers. In *Just War Against Terror* (2005), Elshtain unblushingly presents the United States as a noble, selfless, law-abiding superpower that must, by default, take on the burden of enforcing order in a lawless world.[2] Under conditions of global chaos, with no impartial world body to regulate conflict, the leading moral force must fill a power void owing to its time-honored values of "human dignity" and "equal regard."[3] Thus: "At this point in time the possibility of international peace and stability premised on equal regard for all rests largely...on American power."[4]

In a universe where American power, strengthened by armed empire and corporate globalization, has grown more authoritarian, the claims of such academics as Bacevich and Elshtain make sense only as ideological platitudes, self-serving legitmating myths. As detailed in the first two chapters of this book, ritual assertions that Washington has always been dedicated to the spread of democracy, human rights, and rule of law around the globe cannot stand the test of even minimum empirical scrutiny. Such claims derive from a revived national exceptionalism fueled nowadays, as before, by an ethos of imperial arrogance and entitlement—the essence not of democracy, even loosely defined, but of elitism and authoritarianism on a grand scale. In his book *Nemesis* (2007), Chalmers Johnson argues that empire ultimately gives rise to some form of domestic tyranny, built as it is on a foundation of war economy and security state.[5] If oligarchic politics is one national outcome of imperial power, then its global equivalence is chaos, war, and lawlessness—all components of a Hobbesian state of nature projected, as we have seen, by American leaders and opinion-makers. Americans today experience hierarchical organization across the entire landscape—government, workplaces, schools and universities, media, technology, daily life—even as politicians and the media celebrate the vitality of democratic values. Far removed from these convenient fictions, Chris Hedges has arrived at a far more realistic (and jaundiced) view of the American predicament: "At no period in American history has our democracy been in such peril or has the possibility of totalitarianism been as real. Our way of life is over. Our profligate consumption is finished. Our children will never have the standard of living we had. And poverty and despair will sweep across the landscape like a plague. This is a bleak future."[6] That "future" cannot be grasped without critical understanding of an existing power structure that forces us to strip away familiar illusions and myths.

Corporate Rule

More than two centuries of modern capitalist development has given rise to mammoth centers of economic wealth, accumulation, and power, a continuously expanding system of corporations and financial enterprises. Early capitalism meant the commodification of virtually anything related to human activity: production, work, administration, social life, culture, politics. Over time, capital came to engulf the whole public terrain, as it drove toward economic and geographical expansion geared to profits, growth, and domination. In this context, historical capitalism (as opposed to the capitalism of textbook theories) generated a ruling stratum built on class domination, social division of labor, and ideological hegemony. In the *Communist Manifesto,* Karl Marx wrote that "The bourgeoisie, during its rule of scarce one hundred years, has created more massive and more colossal productive forces than have all preceding generations together." The scope of this transformation signaled a gradual enlarging of the field of domination since "the bourgeoisie cannot exist without constantly revolutionizing the instruments of production, and thereby the relations of production and with them the whole relations of society."[7]

This epic transformation was fueled by the expansion and integration of economic, social, and political forces, with far-reaching historical consequences. Commodification of the world was not accompanied by free markets so much as a growing system of integrated power in which state and capital, society and economy would progressively converge; the productive (and financial) apparatus was destined to impact every realm of public life, imparting to it the logic of market relations (what Marx called the "fetishism of commodities" and George Lukacs later referred to as the process "reification"). While capitalist development typically brought with it—notably in Europe and North America—the spread of liberal-democratic ideals and practices, compatible with nascent democratic institutions, it also led to concentrated forms of economic power owned and managed by a relatively small oligarchy, as capitalism and democracy entered into a deeply conflicted legacy. Given the intense economic competition that drove out smaller enterprises, Marx concluded that larger concentrations of capital were destined to prevail over time, resulting in monopoly power and greater solidification of the ruling elite. Such concentration would be the genesis of the present-day corporate enterprise whose chieftains would, beneath the surface of liberal-democratic processes, strive mightily toward the most effective institutional and ideological controls. To further consolidate their leverage, the prime movers of capital would be driven to globalize their operations, enhancing not only their profits but their economic mobility and flexibility—and thus their greater advantage over labor forces. As Marx put it, "The need for constantly-expanding markets for its products chases the bourgeoisie over the whole surface of the globe."[8] Later, it would be necessary to add the search for cheap labor and natural resources and then, with mounting national conflicts, the quest for geopolitical supremacy.

By the twentieth century, and especially after the great 1930s market crash, a more efficiently organized and managed capitalism would become an established fact of modern life, whether under fascism, social democracy, or Keynesian liberalism, as in the United States. Understood as the progressive convergence of corporate and governmental power, what might be labeled "state capitalism" was analyzed by such theorists as Max Weber and Joseph Schumpeter along with thinkers associated with Austro-Marxism and the Frankfurt School of Critical Theory. At this time Marx's prophesy regarding capitalism moving inexorably toward concentrated and centralized power had been confirmed, though not always the crisis-tendencies that Marx also predicted. For Marx, the advent or rationalized capitalism did not mean *state* capitalism based on social priorities, deep government involvement in the economy, and regulation of class conflict. This was a power structure that Marx, whose outlook was shaped by nineteenth-century realities, could not have foreseen. Turning to postwar America, C. Wright Mills would carry this perspective further, focusing on the rise of a *militarized* state capitalism—that is, a merger of corporate, government, and military interests compatible with the U.S. role as leading world superpower requiring a huge war economy and security state. For Mills, despite its liberal-democratic façade, the American power structure had achieved an unparalleled capacity to dominate both nationally and globally: "As the institutional means of power and the means of communication that tie them together have become steadily more efficient, those now in command of them have come into command of instruments of rule quite unsurpassed in the history of mankind."[9] As for the economy, the system was now (1950s) controlled by just a few hundred large corporations destined to expand more dramatically over time. What gave this system its unique power, aside from its global military presence, was a set of exceptional historical conditions (including the absence of feudalism). Thus: "The American elite entered modern history as a virtually unopposed bourgeoisie. No national bourgeoisie, before or since, has had such opportunities and advantages."[10] Mills' comment here reflects the true essence of American exceptionalism.

Such an integrated system of power could never have been sustained, much less broadened and globalized, if it had not rested upon an elaborate foundation of myths, values, traditions, and social relations that frequently come under the general category of "political culture." In the United States, the widely taken-for-granted belief in a uniquely democratic politics has always been central to this ideological foundation. Any understanding of the American corporate state, including its postwar militarized phase, must therefore take into account Antonio Gramsci's concept of ideological hegemony, which points toward the consensual basis of both corporate and state power—a phenomenon that has surely grown in relevance with the ascending importance of both the mass media and popular culture in such advanced industrial societies as the United States. Mills's otherwise brilliant work on the power elite unfortunately did not systematically engage this motif. Michael Parenti, in *Land of Idols*, establishes the argument that "capitalism is not only an economic system but an entire social and cultural order...While their cultural hegemony bolsters their state power, they also use their state power to finance and expand their cultural hegemony. This cultural dominance sustains the existing politico-economic system in several ways"—ways that include control of the communications and entertainment industries, support for such institutions and schools and universities, and the sponsoring of "good works" in the arts and elsewhere. Thus hegemony is solidified "not only by propagating the right values, attitudes, and beliefs, but by actually performing vital social functions that have diffuse benefits."[11]

Enough has been written about corporate power and its destructive impact on modern social and political life to fill many volumes, so here the focus will be on the profoundly antidemocratic implications of this critical analysis. In this and succeeding chapters, attention is devoted to a variety of consequences that corporate power has for democracy, starting with a view of the American ruling elite shaped by a network of economic interests, political arrangements, and ideological beliefs grounded in an expanding militarized state-capitalism. My argument is that corporate power subverts democratic politics across the entire public landscape: workplace, media, educational system, government, elections, and social relations. Its capacity to erode participatory norms is reinforced by a confluence of factors globalization, technology, deregulation, oligopolistic tendencies in the economy, media concentration, growth of lobbies, bureaucracy, vastly increased role of money in politics, and expansion of the war economy. As the wildly ambitious elites atop this power structure continue along their path of domination, accumulation, and destruction, the extreme corporate model engulfing virtually everything before it seems more impenetrable with each passing year.

The earlier trajectory of American state capitalism, extended to the military, was brilliantly dissected by Mills in *The Power Elite* (1956). Mills described an oligarchical power structure presided over by a tightly knit circle of corporate, government, and military elites, their roles mostly interchangeable and largely detached from the sphere of popular interests and demands. Writing after the war economy had become a "permanent" fixture, Mills observed: "As the institutional means of power and the means of communication that tie them together have become steadily more efficient, those now in command of them have come into command of instruments of rule quite unsurpassed in the history of mankind."[12] For Mills, envisioning an even more concentrated power structure in the decades ahead, the growth of militarized state capitalism was destined to clash with the requirements of democracy and free markets, generating a distinctly authoritarian logic. The American behemoth was a product of World War II, when "the merger of the corporate economy and the military bureaucracy came into its present-day significance,"[13] leading to a deepening convergence of "private" and "public" interests. An eclipse of democratic citizenship and institutional accountability was, for Mills, endemic to this system. It is a great tribute to Mills that, attuned to the war economy and security state, he could already write that "...the structural clue to the power elite today lies in the enlarged and military state" where "virtually all political and economic actions are now judged in terms of military definitions of reality."[14] In a period of expanded state capitalism today, with corporate and military interests more entrenched than ever, Mills surely would have found the idea of independent government functions laughable. And Mills was correct, then and now, for it is hard to conceive of state power operating autonomously relative to the irrepressible sway of privileged interests. Of course, the power structure that Mills probed in the 1950s has only become more authoritarian (and global) in the aftermath of several wars, skyrocketing military spending and deployments, a consolidated security state, and neoliberal globalization.

If American society is structurally and ideologically integrated at the summits of power, this is no radical break with the past much less the work of conspiratorial forces; it is the product of merging class and institutional forms of domination congealed across more than two centuries. By the early twenty-first century Fortune 500 corporations had amassed some 60 percent of total wealth in the United States, with assets spread across the planet. Such inequality has given elites, never comprising more than a tiny percentage of the population, considerable insulation from public leverage and access. American corporations gained hegemony under laissez-faire capitalism during the nineteenth century, given special legal momentum when the Supreme Court ruled in 1886 that these enterprises possessed "rights" as "recognized citizens" under the Constitution. With only rudimentary state regulations and planning, a corporate system driven by the Rockefeller and Morgan empires was able to consolidate its hold over the economy in the decades before World War I. By the 1930s and 1940s, pushed forward by the New Deal and World War II, the marriage of government and big business was officially consecrated, remaining intact across subsequent decades. Given its perpetual growth obsession, its internal hierarchy, its fierce opposition to social reforms, its ideological uniformity, and its profit-driven agendas, this state-corporate system, contrary to myth, became a mortal enemy of democracy as its goal was always *domination* in the service of freewheeling "private" economic agendas.

Whether this system morphed into something called an oligopoly or plutocracy is no doubt a matter of semantics, the point being that neither model is compatible with any ideal (or practice) of self-governance. Following Reagan-era attempts, partly successful, to roll back New Deal gains and deregulate the economy, corporate power was able to reach new heights of domestic and global domination, empowering the elite with unfettered confidence. By the 1990s new technology, financial speculation, and advancing globalization opened up new avenues of growth and power. An emboldened aristocracy of wealth flourished as the top one-tenth of one percent of fortunes soared, creating hundreds of new multibillionaires with the richest of them, Microsoft's Bill Gates, seeing his wealth increase from $2 billion to $85 billion in just a decade while the top 400 increased their average net worth to a staggering $2.6 billion by 2000. At this juncture the leading 100 corporations, many tied to finance and technology, had amassed more than one-third of total American assets.[15] The predictable result was massive increases in social inequality, scandalous business practices, depletion of public services and infrastructure, and further corporate growth enhanced by greater capital mobility made possible by globalization. Profits escalated while many business operations moved abroad and the domestic economy was beset with massive deindustrialization, leading to loss of millions of better-paying jobs. By 2006, benefitting from Bush's huge tax breaks for the rich, the wealthiest one percent of Americans held 34 percent of the total wealth, with the richest 20 percent controlling 85 percent. None of these far-reaching developments was subjected to much political debate or grew out of public decision-making processes, for corporate CEOs and boards of directors were beholden only to stockholders obsessed with quick monetary returns. Aside from some government responses to financial scandals—for example, the Savings and Loan debacle and, later, the Enron collapse and a few Wall Street shenanigans—Reagan-era deregulations kept political authority at bay. For ordinary citizens this plutocratic turn—allowing conglomerates in finance, technology, the military, media, and pharmaceuticals among others enormous freedom to operate—turned into a nightmarish drama that would more fully hit American society with the great economic meltdown of 2008–09. Finance, trade, investments, social priorities, jobs—these crucial issues and others ended up mostly in the hands of officials and managers never elected by voters. As for profits, they flowed mainly into the coffers of owners and executives, only marginally improving the lives of workers, consumers, and communities. These same elites benefitted from new tax breaks and more lax regulatory controls during the second Bush presidency. Even conservatives like Kevin Phillips were forced to conclude that "simply put, voters...were losing political and popular governance of the economy."[16]

The corporate elite can be said to constitute the dynamic component of a U.S. business sector that owns industrial firms, banks, service enterprises, and agribusiness, what William Domhoff labels the "corporate community."[17] While the very reference to corporate domination runs against conventional American opinion, its long and well-documented history is hard to dispute, especially given its increasing capacity to penetrate and reshape virtually every realm of public life. Indeed corporate hegemony, today the expression of some 500 giant corporations whose owners and managers share roughly the same interests and outlooks, has been remarkably stable across many decades, challenged only occasionally with mostly limited success. With tentacles into all areas of economic life, these enterprises command a preponderant share of national wealth, enabling them to heavily influence resource allocation, governmental decision-making, and the mass media. As Domhoff puts it, "This combination of economic power, policy expertise, and continuing political success makes the corporate owners and executives a *dominant class,* not in the sense of complete and absolute power, but in the sense that they have the power to shape the economic and political framework within which other groups and classes must operate."[18] Elite ideological cohesion flows not only from broadly identical class interests but from solidarity tied to common social involvements, cultural values, and educational backgrounds. History convincingly shows that, on the larger issues (economic and foreign policy), the elites typically close ranks, differing only when it comes to social issues removed from questions of wealth and power. The capacity of elites to mobilize their resources depends on a number of mechanisms: campaign financing, lobbies, think tanks, foundations, the media, and legal statutes endowing corporations with nearly total control of their workplaces. The power of modern American corporations to invade crucial zones of social existence is nearly total. What renders this authoritarian public sphere even more daunting is the relative, and in many ways growing, weakness of countervailing forces such as labor, small businesses, and popular movements.

As Domhoff observes, in recent decades corporations have won most battles they have waged against liberal or labor opponents, with 1973 passage of Occupational Safety and Health Administration (OSHA) (during a Republican presidency) one of the few major exceptions. The leading corporations, including the medical industry, insurance companies, and Wall Street firms, have benefitted greatly from regressive taxation, huge subsidies, deregulation, and bailouts. Corporate money spent on lobbies, think tanks, election campaigns, and R&D—not to mention direct ownership of megamedia outlets—cannot be matched by oppositional groups. There are no actual labor or progressive counterparts to the American Enterprise Institute, Cato Institute, Heritage Foundation, Hoover Institute, Council on Foreign Relations, and Business Roundtable—all with special access to corporate media outlets. As Domhoff rightly points out, these instruments of opinion formation amount to a propaganda network in the service of big-business interests. On the major issues—war, investments, trade, labor relations, social programs—debate is rarely allowed to challenge this well-constructed hegemony. In Domhoff's words, "structural economic power and control of the two parties, along with the elaboration of an opinion-shaping network, results in a polity where there is little or no organized public opinion independent of the limits set by debates within the power elite itself. There is no organizational base from which to construct an alternative public opinion."[19] The United States has been blessed, or cursed, with a national exceptionalism that has allowed corporate domination to gain (and sustain) the unique leverage it enjoys. The absence of feudalism meant diminution of class conflict and ideological divisions, helping to explain why Democrats and Republicans, liberals and conservatives could share common interests and outlooks for more than a century. The frontier bolstered colonial expansion, an ethos of "rugged individualism," and social Darwinism that still infuses the political culture, endowing American capitalism with its peculiarly harsh features. Early U.S. development gave rise to superpower ambitions and imperial power that would later help stabilize the war economy and security state.

The *internal* structure of modern corporations has followed distinctly bureaucratic lines, with no semblance of democratic participation (or even claims thereof). The only (increasingly marginal) leverage exercised by workers, consumers, and citizens has been through labor unions and some modest legislation, but unions have been steadily marginalized and by 2000 represented less than 20 percent of the total work force. The structure of authority in enterprises like AT&T, Microsoft, Bank of America, IBM, and Disney Corp. permits no opposition to managerial control, whether on matters of working conditions, pay scales, production, or free speech. Even the freedom to unionize—long recognized as a universal human right—is effectively denied by most American corporations. Michael Moore, interviewed by Naomi Klein following release of his film *Capitalism: A Love Story* (2009), put the matter quite succinctly: " we spend eight to ten to twelve hours of our daily lives at work, where we have no say. I think when anthropologists dig us up 400 years from now—if we make it that far—they're going to say 'Look at those people back then. They thought they were free. They called themselves a democracy, but they spent ten hours of every day in a totalitarian situation and they allowed the richest one percent to have more financial wealth than the bottom 95 percent combined."[20] The official governing body of most large corporations, the board of directors, is comprised of 10 to 15 (mostly white male) members whose decisions regarding production, labor, and social issues are virtually iron-clad, accountable only to major stockholders. As Domhoff notes, "Boards of Directors...are the institutionalized interface between organizations and social classes in the United States, [in other words] the intersection between corporations and the upper class."[21] The Board has nearly total power over its workforce, all the more so at times of economic downturn and rising unemployment.

Class domination of the corporate workplace is close to a totally administered system in which even talk of democracy is unthinkable, especially at a time of growing economic concentration, emphasis on technology, a flourishing service economy, high unemployment, and globalization. Indeed it is at the workplace that unequal wealth is most visibly translated into naked institutional and social power. Workers' health status, education, cultural pursuits, and family lives—not to mention civic participation—inevitably suffer as corporations intensify their hierarchical controls and global reach. The decline of general infrastructural and social supports has only aggravated this misery. The tens of millions of American workers who live in grinding poverty—the vast majority black and Latino—see few escape mechanisms, their hopes blocked by material and institutional controls over their capacity to improve their lives.

In *The Retail Revolution* (2009), Nelson Lichtenstein details horrifying working conditions for millions of people stuck in low-end jobs at Wal-mart and kindred massive retail outlets.[22] Wal-Mart operates some 4200 U.S. stores where hundreds of thousands of workers barely earn a minimum wage, have few benefits, suffer harsh conditions, and face implacable opposition to unionizing efforts, while at the same time pervasive high-tech surveillance tracks their every move. Menial workers are sucked into a corporate subculture that

Wal-Mart managers tout as "family" rooted in old-fashioned values. The near-total control managers exert over retail employees leaves no room for creativity or participation within a transmission belt, from top to bottom, designed to run with smooth bureaucratic efficiency. Advanced use of computers and other technology permits the kind of routinized workplace that founders of scientific management, or Fordism, more than a century ago would have heartily celebrated. Workers are meant to function within this retail matrix as trained, interchangeable, disposable automatons, whether at stores or the massive warehouse networks housing imported Asian goods and employ mostly "permanent temp" workers earning perhaps $20,000 yearly at a time (in 2008) when CEO H. Lee Scott reported income of $60 million.[23] A retail empire with nearly 2 million workers globally, Wal-Mart exemplifies the severely exploitative, authoritarian model of early twenty-first century labor relations in the United States, as the aim of processing goods worldwide as swiftly, efficiently, and cheaply as possible triumphs over all competing interests. Similar trends define the vast service economy, known as "MacDonaldization," a phenomenon more fully explored in chapter 4.

As corporate power extends aggressively into virtually every social, cultural, and political space, Wal-Mart and other massive retail operations set the pace. Marketing priorities channeled through advertising, public relations, lobbies, think tanks, and polling emphasize ideals (free markets, democracy, individual choice, etc.) that resonate little with the daily experiences of ordinary workers reduced to objectified components of a vast institutional system that values profits, market shares, efficiency, and control over everything. As Jamie Court writes in *Corporateering* (2003), "the industries' arguments are that commercial concerns—aka economic advantages—always trump social consideration, such as the quality of health care...Beyond policymaking, corporations use the same paradigm to replace social standards and ethical rules benefitting the individual with corporate rules and logic that emphasize the commercial."[24] This "logic" ensures a steadily diminishing realm of individual (and collective) control and autonomy—that is, a death knell to any prospects for local democracy. Corporate shibboleths like "flexibility," "efficiency," "collaboration," and "teamwork" in effect represent a move toward heightened managerial domination over workplace and community. The historical thrust of corporate power, notably where regulations and controls are relaxed as in the United States, is debilitating for any realization of the general interest. Chris Hedges writes: "We have to grasp, as

Marx and Adam Smith did, that corporations are not concerned with the common good. They exploit, pollute, impoverish, repress, kill, and lie to make money. They throw poor families out of homes, let the uninsured die, wage useless wars to make profits, poison and pollute the ecosystem, slash social assistance programs, gut public education, trash the global economy, plunder the U.S. Treasury, and crush all popular movements that seek justice for working men and women."[25]

The growth of corporations domestically generates a globalizing dynamic engineered by transnational business interests tied to the intensified search for natural resources, cheap labor, and new markets. Within a familiar neoliberal regime marked by incessant expansion, drive for superprofits, and deregulation, international capital—centered in the leading industrial nations—has achieved higher levels of mobility and flexibility, mostly at the expense of labor, local communities, and weaker national governments. Globalization has meant accelerated integration of big capital with governmental systems, sophisticated communications technology, international agencies like the World Bank and World Trade Organization, and a worldwide media network. Despite the well-known domestic (U.S.) attack on Keynesian policies, chieftains of transnational corporations rely heavily on all manner of public assistance and supports to advance their interests, always backed up by military power where normal institutional and ideological modes of control falter. As certain resources (oil, gas, timber, rare metals and minerals, etc.) become increasingly scarce, moreover, stepped-up national and corporate competition is destined to intensify along the lines of resource wars, leading to the heightened use of military force among numerous parties. In the case of the United States, a superpower bent on world domination, this dialectic figures to be especially potent—and indeed is already visible in Washington's efforts to recolonize the Middle East. Resource wars are likely to be the bedrock of U.S. foreign policy for decades to come, especially when the effects of peak oil are more pronounced.

The rise of global neoliberalism has taken authoritarian (and oligopolistic) tendencies inherent in modern corporate power to new levels. Not only is the scope of economic power far greater than before, that power is increasingly beyond the reach of most governments and other potential sources of opposition. As capital becomes more fluid and flexible, it essentially disempowers workers everywhere. Neither the transnational corporations nor the international bodies that do their bidding have mechanisms of popular control. Arenas for public debate and interventions—whether in the media, technology, or politics—scarcely exist. Military interventions further magnify these repressive elements of the global system.

Enlarged corporate power signals the ideological eclipse of familiar liberal verities such as market relations, individualism, free choice, and the comfortable equation of capitalism with democracy. In the United States, militarized *state* capitalism long ago dismantled and superseded classical liberal illusions that, however, survive today within a political culture transformed by corporate propaganda shared by the major parties. Meanwhile, with intensified organizational control over the workplace come broader forms of disempowerment, just as Mills anticipated many decades ago. These trends have only been further reinforced by the logic of corporate globalization.

The War Economy

The warfare state took shape in the decades following World War II, but it has deeper origins in U.S. history, the extension of a proud tradition of military power going back to the revolutionary war. Perpetual military engagements signaled a convergence of economic and armed forces interests as the business sector stood to profit immensely from the heightened demand for base constructions and supports, munitions, equipment, vehicles, and other combat-related material. Referring to World War I—a rather brief intervention in terms of the American experience—retired Marine general Smedley Butler could write, in *War is a Racket,* that warfare is nothing but a bloody profit-making enterprise conducted for the benefit of the very few, at the expense of the very many," adding, "Out of war nations acquire additional territory, if they are victorious. They just take it. This newly acquired territory promptly is exploited by the few—the self-same few who wrung dollars out of blood in the war. The general public shoulders the bill."[26] Although the United States annexed no new land during the Great War (as it had done earlier), the mobilization did result in a new generation of millionaires and billionaires profiting from steel production, mining, and shipbuilding as well as financial speculation, at a time when President Woodrow Wilson was justifying U.S. intervention to "make the world safe for democracy." Federal wartime spending of $52 billion netted some $16 billion in profits for such corporations as U.S. Steel, DuPont, Anaconda Copper, and of course the sprawling Rockefeller interests, all dressed up in noble patriotic and democratic ideals.

The World War I splurge prefigured a more full-blown expansion of Pentagon capitalism that, during the Cold War, gained much of its momentum from four years of state-engineered war mobilization during World War II. As is well known, the much-anticipated post-war demobilization never occurred—the fascist enemy having been quickly replaced by an even more sinister Communist menace that rationalized exorbitant levels of military and intelligence spending augmented by a rapidly growing nuclear force. Fear of new external threats helped legitimate the war economy, given full and equal backing by Democrats and Republicans, who routinely and happily passed military expenditures dwarfing those of the Soviet Union, China, or any other country. War had indeed become the racket of all rackets in Washington D.C., feeding the profits of literally thousands of arms contractors and subcontractors located in every state. Eventually trillions of dollars would be spent to subsidize a vast global network of armed-forces bases—in the year 2010 more than 700 in roughly 130 countries. Seymour Melman, the first theorist of Pentagon capitalism, would observe that the war economy was simply "part of the industrial system where goods are sold before they are produced, where profitability is assured, and where the prime and subcontracting firms are subordinate to the world's largest central managerial office."[27] Melman noted that the huge labor force (usually millions at any given time, including military personnel), resources, managers, administrators, corporations, technology, and global deployments were part of a massive state-planning apparatus—a dynamic economic system integral to, and not separate from, the larger capitalist edifice. From this standpoint, the war economy fed directly into the trend toward statism, concentrated economic power, and lopsided investment priorities working to the disadvantage of the public infrastructure and social programs.

Melman's conclusions paralleled those of Mills, for whom the war economy was a driving force behind state-capitalism, a set of interests crucial to the merging of governmental and corporate power. In *The Power Elite,* Mills observed that "the structural clue to the power elite today lies in the enlarged and military state... The warlords have gained decisive political relevance, and the military structure of America is now in considerable part a political structure. The seemingly permanent military threat places a premium on the military and upon their control of the men, materiel, money, and power; virtually all political and economic actions are now judged in terms of military definitions of reality."[28] What both Melman and Mills observed several decades ago was just a glimpse of the much larger historical trajectory.

Crucial to maintenance of the American state-capitalism has been the growth of U.S. imperial power and its requisite war system, situated within a framework of economic, cultural, and political relations so pervasive as to be seemingly invisible. A nation long driven by ambitions of international supremacy—what the Pentagon would eventually call full-spectrum dominance—has erected a behemoth rooted in authoritarian controls, economic coercion, and military force, both domestically and abroad. While predictably denied by government and Pentagon officials, militarism has become a pervasive ideology ritually given legitimacy by politicians, the media, corporate elites, and academia, its essential imperial premises sacrosanct within the established public sphere. The historical turning point associated with what Sheldon Wolin calls a new "power imaginary" grew out of war mobilization and military Keynesianism during and after World War II.[29] As James Cypher notes, "In the U.S. militarism is and has been since the late 1940s a hegemonic societal perception—the prism though which global political events and U.S. foreign policy are interpreted."[30] The outlook, it should be emphasized, is hardly the product of a few neocon extremists or the result of a Bush-Cheney coup to push the United States along the path of a more adventurous foreign policy, but rather should be viewed as an *extension* of American traditions rooted in national exceptionalism, conquest, and expansion.

The U.S. military achieved a postwar global reach without historical parallel, based in a permanent war economy that Melman linked to a byzantine web of political, bureaucratic, cultural, and international as well as economic processes. The economic sphere calls attention to a system of production and consumption within the war machine, including budgetary allocations and taxation, stimulus to corporate power, R&D, technology, labor relations, and the larger ramifications of a militarized society central to U.S. imperial power covering the world's land, seas, air, outer space, and even cyberspace. Elevated military preparedness and planning, a legacy of World War II, has rarely slackened, reaching peak levels during the Bush-Cheney years. The wartime threat of Nazis and fascists was soon enough transferred to the new menace of international communism, which justified the kind of Pentagon expansion that President Eisenhower in 1961 would famously label the "military-industrial complex." The United States gladly took on the role of world's leading superpower, steadily widening its lead over rival USSR as the Pentagon budget would soon exceed the entire gross domestic product of all but a few industrialized nations. In the mid-1950s Mills could write: "It is not only within the higher political, economic, scientific, and educational circles that the military ascendancy is apparent. The warlords, along with fellow travelers and spokesmen, are attempting to plant their metaphysics firmly among the population at large."[31] Looking to the future, he added: "American militarism in fully developed form would mean the triumph in all areas of life of the military metaphysic, and hence the subordination to it of all other ways of life."[32]

Writing only a few years after Mills, Fred Cook, in his seminal *The Warfare State* (1962), projected this military trajectory with similar clarity, identifying a radical growth of Pentagon influence throughout American society that would forever reshape American politics, economic life, and culture, not to mention foreign policy. Observed Cook: "The crutch of the Warfare State is propaganda. We must be taught to fear and to hate or we will not agree to regiment our lives, to bear the enormous burdens of ever heavier taxation to pay for ever more costly military hardware—and to do this at the expense of domestic programs like medical care and education and healthy urban development."[33] According to Cook, the 1946 elections signaled the first real triumph of a military-corporate-government alliance that would be embellished by Democrats and Republicans equally across the decades. It marked a gradual movement away from FDR's liberal emphasis (before the war) on social Keynesianism toward a military Keynesianism that would quickly become institutionalized. As Pentagon agendas helped shape the "American way of life," Cold War bipartisan consensus meant that dissent would be treated as un-American, even treasonous. As the arms race with the USSR intensified, Cook wrote: "The picture that emerges is the picture of a nation whose entire economic welfare is tied to warfare,"[34] a theme later emphasized in the work of Melman.[35] Anticipating destructive trends that would take decades to fully unfold, Cook reflected: "The time has come when we can see clearly and unmistakably before us our chosen destiny. The Pied Pipers of the military and big business, who have been drumming into our ears the siren song of 'peace through strength,' can no longer quite conceal the brink toward which they lead us."[36] Like Mills, Cook was convinced that the increasing militarization of American society would spell the eclipse of what remained of democratic politics.

Postwar U.S. development followed a process of structural and ideological integration as corporate, government, and military interests converged to sustain authoritarian power. Military Keynesianism reinforced U.S. imperial designs as well as domestic elite power, boosting profits and helping open the terrain for global investments and markets. The great staying-power of the war economy depended on numerous factors: corporate lobbying, bureaucratic power, scientific and technological work, armed-services jockeying for advantage, the entwined ideological priorities of the dominant parties. Every postwar American president, from Truman to Obama, has given full blessings to a Pentagon behemoth that has over time achieved a dynamic life of its own. Some of the most aggressive military interventions—Korea, Vietnam, Central America, and the Balkans—were launched by Democrats, the reputed party of peace, diplomacy, and cooperation. A highly institutionalized power structure would permit few significant elite differences at the summits of governance.

The permanent war apparatus today amounts to a global network of more than a thousand military facilities spread across 40 states and more than 70 nations, from Latin America to Africa, Europe, the Middle East, Asia, and scattered islands across the Pacific and Atlantic oceans. Its sophisticated arms, intelligence, and surveillance webs of power extend to every corner of the Earth and into outer space, fueled by a production and distribution system of several thousand industrial companies and subsidiaries. It is intimately connected to such powerful, and typically secretive, institutions as the Central Intelligence Agency (CIA), National Security Agency (NSA), Federal Bureau of Investigation (FBI), Bureau of Alcohol, Tobacco, and Firearms (BATF), and the National Aeronautics and Space Administration (NASA). Its ideological influence on the mass media, think tanks, universities, popular culture, and the Internet goes largely unchallenged, legitimated as it is by deep patriotic attitudes. The Pentagon labyrinth itself, located in Washington D.C., lies at the hub of this activity, the symbol of American global power since 1947, with 28,000 employees, 30 acres of offices and meeting rooms, and 17.5 miles of hallways. It is a nerve center of communications, transportation, social life, and political maneuvering while functioning as the National Military Command Center, which collects information from around the globe. It is the bureaucratic center of a sprawling network employing 1.6 million armed-services personnel, 800,000 reserves, and some 2 million workers in the industrial sector. In providing far-flung support for troops, logistical operations, and civilian employees, the Pentagon manages vast numbers of information sites, entertainment centers, hospitals, schools, family dwellings, officers' and enlisted clubs, churches, restaurants, sports facilities, and transportation systems.

By fiscal year 2010 Pentagon spending had reached nearly $1 trillion (including veterans' funding), nearly three times what all potential U.S. adversaries were investing together (with Russia and China combined at less than $200 billion). The United States and its (mostly European) allies were spending roughly 75 percent of total global military allocations in 2009, with Washington alone counting for about half the total. This amount does not include money for intelligence agencies (nearly $100 billion in known resources for 2009), for homeland security (another $50 billion), or for the occupation of Iraq (untold tens of billions more)—and these numbers are bound to increase with new military ventures in the future. These national commitments, without parallel in history, reflect the ethos of something akin to a garrison state, its voracious needs routinely oiled by lobbies, politicians of both parties, think tanks, the media, universities, and of course hundreds of military contractors. Arms producers yearly donate several million dollars in campaign funding: Lockheed-Martin, Raytheon, TRW, and Boeing gave more than $6 million to both Democrats and Republicans during the 2000 elections. Such corporations, obviously, benefit hugely from new weapons contracts as well as lucrative overseas arms sales, which totaled a staggering $156 billion between 2001 and 2008 (41 percent of world sales). As the ideological apparatus holds out the familiar threat of new enemies (real or imagined), profit-driven corporations seek aggressive military overtures to fight rogue states, terrorists, drug traffickers, and other fears. Leading military contractors were anxious to see NATO's push eastward culminating in the 1990s Balkans interventions for both geostrategic and economic reasons. Lockheed-Martin, among others, secured billions in arms sales to Poland, the Czech Republic, Romania, and Croatia starting in 1999, just after the U.S./NATO bombing campaign against Serbia.

The war economy thrives on a confluence of several factors: a deeply embedded military culture, bureaucratic leverage, political conservatism, worship of technology, equation of corporate (and military) power with "freedom" and "democracy"—all underwritten by national exceptionalism and imperial hubris. Helen Caldicott observes that "one could readily diagnose the attitudes of the Pentagon as clinically sick and suggest that all people who subscribe to those theories [e.g., about world domination] need urgent counseling and therapy."[37] Of course, the seductive power, material, and status rewards derived from an immense web of contracts, jobs, and deployments could help ameliorate the need for psychological assistance. A more accurate rending of Pentagon power lies in its business-as-usual trajectory within militarized state capitalism, where elites are viewed as pursuing mostly rational objectives. The warfare system thrives on a corporate oligopoly, fully at conflict with norms of free enterprise insofar as the contractors' profitability from sales to government alone is routinely ensured. By 2000 the leading military corporations had been reduced in number to just five: Lockheed-Martin, Boeing, Raytheon, General Dynamics, and Northrop-Grumman. In 2003 the largest of these remained Lockheed-Martin, the result of 1990s mergers involving Lockheed and Martin Murietta, Loral Defense, General Dynamics, and scores of smaller companies forming a $36 billion empire that tirelessly champions aggressive U.S. military policies. After 9/11 these corporations adapted their modus operandi to accommodate new demands for space militarization, homeland security, and the war on terrorism, entailing a shift toward high-tech production to fit the (more expensive) Bush-Cheney-Rumsfeld emphasis on technowar. In 2006 it cost more than $1 million to dispatch a Tomahawk missile, about $2,500 an hour to operate a single M-12A tank, more than $3,000 an hour to fly an F-16 fighter plane, and roughly $40,000 an hour to keep a navy destroyer active. With everything taken into account, moreover, by 2009 it cost more than $1 million to deploy and equip a single first-line soldier to Iraq or Afghanistan for a year.

Military Keynesianism has long relied on science and technology: since World War II upwards of 70 percent of all resources devoted to R&D has been Pentagon-sponsored. With emphasis on remote aerial warfare, robotics, and elaborate communications systems, technowar has been a durable U.S. military tradition at least since the Vietnam War. By the 1990s, however, Pentagon technology, refined by computerized systems, made quantitative leaps forward, a paradigm shift that would be labeled a "revolution in military affairs" (RMA). Military resources favored high-tech weapons systems, surveillance, space operations, information networks, and lighter, more mobile combat units for all branches of the armed services. A high-tech military would presumably give the United States improved full-spectrum dominance, wedding flexibility, mobility, and computerized responses to an already massive weapons arsenal. A champion of RMA, Secretary of Defense Donald Rumsfeld, envisioned a new phase of military development, pushed forward by the Bush-Cheney administration. In fact RMA had been vigorously set in motion during the Desert Storm, with the Pentagon relying heavily on high-tech communications and weapons systems to create an integrated electronic battlefield. While technowar permits quicker, more flexible, often more deadly use of armed force, it is also extremely costly and limited in the context of asymmetric warfare like that faced by the United States in Iraq and Afghanistan. RMA innovations include pilotless aircraft like the Global Hawk and Predator, used in Afghanistan and Pakistan against dispersed and hard-to-reach military targets like Al Qaeda base camps. In December 2009, the United States escalated its drone strikes in both Afghanistan and Pakistan, against Al Qaeda and the Taliban, as Obama revealed his preference for high-tech assaults (risking few if any American lives) that in this case extended to targets in densely populated urban areas like Quetta, Pakistan. Such risky and costly operations—run mostly by the CIA—coincided with the 2009 U.S. "surge" strategy in Afghanistan involving significant escalation of military commitment.

As the war economy thrives, the marriage of government, business, and military tightens; "privatization" of military functions simply comes with the terrain, as many corporations take on greater "battlefield" responsibilities. Since the early 1980s more U.S. armed-forces operational tasks have been carried out by private firms, usually staffed by retired military personnel looking for a mix of adventure and fortunes. Enterprises like Military Professional Resources, Inc. (MPRI), Vinnell, Blackwater, DynCorp, Halliburton, and Bechtel have been hired by the Pentagon or State Department to train and assist military and police agencies in countries deemed strategically vital to the United States. These contractors perform many jobs—planning, engineering, security, infrastructure rebuilding, etc.—almost entirely beyond public or legislative oversight. Until Blackwater operatives went on a Baghdad shooting rampage in late 2007, accused of killing at least 17 Iraqi civilians, the PMCs worked largely beneath the political and media radar. Yet their strategic role in the Middle East, with reportedly more than 100,000 "contractors" in Iraq alone (as of 2009), has been crucial to both the Pentagon and State Department. Ken Silverstein, in *Private Warriors* (2000), wrote: "These private warriors have a financial and career interest in war and conflict, as well as the power and connections to promote continued hard-line policies. Their collective influence is one reason the United States seems incapable of making the transition to a post-Cold War world."[38] MPRI, founded in 1987 by retired Army General Vernon Lewis, has helped keep the harsh Saudi Arabian regime in power, working behind the scenes to assist its coercive military, intelligence, and police organs— vital to U.S. oil interests in the region. The company received more than $500 million in the 1990s to train similar forces in Bosnia and Croatia under equally repressive governments. Corporations like MPRI and Vinnell have received billions of dollars to protect dictatorial regimes in Central America, Indonesia, South Korea, Kuwait, and Saudi Arabia. Joint Pentagon-corporate programs have funded and trained thousands of operatives yearly at military schools and training camps in the United States and elsewhere. PMCs in collaboration with arms contractors have reaped hundreds of billions of taxpayers' dollars. Such "privatization" of war and related functions, more important than ever, allows the Pentagon, working with the CIA and NSA, to more easily escape public scrutiny. Annual PMC contracts, subsidized mostly by the Pentagon and State Department, have been estimated to reach as high as $100 billion, according to Sourcewatch, thus amounting to as much as nearly $1 trillion in the period 2000 to 2010.[39]

The permanent war system simultaneously legitimates and reinforces state power on a grand scale, as few politicians are willing to risk opposing or seriously questioning the imperial behemoth. For most citizens, a sprawling Pentagon edifice represents American status and power in a threatening world. In a nation that consumes more than 30 percent of the world's energy supplies and depends on a steady flow of cheap labor, markets, and resources from abroad, imperial wars will continue to underpin statist economic and political arrangements even as elites and opinion-makers loudly champion small government and free markets. Yet, while lopsided Pentagon spending helps drive economic growth, such growth (technology-intensive, top-heavy, wasteful, destructive) is increasingly detrimental to the social infrastructure, jobs, and public services. The American growth model favors the military sector, neoliberal global agendas, Wall Street investment strategies, and corporate deregulation over tax-supported civilian programs. Fred Cook's description of a "nation whose entire economic welfare is tied to warfare"[40] still resonates decades later, at a time when the cumulative Pentagon budget has reached a staggering $25 trillion. Unfortunately, such unbelievable material, human, and technological resources have produced little beyond devastation and waste, the former totaling millions of human lives since World War II. Put differently, the military sector has contributed little to useful modes of production and consumption or to the general welfare, except peripherally in the case of a few technological spin-offs. More than that, the war economy by its very logic reproduces material decay, social inequality, cultural tensions, and political hierarchy at the very moment it helps sustain an advanced industrial order. For the United States, as is well known, the end of the Cold War brought a modest and brief decline in military spending as many politicians spoke of armed services reductions, troop demobilizations, and base closings in step with the much-anticipated "peace dividend." A modest shift in this direction did occur, but the goal was *modernization*: cutbacks in domestic bases and personnel along with a phasing out of older weapons systems in favor of a higher-tech military. The newer arsenals, of course, packed much greater firepower and efficiency than what they replaced. After 9/11, quite predictably, the Pentagon budget soared, fueled by interventions in Afghanistan and Iraq combined with the war on terrorism.

With the American people asked to endure burdensome costs and sacrifices for war and preparation for war, mechanisms of legitimation take on new meaning. Empire, a bloated war economy, recurrent armed interventions, hardships on the home front—all these must be made to appear "natural," routine, even desirable if not noble. The historical myth of national exceptionalism, recycled as hubris derived from economic, technological, and military supremacy, satisfies this ideological role. To translate this ideological syndrome into popular language and daily life, to incorporate it into the political culture, is the task not so much of classical state-run propaganda as forms of ideological hegemony reliant on education, the media, and popular culture. In the United States, media culture is an outgrowth of megacorporate power that lies at the core of the most far-reaching ideological and cultural apparatus in history. Hollywood films alone have for many decades performed crucial services for imperial legitimation.[41] The endlessly repetitive fantasies, illusions, myths, images, and storylines of Hollywood movies (along with TV and other outlets) influence mass audiences in rather predictable ways, in the fashion of advertising and public relations. One popular response to the flood of violent combat, action-adventure, sci-fi, and horror films—and their companion video games—is readiness to support U.S. military ventures, except where American casualties are deemed excessive. Without such ideological legitimation even the most authoritarian corporate, military, and government structures are destined to crumble.

Despite its command of institutional power, tools of violence, and material resources, therefore, the imperial system cannot long survive without a pervasive *culture* of militarism. Across the postwar years U.S. military power has been elevated into an ideology reproduced through media culture, political communication, academic discourses, and patriotic indoctrination. If the linkage between militarism and social life has a long history, it has tightened with the remarkable expansion of corporate media and popular culture over the past few decades. If strong popular belief in the efficacy of military power lends warfare a deeper sense of meaning and purpose,[42] it also keeps intact a hegemonic façade behind which elites can more freely operate. Decay of the American public realm cannot be grasped apart from this destructive cycle—bound to worsen as the rulers strive to maintain empire against potentially explosive challenges. By the early twenty-first century it seemed that war, and orientation to war, had become a way of life in the United States, a society apparently growing addicted to war. If the United States does not yet reach the level of a full-fledged "warrior society" in the mode of ancient Sparta, Nazi Germany, interwar Japan, or even Israel today, the consequences of military power could be in some ways even more far-reaching owing to the mere *scope* of American global reach.

Who could expect otherwise at a time when the Pentagon runs its own vast propaganda network with scores of newspapers, magazines, and documents, invests in hundreds of movies and TV programs, has a vast repertoire of state-of-the-art video games, exerts influence on many academic disciplines, and remains by far the largest sponsor of R&D. What might be called the militarization of American higher education is reflected in the capacity of the Pentagon to shape research at such respectable universities as University of California at Berkeley, MIT, Stanford, Johns-Hopkins, Penn State, and Carnegie-Mellon—a few of the more than 350 institutions routinely obtaining military contracts. Within the familiar umbrella of national security, a convergence of military, corporate, and academic interests have converged around U.S. imperial agendas.[43] Tens of billions are targeted annually for high-tech warfare agendas: urban-assault counterinsurgency methods, satellite technology, nuclear modernization, robotics and other forms of remote combat, laser-guided weapons, war-gaming, and data-base collections among others.[44]

The high-tech U.S. military has pursued new openings—cyberspace—in the wake of revelations that Google and other technology corporations have been targeted by hackers. The spread of cyber-espionage after 2006 especially bolstered prospects for large military contractors to intensify their focus on defending computer systems and networks, at the very moment weapons production has entered into something of a decline. According to Loren Thompson, policy analyst for the Lexington Institute, "Cyber security is shaping up to be a major growth opportunity for the defense industry. We've spent the last 20 years putting all of our information onto computers. Now we don't have any choice but to defend ourselves against foreign intrusion."[45] Many Pentagon contractors, having already done extensive work protecting corporate and government computers, are well-positioned to exploit this new market, which could exceed $100 billion in revenue in the decade after 2010. Thompson noted that "each of these companies recognizes the growing demand for cyber skills could help cover any shortfall in revenues."[46] According to deputy secretary of defense, William J. Lynn, some 90,000 people were already hired to administer, monitor, and defend no less than 15,000 networks connecting 7 million computers. Cyber-security efforts were expected to increase 8 percent after 2010. To this end, Northrop acquired Essex Corporation, specializing in encryption technology used by the NSA and other intelligence agencies. Northrop also created a cyber-security research consortium involving MIT, Carnegie-Mellon, and Purdue University. Meanwhile, Lockheed-Martin, not to be outdone, assembled a cyber-security alliance involving Microsoft, Dell, and Cisco Systems to develop measures to fight hackers. The largest military contractor also established a 5000 square-foot facility in Maryland dedicated to cyber research.

In a militarized society the armed forces naturally touch the lives of tens of millions of people, often extensively, and often outside the military orbit itself. In her study of the American "homefront," Catherine Lutz comments: "In an important sense...we all inhabit an army camp, mobilized to lend support to the permanent state of war readiness that has been with us since World War II. No matter where we live, we have raised war taxes at work, and future soldiers at home, lived with the cultural atmosphere of racism and belligerence that war mobilization often uses or creates, and nourished the public opinion that helps send soldiers off to war... All experience the problems bred by war's glorification of violent masculinity and the inequalities created by its redistribution of wealth to the already privileged." Lutz adds that "we all have lived with the consequences of the reinvigorated idea that we prove and regenerate ourselves through violence."[47] This experience is even more all-consuming for military personnel and civilian residents of towns like Fayetteville, North Carolina—home of the sprawling Fort Bragg army base—that Lutz selected for her research. It is here that the many contradictions of U.S. militarism come home to roost—a "dumping ground for the problems of the American century of war and empire." It is here that we find exaggerated problems of poverty, crime, child abuse, alcoholism, prostitution, homelessness, and a wide range of physical and mental injuries.[48] These are the fruits of a permanent war system that transfigures daily life for those within and close to the "homefront" of the empire.

This is unquestionably a world geared to warfare, preparation for warfare, killing, and the refinement of instruments for killing. In her classic work *Military Brats* (1991), Mary Edwards Wertsch brilliantly weaves together narratives of life in the military, focusing on two lingering motifs—the warrior ethos and authoritarian social relations. She writes: "Growing up inside the fortress [as she did] is like being drafted into a gigantic theater company. The role of the warrior society, even in peacetime, is to exist in a state of perpetual 'readiness': one continuous dress rehearsal for war. The principal actors are immaculately costumed, carefully scripted, and supplied with a vast array of props. They practice elaborate large-scale stage movements—land, air, sea exercises simulating attacks and defenses."[49] Everything revolves around a pervasive socialization process that Wertsch expertly unravels. Well before 9/11 and subsequent wars, she remarks that "this is a society prepared to wage war with the same relentless attention to detail it brings to every moment of every day."[50] In such a culture hierarchical norms inevitably prevail: "The Fortress, in short, is an authoritarian society. The masks worn there are authoritarian masks, each exactly like the others of its rank, each subservient to those of high rungs. The notions of conformity, order, and obedience reign supreme."[51] She adds: "The great paradox of the military is that its members, the self-appointed front-line guardians of our cherished American democratic values, do not live in a democracy themselves. Not only is individuality not valued in the military, it is discouraged. There is no freedom of speech, save on the most innocuous level. There is no freedom of assembly for anything that is not authorized. There is not even a concept of privacy..."[52] God, community, family, nation—the entire ideological panorama is glorified through mediations of warfare, violence, hierarchy, and aggression.

In this as in other ways the permanent war system erodes democratic politics at every level. A military culture reinforces not only the warrior attitudes mentioned by Wertsch but also hierarchy, discipline, secrecy, surveillance, lopsided budgetary allocations, and narrowing of political debate. In broader terms, Richard Falk perceives an epic shift toward fascism in the global order that, he argues, likewise permeates American domestic society as concentrate power and wealth come to dominate the field of decision-making.[53] An imperial arrogance that dwells on U.S. exceptionalism and subverts universal legality while embracing full-spectrum dominance ultimately nourishes an atmosphere of lawlessness and violence at home. A Hobbesian milieu, after all, recognizes no political boundaries. Falk notes that such a drastic authoritarian turn will be momentarily disguised as an urgent security imperative to fight global terrorism.[54] While this scenario has gained momentum since 9/11, the pattern was actually set solidified during World War II, when the war economy and security state first gained ascendancy. Further, as discussed in earlier chapters, the United States has throughout much of its history worked tenaciously *against* democratic possibilities outside its own borders. The neocons, as we have seen, uphold the primacy of American power (while preaching "democracy promotion") said to be driven by superior U.S. values and traditions. Falk argues: "...I consider it reasonable to think of something one might call global fascism as the mentality of those seeking to regulate the world, from either above or below, according to their extremist beliefs."[55] In both cases—home and abroad—the rules and laws of political behavior are set and constrained by the most powerful and wealthy forces in society.

When it comes to the actual *making* of U.S. foreign policy, therefore, even pretenses of democratic participation quickly vanish into thin air as American global initiatives are framed, justified, and carried out at the summits of state capitalist power. Only a tiny minority of Americans has shown much interest in foreign policy, the vast majority routinely bombarded by patriotic, elitist warnings to leave grave issues of war and peace to the (mostly white-male) "experts." Most people uncritically follow the dictates of U.S. imperial strategy as set by the rulers. The Constitution, an antiquated document that formally endows Congress with warmaking powers, rarely enters the decision-making process: virtually every U.S. military intervention, from Mexico to Iraq to Afghanistan, has been framed, decided, and implemented by executive power. Support is readily generated on a foundation of "national security" threats marketed by huge military lobbies, think tanks, and the media. The long U.S. history of national expansion, conquest, and war has moved along this markedly undemocratic trajectory. The imperial presidency, already well-established in the nineteenth century, has only grown in scope and legitimacy across the postwar era. Genuine debates over U.S. global objectives have been rare, whether on TV, talk radio, Congressional deliberations, "expert" testimony, or presidential debates. Elites possess great autonomy when it comes to the pressing issues: military, the budget, arms sales abroad, foreign interventions, support for Israel, covert operations, surveillance, space militarization. One departure came during final years of the Vietnam War, when a few sectors of the dominant class (joined by disillusioned elements of the media) grew disgusted with a costly military disaster that was also leading to widespread civic unrest. Even here, however, disagreements with official policy revolved mainly around the *failure* of that policy to bear results; the ends were taken as just and honorable.

Postwar examples of executive-driven interventions abound, from Korea to Vietnam, Laos, Cambodia, Central America, the Balkans, Iraq, and Afghanistan, all launched by the White House with minimal if any Congressional involvement, and all justified by a similar litany of distortions, myths, and deceptions. Enough has already been written about the unprovoked and illegal Iraq War, here and elsewhere, to reveal an totally manipulative process despite Bush administration (belated) claims of purely democratic motives. We know that Bush and the neocons were determined to launch the war, confident it would be fully endorsed by politicians of both parties. In December 2001 the House voted 393 to 12 to brand any Iraqi rejection of new arms inspections (after the Hussein regime had long been disarmed) an "increasing threat" to U.S. security—although few politicians or media outlets questioned how a small, distant nation weakened by years of harsh sanctions, covert actions, and bombings could be a threat to the world's leading superpower, or indeed to anyone. By late 2002 the fashionable discourse of regime change (a clear violation of international law) had become something of an obsession among elites and media pundits. The famous 1998 PNAC statement made it clear that no evidence of terrorist links or WMD possession was needed to justify U.S. military action; only later, for public edification, did the propaganda machine arrive at such outrageously flimsy pretexts. By mid-2002 the war drums had picked up momentum, with Congress voting overwhelmingly in November to support military force against Iraq—the Senate by 77 to 23, the House by 296 to 133, all "debates" confined to questions of timing, logistics, and strategy. By the end of 2002, therefore, despite mounting antiwar sentiment across the country, Democrats were eagerly subscribing to an imperial Republican foreign policy scheme destined to profoundly influence global and domestic politics for years if not decades into the future.

At a critical turning point in U.S. history, therefore, Democrats were able to produce no alternative responses, perhaps fearful they would be branded unpatriotic or soft on terrorism; bipartisan consensus once again prevailed. The bankruptcy of Bush's rationale for war went scarcely contested within the political arena, where fear and uncertainty ruled the day. House majority leader Dennis Hastert (R-Illinois) loudly proclaimed: "We must not let evil triumph!", and Democrats quickly took up the rhetoric. Representative Tom Lantos (D-Calif) spoke for many Democrats when he said: "Just as leaders and diplomats who appeased Hitler at Munich in 1938 stand humiliated before history, so will we if we appease Saddam Hussein today."[56] The silly equation of Hitler's war machine with Hussein's weak, beaten, surrounded, impoverished nation of 23 million was never made an issue in Congress or the media. However, Senator Robert Byrd (D-W. Va.) would say: "I'm in my 50th year in Congress and I never thought I would find a Senate which lacks the backbone to stand up against the stampede, this rush to war."[57] That the United States could launch bloody warfare against Iraq, without UN Security Council approval and in violation of international law—in the absence of mainstream dissent—speaks volumes about the stifling narrowness of American politics.

James Bamford has thoroughly documented the shameful trail of propaganda that paved the way toward a war Bush and the neocons had decided to carry out months and even years before the March 2003 invasion. The Pentagon, CIA, and White House utilized the sprawling public relations network of the John Rendon Group to wage "perception management" of epic proportions, helping establish the ideological terrain for intervention in the absence of any credible Iraqi threat. The campaign succeeded through large-scale saturation of the media with false reports, misleading intelligence "data," distorted alarms (visions of "mushroom clouds"), and a variety of contrived prowar narratives from writers like Judith Miller of the *New York Times*. Bamford writes that "never before in history had such an extensive secret network been established to shape the entire world's perception of a war."[58] That is not all: with U.S. military occupation solidly in place by late 2003, it was revealed that Pentagon contractors regularly paid Iraqi newspapers to publish glowing stories about the war and the role of U.S. troops as benevolent "liberators," a propaganda enterprise hidden from the American public. The Washington D.C.-based Lincoln Group was awarded tens of millions of dollars to infiltrate Iraqi media over a period of nearly two years.[59] The war unfolded within a cynical framework of sustained domestic and international media manipulation, the success of which, at least on the home front, cannot be discounted in the face of enormous material and human costs on both sides.

What is less known is that, in the buildup to regime change, Washington had for years carried out numerous programs and schemes—mostly secret and illegal—to complement deadly economic sanctions between 1991 and 2003 that killed upwards of 500,000 Iraqi civilians. Dilip Hiro, in his revealing book *Iraq* (2002), describes ongoing covert actions, sabotage, arming of opposition groups, and even a coup attempt, often under cover of the UN inspections regime, undertaken by the CIA and other clandestine agencies.[60] American operatives, posing as weapons inspectors, collected intelligence data that would be used for later military operations. Hiro details aborted CIA coup efforts in June 1996 after the "White House [Clinton] decided to accelerate its plan to overthrow Saddam and replace him with a small group of generals"—a plan that collapsed when Hussein learned about the conspirators.[61] All these unlawful activities took place fully outside any public debate or scrutiny in the United States.

Other episodes of virtually autocratic U.S. foreign policy interventions are much too numerous to be catalogued here, even if restricted to the postwar years. Lawrence Davidson, in his *Foreign Policy, Inc.* (2009), chronicles in some detail several noteworthy cases, revolving around the powerful Cuba and Israel lobbies that for decades have decisively impacted key areas of American global behavior, once again beneath the public radar.[62] Since the early 1960s strong anti-Castro lobbyists, based mainly in Florida, have worked tirelessly to isolate Cuba—through diplomatic maneuvers, propaganda, embargoes, and cultural boycotts, although the island regime posed no recognizable threat to the United States or anyone else, and the stated goal of democracy promotion had little resonance. Congress continued to pass harsh anti-Cuban resolutions even though American public opinion reflected indifference.[63] The power of the much-larger Israel lobby, comprised of several wealthy and influential organizations, has been more far-reaching in its tenacious and largely successful campaigns to discredit even tepid opposition to Israeli treatment of Palestinians (much of it against universal human rights and legal norms), as "anti-Semitic" and harmful to U.S. interests in the Middle East. As Stephen Walt and John Mearsheimer convincingly show in *The Israel Lobby* (2007), American elite consensus behind Israeli oppression of Palestinians typically *conflicts* with U.S. strategic interests in the Middle East, not to mention international rules and norms.[64] Open discussion of these policies has long been taboo within mainstream political and media venues. Any elected member of the U.S. Congress publicly opposing Israeli policies will be quickly rebuked and driven from office—witness the example of Rep. Cynthia McKinney (D-Georgia) in 2006. Powerful and wealthy lobbies with perhaps tens of thousands of members have thus managed to engineer U.S. foreign policy well beyond the reach of any political mechanisms. Such lobbies, moreover, have enjoyed a long symbiotic relationship with think tanks, foundations, and universities as well as the mass media.

Still another instance of corporate-military agendas subverting democracy is what has been called "the secret U.S. war in Pakistan," where the CIA, Special Forces units, and private military contractors have combined, inside and just outside the borders of Pakistan, to carry out intelligence-gathering, covert actions, and drone bombing campaigns directed against Al Qaeda and Taliban targets in Afghanistan and Pakistan. The drone strikes were actually increased after Obama took office, often with extensive civilian casualties. Though fraught with potentially disastrous outcomes for the region, such initiatives never received official Congressional approval. As Jeremy Scahill, writing in *The Nation,* observes: "The use of private companies like Blackwater for sensitive operations such as drone strikes or other covert work undoubtedly comes with the benefit of plausible deniability that places an additional barrier in an already deeply flawed system of accountability."[65] And of course this kind of "secret" warfare scarcely departs from U.S. historical precedents.

The American imperial Leviathan has only grown more powerful and audacious over time. If Manifest Destiny called for conquest of the frontier, the American Century—symbolic of more global aspirations—meant that the United States had the duty, and right, to liberate and transform the world. The result has been an international military presence, accompanied by perpetual interventions, far beyond anything needed for national defense. On the contrary, insofar as imperial ventures are sure to produce blowback, they wind up counterproductive to the requirements of territorial security. The problem is that military power—and global projection of that power—has become increasingly central to national identity, a mark of strength and progress that the vast majority of Americans take for granted. Andrew Bacevich notes that "the citizens of the United States have essentially forfeited any capacity to ask first-order questions about the fundamentals of national security policy."[66] Foreign policy consensus is so overwhelming that even mild criticisms of U.S. behavior—not to mention out-of-control Pentagon spending—appear within the establishment political system and media as wacky, irrational, off-limits. The warfare state, solidified throughout the postwar decades, has become firmly embedded in the political culture, immune to messy public deliberations.

National Security State

The modern security-state, formed in the aftermath of World War II and start of the Cold War—and given new powers across the postwar years—was a logical outgrowth of the U.S. superpower presence. Built on a wide ensemble of intelligence agencies, the national security state (NSS) depends on a rich diversity of operations: surveillance, field investigations, high-tech communications, covert activities, espionage, law enforcement. It is simultaneously a product of, and boost to, the authoritarian state bolstered by the war economy. It reflects the degree to which liberal-capitalism gives way to rationalizing tendencies of the corporate state where crucial elements of the free market and popular governance are weakened or negated, often in the name of "national security," with the state apparatus a major organizing principle of public life. Beneath an ideology of economic freedom and political self-rule, the elites work assiduously to meld together government and society. In his classic *The Ecology of Freedom*, Murray Bookchin writes: "In restructuring society around itself, the state acquires superadded functions that now appear as political functions. It not only manages the economy but politicizes it; it not only colonizes social life but absorbs it. Social forms thus appear as state forms and social values as political values. Society is reorganized in such a way that it becomes indistinguishable from the state."[67] Left out of Bookchin's equation here is the role of corporate power, but his emphasis on growth of the authoritarian state—whatever its definition, functions, and legitimation—nonetheless holds. In the case of American society, as mentioned, the presence of a huge military apparatus brings new meaning to authoritarian power.

In the United States the security-state restricts and narrows political discourse and institutional practices in favor of supposedly more urgent (military, patriotic, self-protective) agendas that surface continuously within the government and media. The ethos of "bipartisanship" in the fight against threats to national security long ago colonized the area of foreign and military policy, understood as the domain of "experts" plying their experience and skills at the summits of national power. In time the NSS has rendered citizen participation increasingly problematic, all the more so in a Hobbesian universe filled with imminent state and nonstate. Noting U.S. possession of economic, technological, and administrative resources of domination without historical parallel, Herbert Marcuse concluded (in 1972) that the power structure "may be forced, under the threefold impact of setbacks in its imperial expansion, internal economic difficulties, and pervasive discontent among the population to set in motion a far more brutal and comprehensive machinery of control."[68] As the many post-9/11 maneuvers of the Bush administration reveal, however, none of these preconditions is absolutely required for the NSS to tighten its authoritarian regime over American society.

Postwar America has seen the dramatic growth of an imperial power structure based on the war economy, bolstered executive power, weakened Congress, bipartisan consensus, and diminished checks-and-balances. The steady rise of an imperial presidency, coinciding with the spread of American global power, has meant heightened flexibility vital to the national security state and to a foreign policy that, as President Truman affirmed just after World War II, would allow the United States to aggressively pursue its national interests anywhere on the globe. In *War Powers* (2005), Peter Irons writes that "Never before has the planet faced a worldwide 'marshall' with such a massive arsenal at its disposal and with no institution, domestic or international, willing or able to restrain him."[69] The motif of Irons' book is summed up by his comment that "in a very real and very dangerous sense, the imperial presidency has hijacked the Constitution, to serve the interests of the American empire."[70] The extent to which the Constitution was actually "hijacked"—as opposed to being largely irrelevant—is rather problematic, but Irons is correct in noting the dynamic of heavy-handed executive power. The postwar entrenchment of U.S. global power, spread across an interminable network of financial and corporate centers, client states, military bases, surveillance operations, and diplomatic venues, has indeed profoundly authoritarian consequences. Such an empire demands an ensemble of institutions to fight myriad challenges, and these institutions need *legitimacy*: military force by its very nature depends on popular appeals to patriotism, loyalty, discipline, and violence. For the United

States, however, with its permanent military-industrial apparatus, the ideological supports must be even more broadly internalized. Military values extend far beyond the Pentagon fortress itself, insofar as U.S. global behavior is fueled by a drive for resources and markets, the cult of technology, national exceptionalism, and imperial hubris— all serving to relegitimate elite power, especially at a time when economic crisis weakens ideological supports. In this setting, elements of a quasi-fascist ideology have already surfaced, consistent with the U.S. quest for world supremacy. With power more concentrated, it penetrates larger regions of economic, social, and personal life, reducing zones of privacy and freedom.

The NSS is grounded in a highly rationalized system of bureaucratic and coercive functions: the military, law enforcement, surveillance, security apparatus, an imperial presidency emboldened by the concept of "unitary" powers. Contrary to much received wisdom, this apparatus was no invention of the Bush-Cheney gang or the neocons, as its antecedents were already present in the Theodore Roosevelt administration. It gained new ascendancy with the Cold War and appearance of the CIA and NSA on the scene. With fears of global Communism looming at the summits of power, the notion of expanded presidential powers—that is, maximum leadership flexibility to handle imminent global challenges—took firm hold in the political culture. "Crises" meant that lengthy deliberations over courses of action, involving matters of war and peace could be disastrous. Not surprisingly, President Truman was the first to seize on the concept of independent or "inherent" executive powers about which the Constitution had been largely silent. Whatever limits the political system might have imposed on the executive—through the famous checks and balances or "advice and consent"—were to be overridden even while honored in theory. The urgent discourse of "national security" took on features of an uncompromising principle, crucial to the postwar evolution of international Machtpolitik.

Postwar history is marked by such presidential "takeover" of foreign policy by Democrats no less than Republicans. Military interventions always came at the whim of the executive, with Congress assigned the role of writing the checks: Truman in Korea, JFK in Vietnam, Nixon in Laos and Cambodia, Reagan in Central America, the first Bush in Panama and Iraq, Clinton in Somalia and the Balkans, the second Bush in Afghanistan and Iraq, and Obama in Afghanistan. Presidential autonomy suited U.S. needs for maneuverability in a threatening world. Scores of initiatives (covert operations, surveillance, proxy warfare, etc.) have been undertaken in secrecy, were illegal, or just routinely approved by compliant or intimidated legislators. Many crucial international agreements—between the United States and Israel, for example—have come under the heading of "executive agreement," with Congressional input essentially by-passed. Presidents often view Congress as a weak and indecisive obstacle that must be finessed: legislators might be "consulted" or "informed," but rarely invited as full partners in decision-making. Even the famous War Powers Act, passed in 1971 to restore Congressional "consent" following the Vietnam War outrages, has been ritually and easily sidestepped by imperial presidents. President Reagan, great champion of limited government, outwardly despised this Act and pressed for greater expansion of military leadership to counter the "evil empire."[71] The two Bushes, Clinton, and Obama have all upheld and utilized vital features of the security state.

The Bush-Cheney administration took this authoritarian diktat to new levels, embracing greater "unitary" powers, preemptive military strategy, secrecy, expanded intelligence and surveillance, and license to sidestep, finesse, or even violate widely held legal norms (such as those prohibiting torture and warrantless wiretapping). The 9/11 attacks provided new ideological rationale for stronger executive authority, as Bush anointed himself a "war president" immune to any serious constraints on White House power. As Charlie Savage notes: "The object wasn't just to strengthen President Bush's powers personally, but rather to strengthen the office institutionally, for all future president of both parties."[72] Government agencies and initiatives would be directly subordinate to the White House, with few intermediaries. The war on terrorism would justify virtually any executive action, no matter how costly or risky. New memos were drawn up at the Attorney General's office establishing legal arguments for "extraordinary rendition" by the military and CIA. Douglas Feith's special intelligence office at the Pentagon routinely bypassed ordinary information-gathering venues, bolstering the case for the Iraq war with bogus "intelligence" about WMD and Hussein terrorist connections. Of course the Bush-Cheney team hardly created this security apparatus de novo, as rules, norms, and procedures of the imperial presidency had long been integral to American politics, as we have seen. Something akin to an iron law of authoritarian leadership is at work here for, in Savage's words: "The accretion of presidential power, history has shown, often acts like a one-way ratchet: it can be increased far more easily than it can be reduced."[73]

The security state thrives on a highly rationalized system of bureaucratic and coercive functions: military, law enforcement, surveillance, political controls. Historically the main ideological rationale was provided by the threat of world Communism and Soviet power, but eclipse of the Cold War witnessed as shift in focus toward global terrorism, rogue states, and radical Islam. Public support for coercive measures was always easy to mobilize with foreign enemies—real or contrived—on the horizon. This was emphatically true for Bush in the aftermath of 9/11, when the specter of new attacks brought an upsurge in patriotism and militarism fueled by widespread fear and insecurity. This was, after all, the "new Pearl Harbor." In 2002 the Pentagon accelerated its procurement of high-tech weaponry, its reliance on mobile antiterrorist units, and its plans for space militarization that, combined with astronomical spending on homeland security, passed through Congress with only perfunctory debate. If terrorist operations were intended to destabilize the imperial system by weakening its pillars of support, as dictated by the famous "strategy of tension," their consequences for American power turned in the opposite direction: the state gained new legitimacy in the midst of grave challenges and a popular mood of vulnerability, allowing the security apparatus to renew its license to expand. Such "wartime" mobilization produced a series of responses that won nearly automatic legislative approval, resulting in heightened levels of military, surveillance, intelligence, and law-enforcement capabilities. This was further enabled by rapid growth of new technologies, including space-based surveillance and tracking, championed by the Pentagon, NASA, and the intelligence community.

The Homeland Security office was set up in November 2001 to coordinate some 40 government agencies. To face an expected perpetual state of alert, such agencies as the CIA, FBI, NSA, and Immigration and Naturalization Service (INS) now commanded far more resources and institutional reach—meaning far greater control over peoples' lives—with less accountability. The USA Patriot Act anti-terror bill was passed in October 2001 by a vote of 337 to 79 in the House and 96 to one in the Senate, moved to resolution with little public input or congressional deliberation. Representative Barney Frank (D-Mass) remarked that passage of this landmark legislation involved "the least democratic process for debating questions fundamental to democracy that I have ever seen." The 342-page document gave the federal government sweeping new powers to investigate and monitor electronic communications, personal and financial records, computer files, and other materials. Wiretap authority was greatly broadened. Due process was suspended in many areas of criminal justice—for example, the right to a speedy trial, freedom from arbitrary police searches, prohibition against indefinite jailing, and incognito detentions—that would later create problems at Guantanamo. More ominously, the bill laid out an elastic definition of terrorism, making it possible for law enforcement to criminalize ordinary acts of dissent and protest, threatening a range of Constitutional rights of free speech and assembly at a time when public discourse was already severely narrowed. (Animal-rights groups, among others, would later be targeted by these prohibitions.) By 2002 the war against terrorism took the United States into a new realm of governmental controls and surveillance that fed off an atmosphere of paranoia and fear.

With an antecedent in President Clinton's antiterrorist legislation of 1996, Bush's Patriot Act was a recycling of earlier repressive measures: the Alien and Sedition Act, post–World War I Palmer Raids, Smith Act, House Un-American Activities Committee, McCarthy witch hunts, and COINTELPRO operations during the Vietnam War era. In the wake of 9/11, moreover, coercive moves against social protest, unpopular views, and perceived foreign threats were easily cloaked behind the façade of patriotic appeals in the midst of grave national threats—and they were just as quickly embraced by the general population. Nancy Chang was scarcely exaggerating when she wrote: "The Act stands as radical in the degree to which it sacrifices our political freedoms in the name of national security and consolidates new powers in the executive branch.[74] Loose definitions of terrorism and related actions permit easy abuse by law enforcement. Citizens' rights to privacy, already eroded in the electronic age, were placed under further challenge: Section 213 permits federal agents to conduct "sneak and peek" searches—covert investigations at homes and offices—with no advance notice, while Section 215 extended the 1978 Foreign Intelligence Surveillance Act (FISA) permitting easy seizure of people's books, tapes, and computer disks in connection with suspicions of "international terrorism." Many restraints on government surveillance (discussed later in this chapter) were stripped away. According to Section 216, federal agents can track Internet transmissions with few guidelines to hold them accountable. Many feared this could lead to widespread abrogation of Fourth Amendment rights in an ideological milieu where mechanisms of appeal have been weakened.

Following 9/11 the FBI, INS, and local police initiated a wave of investigations, aggravating public fears as citizens were asked to report on the activities and beliefs of neighbors and coworkers (a scheme that ultimately failed). The patriotic mettle of individuals often came under challenge. The list of "terrorist" organizations grew rapidly, extended to virtually any group identified as Arab, Muslim, or anti-war. Working through the vast Homeland Security apparatus, with its 180,000 employees, the act created a system of databases to detect potential threats—intelligence surely needed to prevent future terrorist strikes, although guilt by suspicion or association was now easier to presume for anyone involved in, or donating money to, protest groups like those involved with the antiwar mobilizations of 2002–03. Mere conjecture that violence might accompany protest actions could be grounds for a federal probe along lines of COINTELPRO, the counter-intelligence program launched by the FBI. Consequences for people's jobs, careers, reputations, and even personal freedoms recalled the scourge of the McCarthy period and earlier Palmer Raids. As before, a threatening political environment was seized upon by the administration as pretext for expanding coercive governmental powers while restricting the ability of the press, the public, and legislatures to hold officials responsible for heavy-handed actions. Although xenophobic responses to the 9/11 events waned after a few years, strong features of the Patriot Act and Homeland Security operations remained intact, still geared to a menacing world rife with terrorists, rogue states, and similar threats. Meanwhile, the much greater *technological* capabilities of the modern security state endowed it with vastly superior military, policy, and surveillance powers than anything preceding it.

In 2002 the Bush administration listed 153 terrorist organizations, enlarging Clinton's smaller list assembled in 1995 and 1996. Anyone belonging to such organizations, even remotely or fleetingly, could under new laws be interrogated, arrested, deported, or have their assets frozen. With combined resources of the Departments of Treasury, State, Justice, and Defense, the federal government was more empowered than ever to fight not only terrorism but any challenge to its power, with groups and individuals targeted according to often vague, arbitrary criteria and protest movements vulnerable owing to their "violent" or "disruptive" character. (While repressive acts under the Patriot Act had by 2010 been rather limited, the potential for more far-reaching crackdowns against political dissent and popular movements had been established.) At the same time, local law enforcement was assuming a more central role, cooperating with the FBI, CIA, and INS to create its own intelligence units and anti-terrorist squads, while building dossier systems to help enforce the Patriot Act. Joint task forces were set up by the FBI, operating out of war-room style centers in urban areas and allowed to investigate personal documents and even seize records of bookstores and libraries to collect data on people's reading habits. During the period 2002 to 2006 the FBI employed a variety of improper and illegal methods to obtain phone records in terrorism investigations—not only of suspects, but of journalists and others—according to a 2010 report issued by the inspector general at the Justice Department. These tactics were approved at the highest levels of the bureau, which sent out "exigent letters" to phone service providers.

An alarming trend since the mid-1990s is deepening military participation in law enforcement. Especially noteworthy has been Pentagon involvement in high-tech surveillance, coinciding with its increased role in immigration and drug enforcement along the U.S.-Mexico border. The protracted and disastrous war on drugs figures centrally in this trend, going back to President Nixon's first crusade and then, in early 1980s, to President Reagan's identification of crime and drugs as twin evils to be eradicated as a cornerstone of national security. This "war" has been partially militarized, with destabilizing consequences, in such regions as Mexico and Colombia. Like terrorism, communism, and kindred designated horrors, drugs (though overwhelmingly an issue of *domestic* consumption and abuse) were depicted as a *foreign* scourge, meaning that interdiction would become a joint police-military task. U.S. armed forces and law enforcement work in tandem as agencies not only to police but to *control*—an underlying motive behind the war on drugs from the outset. Local police paramilitary units (PPUs), modeled after the Navy SEALs, have carried out thousands of drug raids yearly, in some cases broadening their reach to counterterrorism. By 2002 most large American cities had PPUs that conducted extensive surveillance, made routine arrests, and engaged in occasional shootouts with criminal suspects. While the Pentagon saw this partnership as an opportunity to expand its power, local law enforcement came to accept (if reluctantly) federal intrusion onto its terrain as a step toward greater empowerment. This development, made easier after 9/11, led to erosion of the famous Posse Comitatus Act of 1878 outlawing military intervention into domestic police operations.

Militarization of law enforcement merged with Bush's strenuous efforts, mixed in their outcome, to extend presidential clout beyond

the reach of Congress and the courts. Arguing that the terrorist menace places the United States under warlike conditions, Bush moved
in early 2002 to apply rules of armed combat to terrorist suspects,
meaning virtually anyone could be detained without charges, incar-
cerated indefinitely without due process, and otherwise be denied
rights normally applicable to the criminal-justice system. Military tribunals would be set up in a context where most legal and civil rights
could be suspended. Laws of warfare are so vague as to allow the
most permissive interpretations—for example, allowing "suspects" to
be abducted from foreign countries, subjected to "harsh interrogation methods," or even summarily killed. Bush was determined in his
nearly autocratic views: he sought unfettered power, as commander-
in-chief, to cope with any "state of emergency," insisting that executive actions should be immune from judicial review. For several years,
Bush and his lieutenants did pursue a secretive and heavy-handed
modus operandi, where possible. At the same time, two federal court
challenges in 2003 and 2004 ruled against Bush, stating he had overstepped his constitutional authority. The outcome of several federal
court cases after 2004—on both the scope of presidential authority and legitimacy of military courts—was decidedly mixed, but the
security state emboldened by 9/11 and the Patriot Act remained fully
intact, to be inherited by the Obama administration.

The expanded scope of U.S. (should this be spelled out?) criminal justice over the past few decades—police, courts, prisons, jails,
surveillance—can be understood as intersecting with the always-
elastic dictates of "national security." With more than 2.2 million
prisoners housed in hundreds of federal, state, and local prisons (the
most by far in the world), what might be called the "penal state" consumed (in 2009) 15 percent of the total civilian budget, an amount
that (like military spending) seems impervious to public challenge
owing to public fears combined with the power of law-enforcement
and prison lobbies. The war on drugs, as it accounts for more than
half of all federal prisoners, effectively drives a penal system obsessed
with incarceration as a mode of social control. Evidence shows that
incarceration rates are strongly equated with race, inequality, poverty, joblessness, and feelings of powerlessness. The jail population
has more than doubled since President Clinton's 1995 "reforms" that,
among their many purposes, drastically expanded the war on drugs
by lengthening prison sentences. With rehabilitation programs virtually nonexistent, levels of recidivism are high; ex-offenders have great
difficulty reentering society, easily falling prey to flourishing criminal

and gang subcultures that, in turn, help further empower the security state. While some argue that the bloated American penal system coincides with the ascendancy of harsh neoliberal economic policies, the imperial state no doubt contributes equally to this development.[75]

Even more ominous, the new circumstances have reinvigorated an already swollen intelligence apparatus, after its status was slightly weakened in the 1990s and its competence questioned after teams of well-paid operatives failed to anticipated the 9/11 terrorist attacks. Whatever their previous ineptness, the FBI, CIA, INS, ATF, NSA, and other police and surveillance organizations now commanded greater resources, had broader powers, and were more deeply embedded in American social and political life. With the Homeland Security office erected to coordinate the work of intelligence and law-enforcement groups, the Pentagon and these other agencies were to become more integrated—as were the international and domestic sections of intelligence. The capacity of this sprawling security apparatus to invade personal freedoms and privacy on a large scale—indeed unprecedented given almost daily technological innovations—cannot be overstated, as the Orwellian specter holds independently of what leader (or party) occupies the White House. Further, as the 2010 WikiLeaks revelations made clear, the security-state has long been active in gathering various types of global information. Washington directives were routinely sent to U.S. diplomatic personnel around the world, ordering them to collect personal, technical, and political information on their counterparts at embassies, consulates, and elsewhere. Spying on UN members had become routine. With the help of the NSA, CIA, and other agencies, an elaborate system of espionage was set up in the guise of conducting foreign relations.

While the American public is vaguely aware of such agencies as the CIA, FBI, and INS, the far more powerful—and intrusive—work of the NSA takes place in the dark, largely outside political oversight and accountability. Its empire of nearly total surveillance remains largely impervious to monitoring or even mild questioning. Yet by 2009 the NSA had become the largest, most costly, most technologically sophisticated intelligence organization in history, with its over 200 million computers processing tens of millions of communications items literally every hour, linked to thousands of miles of fiber-optic cable and dozens of satellites circling the planet. With more than 75 acres of floor space near Washington, DC, the agency shares global information with dozens of military and law-enforcement groups, now part of the barely known National Security Operations Center

(NSOC) set up after 9/11. The NSA has close working relations with military contractors like Raytheon and Lockheed-Martin, as well as telecommunications giants like AT&T. Following 9/11, as the security state moved toward full-spectrum surveillance, President Bush issued a secret order to step up warrantless wiretapping under the auspices of the NSA. In the summer of 2007 Bush pushed through crucial FISA reforms giving the NSA a freer hand in its ubiquitous work—for example, making it easier to monitor electronic calls and transmissions without warrants.[76]

The capacity of the NSA to build vast data warehouses gave it unmatched power to spy on ordinary Americans with little if any requirement for legal justification. An invisible fortress, the NSA remains as secretive and mysterious today as when President Truman established it in the late 1940s—without the approval or even knowledge of Congress.[77] It oversees thousands of operatives and analysts with unique access to the worldwide flow of phone messages, radio transmissions, and Internet transactions. The little-known U.S. Echelon program is designed to intercept millions of communications items, both domestic and global, military and civilian, with no worry about political scrutiny. According to James Bamford in his eye-opening study of the NSA, *The Shadow Factory* (2008): "The principal end product of all hat data and al that processing is a list of names—the watch list—of people, both American and foreign, thought to pose a danger to the country."[78] The agency has always fiercely resisted even modest demands for accountability. While illegal spying is surely its normal modus operandi, the NSA operates in an even more rarefied, secret, high-tech environment than other intelligence organizations, its directors rarely appearing before Congress or the public. Meanwhile, the relationship between the NSA and telecommunications industry continues to be cozy and secret, allowing the agency open access to the databases and technology of such corporations as Bell, Verizon, Microsoft, and AT&T. According to one AT&T employee interviewed by Bamford, "it appears the NSA is capable of conducting what amounts to vacuum-cleaner surveillance of all data crossing the Internet—whether that be people's email, Web-surfing, or any other data ... What I saw is that everything's flowing across the Internet to this government-controlled room. The physical appearance gives them everything. A lot of this is domestic."[79]

The Orwellian potential of the security-state is indeed frightening: owing to technological developments, the NSA, working with corporations, the military, law enforcement, and other intelligence groups, is pushing the security apparatus into a world of total information awareness. Bamford reports that the NSA is ceaselessly looking for heightened surveillance potential to monitor phone calls, credit card receipts, social networks, global positioning system (GPS) tracks, Internet transmissions, and Amazon book purchases. An eventual goal is to determine where people are, what they are doing, even what they are thinking—all far removed from public knowledge of what is taking place. Such prospects, only dimly glimpsed in the 1998 Tony Scott film *Enemy of the State,* suggest a scope of domination that is unprecedented. The confluence of bureaucracy and technology further strengthens militarized state capitalism, in the process reducing the public sphere and eviscerating what is left of democratic politics. The permanent machinery of government, with its institutionalized rules, norms, and procedures, grows ever more entrenched—a seemingly irreversible trend in the age of an imperial presidency facing perpetual global challenges. With an international surveillance network all interests and forces at the summit—corporations, military, government, intelligence and law-enforcement agencies—congeal to solidify a mammoth system of wealth, power, and violence.

The Democratic Facade

While free and open elections based on universal suffrage are generally considered the sine qua non of democratic politics, the idea that popular sovereignty has been historically subverted by a combination of institutional and ideological pressures is hardly alien to theorists, going back to Marx and Engels and later radical critiques of anarchism, council communism, the "elite theorists," and Frankfurt School. When electoral and legislative activity is framed against the larger ensemble of class and power relations, according to such views, it is easy to see how governing mechanisms—however democratic in design—can be systematically controlled and manipulated to the benefit of elites possessing superior resources (organization, education, skills, wealth, etc.). No matter how "free," elections cannot in themselves decisively alter the reality of class domination; where power and capital are so highly concentrated, as in most advanced capitalist societies, "choice" frequently turns into an illusion. Behind the network of parties, elections, and elections there are the deeper, corrosive workings of corporate power, the state, and bureaucracy. As Gaetano Mosca, an "elite theorist," wrote roughly a century ago, all societies are comprised of two classes, "a class that rules and a class that is ruled. The first class, always the less numerous, performs all the political functions, monopolizes power, and enjoys the advantages that power brings, whereas the second, the more numerous class, is directed and controlled by the first in a manner that is now more or less legal, now more or less arbitrary and violent."[80] A second "elite theorist," Vilfredo Pareto, defined liberal-capitalism as a system of "demagogic plutocracy" while a third, Robert Michels, believed that all modern large-scale organizations—whatever their political functions or democratic objectives—inescapably come under the grip of an "iron law of oligarchy," or rule of the privileged few. Consistent with critiques of liberal-democracy put forward by Marxists, these critics understand "democracy" as just another cosmetic façade, a political formula to legitimate ruling-class domination.

Both Michels and the Marxist Antonio Gramsci, critical observers of early twentieth-century European politics, arrived at similar conclusions but from contrasting points of departure: an illusory form, the parliamentary system could never serve as an arena for fundamental change—that is, nothing but limited reforms. For Michels, large-scale economic and institutional power ultimately prevails over the freest and best-intended of electoral processes. Owing to the privileged resources and capabilities of elites, along with the inclination toward passivity and cynicism of the masses, the former are destined to rule according to a lawful formula—the technical and psychological indispensability of strong leadership. As Michels noted in *Political Parties*: "Every party organization represents and oligarchical power grounded upon a democratic basis: we find everywhere electors and elected. We find everywhere that the power of the elected leaders over the electing masses is almost unlimited."[81] Roughly a decade later, at the end of World War I, Gramsci would refer to the Italian parliament (even with its strong Socialist presence) as a "political circus," a fraudulent system of representation cynically manipulated by the ruling bourgeoisie to serve the interests of capital. Basic change would have to be directed outside liberal-democratic institutions, "understood in the sense of action which immobilizes parliament, strips the democratic mask away from the ambivalent face of the bourgeois dictatorship and reveals it in all its horrible and repugnant ugliness."[82] As is well known, Gramsci's answer to that predicament came first in the form of local councils, then in the form of a revolutionary (Leninist) party.

Could these jaundiced views of liberal democracy, so roundly dismissed by mainstream observers and social scientists in Europe and

North America, have relevance to the contemporary American context? After all, the elite-driven processes theorized by Marxists, anarchists, and others—centered in corporate power, bureaucracy, the authoritarian state—now appear *more* all-encompassing than what prevailed nearly a century ago. More than that, the American power elite, to a degree greater than any other, accrued more awesome instruments of control through its permanent war system, globalized economic reach, and capacity for ideological domination through the mass media and popular culture, scarcely foreseen in the earlier days of capitalism. Mills, as we have seen, projected as much already by the mid-1950s. A few decades later, Bertram Gross, in *Friendly Fascism,* could write, echoing Gramsci: "Protests channeled completely into electoral processes tend to be narrowed down, filtered, sterilized, and simplified so that they challenge neither empire nor oligarchy."[83] In other words, despite its capacity to deliver reforms, electoral politics operates as an intricate and seductive device for legitimating and perpetuating the status quo.

Throughout most of American history, as we have seen, the ruling elites have comprised the most politically engaged sector of the dominant class based in manufacturing, banking, agriculture, and other large-scale business. Today, of course, those elites have a durable presence across the landscape—not only the familiar modes of production but in Wall Street, insurance, pharmaceuticals, the media, popular culture, universities, and the military. It is from within this realm that American politics is largely shaped, from elections to parties, lobbies, legislative work, and selection of government personnel. Whether in federal or local politics, Congress or the presidency, Republicans or Democrats, wealth has always strongly influenced political life in America, despite opinion-makers' pretenses of equality, democracy, and pluralism. Elections have degenerated into commodified spectacles—ritualized campaign tributes to family values, economic growth, material prosperity, the free market, and peace through strength that have little meaning for ordinary people, or indeed policy formation. The idea of freely competing parties within open democratic structures has turned into a sad farce, as corporate penetration transforms politics into a mixture of patronage and theater, with parties and candidates following the highest bidder. Ralph Nader's famous statement in 2000, that "the two parties have morphed together into one corporate party with two heads wearing differing makeup," seems more resonant a decade later. The greater the power of modern corporations, the more extensive the rollback of popular access and participation. In such a world—reconfigured through intensifying corporate globalization, empire, bureaucracy, and media culture—the entire public sphere is being confined to an ever-narrowing elite stratum. As ostensible arbiter of multiple and freely competing interests, the liberal state now stands as a façade behind which systemic concepts of representation and competition are subverted and detached from everyday reality.

In fact this system of oligarchical rule has been in place, to varying degrees, since the American political order was first established. The Founders, moreover, had no desire for democratic governance: fearful of mass insurgency, they hoped to protect their wealth and privilege by means of centralized state power. The Constitution, progressive in many ways for its time, was framed by a small handful of white European men immersed in class, patriarchal, and racial supremacy, dedicated first and foremost to the preservation of private property (including slavery). Political engagement depended almost exclusively on moneyed resources, a tradition that, in different ways, has been protected and extended over time. An elitist distrust of democracy meshed with a liberal view of freedom rooted in the virtues of commerce, property, and trade. A document that repudiated monarchy, aristocracy, and state church, the Constitution nonetheless permitted—indeed encouraged—what can only be described as plutocratic rule. The later development of parties and elections in the United States has, despite a steady broadening of the franchise, continued to favor this wealth-based politics.

The American two-party system is so tightly integrated that it effectively excludes alternatives to corporate domination, as the wealth/power nexus means that mainstream politicians—legislators, mayors, governors, presidents—are indebted to big-business largesse: Wall Street, banking, industry, medicine, insurance companies, agribusiness, military contractors, etc. To win elections, Republicans and Democrats compete for roughly the same sources of campaign financing. For this reason differences between the two parties are visible on peripheral social issues, but on matters related to class and power relations (including foreign policy) the ranks close into a familiar politics of bipartisan consensus, the more so as we move to the higher circles of governance. Single-member, winner-take-all districts nullify third-party challenges while Republicans and Democrats, to gain electoral majorities, are forced toward a comfortable "middle" and away from the "extremist" alternatives. Electoral success hinges on a candidate's ability to raise millions (in some cases tens or hundreds of millions) of dollars in "private" funding. In the absence of public campaign funding, the pressures of corporate financing and media advertising dictate that electoral competitions will follow three inviolable imperatives—focus on personalities and tangential issues, reliance on ideological platitudes (family values, economic growth, fiscal restraint, national security, etc.), and avoidance of discourses calling into question the blessings of corporate and military power. Electoral culture sustains distance between ideological rhetoric ("change," fighting bureaucracy and corruption, sweeping out the "insiders," attacking big government) and actual policies. Congress itself reinforces a sort of political immobilism, with power dispersed among multiple overlapping committees and agencies, a bicameral structure favoring rural and small-state representation, and a legislative maze permeated by moneyed interests. Anything outside this institutionalized matrix of power is quickly jettisoned as too "extreme," ideological, or unrealistic, that is, not worthy of debate. The postwar history of American electoral politics fits this trajectory almost ideally, as party and legislative arrangements could hardly be more perfectly designed to protect and reproduce elite power.

Members of Congress and the White House, both liberals and conservatives, tend to agree (indeed are *expected* to agree) on fundamental priorities: support for big-business, aggressive foreign and military policies, a strong global presence, family values, patriotism, and subscription to religious values. Disagreements over gay rights, abortion, gun control, and school prayer—for example, issues having little bearing on class and power relations—are drawn to the center of political and media attention. Reductions in military spending, altered Middle East priorities, tight Wall Street regulations, ecological sustainability, a national health care system—none of these has been seriously addressed within a two-party system dominated by corporations. The political system theoretically guarantees free electoral competition, but only so far as the parameters of campaign financing, lobbies, and the media will allow. American politicians invariably emerge from the top ten to 15 percent on the income ladder, with legal and professional backgrounds prevalent and white males (75 percent of the Senate) still a powerful majority; few rise from poor or working-class backgrounds.[84] The influence of wealth on elections and legislative work far exceeds that wielded by unions, community groups, and social movements. Despite various reforms here and there, this plutocratic system is sturdier than ever at the start of the twenty-first century.

National success for Republicans and Democrats alike depends on the role of Political Action Committees (PACs), advocacy groups, individuals, and conservative organizations that funnel corporate money. Business funding supports thousands of lobbies in Washington and state capitols. From 1998 to 2009 the leading overall federal interest-group spenders were: the Chamber of Commerce ($527 million), American Medical Association ($212 million), and General Electric ($191 million), followed by the American Hospital Association ($168 million), PHrMA ($161 million), AT&T ($151 million), Northrop-Grumman ($144 million), and Exxon-Mobil ($131 million). In 2009 alone Washington lobbies spent more than $2.5 billion to influence legislators.[85] In 2008 the leading contributors were the medical, insurance, banking, oil and gas, and pharmaceutical companies—the very interests with the most pending Congressional measures. For her 2008 House campaign Speaker Nancy Pelosi (D-Calif) spent $2.7 million, her biggest donors being banks, insurance firms, law corporations, and real estate. Senate majority leader Harry Reid (D-Nev) spent $13 million for re-election in 2004, the bulk coming from casinos, Wall Street, law corporations, and real estate. A leading Senate conservative, Rich McConnell (R-Ky), spent $21.3 million for his successful 2008 campaign, provided mostly by medical corporations, Wall Street, law firms, and real estate. House minority leader John Boehner (R-OH) spent $5.1 million on his 2008 election, aided by the generosity of medical and pharmaceutical industries, Wall Street, and utilities. In the Senate, Charles Schumer (D-NY) had by late 2009 raised $8.8 million for his 2010 campaign, thanks mainly to Wall Street, insurance companies, law firms, and real estate.[86] Christopher Dodd (D-Conn), chair of the Senate Banking Committee at the time of the financial meltdown, has long received generous contributions from Wall Street, so it was hardly shocking to find he had failed to aggressively investigate the subprime mortgage catastrophe (among others) while later helping engineer a $700 billion bailout the nation's largest banks. Dodd was also revealed to have been among the "Friends of Angelo" who received preferential mortgage rates from Angelo Mozilo's Countrywide Financial Corp. These limited examples only hint at the extent to which corporate funding dominates the American political scene.

The 2008 Presidential campaign, reputedly a contest between a Republican with close ties to big business and a Democrat attached to popular constituencies, broke all spending records, with Obama the "populist" raising an all-time record $730 million, more than double John McCain's $333 million total. Running as a "change" candidate, Obama far outmaneuvered McCain on the corporate front, assisted by PACs and individuals working for large business interests. Obama's great fundraising coup was made possible by such firms as Goldman Sachs ($995,000), Microsoft ($834,000), Google ($803,000), Citigroup ($701,000), J.P. Morgan Chase ($695,000), Time-Warner ($590,000), IBM ($518,000), and Morgan Stanley ($514,000).[87] Looking at such largesse, familiar reports of Obama's historic grassroots efforts to raise money through Internet sites—while surely impressive—were dwarfed by this plutocratic side. At the end of the 2008 election cycle, therefore, the three leading Democrats (Obama, Pelosi, and Reid) all owed their political fortunes to heavy corporate financing. Obama's first year in the presidency furnishes a prime case study in how corporate wealth gets translated into out-right political influence. Two defining issues of this period—financial crisis and health care reform—were "resolved" in favor of those "private" interests having greatest investment in the outcomes. (The health care bill, gutted of any public option, Medicare extension, or caps on drug prices, turned into a massive boondoggle for the insur-ance and pharmaceutical industries—a legislative debacle taken up more fully in chapter 5.) While Obama ran as a populist intent on curbing Wall Street power and fighting corporate greed, his modus operandi once in office could not have been more removed from the campaign messages. His first move was to appoint an economic team of bankers, ex-bankers, and Wall Street insiders, the same corporate elites largely responsible for the financial chaos in the first place. In fact Obama's economic strategy deviated little from what preceded it, as liberals, progressives, and Wall Street critics were banished from the inner circle of advisers and decision-makers. The influence of Bob Rubin, former Goldman Sachs chair and veteran Wall Street opera-tive, was dominant from the outset. Michael Froman, high-ranking Citigroup executive and leading Obama fundraiser, was named head of the transition economic team that immediately called for extended corporate bailouts, continued deregulation, free trade, and a litany of "free-market" bromides championed by the Bush administration and the conservative Hamilton Project. Rubin protégé and Wall Street mover Timothy Geithner was named secretary of treasury, a prelude to the $306 billion taxpayer bailout of Citigroup, prompting Matt Taibbi to comment: "Geithner...is hired to head the U.S. Treasury by an executive from Citigroup—Michael Froman—before the ink is even dry on the massive government giveaway to Citigroup that

Geithner himself was instrumental in delivering."[88] (Rubin himself had received $126 million from Citigroup for work over several years.) This bailout, like several others that quickly followed, was not contingent on any significant reforms: no new regulations, no executives replaced, no caps on pay and bonuses for the upper tier of managers. Of course, Wall Street was euphoric about the Citigroup bailout, the stock market jumping by nearly 12 percent virtually overnight.

Instead of a populist assault on the centers of financial power implicated in the 2008 meltdown, therefore, Obama's presidency signaled just the opposite—more of the same for Wall Street. The National Economic Council (NEC), charged with executive policy coordination, was dominated from the start by Froman, Rubin, Geithner, and Rubin protégé Larry Summers along with such financial elites as Diane Farrell (Goldman Sachs) and David Lipton (Citigroup). Peter Orszag, a Hamilton Project veteran, was appointed head of the Office of Management and Budget. These people shared essentially the same outlook: give the corporations, banks, and wealthy relatively free reign while accepting modest regulations and endorsing limited reforms for the middle class, a slightly more liberal variant of Reaganomics. Taibbi writes: "Taken together, the rash of appointments with ties to Bob Rubin may well represent the most sweeping influence by a single Wall Street insider in the history of government."[89] These Obama lieutenants had all gotten rich from their own financial dealings, Summers having made $5.2 million in 2008 alone as director of the D.E. Shaw hedge fund. Rahm Emmanuel, Obama's chief of staff, walked away with millions from his Wall Street involvements. Could these Democrats, pushing financial bailouts worth potentially trillions of dollars, actually have set out to reform, much less challenge, the very system that had rewarded them so handsomely? Even the Consumer Finance Protection Agency that Obama set up in 2009 was riddled with so many exceptions and loopholes as to be mostly worthless in restraining corporate greed. In the end, the huge financial oligopolies—main culprits in the catastrophic economic downturn—were allowed to remain intact, with regulatory and oversight bodies (themselves riddled with corporate interests) scarcely able to tame the capitalist juggernaut.

The 2010 national midterm elections revealed, perhaps more lucidly than ever, the plutocratic dynamics of American politics. Republicans achieved a series of congressional victories, wresting power in the House from Democrats in dramatic fashion, fueled in great measure by an insurgent Tea Party movement promising to roll back "big government." While Tea-Party-backed candidates routinely lost contested Senate seats, their takeover of the House—and many state legislatures—was energized by a carefully manufactured image as antiestablishment "outsiders" dedicated to overturning business-as-usual. Senator Jim DeMint (R-So. Carolina) noted that "Tea Party Republicans were elected to go to Washington and save the country, not be coopted by the club."[90] This sentiment echoed the right wing consensus, which targeted Obama and the Democrats as having delivered the country over to "socialism" or some nightmarish equivalent. Republicans won on a platform of small government, lower taxes, deficit reduction, and loosened corporate regulations, though it was vague on specific programs. Many Tea Party candidates vowed to repeal Obama's health care reforms, and then take on even Medicare and social security.

One problem with this "insurgency" was that it was entirely fraudulent, bereft of any political consistency or efficacy. Rather than being a triumph of "outsiders," Republican gains actually meant a great advance for big business, the certain beneficiaries of deregulation, tax cuts for the wealthy, and continued free reign for Wall Street. The most expensive midterm election in U.S. history, its outcome signaled an even firmer entrenchment of oligarchic power—more than anything, a corporate assault on democracy and social programs masked as populism. Tea Party surges depended wholly on a massive infusion of corporate funds channeled through such organizations as the Chamber of Commerce, Karl Rove's Crossroads GPS, and Americans for Prosperity as well as from billionaires like the Koch brothers, who helped back the Tea Party and such candidates as Carly Fiorina in her California senate bid. The Supreme Court decision on *Citizens United vs. FEC,* allowing corporations to spend unlimited amounts on electoral campaigns, meant that such largesse might not only skew the electoral process but would be held secret from the public. That hundreds of corporate-backed politicians, most of them fanatically devoted to the rich and powerful, could be viewed as "outsiders" wanting nothing but a clean sweep is best attributed to effective media propaganda at Fox TV and kindred outlets. Unprecedented levels of campaign spending (some $5 billion) went overwhelmingly to Republicans and Tea Party representatives, all in the guise of fighting "special interests" and dismantling "big government."

Matching the Tea Party love of big corporations—the more unregulated the better—is their love of big government behind phony libertarian rhetoric. Conservatives scream that government is too big, has too much control over people's lives, is stifling the "free market," and tramples individual freedom and political democracy. At the same time, however, they lend their uncritical support to a bloated state machinery in several crucial areas: the permanent war economy, national security-state, federal bailouts for banks and corporations, a massive intelligence apparatus, the prison-industrial complex, and the costly, intrusive, and failed war on drugs. Indeed at not point have Tea Party activists or their representatives in Congress even mentioned possible reductions in a military budget that exceeds that of all other nations combined. Tax-and-spend is an exemplary practice so long as it fits special corporate interests and rightwing ideological priorities. In fact the hawkish right cannot spend enough on the gargantuan war economy and security state, as it relishes the ethos of global combat with righteous warfare always just around the corner. What the Tea Party finds objectionable are two completely separate agendas—big-business regulations and social expenditures. This explains a total silence when it came to astronomical federal budgets (devoted mostly to wars) of the George W. Bush administration—budgets creating record governmental deficits. The extreme hypocrisy and mendacity of the Tea Party agenda would be more transparent had it not gotten the sympathetic attention of so much of the corporate media, which takes "libertarian" and "free market" statements at face value. Rightwing attacks on social security, Medicare, and unemployment insurance—safety nets made increasingly indispensable with the economic downturn—have passed for a principles defense of freedom and democracy. That a movement presenting itself as an historical gathering of antiestablishment "outsiders" while simultaneously embracing massive corporate, financial, military, and governmental power is all the more preposterous. With Tea Party largesse coming from such interests as Big Pharma, Wall Street, insurance companies, big oil, and the billionaire Koch brothers, we have the spectacle of a small grouping of billionaires and corporate elites, further empowered by such media outlets as Fox, being able to get the vast majority of American white people (few of them privileged) to support policies favoring lower taxes for the wealthy, loosened business regulations, eroding social services, a declining public infrastructure, and more poverty—that is, policies generally working against their own interests.[91]

Mainstream observers often claim that money is not all-decisive in political campaigns—that it does not ensure victory, more often determined by other factors such as party affiliation, personal image, and stand on issues. Thus independently wealthy Meg Whitman spent $142 million on the 2010 California governors race, which was won by Jerry Brown with his relatively paltry total of $24 million spent (along with $27 million from other sources). Whitman, like another rich former CEO, Carly Fiorina, who lost the California Senate race to incumbent Barbara Boxer, failed to simply buy her way into political office. These outcomes, however, were hardly the norm, either historically or for the 2010 midterm elections that gave national Republicans decisive control of the House thanks in part to Tea Party support. According to Public Citizen, no less than 58 of the 74 electoral contests in which power changed hands went to Republican candidates who overwhelmingly outspent their Democratic adversaries with funds from conservative PACS, corporations, and wealthy donors. In these and other high-visibility campaigns, prospects for being taken serious as a candidate—much less winning office—within the media and government establishments are negligible. Here it is important to remember that financial resources go well beyond campaign advertising as such, extending to the commercial media, foundations, think tanks, and lobbies with kindred interests. Indeed the 2010 elections reveal that American politics has become more money-driven than ever.

Meanwhile, the power structure expands, consolidating its hold over vast regions of American social and political life. The merger of corporate and government power is endemic to an age of rationalized state capitalism that has come to define the American "developmental model." The power structure demands consolidation of ruling interests at the summit, just as Mills had theorized, meaning that discourses of popular sovereignty, citizenship, and collective decision-making—so essential to democracy—survive mainly as abstract ideals, ritualized beliefs detached from the daily exercise of power. As cherished instruments of political competition and interest articulation, the major parties offer no alternative to this oligarchic model as they, like government itself, wind up submerged beneath an institutionalized behemoth. Not only Mills, but such theorists as the aforementioned Michels and Pareto along with Max Weber, viewed large-scale bureaucratic organization, in its multiple expressions, as innately authoritarian in its daily political workings. For Michels, as mentioned above, even the most ambitious socialist parties with egalitarian and democratic goals could never hope to challenge capitalism since bureaucracy conferred on those at the top a monopoly of such resources as money, institutional leverage, knowledge, and communications skills. Elites within even the most supposedly democratic large-scale organizations constitute a ruling oligarchy, that is, a separate power elite legitimated through its privileged material, psychological, and institutional status. The most visionary objectives therefore mean little in such a context, as party doctrines are routinely eviscerated to fit the requirements of institutionalized power.[92] Viewed thusly, Obama's compromise with Wall Street agendas beneath populist rhetoric should come as no surprise.

The Tea Party phenomenon that took off in 2009 might suggest a departure of major proportions from the regimen on normal politics. Running for office as libertarians, in favor of small government, lowered spending, and free markets, while embellishing a media image of antiestablishment "outsiders" ready to take on the Washington beltway, Tea Party candidates helped Republicans win 60 new House seats in the 2010 midterm elections. There was an aura of change, even insurgency, sweeping American politics. These were, after all, the heir of the great Ronald Reagan revolution against big government. The problem with such simplistic claims—dutifully parroted by corporate media outlets—is that they had no regard for historical facts: Reagan, like the Bushes who succeeded him, was an architect of huge governmental power built on massive spending for the military, wars, law enforcement, intelligence, and kindred projects. The rhetoric had no connection to actual outcomes. As for the Tea Partiers, they rail against "big government" but have nothing to say about the trillions of public dollars spent on the Pentagon and the empire it protects through wars, covert operations, surveillance, proxy engagements, and other forms of intervention. Nor do these faux libertarians have anything to say about increasing corporate and financial power that colonizes the entire public landscape: politics, government, media, popular culture, health care, the workplace, and daily life. The notion that the Tea Party represents some kind of outsider insurgency is based on sheer fiction and hypocrisy—that is, insiders drenched in wealth and privilege and dedicated to massive state power masquerading as crusaders for economic and political freedom.

In this historical context—where corporate power and its right-wing operatives pretend to stand for freedom and democracy—American liberalism has weakened to the point of virtual collapse. As Chris Hedges persuasively argues, the very pillars of liberal politics (unions, religion, academia, the media, Democratic Party) have become little more than appendages of corporate interests, as the elites set out to destroy the last vestiges of reform and regulations.[93] Even modest attempts to soften the harsh edges of an increasingly aggressive and freewheeling capitalism represent an intolerable threat to elite wealth and power. Hedges writes: "In killing off the liberal class, the corporate state, in its zealous pursuit of profit, has killed off its most integral and important partner. The liberal class once ensured that restive citizens could settle for moderate reforms. The corporate state, by shutting down reform mechanisms, has created a closed system defined by polarization, gridlock, and political theater. It has removed the veneer of virtue and goodness provided by the liberal class."[94] Liberal collapse has left a political void filled by financial speculators, war profiteers, media hucksters, and Tea Party frauds as party competition degenerates further into a commodified spectacle.

As the political culture moves ever rightward—and as corporate power is further liberated to carry out its exploitation, fraud, criminality, and propaganda—Democrats become less distinguishable from Republicans, even as the latter scream about a descent into "socialism" or "communism" at the first glimpse of social reforms. President Obama's failure to pursue a liberal agenda should therefore come as little surprise to careful observers of the American political scene. Corporate power exercises such enormous leverage over the political system, as we have seen, that no occupant of the White House nowadays can hope to chart an independent course; presidential autonomy is a myth. Tariq Ali, in *The Obama Syndrome,* writes that "A modern American president—Republican or Democrat—operates as the messenger-servant of the country's corporations, defending them against their critics and ensuring that no obstacles are placed in their way."[95] The decision by Obama to immediately staff his administration with Wall Street insiders and Pentagon hawks should have been predictable enough. Ali points out that, "In reality, Barack Obama is a skillful and gifted machine politician who rapidly rose to the top. Once that is understood there is little about him that should surprise anyone: to talk of betrayal is foolish, for nothing has been betrayed but one's illusions."[96]

Despite its stated hostility to bureaucracy, centralized power, and big government, therefore, American conservatism (consistent with longstanding liberal-capitalist practice) embellishes precisely the opposite—incessant expansion of corporate, military, and governmental power. In the United States, the permanent war system has established a momentum hard to reverse. As Cornell West concludes in his *Democracy Matters*, reflecting on this trend: "In short, we are experiencing the sad imperial devouring of American democracy."[97]

Superficial tropes about free markets, limited government, and citizen participation today have little if any policy repercussions. Integrated power at the summit constricts politics and deflates citizenship, reflected in the corporate takeover of virtually every facet of governance; power resides largely outside the sphere of elections, parties, and legislation, especially at the national level. Traditional ideologies have grown increasingly stale and irrelevant. If corporate power decisively shapes the flow of capital, natural resources, commodities, information, and technology, its reach mostly escapes the orbit of parties and elections.[98] If the oligopolistic tendencies analyzed by Weber and Michels—and later Mills—persist many decades later, we should not be astonished to encounter a political culture of phantom discourses, rife with illusions and fantasies, and inclined toward citizen passivity, resignation, and cynicism—all signs of a social order in precipitous decline. As we have seen, the Obama presidency might well do more to hasten, than to arrest or delay, this downward historical trajectory.

4

The Many Faces of Corporate Power

In contrast to familiar myths about free markets, pluralism, democracy, and freedom of choice, the postwar American landscape has reflected just the opposite: steady growth of corporate power with its increasing stranglehold over elections, government, media, workplace, universities, and other arenas of public life. Big-business interests, in collaboration with the state and military, have developed more power than ever to colonize the entire society. Potentially countervailing forces—in labor, the media, education, popular movements, communities—have correspondingly weakened over the past few decades. Mass constituencies are more atomized, dispersed, and depoliticized even as popular anger festers and occasionally surfaces, as in the epic Seattle protests of 1999, recurrent antiwar mobilizations as in 2002–03, immigrants-rights movements, and of course the Tea Party phenomenon of 2009–10. The gap between rich and poor widens as poverty, unemployment, and erosion of social services dramatically worsens in the wealthiest, most powerful nation in history. With the corporate system dominated by just 500 giant companies in command of preponderant wealth and resources, the question arises as to whether even a minimalist democracy can survive under such burdensome conditions. Could there be anything resembling democracy where the vast majority of people are subjected to such gross disparity of income, resources, status, and control within workplaces, government, and other spheres of daily life? The critical analysis I laid out in earlier chapters suggests the answer must be a depressing but resounding negative. In this chapter, the main focus is on the authoritarian consequences of corporate domination for five crucial areas of public life—the media, government decision-making, financial institutions, workplace, and institutions of higher education.

Media Oligarchy

Concentrated media power has been a major (in some ways dominant) force behind the subversion of democratic politics in the United
States, a force driven by commercialized images and narratives, celebrity and sports spectacles, profit-making, and mostly conservative
opinion—all resulting in a narrowing of the public sphere. Recent
trends have involved oligopolistic ownership, deregulation, expansion of advertising, and rightward shift in political content. Expanded
corporate control—over film, TV, cable, radio, print journalism, the
Internet—has meant a steady decline of citizenship coinciding with
the spread of political alienation discussed elsewhere in this book. As
media culture becomes more integral to all realms of American public
life, its effects have been profoundly depoliticizing and thus undemocratic. The fact that the leading media oligopolies (Viacom, Time-
Warner, NewsCorp, General Electric, Disney, and Sony) now flourish
endows them with far greater leverage over resources and at the very
moment growing deregulation frees them to pursue their own agendas. Given its command over technical resources, its capacity to com-
bine political messages with "entertainment," its sheer scope, and its
legitimacy as part of a "free press," the corporate media attains great
effectiveness as a propaganda apparatus, infinitely beyond what could
be achieved by a heavy-handed state system. Beyond Orwellian Big
Brother, American media culture functions incessantly to transform
popular consciousness within the contours of a dominant ideology
shaped by consumerism, ersatz forms of liberation, visual spectacles,
and of course patriotism—all defined and transmitted by a tiny stratum of communications elites. As Robert McChesney notes: "The
corporate media cement a system whereby the wealthy and powerful
few make the most important decisions with virtually no informed
public participation."[1]

A vibrant, democratized communications system would of course
impose relatively few limits to political discourse, especially on issues
(finance, jobs, the environmental threats, warfare) of urgent importance to public welfare. Media culture largely defines how crucial
issues are framed, valorized, and contextualized, what is emphasized,
what is trivialized, and what is ignored or dismissed altogether. It
establishes the range of views permitted and who is allowed to express
those views. While media and popular culture *appear* open and diversified, in fact those who manage this trillion-dollar empire devote
abundant time and resources to governing the flow of information.

Media capacity to shape popular consciousness—or forge ideological hegemony—turns on both structure and content of communications transmitted across the terrain. In advanced state-capitalist society, and especially the United States, media culture appears as the dominant and in many ways all-consuming mode of communication. Here we refer to more than just information since the media reproduces images, stories, myths, and spectacles that, in diverse ways, help sustain existing institutions, practices, and values. In this complex modality, corporate media forms a uniquely thriving propaganda system, reaching into every corner of society with high levels of technological sophistication, material resources, and ideological legitimation.

Enough has been written about the oligarchic nature of American media culture as to render superfluous much further elaboration here. Suffice it to note, following the work of Ben Bagdikian and Robert McChesney, that concentrated business ownership and control has tightened over the past few decades, reinforced by globalization, a wave of mergers and conglomerations starting in the 1990s, and effects of the 1996 Telecommunications Act (refined through later initiatives) further empowering corporate interests across the communications terrain.[2] As elsewhere, markets are dominated by fewer and fewer giant enterprises, reducing diversity, access, and local control. The rise of a global media oligopoly demonstrates once again the fiction of free markets, even as the Telecomm Act promised new political and economic freedoms with deregulation, a process that actually gave enhanced freedom of maneuver to those megacorporations listed above. Five large global media empires have come to dominate the public terrain—led by Time-Warner, Disney, and NewsCorp—each with strong holdings in film studios, TV networks, satellite TV, music, retail stores, print outlets, radio, sports teams, and global venues. Never in history have so few media centers been able to exercise such largely unrestrained international economic, political, and cultural power. Massive business interests, driven overwhelmingly by profits, have ushered in a new era in which production, banking, government, communications, culture, and even education have fully merged. The issue as to whether these oligopolies can coexist with even limited notions of democracy is clearly a pressing one.

Critics like Bagdikian, McChesney, Noam Chomsky, and Edward Herman have rightfully called attention to the vast expansion of media power as not only a source of ideological hegemony but as a threat to democratic politics. Yet it is media *content* that more decisively shapes popular beliefs and attitudes: where ideological messages are roughly identical—as dictated by the priorities of corporate media—then the precise number of outlets will be of secondary importance. Oligopolistic structure does, of course, enhance the ruling elite's capacity to manufacture public consent, but it is media substance that essentially determines the nature and degree of that consent. In the United States, the recent three decades or more have witnessed a steady, seemingly inexorable, rightward shift in media culture, reflected above all in TV news, cable offerings, Hollywood spectacles, talk radio, and op-ed pages of most daily newspapers. Given the powerful role conservative think tanks, foundations, lobbies, PACs, and otherwise sheer corporate leverage, the entire media landscape has been profoundly altered by right-wing ideas—fiercely pro-business and anti-labor while backing corporate deregulation, aggressive foreign policies, massive arms spending, and politics grounded in religious beliefs and "family values." In *The Republican Noise Machine* (2004), David Brock details at length a protracted, orchestrated, and well-funded campaign waged by hundreds of conservative groups to transform the American media, a strategy informed by "savage partisanship."[3] The rapid emergence of NewsCorp since the early 1990s, marked by the great success of the Fox TV Network, testifies to the explosive impact of this strategy. Thus, political views considered extreme in the 1960s and 1970s, above all in foreign policy, had become increasingly mainstream by the time Bush and Cheney rose to power. Hawkish ideas once espoused by fanatical neocons had permeated the ideological outlook of both major parties, as shown by the continuity from Bush to Obama.

The corporate media has evolved into an ideological tool that would have been the envy of Nazis and Communists restricted to heavy-handed, Orwellian methods often met with public cynicism and ridicule. Talk radio, for example, has become into a haven for right-wing extremism—a nearly monolithic source of attacks by mostly white-male hosts on a long list of demons: liberals, feminists, environmentalists, peace activists, intellectual critics, anyone seen as influenced by 1960s culture. At the hands of Rush Limbaugh, Glenn Beck, Sean Hannity, and their legions of clones and followers, even modest critics of the status quo were routinely savaged as Nazis, communists, terrorists, godless, and traitors, without fear of being questioned much less targeted for attacks. As such bombast gained respectability, feeding into the "tea-party" mania of 2009–10, it helped galvanize new strata of right-wing populists. Talk radio outlets served as the main conduit of myths like "death panels" and "communist takeover" used to discredit Obama's tepid health care reforms and financial regulations. As of early 2010, more than half of all talk radio venues—mostly closed off to liberals—were owned by the fiercely-conservative Clear Channel Corp, which offered no pretense of media objectivity or fairness. Nearly half of all Americans were reported to be regular listeners to the talk shows. For right-wing media crusaders, as Brock notes, "the battle is not simply for political control, it is for re-establishing control of America's institutions."[4] It is a battle that has largely been won.

In a media complex dominated by a handful of corporations wedded to commercial interests, no one should be astonished to find a narrowing of public discourse to fit the imperatives of that paradigm. An oligopolistic media can allow for only that degree of diversity, multiculturalism, and experimentation that falls short of challenging those interests. The seeming openness and balance of corporate-sponsored film, TV, radio, and print journalism meets stringent limits, some imposed by simple elite bias, some by the demands of advertising, some by ideological bias. "News" and "perspective" is subject to greater controls than entertainment, though in a tabloid culture that dwells on celebrity and spectacle the boundaries that separate information from diversion easily vanish. Beneath the façade of a "free" media culture, however, information and diversion equally serve hegemonic ends. When it comes to providing information and context that might enlighten audiences regarding crucial issues of the day—surely vital to any democratic process—the corporate media fails miserably, in several ways. A wide range of issues is basically "censored," that is, kept entirely from public view. Other issues are covered, even obsessively, but from a hegemonic point of view that crowds out competing opinions. Some issues are simply trivialized, reduced to so much infotainment. Still others (for example, military interventions) will be a source of constant media attention, but framed within a spirit of boosterism and cheerleading. Of course there is the omnipresent and growing spectacle of tabloid journalism that is fixated on celebrity scandals and the like. Finally, there are regular media-sponsored debates ostensibly claiming to put liberals against conservatives, but where opinions are confined to safe ideological boundaries. Viewed thusly, media culture follows no classical propaganda model—that would actually be counterproductive—but enters popular consciousness in a far more subtle and unsuspecting fashion.

It is worth considering precisely what issues have been "censored" or kept from public view in recent years. What subject matter are audiences for TV news, talk shows, radio, and kindred other venues likely to miss? There are in fact dozens of such examples, including many crucial to an understanding of global and domestic politics. According to the volume *Censored 2010,* this includes news and analysis concerning issues related to the World Bank and International Monetary Fund, the Federal Reserve Board, U.S. arms trade abroad, the complex workings of Wall Street (beyond stock-market reports), interests behind the war on drugs, Pentagon role in space militarization, the true costs of war, environmental problems, sources of the cancer epidemic, and mounting challenges associated with nuclear power.[5] To this could be added other examples: the role of animal-based agriculture in global warming, horrors of the fast-food industry, true "side effects" of Big Pharma, the extent of U.S. war crimes in Iraq alone, and the true public costs of telecommunications deregulation. It hardly need be added that press coverage of such supersecret, yet central, agencies as the NSA, NSC, and CIA has been virtually taboo, ruled off-limits. How any population deprived of such political information and historical perspective on issues of urgent public concern could hope to exercise informed citizenship has yet to be explained by gatekeepers of the "free press."

At the same time, other topics of public interest have received almost obsessive media coverage, but that coverage is so one-sided as to render alternative opinions "irrational." On questions of foreign policy, for example, free and opens exchange of views is either ruled out or reduced to simple differences over tactics and methods. The U.S.-Israeli relationship probably offers the base case study of a global issue that the mainstream press treats monolithically, so that even moderate criticism of Washington aid to Israel—not to mention Israeli oppression of Palestinians—is considered illegitimate, a reflection of what Edward Said once called "America's last taboo."[6] Where strong criticisms do occasionally surface, a loud chorus of "anti-Semitism" charges—in and out of the media—is usually enough to silence the dissent. Routine Israeli behavior has for decades been so criminal, including unlawful occupations, land seizures, property and resource theft, illegal detentions, and military assaults, that had it been conducted by any other country it would have been fiercely denounced in every media outlet. Instead, the American public is treated to either silence or apologetics from a rapt media, which offers no in-depth information or historical context regarding the Israeli-Palestinian conflict.

The supposed Iranian threat provides yet another instance where media outlets have fallen quickly and completely in line with government agendas. Everyone knows that Iran was developing its own nuclear program, although few were informed that it was clearly operating within its Nuclear Nonproliferation Treaty (NPT) rights to a civilian energy project, and neither the International Atomic Energy Agency (IAEA) nor any intelligence agency has presented evidence of an Iranian weapons program. A member of the NPT, Iran had in fact allowed foreign inspections but such unpalatable facts too were generally hidden in U.S. media accounts of an imminent Iranian military challenge. Also conveniently left out of most news accounts were the real military threats that Iran faced with huge concentrations of both conventional and atomic weaponry while Israel refuses NPT membership and, of course, any inspections regimen. Also ignored has been long-standing Washington support for outlaw nuclear regimes in Pakistan and India, as well as Israel—all beyond the reach of NPT guidelines and strictures. Nor has the media informed Americans that Iran, in cooperation with Egypt and other states, proposed a nuclear-free zone for the Middle East, an overture arrogantly rejected by U.S. and Israeli leaders intent on preserving their own nuclear monopoly. After 2007 the media has especially become obsessed with the hypothetical Iranian WMD menace, focused on an urgent need for sanctions, diplomatic isolation, and even military operations to confront the Iranian "failure" to heed international norms. Larger questions regarding the NPT, Israel, the Middle East, and U.S. geopolitical goals were obscured or ignored.

Media power also extends to what might be called "news abuse," meaning coverage of issues where fairness and balance seem credible but where "debates" serve to obscure far more than they reveal. The issue of global warming fits this pattern: while the worldwide scientific consensus presents grave warnings about what climate change augurs even in the near future, a few corporate-sponsored naysayers are afforded equal time on TV news, talk shows, documentaries, and political debates. The truth about human-caused warming, from carbon dioxide buildup, leading to drastic weather changes, threatened wildlife, and deforestation, for example, is scientifically ironclad and ought to be well beyond controversy, yet the American media adheres to the fiction that two sides deserve equal attention, as if they were equally credible. No global media outlets provide equal forums to achieve "balance." Knowledgeable experts view this phony equivalence as another case of U.S. corporations refusing to accept limits on their growth and profits that, of course, genuine reforms to fight global warming would signify. Similar "news abuse" afflicted media treatment of Obama's health care proposals in 2009–10, when emotional debates over a modest "public option" (quickly withdrawn) obscured the fact that such an "option," in universal form, is taken as a basic human right throughout the industrialized world. European conservatives would have rejected these reforms as entirely too restrained. The media rarely devoted attention to this or related facts, including research showing European health care indicators to be far superior to those in the United States for systems less expensive, more accessible, and more efficient. Nor did it inform audiences that the U.S. military—indeed *most* of the public sector—has long been a beacon of "socialized medicine" that its grateful recipients uniformly consider sacred. Indeed the corporate model of health care, where gargantuan insurance companies operate as little more than conduits of parasitic, bureaucratic waste, was taken as a fixed reality, criticized at times merely for excesses. References to threats of a communist-style "government takeover," financed by the rich medical lobbies, crowded out all serious health-related discourses.

While many critics point to the rise of "infotainment" and trivialization of serious news stories, the reality is that media culture approaches most issues and events seriously, often obsessively—none more so than coverage of U.S. military interventions. Indeed war has become one of the great spectacles of American society, as it merges elements of military violence, flashy technology, battles against demonic enemies, and flag-waving mobilization bearing resembling a sports extravaganza. Technowar turns out to be not only good business but also good media, at the same time deadly serious news for mass audiences riveted on accounts of Pentagon-embedded reporters. The 1991 Gulf War first brought this phenomenon to the fore, inspiring tens of millions of Americans to display flags and yellow ribbons as the U.S. military set out to extinguish the "Vietnam syndrome" for all time.[7]

As Norman Solomon shows in *War Made Easy* (2007), the American media has long worked as a propaganda tool smoothing U.S. readiness for war—its coverage reduced to patriotic cheerleading, its images keyed to the excitement of military triumphs, its "news" derived from official sources and military "experts," its reporters usually assigned to U.S. armed forces units, its journalists rarely willing to question White House and Pentagon claims justifying war.[8] The media prefers to view its herculean efforts at "coverage" of U.S. military interventions as auxiliary to war efforts, in the face of established norms of journalistic objectivity. Viewers of TV news and readers of local newspapers will be treated to virtually the same narratives: the United States as noble superpower reluctantly combating foreign evil in defense of human rights, democracy, and the fight against tyranny and/or WMD. In Iraq the media performed its most dutiful propaganda mission of all, incessantly repeating the litany of government lies, myths, and distortions that laid the groundwork for U.S. invasion and occupation. Saddam Hussein was yet another incarnation of Hitler, implying that anyone questioning the legitimacy of an illegal war was a simple "appeaser" or sympathizer of tyranny. Few media outlets went beneath the surface to question, much less investigate, the bogus rationale for war. No attention was devoted to clear violations of international law and the UN Charter that unprovoked war against a weak, beaten, defenseless nation involved, or the war crimes endemic to a bloody occupation regime. Any close reading of history in such disparate locales as Indonesia, Central America, Vietnam, Colombia, Turkey, and Israel, where U.S. support for tyranny, proxy wars, and human rights abuses is well-known, would have given rise to media skepticism about American claims, but this never occurred. And no skepticism was likely to emerge from among the dozens of national security "experts" routinely appearing on the TV and radio talk shows: military boosterism was the order of the day.

What, then, about domestic politics—where the structures and practices of democracy are supposedly beyond question? When it comes to executive power in the era of the national security state, public access has been virtually absent, a trend heightened during the Bush-Cheney years, when secrecy was cherished. According to a 2004 Congressional report, the Bush White House made ambitious efforts to keep even routine government activity from public scrutiny, rewriting laws to compromise transparency that were often justified by the war on terrorism.[9] Congressional oversight was steadily whittled down, along with the public right to know, usually in accordance with "state secrets privilege," closing off media access in the process. Between 2001 and 2005, nearly two-thirds of 7,000 federal advisory committee meetings were closed to the public, creating little media fanfare. Representative Henry Waxman (D-Calif) proposed legislation to widen public and media access, but it was never so much as debated on the House floor.[10] There were few stirrings from within the corporate media for greater transparency involving everyday governmental processes.

Electoral campaigns, for their part, naturally occupy a central place in American political folklore as vehicles of both citizen participation and public debate. The belief that elections allow for a general airing of political views is widespread, and there is always just enough reality to sustain that belief. The actuality, however, mostly conflicts with this ideal formulation: for decades campaigns at all levels have been largely scripted to avoid unsettling topics and opinions, especially for presidential contests. Off limits in 2008 were such pressing issues as global warming, Pentagon spending, the Patriot Act, U.S.-Israeli relations, nuclear energy, universal health care, the Federal Reserve Board, campaign finance, and lobby restrictions. Similarly excluded were in-depth looks at such chronic problems as the cancer epidemic, war on drugs, homelessness, and child care. At the forefront were the well-worn narratives of military experience, personal habits, number of trips to the Middle East, and readiness to confront the Iranian "threat." In fact Obama and McCain scandalously negotiated a secret contract dictating terms of the 2008 presidential debates, including participants, format, and topics to be raised (and excluded). Keeping out independents and restricting content, the debates were designed to maintain a cozy duopoly in which Democrats and Republicans agree to be amicable. Throughout the long electoral charade—both in debates and on the campaign trail—the word "corporation" was never mentioned, nor were questions related to economic globalization ever meaningfully addressed. There is a logic to this game: since 1988 presidential debates have been sponsored by the Commission on Presidential Debates, funded by tobacco, beer, and other large business interests never known for upsetting the political consensus.[11]

The final dimension of media power—infotainment—has come to dominate a public landscape increasingly fascinated with spectacles tied to warfare, crime, sports, and celebrity gossip. A major (but hardly sole) venue of such infotainment is the tabloids such as *The National Enquirer, Star, Globe* and *People* magazine, along with their cable TV equivalents, but tabloid styles have crept into mainstream outlets as well. Tabloid circulation dwarfs that of the conventional magazines and daily newspapers, often reaching more than 10 million readers for the *Enquirer* and *People*. Stories featured in these outlets—celebrity trials, sex scandals, bizarre tales, exotic murders, etc.—are increasingly covered in the mainstream press. Reports on salacious narratives involving New York governor Elliott Spitzer, Anna Nicole Smith, John Edwards, Tiger Woods, Michael Jackson, and Michael Phelps, to name just a few, occupied nearly as much space in the conventional media as in the tabloid press, typically pushing out more "serious" news and features. According to *Project Censored,* "junk-food" stories dominated the media landscape during 2008–09, including the trivial Michael Phelps pot scandal, Michelle Obama's fashion choices, Michael Jackson's death, the continuing saga of Brad Pitt and Angelina Jolie, and the Boston arrest of Harvard professor Henry Louis Gates. Few such topics, of course, intersect with more urgent domestic or global concerns, nor do they reveal much about the plight of ordinary Americans who, during the same time span, were facing an economic crisis of calamitous proportions.[12]

At the time when media culture dominates the ideological terrain in most advanced industrial societies, the American power structure has come to revolve more around the sway of corporate interests. The entire communications system, from politics to news to entertainment, revolves around this pervasive form of commercial propaganda. The large-scale media amount to little more than a massive sales project for corporate goods and services—indeed for commodification of a world in which consumer and material values rule. Sut Jhally goes further, arguing that "twentieth-century advertising is the most powerful and sustained system of propaganda in human history and its cumulative cultural effects, unless quickly checked, will be responsible for destroying the world as we know it."[13] In the advertising discourse, according to Jhally, all societal and ecological values are subordinated to a corporate regimen of endless consumption, growth, waste, and destruction.[14] Devoting hundreds of billions yearly to the incessant movement of products, advertising has grown beyond its instrumental sales function into a more comprehensive *ideological* mechanism pervading every corner of society. In Michael Lowy's words, "Advertising pollutes the mental, just like the urban and rural landscape: it stuffs the scull like it stuffs the mailbox. It holds sway over press, cinema, television, radio. Nothing escapes its decomposing influence: in our time, we see that sports, religion, culture, journalism, literature, and politics are ruled by advertising. All are pervaded by advertising's attitude, its style, its methods, its modes of argument."[15] This describes the all-consuming American media in a capsule.

The corrosive role of advertising—dominated in the United States by eight major firms—is notably troublesome for American politics, where commercialism strives to colonize as much terrain as possible. A phenomenon created to sell commodities produced by large corporations, advertising has given rise to an entirely new paradigm not only for media culture but for political discourse, as modes of communication become increasingly geared to consumerism, with the "consumer" taking precedence over the "citizen" in public life. Robert

McChesney writes: "As a driving force in our media system, advertising has brought commercial values into our journalism and culture in a manner unforeseeable in classical democratic theory and incompatible with traditional notions of a free press."[16] By early twenty-first century U.S. electoral campaigns revolved increasingly around TV and other media-centered frames of communication, that is, commercial sales and marketing. An oligopolistic economic system depends on corporate lobbies, public relations, advertising, and a friendly media, all of which serve to recast citizenship within the orbit of passive consumption. McChesney notes that "in hyper-commercialism, corporate power is woven so deeply into the culture that it becomes invisible, unquestionable."[17]

Like the political system, the media is a haven for strong lobbies, the pervasive influence of which goes largely unnoticed. Dozens of registered lobbyists, public relations operatives, corporate executives, and business strategists appear regularly on such TV outlets as Fox, CNN, MSNBC, ABC, NBC, and CBS, often without being identified as such Their function: to manage public images of issues and events, promote financial interests, and further elite agendas. Many "guests" who appear on these outlets, usually cast as government, military, or business experts, are regulars like the military analyst Barry McCaffrey at NBC, who works for the private contractor DynCorp with links to economic and military interests in the Middle East. Health care experts with authoritative opinions on the Obama reforms, inevitably critical of the "public option", frequently turned out to be lobbyists or consultants for Big Pharma or the insurance industry. Alternative views were rarely given a voice, even when they might have been more aligned with majority opinion. The range of views expressed on other topics—the wars in Iraq and Afghanistan, for example—were similarly tightly restricted. Although considerable media bias results from outright lobbying power, rarely is this crucial information made available to the audience.

Corporate media domination of the political culture raises serious questions about the nature and validity of "public opinion" in American society and, by extension, its role in the governmental process. If, as suggested above, public views, attitudes, beliefs, and preferences are so powerfully shaped by business interests, the citizen awareness and participation is effectively managed. Wolin, in *Democracy, Inc.*, refers precisely to the hegemonic workings of "managed democracy," though whether such a "managed" process could still be regarded as "democratic" is highly questionable. The main point here is that, in Wolin's terms, elites "manage" or control a legitimation process in the service of a power structure that regards democracy as a troublesome obstacle to be fought and contained. "Public opinion" within this context—however "scientific" or representative the surveys—has no autonomous status but rather constitutes an ensemble of beliefs, attitudes, and preferences to be channeled and managed, especially on matters of economic and foreign policy.[18] Domhoff, among others, calls attention to an "opinion-shaping network" comprised of lobbies, think tanks, public relations firms, and the media supported by and designed to facilitate explicitly corporate agendas. Elites spare no effort or resources to mobilize public opinion that fits their priorities, around such discourses as "free markets," individual freedom, consumer values, big military, and patriotism— all now broadly accepted by the American public. Critics at odds with such discourses are either banished from the media or marginalized as ideological "extremists." According to Domhoff, "The opinion-shaping network achieves its clearest expression and greatest success in the area of foreign policy, where most people have little information or interests, and are predisposed to agree with top leaders out of patriotism and a fear of whatever is strange or foreign."[19] It should be remembered, of course, that the media itself works to instill such beliefs and fears among its patrons.

Any clear framing of "public opinion," therefore, must recognize an amorphous mass electorate juxtaposed to a system of well-funded, tightly organized interests—that is, a lopsided and distorted playing field. In media culture, as elsewhere, ownership and control is highly concentrated, structured, and ideologically driven. And the huge lobbies easily merge with this culture, enhancing its power: Burston-Marsteller, PHrMA, Cassidy and Associates, Alston and Byrd, Whitman Insight Strategies, Rendon Group—these and kindred firms easily outweigh the leverage of consumer, labor, and community groups. Burston-Marsteller, with 63 offices in 32 countries and clients like General Electric and Philip Morris, has revenues of $300 million yearly while its gigantic parent owner, Young and Rubicam, earned a staggering $10 billion in 2001 alone.[20] The role of the Rendon Group in propagandizing for the Iraq war has already been detailed. Here "liberal" public opinion, even when it surfaces as on some economic and lifestyle issues, readily gets lost in the loud cacophony of conservative voices. Liberal access is negated by the long march of corporate-friendly experts, lobbyists, think tank representatives, public relations operatives, and ideologues of the sort that dominate talk radio.

The dramatic right-wing shift in American political culture, documented by Brock, McChesney, and others, would probably have been impossible without the great success of the Fox television network. Surely the Tea Party insurgency and the Republican takeover of the House after the 2010 midterm elections owes much to this propaganda machine, which reaches into tens of millions of American homes on a daily basis. When Rupert Murdoch introduced the Fox operation in 1996, his singular goal was to dominate the media terrain in order to win over mass audiences for an unabashedly pro-corporate, pro-military agenda. By featuring a stable of arch-conservative firebrands like Bill O'Reilly, Sean Hannity, and (later) Glenn Beck, Rupert and Fox president Roger Ailes hoped to transform the very contours of political debate in the United States—and indeed were able to do so within a decade or less. Beck, whose tirades were directed against multiculturalism, gay marriage, Venezuela, immigration, antiwar protesters, the liberal media, and of course Democrats, was fond of labeling Obama (and indeed any critics of Fox News) as "Marxist" or "communist." Sarah Palin was hired as a "news analyst" in 2010 after quitting as governor of Alaska. The Tea Party, meanwhile, was beneficiary of virtually round-the-clock coverage, replete with special features, interviews, and commentary. Architect of surely the biggest propaganda outlet in history, Murdoch and his lieutenants made no apologies for endowing "news" and "commentary" with a sharply conservative thrust even as they upheld the fiction of Fox being "the most trusted name in news."

What John Nichols and Robert McChesney refer to as the "money-and-media-election-complex" has assumed rising importance for American politics with each passing year, as shown by the conservative takeover of the House of Representatives at the 2010 midterm elections.[21] Among other trends, political advertising had become a vast source of revenue throughout commercial broadcasting, with thirty-second ad spots going for as much as $5,000 at outlets owned by a small handful of corporations. Pro-Republican advertising outspent that of the Democrats by seven to one, according to the Center for Media and Democracy. Campaign spots are totally unregulated for veracity. Nichols and McChesney observe that "as ads become the primary source of political information, we create a politics based on lies or, at best, decontextualized quarter-truths," precisely at a time when the news media has deteriorated as a source of coverage and analysis. They add, reflecting on the corrosive impact of the money-and-media-election complex: "How ironic that, just as demographic trends are moving in a decidedly progressive direction—as minorities begin to from majorities in our states, and as young people move increasingly to the left on social and economic issues—the electoral system is becoming a bastion of reaction." The result is "radically different electoral landscape than anything Americans have known since the Gilded Age."[22]

The very nature of media culture thus reveals enormous obstacles in efforts to accurately interpret "public opinion." Where people are bombarded with corporate-driven messages, as at Fox, and where political language mostly revolves around commercial advertising with its rapid flow of images and quick sound-bites, questions regarding the actual source of popular "consent" inevitably arise. In other words, to what extent are public views, attitudes, and values manipulated to suit the dominant interests? Without clear answers to such questions—or even attempts to pose them—facile references to polls and surveys on most topics ought to be treated with suspicion. Abundant evidence shows that the corporate media in fact employs its seemingly infinite resources to indoctrinate, typically with great success—as reflected, for example, in the health care discourses of 2009–10. How to explain the pervasive American belief in a benevolent (though nonexistent) "free market," blind faith in the workings of democratic governance, satisfaction with a fair and balanced media, or support for a costly and bloody, though illegal and unnecessary, war in Iraq? Are people offered genuine alternatives to such hegemonic discourses? We know the vast majority of Americans does go along with business-as-usual, tolerating if not endorsing the most harmful practices of corporations and military. Populist anger has been on the rise, but more often than not it is directed against "big government" rather than the immense power of banks, insurance companies, and military contractors. The focus of such anger is also rather contradictory, as in the call for "reduced government" by the same people arguing for a bigger, stronger, more globally active Pentagon along with beefed-up law enforcement. The outbursts, moreover, are blocked in their political capacity, as they are tied to a conservative outlook that steadfastly refuses to disturb the status quo. Filtered largely through media culture, the anger ultimately helps reproduce and strengthen a rather closed political universe.

The Great Lobby Complex

The powerful media lobbies mentioned above, operating across the political landscape, have become the lifeblood of corporate interests and agendas. With the progressive institutionalization of state capitalism, government and business forces, intersect and overlap as the familiar distinction between "public" and "private" realms declines and then evaporates. Here literally thousands of well-funded, tightly organized lobbies enter the governing realm at every level, building spheres of power and wealth, often behind the scenes and at the expense of popular awareness and control. Lobbies use their vast resources—money, organization, social contacts, expertise, media power, etc.—to shape legislation, win tax breaks for the rich, get lucrative contracts, gain state subsidies, block regulations, and take over public agencies. Given the postwar expansion of lobby power, the division separating legislators and lobbyists has shrunk dramatically. Arianna Huffington notes, in *Third World America,* that "with this merging of state and private power, we're getting to the point where the only difference between senior congressional staffers and the lobbyists and influence launderers whose ranks they'll join soon is the size of their paychecks."[23] Indeed members of the legislative branch could expect as much as $6.5 million in corporate largesse during 2009, thanks to the tireless energies of some 14,000 lobbyists. The quaint political-science image of a balanced system of "interest groups" competing more or less equally to influence legislation was long ago obsolete. Business groups representing banks, insurance, pharmaceuticals, agribusiness, energy, and military easily dwarf, in numbers and resources, groups advocating for labor, consumers, and communities. Their interests are rather neatly framed—to maximize corporate power and wealth—and have usually been secured with the defeat of their competition in the "liberal-labor coalition."[24]

A thorough recent critique of American lobbies is Thomas Frank's *The Wrecking Crew* (2008), in which he charts the steady deterioration of a political system taken over by Washington-based ultraconservatives whose single-minded purpose has been to subvert government and give carte blanche to freewheeling corporate interests. Best known for *What's the Matter with Kansas?* (2005), a treatise on the Republican genius for mobilizing workers and the poor around traditional values to the detriment of their economic self-interests, Frank shifts attention here to the role of lobbies and kindred elite groups working at the summits of power to undermine democratic governance. Ascendancy of the right, spurred by the Reagan Revolution of the 1980s, revolved around a *philosophy* of government (beyond mere electoral tactics) that views the liberal state as a perversion of social values and the "market" a true embodiment of human potential. As the market penetrates and transforms government, as big business takes over more and more state functions, it is possible to see with greater clarity how continuous misrule, incompetence, and corruption are less marks of leadership malfeasance or personal flaws than of well-planned right-wing agendas. A tenacious but well-organized "winger" assault on liberal government and the New Deal social contract that kept it alive is the most visible expression of the "wrecking crew in action," given a new lease on life during the second Bush presidency.[25] For libertarians weaned on reputed laissez-faire principles, the market entails all that is organic and natural while the state is innately coercive and repressive, the very enemy of freedom, democracy, and prosperity.

As Frank argues, however, this revived archaic ideology amounts to little more than shameless cover for unregulated corporate power, the authoritarian and plutocratic elements of which are never acknowledged much less questioned. Its pseudo-libertarianism is simply faux populism, cynically pedaled not only in the D.C. corridors of power but in the Midwestern hinterlands, that legitimates elite rule while displacing citizen participation. Market pretenses allow conservatives to "pass off a patently pro-business political agenda as a noble bid for human freedom."[26] As the second Bush administration was drawing to a close, the nation was beset with severe economic crises, the striking reality was that an arrogant and unprincipled "wrecking crew" was able to make inroads into American domestic and foreign policy to the extent that "Washington [had] truly become a winger wonderland."[27]

The ostensible success of ultraconservatives and their lobbies in disabling—or more accurately colonizing—government historically depended on the capacity of business interests to infiltrate and capture large sectors of the state. Stupendous wealth that helps determine electoral outcomes, "privatization" of government functions, proliferation of right-wing think tanks and foundations, penetration of public agencies, and tightened corporate media ownership all feed into the same oligarchic outcome. Add the influence of D.C.-based lobbies on Congress and the executive, and a sharper picture of corporate hegemony emerges. Frank is adept at surveying the damage these aggressive and well-financed lobbies have inflicted on government, their concern for the public interests (however defined) invisible. After the early 1980s Washington saw a massive influx of lobbyists bringing the total (in 2008) to roughly 90,000—most working in the service of insurance, banking, pharmaceutical, military, agricultural, and media corporations. These interest groups seek, usually with measurable success, to exert leverage over such agencies as the Federal Communications Commission (FCC), Food and Drug Agency (FDA), Environmental Protection Agency (EPA), and the National Institutes of Health (NIH), hoping to weaken or possibly overturn federal and state regulations. In Frank's view, the army of D.C. lobbyists (along with their cohorts in state capitols) are nothing but unscrupulous profiteers masquerading as noble agents of individualism, reduced government, and free enterprise.

One particularly notorious lobbyist was Jack Abramoff, imprisoned for illegal practices carried out across many years, an operative who went from Reagan Youth leader to catalyst of the Washington "bayonet charge" to bring back "free markets" and restore "small government." Abramoff and his circle (including Representative Tom Delay of Texas) were drawn to every ultraconservative issue—South African apartheid, the Afghan Mujahedeen, sweatshop havens, the wars against Iraq, and Darwinian economies bereft of labor and human rights. A world-champion lobbyist involved in projects like Indian casinos and corporate-owned Channel One for high schools, Abramoff became the "field marshal" of the D.C. wingers—someone who could block legislation, get bills passed, and destroy people's careers. With resources for sale at stupendous prices, his obsessive goal was to weaken regulations of the Occupational and Safety Agency (OSHA). Years of exorbitant fees to clients, kick backs, and bribing of government officials eventually brought prison time. Looking for a marketplace utopia, Abramoff and other Washington operatives mounted an ideological crusade starting in the 1980s, abetted by the media, to demonize and isolate liberals who embraced a more jaundiced view of corporate power. Frank describes how, in order to take over and "wreck" government, the wingers sought to extirpate the last vestiges of Keynesianism and with it the hated tax-and-spend panderers to every popular whim. While Frank dwells little on the postwar evolution of bipartisanism, the "winger wonderland" he explores was in fact almost equally inhabited by those extravagant liberals, few of whom (within or outside the Democratic Party) ever managed to stand up against the big-business juggernaut. On the contrary, the vast majority of liberals subscribed to the same "free market" mythology. Frank eventually takes note of this when he says: "It would be nice if electing Democrats was all that was required to resuscitate the America that wingers flattened, but it will take far more than that... [It will require] a reconstructive project of massive proportions."[28]

Frank is hardly alone in arguing the public realm has been extensively colonized by corporate interests, but his central argument—that the ultra right is using lobbies to "wreck" government—raises a host of other issues. The problem with Frank's analysis lies in the absence of historical perspective combined with a rather clouded view of the relationship between corporations and state power. Put bluntly, are "free market" operatives really the dedicated assassins of big government Frank claims they are—or that they themselves claim? Or is their effort to manipulate government toward their own ends simply another instance of business-as-usual? Of course lobbying itself is as old as American capitalism, an indelible part of the public terrain and central to such experiences as urban machine politics, which gained strength as the state began expanding in the 1930s. Nowadays federal, state, and local agencies are routinely infiltrated or dominated by "private" interests, a practice that rarely elicits much controversy or even notice. In a revealing section of his book, Frank mentions FDR's prize Tennessee Valley Authority (TVA) as a seminal example of the public interest in action, an icon of those halcyon days of democratic government said to contrast so starkly with what followed later. According to Frank, the Roosevelt administration was able to resist pressures toward corruption, cronyism, and patronage, holding off "profiteers of the private sector" that would typify later "wrecking crew" schemes set in motion by the Reagan Revolution.

This is sheer fiction, as any cursory investigation of TVA history will show: what we have, instead, is a well-known case of business manipulation of a government agency—the very point made by Philip Selznick in his classic *TVA and the Grassroots,* first published in 1949.[29] Established in 1933, the TVA was to be a new kind of agency dedicated to the public interest, conservation, and grassroots participation, a centerpiece of "democracy on the march." Quickly, however, the TVA faced sharp challenges from both local and national private interests, at which juncture its managers "adapted" to those interests, leaving the door wide open to a reshaping of organizational identity and purpose.[30] Formal authority was soon reconfigured by the power of capital. Initially a worldwide symbol of the "positive, benevolent intervention of government for the general welfare," the TVA emerged as something altogether different, an institutionalized state agency coopted by powerful lobbies such as the American Farm Bureau.[31] Here and elsewhere New Deal progressivism aligned itself with rival interests for the sake of resources and "efficiency," its capacity for democratic planning broken by corporate power. Selznick believed it was naïve even at that time to imagine any large-scale government agency could be immune to big-business predation. In a 1965 revised edition of his book, Selznick wrote that the TVA had sadly become a bête noir of environmentalists, attacked for its support of mining-company interests that led to ruined hillsides, poisoned streams, devastated farmlands, and vast wildlife destruction.[32] So much for the public interest and "democracy on the march." And so much for the fanciful notion that corporate colonization of the public sector originated during the Reagan years. As for the TVA, the same tortured legacy continues: today the agency operates as a massive, federally funded utility, its regulatory functions gutted by industry, leading one commentator to note that "the TVA, the nation's largest utility, has become a poster child for the failure of deregulation."[33] Thanks to the overwhelming power of coal interests, the TVA has been helpless to restrain ecologically destructive practices; on the contrary, "public" and "private" have worked in tandem. One result was the largest industrial spill of toxins in history, following collapse of an earthen dike on the Tennessee River, in December 2009, releasing over one billion tons of muddy waste.[34]

Nowhere in fact has the lobby juggernaut been more active—or destructive—than in its struggle to fight and overturn environmental regulations, always on behalf of free markets, growth, and prosperity. Gains of the 1970s and 1980s, mostly thanks to environmental movements and the EPA, have been challenged and often reversed since 2000, under assault from the major polluting industries (coal, oil, chemicals, mining, timber, etc.), their powerful lobbies, and right-wing groups tied to such think tanks as the Heritage Foundation. This backlash has been funded by foundations like Coors, Olin, Scaife, Castle Rock, Koch, and Bradley.[35] The agenda, here as elsewhere, is to keep the polluting industries as free as possible of regulatory laws enacted by the EPA through the Clear Air and Water Acts combined with other legislation. Backlash ideology framed ecological reforms as a diabolical plot to destroy not only the free market and democracy but the basis of Western Civilization itself—growth, profits, affluence, and progress. As with the ill-fated TVA, corporate strategy—more often successful than not—was to colonize the EPA so that lobbyists representing interests with a stake in deregulation could manage or at least strongly influence those departments involved in environmental policy. Officials recruited from the very polluting industries could thus paralyze EPA regulatory functions, a stratagem perfected by the Bush administration. Leading EPA figures under Bush and Cheney, all closely tied to oil, coal, and utility interests, entered government from such backgrounds as chemicals, oil, timber, and mining. White House director of the Council on Environmental Quality was James Connaughton, former asbestos industry lawyer.

As with the TVA, results have been rather predictable: while the EPA became what Robert Kennedy, Jr. called a "country club for America's polluters,"[36] the very agency entrusted with protecting citizens from environmental harm simply ceased enforcing the law.[37] The government looked away as mining, agribusiness, chemical, and logging interests routinely flouted regulations limiting air, water, and soil pollution. Meanwhile, the White House dropped scores of legal cases against oil, coal, chemical, and agricultural corporations—industries that contributed generously to the 2000 and 2004 Bush campaigns. Gail Norton, director of the Department of Interior, and tied to Coors, Amoco, and the Chemical Manufacturers Association, bitterly opposed the bulk of environmental regulations. With corporate penetration of the Bush administration a fait accompli, the expected outcome, as Kennedy notes, was that "Norton opened up our public treasure to industry plunder."[38] Norton tolerated no dissent from her policy of allowing corporations carte blanche in their reckless subversion of the public commons. Under Bush and Cheney, EPA budgets were slashed, scientific data on ecological challenges massaged, regulations perverted, and legal actions dropped under lobby pressures. This "new orgy or industry plunder" led to a rollback of federal emission standards, relaxation of wildlife protection measures, exemptions for the military, new subsidies for polluters, and efforts to reverse global warming[39]—all in the face of polls consistently showing the vast majority of Americans favor increasingly strict environmental protections.[40]

A related arena of corporate lobbying is the nuclear power industry, expanded during the 1950s as part of the permanent war economy. In 2010 ten firms had more than 60 percent control of the nuclear industry, with Exelon leading the way at 15 percent. Deregulation permitted the rise of two huge consortia—one comprised of Exelon, Duke Energy Corp, and several others, called the Nustart group, which gets vast government subsidies for site and design permits, what Helen Caldicott refers to as a "socialized arrangement that suits the nuclear consortium."[41] Thanks to hyperactive lobbies, the U.S. nuclear industry has maintained veto power over appointments to the Nuclear Regulatory Commission. According to Caldicott, "The NRC, ostensibly an independent body, now virtually represents the nuclear industry...[with] the public effectively eliminated from the nuclear industry's decision process."[42] Again, owing to powerful lobbies, nuclear corporations have over many decades received generous state subsidies for virtually every aspect of their operations—some $13 billion, including tax breaks, in 2005 alone when Congress passed its energy bill. Further, the Price-Anderson Act, enacted in 1957, means that taxpayers will fund up to 98 percent of $600 billion in government insurance in case of nuclear accident. Contained in Price-Anderson, moreover, is a stipulation that individuals cannot claim punitive damages against nuclear enterprises. This exemplary case of corporate welfare was extended by Congress in 2005 to the year 2025.

A sacred yet often pilloried American institution, lobbies have long been active at all levels of government. We have seen, in the previous section, how media lobbies have aggressively shaped news, information, and entertainment, usually behind the scenes. Chapter 3 explored the role of military lobbies in determining U.S. foreign policy throughout the postwar era. Corporate influence long predated World War II, as Smedley Butler observed in his famous 1930s treatise on the causes of World War I. A Marine general, Butler admitted he was a "gangster for capitalism," concluding, "War destroys peoples and societies for the wealth of a few."[43] Pharmaceutical, insurance, and food lobbies have been among the most active and effective interest groups—a motif taken up more fully in chapter five. Financial lobbies, more aggressive since the 1990s, are explored in the next section. Sufficient to note here is that one of President Obama's few progressive moves to confront the economic crisis was a proposed Consumer Finance Protection Agency that would help ordinary people avoid abusive bank practices, but (at this writing, early 2010) so weakened by the influence of Wall Street lobbies as to leave consumers largely unprotected. In these and many other cases, well-funded lobbies do everything in their power to stifle debate, discredit opponents, inject misleading information (as on global warming), and, most significantly, infiltrate and colonize public agencies. Toward these ends they can mobilize resources far superior to those of more dispersed labor, consumer, and community groups.

Lobby power has only intensified over time: in 2009–10, the Chamber of Commerce began a large-scale grassroots operation aided by record amounts of money raised from corporations and wealthy individuals. By early 2010 the chamber had recruited nearly

6 million people to help with lobbying and elections, bolstered by the January 2010 Supreme Court ruling that gives corporations a free-speech right to spend money on candidates, overturning a century of laws that had limited such spending. Resurgent interest-group power fits a trend in which the established parties have lost ground to well-financed "outside" forces, at a time when an increasing percentage of voters (nearly 40 percent) identify as independents. The chamber set up a network called Friends of the U.S. Chamber, inspired mainly by efforts to oppose health care reform. In 2009 the chamber spent $144 million on lobbies—an impressive 60 percent increase over 2008.[44] This was roughly five times what PhRMA, General Electric, and ExxonMobil spent combined. Further, it appears the chamber can now take such largesse from wealthy contributors without serious disclosure worries. As business contributes money to the chamber, advertising can then be sponsored by the chamber for candidates and issues without having to reveal names of specific businesses involved. While the chamber officially represents 3 million companies, internal documents show that it depends overwhelmingly on just a dozen or so major corporations. Supposedly bipartisan, it has routinely favored Republicans: in 2008, for example, 86 percent of the chamber's political contributions went to Republicans.[45]

Viewed thusly, Frank's "wrecking crew" thesis runs into thorny problems, for his argument—with strong empirical conclusions about the role of American lobbies—essentially restates the historic integration of government and corporations that marked the rise of state-capitalism in the U.S. colonization of the public sphere by "private" interests has indeed long been a pervasive motif of American politics. One novel aspect of Frank's work is the attention he devotes to the resurgence of free-market ideology since the Reagan years, although he seems much too willing to accept this establishment discourse at face value. In fact the system has long been statist in many crucial realms: the military, law enforcement, education, regulations, social programs, infrastructural funding, bailouts, federal or local ownership, and more. A government-business partnership has long shaped the entire land-scape, as we have seen. The earlier trajectory of state capitalism (incorporating the military) was long ago brilliantly analyzed by Mills in *The Power Elite*. Mills described an oligarchical power structure presided over by a confluence of corporate, government, and military interests, their roles interchangeable and mostly detached from public inputs and accountability.[46] The anticipated later growth of militarized state-capitalism that would be embraced by Democrats and Republicans equally, inevitably clashed with the requirements of democracy and free markets, yielding to a deeply authoritarian logic. The power of lobbies is best understood in this historical context.

In a period of solidifying state-capitalism, Mills surely would have found the idea of autonomous, unfettered government preposterous. And Mills was right, then as now: it is hard to conceive of state power operating "independent of vested interests."[47] From this standpoint, it was never the goal of lobbies to destroy or "wreck" the state, but rather to colonize and direct the state toward further empowering corporate interests. It is true, moreover, that elites at the summits of power tend to share a common outlook, and it is for this reason that systemic integration has occurred over the years with only minor disruptions. Such integration is naturally reinforced, and ideologically legitimated, by the growth of military and imperial power. Lobbies, though surely less of a factor in the 1950s than in the early twenty-first century, were nonetheless taken for granted, with tales of the "public interest" and "democracy" spun largely to rationalize widespread powerlessness. And such powerlessness extended, then as now, above all to the realm of foreign and military policy, considered the domain of (white male) "experts." In 2008, as the American economy descended into severe crisis, the "small government," free-enterprise champion Bush earmarked hundreds of billions to bail out Wall Street, banks, insurance companies, and other huge businesses—after having spent more hundreds of billions on wars and military occupations. The reality is that Republicans no less than Democrats, "free-marketeers" no less than "tax-and-spend liberals," have worked faithfully to maintain a gargantuan state apparatus, riddled with corporate interests, because it fully coincides with their insatiable drive for power and wealth.

By 2010, the powerful lobbying machines were thriving as never before, more capable than ever of thwarting social reforms. The corporate billions poured into the legislative process is, with a few noteworthy exceptions, entirely legal, part of normal business within the D.C. establishment. Even where lobbyists' behavior might be criticized as disgusting or unethical, it has become so widespread and legitimate as to be impervious to prosecution. Although by 2009 some 20 ex-lobbyists had been charged or convicted of crimes, most operations simply passed beneath the radar; corporate influence-peddling was generally seen as just another American tradition. Even Abramoff complained that he had done nothing wrong, that he was just doing his job like all the others. "I felt my job was to go out there and save the world," said Abramoff. "I thought it was immoral to take someone's money and not win for them."[48] The problem was that he was somehow *better* at his work than other lobbyists. Added Grover Norquist, a guru of the great lobby apparatus, "What the Republicans need is 50 Jack Abramoffs. Then this becomes a different town."[49] And of course thanks to Abramoff and his thousands of cohorts, D.C. did in fact become a "different town."

One consequence of the lobby revolution is the effective corporate subversion of environmental reforms, both state and local, that the ecological crisis has forced onto the political agenda. Well-funded groups representing the energy, chemical, and auto industries have fought tenaciously to block, or at least water down, legislative measures to curb water and air pollution, roll back greenhouse emissions, and stimulate alternative technologies. Few states have been able to mobilize sufficient legislative votes to even modestly address runaway global warming in the face of corporate intransigence. Nationally, neither the House nor the Senate has managed to pass a climate change bill, even with strong Democratic majorities. The tepid Kerry-Lieberman proposals—friendly as they were to big business—quickly vanished without much public notice, once the oil and auto corporations moved to counterattack. Despite the mounting crisis, Congressional agendas essentially favor more of the same: stepped up offshore drilling, auto industry subsidies, emphasis on "clean" coal and gas, and a return to nuclear power. For its part, the Obama administration backed away from its initially aggressive pursuit of global warming legislation. Not only Congress, but agencies within the federal government were so colonized by the energy industry that the agency often stood by while oil and gas giants were simply allowed to self-regulate. Offshore oil drilling permits were given out by the thousands, even for highly problematic ocean depths. It was the Mineral Management Service that essentially looked away as British Petroleum (BP) was given carte blanche to build its Deepwater Horizon rig in the Gulf of Mexico, allowing for the greatest environmental disaster in U.S. history. After the disaster, evidence mounted that BP had largely ignored even its own formal safety procedures.

More startling yet, the vast majority of environmental groups have themselves succumbed to lobby pressures, thereby retreating from earlier progressive stands against global warming.[50] Having grown addicted to corporate largesse, such important organizations as the Sierra Club, World Wildlife Federation, and the Nature Conservancy refuse to push for genuine reforms, fearful of alienating big money sources. Some leaders of these groups have even questioned the science underlying climate change priorities, while others refuse to press for any legislation deemed "unrealistic"—that is, opposed by moderate Republicans, Blue Dog Democrats, and major corporations. With a massive infusion of funds coming from oil giants like Shell, ExxonMobil, and BP, along with the Chamber of Commerce, it is hardly surprising to find that American environmentalism has reached an impasse, even as the famous "tipping point" of ecological catastrophe appears close at hand.

Financial Colossus

The present-day global economy, still dominated by the United States, is marked by multinational corporate hegemony, the increasing power of finance capital, and institutional oligarchy. It is a system based on speculative investment, tightened workforce controls, austerity programs, and maximum growth—while the major national powers—in partnership with the International Monetary Fund, World Bank, and World Trade Organization—impose state-capitalist agendas well beyond the reach of local populations, social movements, and democratic governance. In the United States, as elsewhere, corporate globalization remains unfriendly to labor rights, consumer protections, social services, the environment, and citizen participation. What is commonly referred to as the "financialization of capital" has, in the era of advanced globalization, delivered broader powers to the banking system, Wall Street, and the Federal Reserve Bank. These huge structures work incessantly toward unfettered financial maneuverability, maximum flow of capital, and freedom from legal or political restraints. Their success has been rather dramatic if calamitous.

In this setting, the dramatic U.S. financial meltdown starting in 2008 amounts to a crisis far beyond earlier cyclical downturns. It was, rather, a cataclysm associated with a newer phase of finance capital in which the system, controlled by fewer corporate giants, that spirals out of control owing to its own lack of restraints. As predatory banking practices increase, the system moves toward greater concentration of power—a financial oligarchy—more reliant on the state for deregulation, bailouts, subsidies, tax breaks, and other favorable legislation. The Wall Street collapse has brought governmental supports, implemented by Democrats and Republicans alike, far beyond what even the earlier Keynesians might have imagined. Despite politicians' rhetoric about "free markets," "limited government," and "personal responsibility," efforts to stabilize Wall Street and related financial operations have led to a hollowing out of the public treasury assisted by the

Federal Reserve, with taxpayers footing the bill for larcenous gamblers' debts. President Obama, heavily obligated to Wall Street financiers, has made nearly $12 trillion available to these interests in the form of cash infusions, loans, guarantees, and buy-outs—all pushed heavily by bankers, the Fed, an army of lobbyists, and the media. Meanwhile, the number of mammoth banks has dwindled to a mighty five—Citigroup, JPMorgan Chase, Bank of America, Wells Fargo, MorganStanley—all recipients of massive government contributions, while having gobbled up hundreds of smaller banks. These few giants held 54 percent of total American financial assets in 2009.

Obama's deference to Wall Street reveals nothing so much as the harsh imperatives of capital, having inherited a bailout agenda from President Bush and delivering trillions of dollars to the largest banks and insurance companies said to be vital to economic health, although most of the "stimulus" never reached ordinary Americans desperately needing their own bailouts, jobs, and social programs. Corporations took the bulk of taxpayers' money, enriched their bloated coffers, fought new regulations, and placed more bets within the international economy. Top executives received tens of billions in bonuses, while the "real" main-street economy was deteriorating with lost jobs, new home foreclosures, eroded public services, declining personal income, and shrinking retirement and savings accounts. Meanwhile, the Fed continued to pump cheap money into the financial system as perpetual "stimulus" to the banks. In the midst of this biggest U.S. government spending spree in history—incredulously met with grassroots "tea-party" protests against "big government"—worth noting is that Obama's corporate bailouts could provide 30 years of public (or even private) health insurance for all uninsured citizens. Moreover, as the wave of financial speculation continued, largely detached from production of useful goods and services, some of the mammoth banks started to teeter, still in danger of collapse.

As mentioned earlier, Obama's economic team was recruited almost entirely from the ranks of Wall Street insiders: Robert Rubin, Larry Summers, Timothy Geithner, Michael Froman, Gary Gensler, Rahm Emmanuel, Mark Patterson, and others. Not surprisingly, critics of this already corrupt, oligopolistic system were fully excluded from the deliberations of the ruling circles. We also saw how the first telling decision made by the Obama White House was a massive bailout of Citigroup through public revenues, arranged by the very former Wall Street operatives already deeply implicated in the crisis from the outset.[51] In fact the stock market responded favorably to this initiative as it did to all the succeeding bailouts, content that the giveaways were not combined with new regulations. These same operatives, of course, continued to sing the virtues of "free enterprise" while railing against "big government." It was these same elites, moreover, who had reaped millions of dollars apiece in Wall Street before joining the Obama administration. Even as the banks invested in little that was productive, they were able to rely on the Fed as the always endless, generous "lender of last resort." Matt Taibbi notes that "Wall Street and the government became one giant dope house, where a few major players share valuable information between conflicted departments the way junkies share needles."[52] As in any such rigged economy, the entire communications network grows insular and closed. Not merely the bailouts, but the larger Wall Street agenda embraced (even if ambivalently) by the Obama administration reinforces this concentration of elite power.

As the financial crisis intensified in 2008 and 2009, banks and kindred corporations stepped up their already ambitious lobbying enterprises—hopeful of bailouts and fearful of regulatory reforms that an angry public might be expected to favor. The eight largest banks ramped up lobby spending by 12 percent in 2009, to roughly $30 million.[53] JPMorgan Chase led the way with $6.2 million for 30 lobbyists deployed to Washington alone. The Financial Services Roundtable, representing more than 100 firms, stepped up its efforts to kill any banking regulations such as size limits or caps on hedge funds, which the roundtable denounced as "political interference." Much like the great success of insurance and other medical-related corporations in fighting extensive health care reforms, financial lobbies were able to block legislative action that challenged their room to maneuver. Obama's aforementioned modest (but long-overdue) proposal for a Consumer Financial Protection Agency was destined to be torpedoed or, if passed, so filled with loopholes and exceptions as to be toothless. Financial groups and their Republican supporters sent memos playing on Americans' mounting distrust of government and politicians, saying, for example: "We don't need another federal government agency. What we need is a better approach that promotes accountability, responsibility, and effective oversight."[54] Of course the big problem for consumers—and indeed the system itself—was an out-of-control banking oligopoly that could only be reigned in by stringent public regulations.

In fact the entire political apparatus, from the White House to Congress to the Federal Reserve, is saturated with financial lobbies that today rank among the most powerful in Washington. As we have seen, the system evolved into a vast playground of corporate lobbies across the entire economic spectrum. In 1999, thanks to relentless pressure from Wall Street, Congress passed the Financial Services Modernization Act—followed quickly by the Commodity Futures Modernization Act of 2000—which tore down the venerable Glass-Seagall Act that in 1933 established a much-needed divide between commercial and investment banking. The idea was that freewheeling investment banks should never receive federal backing, which is precisely what they have been given during the Bush and Obama presidencies. After 2000, Wall Street predictably became a gigantic casino investing funds having little to do with actual production or human welfare. The wave of deregulation was spurred by a phalanx of lobbies: real estate, mortgage brokers, insurance firms, credit card enterprises, investment banks, trade groups, private equity companies, hedge-fund operators, and even credit unions. Massive amounts of money flowed from Wall Street into the governing arena after the early 1980s, stepped up again in the late 1990s when loosened regulations produced "oceans of money" for the already wealthy. By 2007 the banks were earning quadruple what they had earned in 1980s, while executive pay doubled and bonuses (already obscene) tripled. Writing about "capital city" (Washington), Kevin Drum notes regarding the lobbies: "Their real power lies in the fact that they've so thoroughly changed our collective attitude toward financial regulation that sometimes they barely need to lobby in the traditional sense at all."[55] But of course lobby they do, with few limits or constraints.

Not only the White House but the Security Exchange Commission (SEC) and Federal Reserve Bank are thoroughly infiltrated by financial lobbies. In Congress, as suggested above, the banks have achieved virtually everything they wanted, as most senators and representatives are dependent on financial contributions to their campaigns. Thus Senator Charles Shumer (D-NY), who routinely raises hundreds of millions from Wall Street for Democratic politicians, has received $14 million himself from the banking industry. In 2009 alone Schumer was given $1.7 million, while his Senate colleagues Harry Reid (D-Nev), Chris Dodd (D-Conn), and Kirsten Gillibrand (D-NY) received about $1 million each. Such banking largesse continues along the roll list in both the Senate and House.[56] While politicians ramble on about "free markets" and "personal responsibility," the symbiotic relationship between Wall Street and government grows even cozier. Not surprisingly—all rhetoric to the contrary—few politicians from either party have been anxious to push for urgently needed banking reforms and regulations. Indeed the few legislative proposals to surface, like the aforementioned consumer protection act, are riddled with exemptions, loopholes, and exceptions. Much legislation, as with the 1999 and 2000 bills referred to above, is actually drafted, edited, and revised by operatives from the banking lobbies. Further, Republicans generally can rely on plenty of help from the "Blue Dog" Democrats (tight with corporate interests) who dominate the House Financial Services Committee. These Democrats too are totally beholden to Wall Street. As William Greider writes: "The odor of money hovers over the Blue Dogs—political money for their next campaigns. The House Finance Services Committee is a prized assignment and known informally among members as a 'money committee', not because it deals with money issues but because its members have an easier time raising campaign funds from the banks and financial firms under their jurisdiction. This is not illegal. It is the way Congress works."[57]

At the very top of this financial pyramid, of course, stands the sprawling Federal Reserve Bank, an all-powerful economic institution since 1913. The Fed epitomizes the merger of government and corporations, public sector and private banking, serving as "lender of last resort," a source of money supply, a regulator of interest rates, and theoretical guarantor of fiscal and monetary stability. It supposedly constitutes a buffer against crisis, a moderator of extreme swings and cycles. The board of governors, ruling the largest financial empire on the planet, is comprised of members appointed to staggered 14-year terms, far removed from any semblance of democratic politics. The chair of the Fed is designated by the president to govern an ostensibly "independent" body. Members of the board, along with those of the 12 regional boards, are overwhelmingly recruited from the banking industry. With no reliance on Congressional funding—it earns money from interest on Treasury securities—the Fed is largely free of political oversight or controls. It has the freedom to operate on its own without prior approval from Congress or the president. The Fed manages a close relationship with many foreign banks, typically outside any public radar. A sign of its enormous clout, in March 2009 the Fed owned $247 billion in gold and held $534 billion in national debt.

The Fed has dramatically expanded its powers over time, with its capacity to shape economic development heightened since the 1970s. It is among the largest, most far-reaching bureaucracies in the United States, though one with no elected leadership. With Alan Greenspan as chair between 1987 and 2006, the Fed achieved nearly mythical status for its continuing efforts to steer the economy. At the same time, board officials typically worked in secrecy with minimum oversight and accountability. As Robert Auerbach shows in *Deception and Abuse* (2009), the Fed was able to manipulate financial markets on its own, provided no transcripts of its meetings, and routinely stonewalled even tepid Congressional investigations.[58] The Fed possesses a unique capacity to bolster elite power as it operates independently of all three branches of government, while its main constituency is the banks and related corporations. It has emerged as perhaps the most indispensable tool of an oligarchic system, all the more powerful given its image as neutral crisis-manager standing above everyday political conflict.

More than any single institution, the Fed has been at the center of desperate elite strivings to arrest the financial crisis, having lent (by early 2010) nearly $2 trillion to failing banks among its numerous initiatives. Wall Street's deep reliance on the public sector thus seems more evident than ever, even as its representatives uphold principles of classical capitalism. Treasury Secretary Geithner remarked in 2009 that the Fed "defends the freedom and security of Americans from existential threats." Ben Bernanke, appointed chair in 2006, carried forward Greenspan's pro-corporate and easy-money policies, for which he was referred to a "Bailout Ben, the patron saint of Wall Street greedheads" and "King Ben, the unelected Czar of a fourth branch of government."[59] As they were writing this about Bernanke, seemingly without tongue-in-cheek, *Time* editors had chosen the Fed chief as their "Person of the Year" for 2009 because "he is the most important player guiding the world's most important economy."[60] Bernanke received this prestigious award because he saved "irresponsible giants of Wall Street only to protect ordinary folks on Main Street."[61] The problem with this accolade is that Bernanke's Fed, fully immersed in the Wall Street larceny, itself contributed to the crisis as the Fed extended Greenspan's laissez-faire approach to the casino economy, issuing easy money, and fighting regulations all the way. Whatever Bernanke's own role in the downturn, however, *Time* magazine's glorification of the Fed chair as autocratic savior of both the domestic and global economy unwittingly pointed toward the vast powers of a profoundly undemocratic system. Predictably, *Time* hoped to soften this recognition by describing Bernanke as "the most powerful nerd on the planet."[62] Bernanke received credit for holding more public meetings, writing more op-ed pieces, and testifying before Congress more frequently than his secretive predecessors, but of course actual decision-making remained just as tightly controlled as ever.

The dramatic financial meltdown of 2008–09 (one that is ongoing) was a predictable outcome of an out-of-control jungle capitalism, a system largely bereft of governmental regulations that was operating beyond real social and ethical constraints. It was a meltdown attributable to far more than a few renegades like Bernie Madoff. Wall Street machinations going back decades, part of a made feeding frenzy among captains of American banking, imploded while political elites simply watched from the sidelines; existing democratic or public controls were simply thrown to the wind. What Robert Scheer calls "The Great American Stickup" amounted to nothing more than a ruthless feeding frenzy on the part of a tiny group of millionaires who, through their reckless greed, push the system toward its greatest crisis since the 1930s.[63] The March 2008 Bear-Stearns collapse augured a series of financial crashes leading to massive bankruptcies, job losses, debt increases, and consumer paralysis with an enormous ripple effect across the domestic and global landscape. The havoc caused by speculative investment practices and banking schemes led to millions of home foreclosures, personal bankruptcies, and fiscal crises in state and local governments. Causes were traceable at least back to Reagan-era deregulations, tax cuts for the wealthy, huge increases in military spending, and a drastic shift from industry to finance, resulting in the shipping of millions of manufacturing jobs abroad. The ascendancy of casino-style capitalism, with its national and worldwide repercussions, thus had deep structural roots in the conservative, anti-Keynesian turn of the 1980s. The entire sordid process was elite-driven from the outset.

Economic reforms, even in the midst of a system-threatening crisis, have been astonishingly tepid. It was Obama's historic task to meet the challenge with political measures that could at least serve as short-term holding measures. As Obama's main lieutenants were Wall Street insiders (see above), efforts to address the underlying conditions of financial crisis were hardly likely to be forthcoming. Congress, moreover, was flooded with hundreds of well-paid lobbyists representing banking interests—and they fought desperately (and for the most part successfully) to block any measures designed to restrict the freedom of Wall Street operatives to continue along the business-as-usual path. With the Recovery Act and kindred reforms, Obama did manage to bring the financial sector—in fact the larger economy—back from the abyss, without which the system would surely have gone into a full-scale depression marked by far more drastic business failures, home foreclosures, job losses, and governmental collapses.

Massive federal bailouts (actually begun under Bush), a huge stimulus package, and infusion of cash into a declining auto industry staved off further crisis. Later, in 2010, Obama pushed through somewhat more ambitious reforms, placing limits on speculative investments, putting restrictions on sleazy credit card lending practices, and creating the Consumer Financial Protection Bureau (mentioned above) that would protect individuals from the worst excesses of the banking industry. Although touted by some as the most sweeping overhaul of financial regulations since the New Deal (and by others as a dangerous move toward "socialism"), these reforms stopped well short of reigning in high-risk trading or scaling back the power of Too-Big-to-Fail banking giants. The powerful Wall Street lobbies were able to subvert far-reaching reform of a banking system that remained on the verge of yet another economic meltdown, all the more probable given the surge in antiregulatory sentiment within the economic and political establishments as well as supposedly outsider insurgencies like the Tea Party movement. Strong Republican gains in the 2010 midterm elections, including a swing of 60 seats in the House, emboldened new lobby efforts to subvert the Democratic legislation. Groups representing Citibank, Goldman Sachs, Morgan Stanley, and JPMorganChase began mobilizing in earnest, dedicated to weaken any measure that might interfere with standard (i.e., risky) Wall Street business. Regulators were under intense pressure from hundreds of banking interest groups pressing their demands without letup, hoping to get the reforms either loosely interpreted or weakly enforced—including those protecting consumers from the worst excesses of lending practices—all the while depicting new regulations as a first step toward draconian socialism.

The dramatic growth of financial wealth and power in the United States, along with the perpetual inequities and crises it generates, has placed in stark relief the great conflict between capitalism and democracy, between "private" interests and public welfare. Increasing concentration of elite power has followed deregulation, reckless investment practices, recurrent bailouts, scandalous lobby operations, and a media all-too-willing to ignore or finesse the true excesses of the financial colossus. While Congress, the White House, the Fed, and media continue to proclaim fealty to "main street," their overwhelming allegiance remains with the Wall Street giants whose interests stand directly opposed to those of ordinary citizens facing job losses, home foreclosures, dwindling savings, crumbling social programs, and a threatening future.

The Authoritarian Workplace

The system of production and labor relations under modern capitalism is uniformly excluded from normative assessments of democracy, even among progressives and leftists, although the workplace has always been central to the lives of most Americans. This is unfortunate, since the workplace has historically been subjected to the penetrating economic, political, and social control of capital, which engulfs so much of human life even for those who never work directly for corporations. The trajectory of state-capitalism moves along well-established lines, despite variations in methods, always seeking to maximize profits, maintain labor discipline, and downsize the workforce while resisting labor autonomy in its myriad forms. The labor process under corporate-state domination is built around a rather fixed division of labor, whether in factories, offices, governmental work, the fast-food industry, or military. In each arena the capitalist aim is to dominate the labor process from the commanding heights, through a combination of methods: state power, material inducements, technological restructuring, bureaucratic controls, and ideological appeals. Where one mechanism of control fails, others can be intensified to manage or avert crisis. For many decades in the United States, this complex system of authoritarian controls worked admirably, reproducing a state-capitalist apparatus that depends on widespread loyalty and obedience, probably nowhere more than at the workplace. In the United States, surely more than any other advanced industrial society, labor has been fully integrated into the prevailing institutions and values, that is, made part of the larger capitalist system of production and consumption.

Historically it was Taylorism ("scientific management"), the genius of Henry Ford and his managers at the turn of the twentieth century, that introduced ways of reducing the labor process to mindless, repetitive operations only those in charge could grasp and coordinate. Later called "Fordism," this method emerged as the guiding model of capitalist industry geared to huge markets, mass production, and the fabled "mass worker" whose activity was to be thoroughly deskilled, robbed of creativity and autonomy. In his *Prison Notebooks*, Antonio Gramsci referred to this process, which by the 1930s was spreading across the globe, as "Americanism" because of its unique success in a country where feudal obstacles never existed to impede capitalist rationalization that was, even then, beginning to pervade the entire society. For Gramsci, this form of capitalism signaled not only an extreme regulation of factory life but the commodification of society—something Marx had foreseen, though he obviously could not yet have grasped its full social totality. "Americanism" had thus essentially become a way of life. This "corporate phase" of industrialization meant the rise of a "new type of worker" to fit expanding requirements of fully rationalized production, not only in auto manufacturing but across the economy.[64] The goal of corporate managers, not always fully realized, was synchronization of the labor process in a way that would regulate and limit class conflict. Whatever the political claims of the ruling elite, democracy clearly had no place in the American system of production, above all labor relations. Elections, collective decision-making, basic rights, freedom of assembly—none of these venerated ideals was to enter the capitalist workplace.

The postwar solidification of corporate power carried forward elements of an authoritarian workplace—managerial controls, bureaucratic routine, fragmentation of the labor force, ideological manipulation, and social discipline augmented by material stresses and anxieties. Key sectors of the economy (notably manufacturing), the Fordist agenda has been strengthened owing to globalization, oligopolistic markets, enhanced bureaucratic power, technological restructuring, and expansion of a media culture that celebrates pro-business attitudes. At the same time, countervailing forces have developed, including trade unions and labor reforms, rising social mobility, economic diversification, and demand for skilled labor. Many counterweights are products of the "new economy," or post-Fordism, in which class and power relations are said to be profoundly altered. Crucial here is the sharp decline in manufacturing—the main historical site of Taylorism—combined with expanding government, technical, and service employment. Conditions for full extension of Taylorism in the modern setting would therefore seem to be negated. But other trends at work in the American economy, such as declining union membership, consolidation of corporate power, and "McDonalidzation" of low-wage work, have conspired to extend rigidly hierarchical and exploitative labor relations into the new historical context. The onset of severe economic downturns only exacerbates these trends.

In *Contested Terrain* (1979), Richard Edwards stressed the great capacity of both technological and bureaucratic forms of control to reproduce Taylorized norms, rules, and procedures in advanced capitalism.[65] This was true not only for traditional sectors like autos and steel but also for electronics, technology, and even much government work, not to mention the emergent fast-food industry. While the new reality departed noticeably from Henry Ford's older and more rigid Taylorism, it did carry forward elements of an authoritarian regime that now revolved around *bureaucratic* mechanisms of control and regulation.[66] In the case of such important corporations as General Motors, IBM, General Electric, and IT&T, hierarchical relations had become institutionalized as "...bureaucratic control constituted the most important change wrought by the modern corporation in the labor process."[67] Beyond Taylorism, however, bureaucratic rule transformed power into something more opaque, impersonal, and out-of-reach. Edwards writes: "Above all else, bureaucratic control institutionalizes the exercise of corporate power, making power appear to emanate from the formal organization itself."[68] A goal of early Taylorism was to submerge the worker's very being into the rhythm and flow of the corporate structure—and in fact this appears to be a signal achievement of modern capitalism. Insofar as this is true, the implications are indeed frightening. As Edwards notes, "Bureaucratic control tends to be a much more totalitarian system—totalitarian in the sense of involving the total behavior of the worker. In bureaucratic control, workers owe not only a hard day's work to the corporation but also their demeanor and affections."[69] In contrast to original Fordism, moreover, the modern rationalized system has much greater social and ideological as well as bureaucratic tools at its disposal. Today, with economic diversification, such corporate domination extends to no more than one-third of the American workforce though it surely influences the entire field of labor relations.

What, then, of post-Fordist notions that a new system of production has fundamentally transformed labor relations, signaling a more open, participatory, creative workplace? Could "re-skilling," flexibility, and loosened managerial controls mean space for democratization? While the American workforce overall has indeed become more educated, skilled, and technically savvy, little evidence supports the claim of a radical break with past authoritarianism; though recast in many ways, corporate management is still able to integrate and control labor with many tools at its disposal. The post-Fordist case, in my opinion, has been vastly exaggerated.[70] Thus the advent of computers is often seen as viewed as emancipatory post-Fordism, but in fact the production apparatus can rely on informational technology to more effectively carefully monitor, supervise, coordinate, and manage the workforce. Power relations within the corporate economy remain little changed as much skilled, "creative" work remains subject to managerial domination and bureaucratic routinization, not to mention social and ideological influences designed to enforce conformity and loyalty. Post-Fordist arguments overlook the extent to which changes in production and management, including new technology, can be readily integrated into the wider division of labor.[71] It further overstates the claim that the era of mass markets and mass production has come to an end. As for "democratization," there is simply no evidence to indicate greater worker participation in vital institutional decisions—even where elements of autonomy and flexibility have appeared. Theories pointing toward such change are driven mainly by wishful speculation.

A further problem with the post-Fordist thesis, though rarely discussed, is the rapid growth of low-wage employment in such areas as retail trade, the fast-food industry, and services vulnerable to harsh forms of bureaucratic control directly in line with earlier Fordist schemes. As the world's largest corporation, Wal-mart, for example, has transformed its massive low-wage army of laborers into something only slightly better than a third-world sweatshop. A huge retailer, the Wal-mart empire operates nearly 4000 mega-stores in nine countries, with a workforce of 1.2 million in the United States that is largely impoverished, weak, without leverage, and nonunionized. Pressures against organizing at Wal-Mart are intense, with even glimpses of disloyalty bringing intimidation and, more often, swift reprisals including job termination. Wal-Mart managers expect total employee immersion in the company, which is why workers (called "associates") face a constant barrage of propaganda behind corporate patriotism and teamwork. Workers must deal with ongoing surveillance and monitoring, which means they are limited in their freedom of movement. Because union power at Wal-Mart is negligible, so too are benefits such as health care and vacation time. According to Robert Greenwald's documentary *Wal-Mart: the High Cost of Low Prices* (2006), corporate managers frequently mislead workers with false promises of pay raises, job promotions, and extra benefits to induce commitment. Barbara Ehrenreich, who worked at Wal-Mart for several months in connection with her book *Nickle and Dimed* (2001), reports that store bosses were continuously monitoring people for "time theft," warning employees about the perils of talking to fellow workers or otherwise wasting time.[72] The famous "Wal-Mart Cheer" was required at frequent meetings. This insular, Orwellian corporate culture surely fits the spirit if not the exact content of previous Taylorized labor relations.

This system of harsh labor controls extends well beyond the shopping empires to a vast production, distribution, and warehousing network that provides millions of Americans daily with cheap goods. In the case of Wal-Mart, there is a vast network of sweatshops the company operates in China, where poverty wages and grinding conditions are the norm. Inside the United States, sprawling distribution centers hire tens of thousands of workers at roughly minimum wage, mostly temporary Latino immigrants, to rapidly process goods imported from Asia. Huge warehouses owned by commercial realtors transfer products to such retail outlets as Wal-Mart, Target, and Home-Depot under the most strenuous conditions, including lack of heat or air conditioning. Temporary workers earn barely over $20,000 yearly, while union representation is nowhere to be found, allowing management essentially free reign.[73]

The fast-food industry, from factory farms through slaughterhouses and outlets, hires tens of millions of superexploited workers within a system that borrows heavily from Taylorism. The leading symbol of this sector, McDonalds alone employs more than 1 million people at 30,000 franchises worldwide, mostly located in the United States. Exuding boundless faith in workplace technology, McDonalds—like other fast-food venues—stands at the forefront of bureaucratic routinization. Enabling its management to control an unskilled labor force, rationalize production, and industrialize the modern kitchen. Workers, mostly drawn from minority groups, receive low pay, have few hopes of upward mobility, get little in the way of benefits, and have scant control over labor conditions. As in the case of Wal-Mart, McDonalds and other kindred businesses fiercely resist unionization, usually with success. Despite its horrendous impact on the economy, health, environment, and agriculture, the fast-food sector benefits generously from the public treasury. As Eric Schlosser notes, "While publicly espousing support for the free market, the fast food chains have quietly pursued and greatly benefitted from a wide variety of government subsidies."[74] The huge slaughterhouses that process meat for these chains are today among the most dangerous and exploitative workplaces in America, with an injury rate (roughly 45,000 a year) three times higher than the factory norm.[75] At slaughterhouse giants like ConAgra, IBP, and Excel, a largely migrant industrial workforce is exposed to nightmares of the killing floor, constant production speedups, close surveillance, and extreme dangers to mind and body, with little recourse to federal regulations and even less assistance from unions. Visiting the sprawling ConAgra complex in Greely, Colorado, Schlosser observed a low-paid, deskilled, power-less labor force not far removed from what Upton Sinclair described in *The Jungle* (1906). Similar plants, often located in small company towns, are spread across Colorado, Texas, Kansas, Iowa, Nebraska, and other states. Reports indicate that employee abuse, pollution, crime, and drugs are rampant. With only limited union presence and lax enforcement of regulations, managers have nearly total power to hire, schedule, discipline, and fire workers.[76]

Analyzing the fast-food model, George Ritzer shows how "McDonaldization" carries forward established Fordist procedures into the new environment. Workers at McDonalds and other chains are subjected to a matrix of routinized norms, rules, and expectations shaping restaurant operations from one locale to another, designed to ensure uniformity, speed, and predictable results. The outcome is a totally managed system in which "efficiency, predictability, calcula-bility, and control through nonhuman technology can be thought of as the basic components of a rational system"—exactly what Henry Ford might have anticipated many decades earlier.[77] The founders and designers of McDonalds, like chieftains of the auto industry, under-stood clearly how strict bureaucratic methods—when combined with the capitalist whip—could be used to maximize control. Ideally, people would come to resemble human robots, incapable of critical thought or rebellious impulses, within a seamless web of rational structures. Workers thus trapped would be unlikely to press for better wages, benefits, and labor conditions—and in any event would have no leverage to do so. Unskilled work lends itself to McDonaldization, which to varying degrees has extended to such chains as Blockbuster, FedexKinkos, Starbucks, and Target as well as Wal-Mart. The very idea of McJobs has come to symbolize highly ritualized and often scripted labor devoid of autonomy and creativity. If there is such a thing as "post-Fordism" in the modern capitalist world, it is far more limited than commonly believed, and of course has little relevance to this mammoth sector of the economy. Democracy? Hardly anyone is so crazy as to even harbor such pretenses.

While the MacDonalds pattern is surely extreme, it fits the general corporate strategy of a workplace emptied of individual (and collec-tive) subjectivity, a commodified and programmed employee posing no threat to the established modus operandi. Where possible, owners and managers would be happy to transform workers into unthink-ing automatons, a prospect less likely to be realized outside of retail and service operations. Unions, of course, can set limits to such authoritarian controls, but the vast majority of American workers (87 percent) belong to no unions. The main point here is that corporations have long strived to mold employees into unthinking receptacles of corporate agendas, where the entire personality is shaped by, and revolves around, preset interests and goals, along lines of the famous "team concept" of Japanese industry that is fashionable among neoliberal academics. We have already seen how Wal-Mart, with its ritual meetings, symbolic interactions, surveillance, and discipline, seeks to integrate the whole worker into the store's modus operandi. The concept of McJobs implies this same commitment to the fully socialized (and administered) worker.

Other such examples abound. Thus the Disney Corporation, proprietor of the "Happiest Place on Earth" (Disneyland), is well-known for its updated Fordism as thousands of employees there have been expected to conform to rigid standards, rules, and procedures. A beacon of the media-entertainment culture, Disney strives for the ultimate corporate milieu, replete with a mania for routinization and control. Though the Disney regimen has weakened is recent years, it has long been a bastion of military-style norms: no facial hair or long hair for men, no short skirts for women, no demeanor considered even mildly noncomformist or "trouble-making," and no offbeat dress or behavior. In what John Van Maanen calls "the smile factory," employees are forced to maintain an upbeat, all-American exterior, including an ever-ready smile that suggests a conventional lifestyle.[78] As at Wal-Mart, supervisors and surveillance cameras are positioned everywhere—many in hidden places—in the perpetual search for "jerks," "weirdos," and "trouble-makers."[79] Habits related to drugs, alcohol, and sex are closely monitored. To enforce the "Disney Way," the corporation emphasizes socialization into loyalty over skills and knowledge, all laid out in a detailed manual consistent with the fast-food model.

Government work, though usually more flexible even at the middle and lower levels, is hardly immune from such Orwellian tendencies. As might be expected, the U.S. military—with more than 2 million armed-services and civilian personnel—sustains, virtually by definition, a strictly authoritarian workplace. This is naturally the standard military formula, likely to change little even with demand for a highly skilled labor force. For the armed forces, moreover, total submersion into the apparatus takes on added ideological, or patriotic, dimensions as the ruling military stratum insists upon absolute loyalty and dedication to explicitly national goals. Further, no counterweights in the form of union or consumer power exist in the military. Mary

Wertsch observes that individuality and freedom are devalued in the armed services, as "the masks worn there are authoritarian masks, each exactly like the others of its rank, each subservient to those of higher rungs. The notions of conformity, order, and obedience reign supreme."[80] Within "the fortress," therefore, success depends on traits of an authoritarian personality: conventional behavior, submission to authority, patriarchal attitudes, stress on discipline and order, rejection of everything that is spontaneous and different.[81] Wertsch emphasizes what is generally known, that "control is the very heart and soul of the military, the very essence of its mission in peace or in war."[82] As both Wertsch and Catherine Lutz further point out, such authoritarian culture readily extends into the families and communities surrounding military bases.[83] What is true of military life surely holds for kindred workplaces across the American landscape: prisons, law enforcement, intelligence, and similar government work.

As mentioned, however, post-Fordist is far from an unvarnished myth: the diversified American economy has permitted, even encouraged, moves toward some independence and creativity, notably in highly skilled technology sectors like those in Silicon Valley. After all, the sharp decline in manufacturing has meant shrinking factory labor at a time when government and professional work is steadily expanding. And if McDonaldization extends to as much as one-third of the work force, it is still far from universal nor could be in a complex modern economy. The newer areas—sometimes referred to as the "professional-managerial class"—are marked by *relative* openness, freer participation, and stronger leverage over pay, benefits, and working conditions; they are minimally democratized. While government employment, for its part, develops along more classically bureaucratic lines, favorable institutional rules and social norms limit the degree of routinization associated with Taylorism. Many fields of public work, moreover, including education, health care, and social services, are unionized, further empowering labor to secure improved wages and working conditions. Also loosening corporate (and government) Fordist agendas have been a series of legislative reforms since the 1930s: National Labor Relations Board statutes, various state and municipal laws, and such federal initiatives as OSHA and EPA. These realities are not sufficient to sustain claims of full-scale post-Fordist democratization, but they do suggest limits to rigid authoritarian controls for significant *parts* of the American workforce.

It should be mentioned that corporations and their managers stand resolutely opposed to even modest trends toward worker empowerment; their hope would be for a return to the heyday of Fordism in which "deregulation" that strips workers of even minimal participation. The prevailing right-wing vision is for a low-wage, nonunionized workforce totally at the mercy of management. In *The Wrecking Crew,* Frank mentions exactly such a free-market utopia upheld by the modern-day "wingers" looking for a return to the good old days of Darwinian capitalism—the Pacific island Saipan under U.S. control. For decades, corporations in Saipan have been importing tens of thousands of low-wage "guest workers" for garment and service industries operating lawlessly outside any regimen of labor codes and human rights. Under this corporate gulag, championed by the right wing as a bastion of free markets and democracy, businesses have been able to invest, manage, and control labor as they choose, with no fear of government "intervention."[84] While local corporations receive generous public subsidies and tax breaks, management proceeds as it pleases in a setting where the labor movement is viewed as a "disease to be wiped out."[85] Frank reports that the infamous lobbyist Jack Abramoff was among the "wingers" who struggled indefatigably to keep Saipan as a modern "free-enterprise" zone to be emulated across the world. Scandal-ridden Tom DeLay joined Abramoff in rising to the defense of "an entire commonwealth organized as a corporate labor camp...".[86] For these advocates, more representative of the corporate establishment than might generally be recognized, Saipan as an island paradise of "freedom" points toward an ideal future model. And there are plenty of trends at work in American society itself to suggest that such a nightmarish scenario—close to being realized in many sectors—should not be fully dismissed from view.

The Corporate University

At first glance, the sphere of higher education would seem to be an oasis of freedom, critical thought, and democracy in a society otherwise dominated by elite power, especially when compared with the media, corporate workplace, the military, and the fast-food industry. After all, Western culture has long cherished traditions of public education, university autonomy, and academic freedom that, in theory at least, insulates academic work from the vagaries of government and corporate influence. And these traditions have by no means vanished in the United States, where university life still possesses a vigorous intellectual and cultural energy combined with strong commitment to independence and tolerance. The liberal ethos of diversity and freedom clearly retains a hold throughout the modern academy, where student and faculty intellectual ferment has become an indelible part of the academy. But that hold is increasingly tenuous at a time when American colleges and universities have forged tightening relationships with corporate, government, and military interests, jeopardizing space for critical thought and political opposition.

The idea that the modern university has evolved into a repository of dominant interests and values conflicts starkly with this fading, if still relevant, liberal ethos. Indeed, at a time when Mills' power elite has consolidated its hold over American public life, it would be hard to imagine the academy as anything less than a microcosm of the larger society. While university-based intellectual culture thrives in time-honored obeisance to academic freedom and scholarly objectivity, irrepressible forces move in opposite directions: corporate influence, bureaucratic controls, social hierarchy, technocratic professionalism, scholarly research benefitting the wealthy and powerful. Genuine intellectual dissent is all-too-often feared, opposed, resisted, and even repressed in a milieu where disciplinary (and political) norms are routinely enforced. While American universities actually have a long history of institutional repression, with extreme periods of academic McCarthyism directed against leftists and other dissenters, the period since the 1970s has seen a much greater emphasis on repressive tolerance with critical views and approaches tolerated, even encouraged, across multiple disciplines—sociology, urban planning, ethnic studies, women's studies, film studies—as part of a professional framework that detaches such views and approaches from politics. Today the modern university has emerged as a site of the "knowledge industry" tied to commercial and technocratic forces that subordinate education to corporate, government, and military priorities.

What is often forgotten is that American universities are subjected to the same process of corporate colonization as the political system. Chapter 5 explores the key role of Rockefeller interests in establishing American medical schools more than a century ago. Mills, as we have seen, analyzed elite penetration of American public life in the years after World War II. It was not until University of California president Clark Kerr's famous embrace of the "multiversity" in 1964 that corporatized higher education would receive its first systematic imprimatur, infused with celebration of an embryonic knowledge industry.[87] What distinguished the contemporary university, according to Kerr, was its convergence with dominant interests in the "surrounding society," its capacity to serve those interests through its intellectual resources, and its dedication to the national priorities of industrial growth and global security. Going beyond traditional notions of academic insularity and intellectual autonomy, the renovated university was destined to "merge its activities with industry as never before," laying the groundwork for a truly American system of higher education. For the first time we are faced with prospects of a corporate academy: as "the university and segments of industry are becoming more alike,"[88] the professor becomes more than anything an entrepreneur happy to dispense knowledge and expertise to the ruling interests. If the university had ever fancied its mission as one of education for citizenship and enlightenment, it would now be a "citadel of training" for banking, manufacturing, agriculture, technology, and of course the military—a relationship accruing to the benefit of all parties.

Kerr's seminal vision of the multiversity turned out to be more prescient than probably even he imagined at the dawn of 1960s campus rebellions. The Berkeley "Free Speech Movement," of course, was a direct revolt against the impersonal, bureaucratic, and instrumental knowledge factory, opposing with its fury the idea of a corporate academy. While the new left was able to carve out some participatory space within the emergent multiversity, across succeeding decades Kerr's agenda has prevailed with a vengeance. Many American universities became sprawling educational centers integrated through bureaucratic power and driven by corporate, government, and military infusions of money. (Since the 1950s the military alone has accounted for 83 percent of all R&D funding.) Faculty and students assumed a fixed place in the vast hierarchy of roles, interests, agendas, and expectations. Nowhere has this been truer, in fact, than at Kerr's old University of California system governed by a 26-member Board of Regents drawn overwhelmingly from the ranks of big business. With 220,000 students and thousands of faculty spread across ten campuses, this small ruling stratum makes virtually all important decisions dealing with structure, basic policies, finances, and investment, essentially insulated from public opinion and accountable to no faculty, student, or employee body. No less than 18 regents are given 12-year appointments by the governor, the others mostly ex-officio. Aside from one faculty and one student delegate—who have no formal decision-making voice—regents typically have little if any academic background. In other words, the main stakeholders in university life are largely bereft of power, reduced to impotent protest in the face of such unpopular decisions as reversal of affirmative action, fee hikes, and employee cutbacks.

As with other major universities, moreover, the University of California Board of Regents is the sole legally sanctioned body: everything is carried out in its name, all legal procedures are initiated (or defended) in its name. The Regents operate their far-flung empire according to a high-tech business model, without hesitation or apology, wheeling and dealing with corporate, federal, and military partners as it pleases. It turns out to be the perfect fulfillment of Kerr's vision. Close scrutiny of other major universities reveals similar power arrangements, with business interests predictably dominant. At Princeton, for example, the 26-member Board of Trustees is comprised of 20 corporate representatives from such firms as Google and McDonnell-Douglas. Washington University in St. Louis is governed by a 54-person Board of Trustees, 48 of whom are drawn from such businesses as Monsanto, AT&T, Bank of America, and McDonnell-Douglas. These boards are self-perpetuating, insulated from the interests of university stakeholders—faculty, students, staff, and impacted community groups. Since the 1970s these governing bodies have presided over the steady corporatization of American higher education, nowadays a technocratic system with few pretenses of democratic governance.

Of course university life has all the *appearances* of a thriving intellectual community, and indeed social and political freedoms are far more extensive than what exists, for example, in the fast-food industry and most government work. Crucial elements of academic freedom have not entirely vanished. Students in particular will find something of a libertine atmosphere, especially at elite institutions throughout the Ivy League and elsewhere. But appearances can be misleading: the educational system, despite undeniable open spaces, is basically authoritarian when it comes to the larger concerns. Thus, while faculty governance finds expression in academic senates and related bodies, decision-making is confined to strictly professional matters, excluding issues concerning university operations, management, fiscal policy, and community relations. Likewise, unions exist to protect faculty interests—for example, the American Association of University Professors and various state unions—but these too are confined to professional issues like faculty tenure. None of these academic bodies has sufficient power to determine overall institutional governance, which is the domain of the board of trustees often in collaboration with state legislatures. Academic freedom survives, but usually within prescribed intellectual and political boundaries that limit what is considered acceptable teaching, research, and writing. In the end, academic constraints on democratic involvement can be measured along several dimensions: (1) the all-powerful role of the board of trustees; (2) institutionalized bureaucracies; (3) external influence of corporate, government, and military interests; (4) the growing importance of foundations and think tanks; (5) outright academic repression of dissident thought; and (6) what might be called "repressive tolerance" as a major legitimating strategy of professions and institutions. The crucial power of university ruling bodies has been elaborated above.

Kerr observed that a major challenge for modern university presidents was to manage a collection of bureaucracies involving huge research programs and centers across many disciplines. In this setting administration was destined to grow more complex in a world of highly specialized knowledge that required constant oversight and coordination. Without doubt the academy today is governed by swollen bureaucracies in which well-paid executives, managers, business leaders, and fundraisers predominate, contributing at best marginally to scholarship, research, and classroom teaching. As campuses are increasingly penetrated by corporate interests, the bureaucratic culture shifts accordingly to reflect the privileged role of business, science, engineering, and medical programs that can win outside funding. Research centers, academic institutes, scientific laboratories, and think tanks all garner lavish contracts to serve external agendas having only a peripheral relationship to student needs. One such example is the right-wing Hoover Institute at Stanford, recipient of billions of dollars mainly from large businesses and wealthy donors and responsible only to its Board of Trustees rather than faculty, students, or the general community.[89] With connections to such conservative think tanks as AEI, Hoover by the 1990s had more than 100 fellows along with 71 visiting scholars and an endowment of $125 million. A vast forum of research, conferences, workshops, and scholarly publications, its political focus has centered on corporate deregulation, reduced government, an aggressive foreign policy, heightened Pentagon spending, and related subsidiary concerns. Other right-wing think tanks, driven by similar priorities, include the Cato, Hudson, Brookings, Heritage, and Manhattan institutes—all theoretically "nonpartisan" but really conservative advocacy centers that help shape academic work across the country. Their funding comes from such corporations as Raytheon, Bank of America, Monsanto, and AT&T, wealthy patrons like Rupert Murdoch, and foundations like Coors, Olin, Bradley, Scaife, and Ford. Professors who cultivate ties to such benefactors are likely to be more successful in getting promotions, research assistance, awards, status, and sabbaticals. The result is a precipitous downward trend in social research, teaching, and stakeholder empowerment.[90]

At University of California at Berkeley, corporate sponsorship of grants, gifts, and projects increased by 35 percent in 2009, rising to $95 million (excluding military contracts) and financed by such interests as Microsoft, Angen, and British Petroleum. In 2007 the Berkeley campus secured a half-billion dollar arrangement with BP to set up the Energy Bioscience Institute for investigating such alternative energy sources as biofuels. The deal, bringing more than 50 BP researchers to campus and provoking a series of student protests, was made backdoor with only a few administrators involved, short-circuiting any faculty or student input.

University of California at Berkeley, moreover, has long operated the bulk of the U.S. nuclear establishment, including the iconic Lawrence Livermore National Laboratory—main center for nuclear research and development since 1952—with a current (2010) $1.5 billion annual budget and 7000 employees. University of California (UC) runs dozens of projects there with Department of Energy funding in partnership with such corporations as Bechtel, Babcock and Wilcox, and URS. Across the postwar years Livermore scientists and technicians, drawn from a wide variety of academic disciplines, designed the Polaris, Minuteman, Poseidon, Lance, and Spartan missiles, among others. In the early 1990s the Lab began the Stockpile Stewardship Program (SSP) to modernize nuclear weapons capabilities without access to a testing regimen that was discontinued in 1992. Today, at a time when the United States is threatening Iran and other countries over nuclear proliferation, Livermore (and kindred labs at Los Alamos and Sandia) is busy with its huge team of academic researchers exploring the properties of highly enriched uranium, as part of missile-defense projects that started with Reagan's "Star Wars" program in 1983. Among its many (largely secret) military-related activities, the UC/Livermore complex has researched powerful laser systems for use in outer space. The lab's board of governors, unaccountable to the university community, makes R&D decisions in partnership with the federal government and numerous military contractors. In 2010 the chair of the board was Norman Pattiz, CEO of Westwood One radio network; the Vice-Chair was J. Scott Ogilvie, president of Bechtel Systems.

Helen Caldicott comments insightfully about the mystical power that nuclear scientists and technicians—usually employed by major universities—have achieved in American society since the days of the Manhattan Project. Not surprisingly, the academic experts who over many decades have directed production of some 70,000 nuclear weapons have been able to create their own insular subculture and language far removed from the mundane realm of university and political life. Their arrogance stems from a mixture of intellectual chauvinism, institutional power, elevated status, and patriotic attitudes amounting to something of a "scientific bomb cult" where, as at Livermore, the world is framed by techno-strategic discourse.[91] In such a world, nuclear weapons end up detached from their potentially horrific consequences, transformed by the physicists, chemists, astronomers, engineers, and computer programmers into objects of veneration, joy, and progress. Needless to say, operational secrecy and esoteric language inform the institutional code of this scientific order, which of course only adds to its mystique. Meanwhile, as U.S. military power expands the vigorous Pentagon R&D agenda simultaneously expands, in the process deeply influencing academic culture at such leading institutions as the University of California, MIT, Harvard, Stanford, and Cal Tech. It might be argued that a qualitative change in the very character and purpose of the physical sciences results from this convergence of Pentagon, corporate, and university interests.

In this setting the very notions of academic freedom and democratic governance wind up reduced to comforting shibboleths. In practice the limits to higher-education discourse take three major forms: outright repression, technological rationality, and "repressive tolerance"—all of them manifestly depoliticizing. Academic discrimination in faculty appointments, promotions, tenure, and awards has long been a reality of American university life, explored many decades ago by Upton Sinclair and others.[92] This state of affairs has recently worsened as the academy is increasingly dependent on external funding at a time the political climate has shifted emphatically rightward. A generation of radical scholars nurtured in 1960s politics and culture faces new obstacles following 9/11 and the ascendancy of Bush and Cheney to the White House. Radical teaching and research in the academy had throughout the twentieth century often exceeded the limits of tolerable discourse, as Marxists, Communists, anarchists, and myriad other dissenters were often driven from university positions—and not just periods such as the 1920s Red Scares and 1950s

McCarthyism. Guardians of academic orthodoxy closely monitored every profession and discipline, all the while claiming adherence to intellectual and political freedoms. Serious questioning of corporate power and U.S. foreign policy was scarcely tolerated, as the apparent openness and diversity of American higher education only concealed deeper authoritarian tendencies. As the academy evolved into something approximating Kerr's "multiversity," the rules and norms of scholarship stiffened and closed off genuine diversity in the absence of any overt McCarthyism. Scholarly work was forced into largely corporate-driven priorities, a narrowing paradigm within which tenure decisions, promotions, grants, awards, and academic status was to be determined. McCarthyite forces did reappear, symbolized in the 1990s and later by David Horowitz's Freedom Center intent on stamping out even moderate dissent as "Stalinist," "anti-Semitic," and "anti-American". During the Bush-Cheney reign right-wing monitors targeted hundreds of radical academic, hoping to intimidate if not destroy anyone deviating from mainstream ideology—though (as of 2010) with limited success.

Perhaps the worst arena of academic repression is the field of Middle Eastern studies, directed against intellectuals critical of Israel. The powerful Israel Lobby, in partnership with such think tanks as AEI and Heritage Foundation, seeks to stifle work related to the Israel-Palestinian conflict hoping to silence or at least marginalize critical scholarly output. Since the 1980s the main pro-Israel organization in the United States—AIPAC—has worked diligently to recruit and train college students to identify campus groups and professors hostile to Israel. Daniel Pipes established the website Campus Watch that publishes dossiers on suspect academics. Books, journals, speaking engagements, university courses, and conferences are closely monitored by this organization and other pro-Israel groups. Opponents are routinely attacked as "anti-Semitic" and fascistic. Pro-Palestinian scholars like the late Edward Said, Juan Cole, Noam Chomsky, and Rashid Khalidi have been investigated and hounded, occasionally even threatened. In the case of outspoken Israel critic Norman Finkelstein, rabid Zionist Alan Dershowitz sought to block publication of his book *Chutzpah* (2007) at the University of California Press, even appealing to the governor for censorship. When that failed, Dershowitz orchestrated a campaign to deny Finkelstein's tenure at DePaul University even after Finkelstein's department (political science) had voted unanimously for tenure.[93] By challenging Israeli policies, Finkelstein had clearly overstepped the bounds of "academic freedom" as understood in the realm of Middle Eastern studies discourses where ideological taboos prevail and McCarthyism remains alive and well.

On the whole, however, McCarthyism remains too heavy-handed to serve an institutional system that prefers more subtle ideological and social mechanisms of control. Within multiversity life the general parameters of discourse are well understood by administrators and faculty: corporate and technocratic values are so firmly embedded in the prevailing academic culture as to be fully taken-for-granted. As we have seen, Kerr's vision relied on prospects for intensified technical specialization linked to the knowledge industry, grounded in a merger of corporate, bureaucratic, and technological interests. David Noble has shown how technology and its rationalizing effects generate an instrumental ethos that takes the shape of narrow scholarly methodologies, fragmented curricula, shrinking political vistas, and such fashions as online teaching.[94] The high-tech mania, according to Noble, diminishes critical thinking, civic skills, and education for citizenship.[95] Technologized education is naturally a great bonanza for such corporations as IBM, Sony, Microsoft, Apple, and Hewlett-Packard, which triumphantly announce the dawning of a new age of learning that is both more efficient and accessible, which brings to mind Herbert Marcuse's prophesies in *One-Dimensional Man* (1964), where technological rationality gives rise to an administered society characterized by a "closed universe of thought."[96]

In many enclaves of academia, however, it is repressive tolerance that seems most appropriate to an understanding of how universities set and maintain discursive boundaries. Critical motifs, theories, and traditions have established a foothold in a wide variety of "softer" liberal-arts fields: urban planning, women's studies, the plethora of ethnic-studies programs, film and media studies, to name some. In many specialized areas, radical approaches—Marxism, neo-Marxism, feminism, ecology, cultural criticism—have gained legitimacy and in some cases even hegemony. Academic tolerance naturally has its limits, but intellectual openness has a certain logic, particularly at elite schools where these approaches are popular, much to the unhappiness of right-wing critics outside the academy. This critical scholarship, much of it falling under the rubric of postmodernism, poststructuralism, and identity concerns, generally falls short of calling into question basic class and power arrangements or connecting such work to the realm of political action. The language is so hyperspecialized, insular, and esoteric—accessible only to a small number of initiates—as to nullify significant political ramifications. Postmodern fashions commonly follow a mode of antipolitics, expressing contempt for organized struggles around state power, valorizing identity preoccupations over more distinctly political discourses. The vocabulary of this work, moreover, is often so abstruse and impenetrable as to negate any broader public intellectual function. Guardians of academic orthodoxy might actually see the legitimizing potential of radical scholarship to the extent it validates pretenses of academic freedom, intellectual tolerance, and political diversity. While some fields of study—economics, philosophy, international relations, etc.—recoil in horror at the thought of such diversity, others (like those mentioned above) are more hospitable in line with the ethos of repressive tolerance.

Returning to the University of California experience—arguably a bellwether of American higher education—it is easy to see how Kerr's "multiversity," viewed decades ago as a universal model of professional work, ultimately triumphed over the radical, participatory values identified with sixties activism. University of California at Berkeley, of course, was a major site of 1960s student and faculty efforts to reorient the university away from the corporate-bureaucratic model that Kerr set forth. A series of new-left insurgencies called into question the knowledge industry that, as Mario Savio so eloquently stated, was a repressive "machine" that trapped students and faculty within an authoritarian structure that regarded stakeholders as manipulable and exploitable objects. The 1960s revolt carried forward, most of all, the classic ideal of participatory democracy that meant education for citizenship rather than training for roles within a fixed, hierarchical system.[97] While the revolt temporarily opened up new social and political spaces, it was soon trampled by the inexorable force of the multiversity.

While corporate involvement in most important areas of university life has risen dramatically around the country, it has often come to be regarded as a routine feature of higher education, even at Berkeley. The new concordat between big business and campuses has typically been met by faculty and students with a sense of resignation, if not approval. At Berkeley, BP employees (16 total) operate their own commercial labs in the middle of campus, doing research that largely fits BP interests, entirely undisturbed—even after the oil giant's criminal malfeasance in the Gulf of Mexico and its generally horrendous impact on the global environment had become widely known. According to many University of California at Berkeley faculty members, the battle to maintain a semblance of academic independence seemed to have been lost in many areas of study—no doubt another legacy of Kerr's "multiversity." Meanwhile, the board of regents would continue to be an arena dominated by corporate interests: one leading regent was Richard C. Blum, billionaire husband of Senator Dianne Feinstein, whose San Francisco investment firm (CB Richard Ellis) owned $700 million in shares of two large for-profit educational corporations. Even as questions arose concerning Blum's approach to higher education and possible conflicts of interest, voices of university dissent were muted. The notion that corporate and university interests had thoroughly converged no longer seemed worthy of critical observation, much less protest.

But the stillness would soon be penetrated by renewed political activity: more than 40 years after the historic Free Speech Movement, not only the Berkeley campus but the entire University of California system became a renewed battleground as stakeholders challenged the board of regents, revisiting the old agenda of democratization. An organization called The Campaign for U.C. Democracy emerged, aiming through direct action and legislative initiatives to reform the board, making it accountable to the people of California as well as students, faculty, and employees within the university community. According to its literature, the campaign looked toward democratic governance in the face of mounting crises: an elitist board, weakened faculty governance, an aloof and bloated administration, skyrocketing student fees, and worsening labor relations. Campaign leaders argued that "current Board structures are hindering the U.C. system's ability to adapt to challenging times, threatening...access, excellence, and public service."[98] It added: "Only by reforming the Board will the public have effective means to defend public education." Foremost among the organization's complaints was nearly total absence of faculty, student, worker, and public representation on the board. This state of affairs reveals how popular struggles against the multiversity—against a corporate-bureaucratic model of university life—first launched in the 1960s, remain central to the politics of American higher education.

5

Medical Tyranny

One of the enduring myths of American society—alongside the familiar fairy-tales of a benevolent free market and democratic foreign policy—is that of an efficient, professional, state-of-the-art health care system. That is embraced to varying degrees across the political spectrum, as shown by the 2009 "debates" over President Obama's reform proposals—the key focus being whether legislators tinkering with the status quo were preparing the way for a "socialist" or "totalitarian" takeover. Even critics who assail the U.S. medical system for its failure to satisfy the health needs of tens of millions of citizens, its poor and expensive insurance for tens of millions others, its wasteful bureaucracies, its shortage of good doctors, and the exorbitant cost of drugs generally agree it is a world-class system with few if any rivals. The main problem, as framed within mainstream discourse is that the health care "delivery system," the apex of scientific and technological medicine, should be made more generally accessible. As research increasingly demonstrates, however, the actual health status of the world's richest nation confounds the established wisdom at every turn, a point graphically made by Michael Moore's 2007 film *Sicko* among other recent documentaries. The wonders of "free-market" or "private" medicine championed by a majority of politicians, economists, corporate elites, academics, and the popular media have failed the reality test for most Americans.

The Rockefeller Legacy

It takes no superior effort to show that medicine in the United States is not only corporate-dominated and profit-driven but institutionally incapable of delivering good care to a majority of citizens, while also lacking wide public access and accountability. Yet the system—high tech, modernized, and staffed at the top by well-trained professionals—might still be regarded as a beacon of success, flawed only in its limited scope of coverage. Sadly, however, all the indicators point to a system more bankrupt than questions of access alone might reveal: Americans spent roughly $2.6 trillion (more than $7,000 per capita) on health care in 2010 (projected to $4.4 trillion by 2018) while the United States, according to World Health Organization data, ranks 37th in the world on measures of overall health performance and 72nd in overall level of health, behind such countries as Portugal and Costa Rica. More than 16 percent of domestic product goes to health care expenditures—three times what is spent on average by other industrialized nations—as the system worsens with each passing year.[1] Viewing these statistics one might argue there exists something of an inverse relationship between resources spent on medicine and results obtained, at least for the United States. The ascending power of medical corporations—the pharmaceutical industry, insurance complexes, hospital networks, research institutions—helps explain not only the health care crisis but, crucial for the main thesis of this book, the rise of an authoritarian and relatively closed network of structures disenfranchises all but the few richest consumers.

Yet even this depressing picture scarcely tells the full story. Judging by any number of indicators—medical tests and reports, surveys, hospital visits, surgeries performed, drugs prescribed, and so forth—as of 2010Americans must be considered the sickest people on earth, their condition barely alleviated by vast reserves of money, technology, and human skills thrown into endless varieties of treatment. Obesity, linked to most health problems and once comparatively rare in the United States, now afflicts over 40 percent of the population, with at least 100 million people yearly testing for extremely high cholesterol. Obesity levels have nearly *tripled* over the past three decades, dramatically elevating the risk for diabetes, heart disease, cancer, and arthritis and defined in 2000 as the number one health problem in the country by the Surgeon General. More than 23 million people in the United States fit the category of morbidly obese—100 or more pounds above ideal body weight. In California alone obesity was projected in 2005 to cost $28 billion in health care expenses, injuries, days off, and lost productivity, leading Kim Belshe, state health and human services secretary, to proclaim it the source of both health and economic crisis.[2] According to a Duke University report, child obesity had risen 15 percent from 2000 to 2004 alone, bringing with it increases in type 2 diabetes, high blood pressure, and other disorders. In 2005 more than 140,000 Americans were scheduled to undergo expensive bariatric surgery to reduce weight.

Health measures across the board are equally depressing: in 2006 there were 60 million Americans with dangerously high blood pressure, 70 million with arthritis and other joint disorders, 25 million with liver disease, and 30 million sexually impotent, to mention some of the most obvious problems. Since the 1950s the death rate from cancer has grown significantly, reaching 470,000 in 2008 and nearly 600,000 in 2009—decades after President Richard Nixon's declared War on Cancer and despite recurrent media-celebrated discoveries of proclaimed remedies.[3] Disorders (physical and mental) are now an ordinary feature of American life, cutting across class, gender, ethnic, and age lines. Further, the medical structure itself is reportedly the cause of at least 260,000 deaths yearly resulting from a variety of mistakes, unnecessary surgeries and other treatments, hospital-generated diseases, and wrong or excessive drug prescriptions.

Not surprisingly, Americans have also become by far the most overmedicated population in the world, with over 200 million people consuming drugs for literally hundreds of medical and psychological problems, not including substances purchased over-the-counter and illegally. Drugs are prescribed in the United States at a rate unheard of at any other time or place, with domestic sales currently (2009) more than 300 billion annually.[4] The ten leading pharmaceutical companies amass greater profits than the remaining Fortune 500 corporations together, based on peak earnings of up to 30 percent of returns on sales (triple that of General Electric and nine times that of Wal-Mart). In the past three decades Congress has given Big Pharma virtual carte blanche to charge whatever the market will tolerate, justified by "free-enterprise" dogma that since the Reagan years has permeated both the health care industry as it has the larger society. Meanwhile, despite an avalanche of celebrated drug "therapies"—along with high-tech interventions, sophisticated testing procedures, high-priced surgeries, and well-trained biomedical professionals—most health indicators worsens with each passing year. The main improvements in the health status of Americans over the past century (in longevity, for example) derive less from enhanced medical treatment than from advances in the public infrastructure and hygiene.

In *Overdosed America,* John Abramson, a medical practitioner in the Boston area for more than 20 years, argues that the U.S. health care establishment has been corrupted by its very modernity, by a hypermedicated system fixated on symptoms over causes, technical fixes over durable solutions, while preferring isolated treatments that largely ignore *contextual* factors such as lifestyle, nutrition, family relations, and environment.[5] He views the system as emphatically iatrogenic (counterproductive and in many ways harmful) insofar as it usually does more harm than good—a thesis influenced by such writers as Ivan Illich (*Medical Nemesis*) and John Robbins (*The Food Revolution*).[6] For Abramson and other critics of the American medical system, the clearest indicator of iatrogenic morass is the drug industry, which now dominates the entire medical terrain.

From his own experience and reading of the medical literature, Abramson grew disillusioned with the scientific pretenses of American health care, writing: "What I found over...two and a half years of 'researching the research' is a scandal in medical science that is at least the equivalent of any of the recent corporate scandals that have shaken Americans' confidence in the integrity of the corporate and financial worlds."[7] This same motif is repeated in the work of Marcia Angell and David Bartlett/James Steele, who also explore the pernicious effects of a corporate juggernaut in which marketing, advertising, and lobbying prevail over the age-old tradition of healing, while the dictates of Wall Street and Madison Avenue take precedence over the needs of the ordinary consumer—an unhappy state of affairs when it comes to producing cars and shoes but positively criminal when it comes to health care.[8] While this development might seem dramatic, it has deep roots in an American history shaped by capitalist industrialization. The emergence of large-scale corporate medicine goes back to the well-known Rockefeller agenda set in motion at the end of the nineteenth century. Expanded and rationalized across each succeeding decade, this system was always fueled and legitimated by science and technology, ultimately transformed into a managerial ideology embraced by a plethora of elite groups: doctors, technicians, hospitals, insurance companies, drug industry, medical schools, and government bureaucrats, all motivated by profits and power over all other concerns. As Richard Brown in his study of "Rockefeller Medicine Men" observes, this achieved its own institutionalized reality that was mostly out of reach of patients, consumers, citizens, and even many professionals, serving primarily class interests.[9]

Under the aegis of Rockefeller, American medicine was consciously linked to forces of industrialization that gained strength across the twentieth century—part of an epic "transformation of institutions."[10] Business and government elites converged around a "union of corporations, philanthropy, the managerial-political stratum, the universities and science spawned by the Rockefeller Medicine Men and their new system of medicine."[11] This broadening empire was socially and politically integrated on a foundation of immense financial, technological, and human resources. It soon evolved into an ideological and institutional force equivalent to a secular religion—one way of understanding the 2009 citizen outbursts against Obama's plan to reform this entrenched network of practices, beliefs, and myths. These outbursts were the product of an ideological mentality unable to grasp the growing dysfunctions of a medical system known globally as excessively costly, inefficient, bureaucratic, political insulated, and cut off from health care alternatives.

The Rise of Big Pharma

The United States is today the most voracious and obsessive drug-consuming nation ever, not only of "illicit" substances but of legal, medically endorsed products found in nearly every home. Pharmaceutical consumption has sharply increased since the early 1980s, after the Bayh-Dole Act of 1984 gave the drug industry freer reign to maneuver, largely outside the realm of public scrutiny and democratic accountability. By 2003 doctors were prescribing 146 medications for every 100 office visits, mostly for such familiar conditions as depression, anxiety, sleeplessness, pain, sexual dysfunction, high blood pressure, excessive cholesterol, and arthritis. As drug sales reached new heights, an average one-year supply cost nearly $2,000. Doctors, pharmacists, therapists, hospitals, health maintenance organizations (HMOs), insurance companies, and government programs like Medicare felt the power of Big Pharma, legally empowered to advertise its goods everywhere—in newspapers and magazines, TV, the Internet, mailings, medical journals—promising the wonders of chemistry for achieving happiness, longevity, physical vigor, mental acuity, good relationships, and sexual vitality. While Big Pharma trades on popular fears of psychological insecurity, depression, and inadequacy, the corporate media—scarcely adverse to such tropes— grows ever-dependent on pharmaceutical advertising revenue that has reached several billion dollars annually.

As Big Pharma superprofits continued to roll in, however, evidence showed that remedies sold by the drug giants more often than not fail to deliver what they promise. Benefits are routinely exaggerated and adverse reactions ignored or downplayed, not only within advertising but, more disturbingly, within the purportedly scientific world of biomedical research. Critics such as Abramson and Angell point out that prescriptions are typically written for conditions stemming from underlying factors that pills can rarely by themselves remedy. Short-term medication for such needs as immediate pain relief or treatment of depression has legitimate rationale, but the astounding fact is that more than 90 percent of drugs are prescribed long-term, often in potentially harmful or even lethal combinations. Data showing adverse reactions (beyond limited "side effects") do not necessarily hurt sales because doctors and patients alike seem caught up in the mystique of what Big Pharma can deliver. Angell, professor at Harvard Medical School and former editor of the *New England Journal of Medicine,* argues that "...we have become an overmedicated society. Doctors have been taught only too well by the pharmaceutical industry, and what they have been taught is to reach for a prescription pad."[12] Under these circumstances health care consumers often feel cheated if they leave the doctor's office without prescription in hand.

The overriding goal of Big Pharma is to produce and sell "blockbusters"—drugs bringing at least $1 billion in revenue yearly. Specific consumer populations are targeted: arthritis patients looking to get rid of pain, middle-aged men wanting greater sexual potency, children with attention-deficit disorder (ADD) and other learning problems, seniors with high blood pressure, middle-aged women seeking hormonal rejuvenation, anyone battling anxiety, depression, and allergies—in other words, a large percentage of the consuming public. The burdensome cost of such pills is justified by the requirements of research and development (R&D). By far the greatest funding, however, goes into marketing and "administration" while the bulk of R&D is carried out through the public sector (universities, the National Institutes of Health, government agencies). Moreover, "new" drugs that supposedly innovative R&D brings to market turn out to be mostly recycled versions of older compounds referred to as "me-too" drugs, and this includes the majority of blockbusters. What further boosts Big Pharma fortunes is that drugs approved by the Food and Drug Administration (FDA) for specific conditions can then be prescribed by doctors for whatever condition they choose. Millions of consumers use two or more drugs simultaneously, often for months and years, although the synergistic and long-term effects of drugs were never tested or monitored by the FDA. In the wake of its huge marketing bonanzas, the drug industry had reached an average profit level (in 2000) of more than 25 percent on revenues compared with the overall Fortune 500 rate of 3.3 percent.[13] Such unregulated larceny is made possible by the collusion of the medical profession, insurance companies, and government programs like Medicare.

In this milieu the pharmaceutical industry is relatively free to employ every method available to bolster its unique corporate status. The United States remains the only advanced industrial nation in the world that does not regulate drug prices, owing to the industry's lobbying power in Washington D.C. and state capitols. Older institutional and legal restraints to protect consumers have been gutted. The FDA, supposed watchdog over the industry, has itself become colonized by the very interests it was originally assigned to monitor. Corporations like Pfizer were able to aggressively market a blockbuster drug like Celebrex, touted as a "super-aspirin" although shown to have harsh side effects and to be no better as a pain killer than much cheaper over-the-counter drugs like ibuprofen. As public awareness of price-gouging spread, Big Pharma had to fight increased competition from abroad—and here it has succeeded in banning imports after tenacious lobbying and advertising campaigns that continue into the Obama administration. (Although drugs are commonly manufactured in dozens of plants scattered across the globe, with distribution more and more internationalized, pharmaceutical companies have sold Congress the fiction about "unsafe" medications slipping into the United States from Canada and Mexico.) Even with import restrictions, tens of thousands of Americans have chosen to buy drugs from abroad, often for one-third the domestic price or less, accounting (in 2008) for roughly $2 billion in Canadian sales alone. In Mexico the custom of "pill tourism" has begun, as Americans visit cities like Nogales, Juarez, and Tijuana, returning with bags of cheap "smiling pills" that can be procured usually without a need for prescriptions.[14]

Not surprisingly, the spectacular growth of Big Pharma has paralleled the sanctimonious "war on drugs" launched by President Nixon and later embraced by the Reagan, Bush, and Clinton administrations, at a cost of tens of billions of dollars. We know the anti-drug crusade only targets *illegal* substances, an agenda zealously pursued by a line of drug czars like William Bennett that has led to the world's largest prison-industrial complex. This "war"—a failure by any measurement—has been carried out ostensibly to protect Americans from the harm done by illicit substances. This claim is laughable. If we glance even superficially at the empirical data, we see that adverse effects (including deaths) of illegal drugs have been comparatively minor—hundreds of mortalities in a typical year from overdoses of cocaine and heroine, even less from hallucinogens, and nothing from marijuana. In contrast, prescribed drugs have been implicated in an average of 100,000 deaths annually plus more than 2 million reactions harmful enough to require hospitalization—and these are just the officially *reported* cases.[15] If we turn to some other familiar legalized drugs, the picture appears even more gruesome: nearly 500,000 deaths yearly from tobacco and more than 100,000 from alcohol.[16] Meanwhile, as the horrors of demon coke and pot are routinely dramatized in the corporate media, this same media contains relentless advertising for pharmaceuticals, tobacco, and alcohol, the same interests that help finance the "war on drugs" frenzy.

The events of 9/11 gave new impetus to a more globalized war on drugs, extending to Mexico, Afghanistan, Colombia, and other regions of South America where this battle—intimately linked to the "war on terrorism"—proceeds within the orbit of U.S. foreign policy. Washington supports right-wing military forces behind the ostensible campaign to eradicate drug production and distribution, spending billions in logistics and aid. U.S. military forces have been deployed to join the fray, as in Afghanistan and Colombia, with predictably horrendous results. While this "war" has been waged with vigor for nearly four decades, its impact on illicit drug use in the United States (the main site of consumption) has been negligible. The campaign has been from the outset a huge, expensive fraud—one, however, effectively sold to the American public at a time when Big Pharma (along with the tobacco and alcohol industries) was spending tens of billions of dollars to advertise far more lethal substances. The underlying thrust of this international war, of course, has little to do with keeping people safe from harmful drugs and everything to do with backing familiar U.S. counterinsurgency programs.

The Controlled Substance Act of 1970 identified marijuana as a drug of maximum danger with no redeeming value, although it and kindred natural substances like peyote have been used for millennia generally without harmful social or health consequences. The Act was pushed through without public debate, its premises taken as gospel by politicians of both parties as well as by media pundits, despite solid evidence to the contrary. Such legislation, both federal and state, has justified a draconian, racist system of punishment incarcerating hundreds of thousands for primarily nonviolent drug-related offenses. All levels of government have invested huge resources to fight the great pot menace even though it is safer than virtually any prescribed drug. In more than three decades of antidrug warfare the facts about the real health impact of pot and other drugs have been met with a wall of ignorance, superstition, and denial among government officials, police, the media, and medical profession. The myth that pot is uniquely addictive, or that it inspires users to take harder drugs as the "reefer madness" scenario conjured, has been thoroughly debunked. Of an estimated 70 million Americans who have used pot regularly since the 1960s fewer than 2 percent chose to even experiment with anything stronger; a much better case for excess and harm could be made regarding *alcohol* consumption.[17] As for addictive properties, studies reveal that cigarette, alcohol, and even coffee habits—not to mention such pharmaceutical habits as barbiturates, anti-depressants, amphetamines, tranquilizers, and painkillers—are more difficult to break than the cannabis habit. The criteria used to criminalize some drugs as opposed to others that are widely marketed and advertised must be considered totally irrational, part of a closed, authoritarian system of discourse.

In a hypermedicated society like the United States, people readily buy drugs at local pharmacies that are far more potent and even addictive than pot and many other banned substances. Over-the-counter drugs, of course, can be disarmingly habit-forming. The prevailing image of "narcotics" in the United States is grounded in hysteria, fear, and ignorance while legal medications are a taken-for-granted part of an addictive culture in which pills serve as chemical fixes for virtually any problem, including those "discovered" by Big Pharma with lucrative drug therapy precisely in mind. One paradoxical result of the war on drugs is that American youth have been more frequently turning to *legal* mind-altering substances to get high: painkillers, antidepressants, tranquilizers, and amphetamines, drugs like Xanax, Vicodin, Valium, and OxyContin that are easily obtained at pharmacies and used by tens of millions of people. With overall drug sales up some 400 percent from 1990 to 2008, use and abuse of prescription medications among youth 12 to 24 has kept pace, with 15 percent of high-school students reportedly "pharming" for recreational purposes.[18] Legal doping naturally has its advantages—drugs are easier to find (often in the family medicine cabinet), costs are negligible, adulteration concerns vanish, and legal risks are minimized. But the kids, much like their parents, typically know little about the dangers of pharmaceuticals, especially when the drugs are mixed or taken in extremely high doses.

These dangers, generally soft-pedalled by the media, doctors, and of course Big Pharma itself, ultimately dwarf those of illicit drugs. And the damage goes far beyond what is tepidly called "side effects," as terrible and even fatal as they might be. The statistics cited above—100,000 deaths and over two million hospitalizations annually—refer only to cases officially reported within the medical system. Adverse reactions include not only side effects but other episodes: accidents, overdoses, wrong prescriptions, severe allergies. Added harm comes from long-term use of substances otherwise safe in more limited or short-term applications, with dependency typically heightened in cases of long-term reliance on a drug or combination of drugs. Contrary to popular belief, such dependency is often more intractable for pharmaceuticals than for outlawed drugs like pot and cocaine.

According to Sidney Wolfe and his associates at the Center for Science in the Public Interest in their volume *Worst Pills, Best Pills,* at least 181 of the 549 most-prescribed drugs should *never* be taken under any circumstances.[19] On the strictly prohibited list are such commonly used substances as Valium, Restoril, Elavil, Vioxx, Celebrex, and Darvon, and a number of other familiar blockbusters. The authors point to some frightening results: at least 166 drugs are known to cause serious depression, 156 produce hallucinations, 129 lead to sexual dysfunction, 77 create dementia, and 59 give rise to extreme dizziness often resulting in falls. Such adverse reactions occur at the rate of nearly 10 million yearly—reactions aggravated by prolonged use. Extensive research has shown that prolonged used of Prozac is linked to violent behavior. As for the medical profession, surveys demonstrate that 70 percent of American doctors have flunked exams testing their knowledge of drugs.[20] Most prescriptions, moreover, are reportedly written before a patient's complete history is taken into account. Where the problem of obesity, for example, is not addressed when treating afflictions like high blood pressure, excessive cholesterol levels, and liver or kidney disorders, the pills end up as just another illusory technical fix at best.

Despite FDA oversight, horror stories resulting from Big Pharma obsession with bringing drugs quickly to market have proliferated. Hormone replacement therapy (HRT) has been administered to millions of women anxious to stave off aging, to reverse the effects of menopause. By 1995 the HRT compound Premarin was one of the best-selling medications in the United States, touted as a miracle remedy and fully endorsed by the FDA. Shockingly, however, the drug was still being endorsed and prescribed long after independent tests showed that regular use of HRT boosted women's risk of heart disease by 50 percent and breast cancer by 66 percent with few noticeable benefits. As with many pharmaceuticals, saturation advertising campaigns wildly exaggerated the benefits of HRT while largely ignoring its dangers. In 2001 Premarin, sold by Wyeth-Ayerst, remained the third most prescribed drug in the United States. Many similar examples can be cited since the 1980s. In 1996 Warner-Lambert brought the kidney medication Rezulin to market after a speededup FDA review; the drug quickly became a blockbuster with $1.8 billion in sales despite questionable patient reports and test findings. The drug was finally taken off the market in 2000 but not before it had caused 391 *reported* deaths from liver disease. It came to light that Dr. Richard Eastman, director of the Rezulin research project, had received $178,000 in "consulting fees" from Warner-Lambert while 12 other researchers were given sizable "grants" from the company. Big Pharma exerted such financial leverage over the FDA, NIH, medical schools, and professional journals (all reliant on drug advertising) that flagrant conflicts of interest came to appear almost ordinary. The Angell and Abramson books are filled with cases of this sort, reflecting deep flaws in so much of the academic research. As Abramson writes, "Studies repeatedly document the bias in commercially-sponsored research, but the medical journals seem powerless to control the scientific integrity of their own pages."[21]

The pharmaceutical giants fight for market privileges to "treat" such common problems as high cholesterol – conditions reversed more effectively, more durably, and more cheaply by means of natural or preventive remedies that, however, have been resisted by the medical establishment. Pills called statins are marketed to reduce cholesterol and, by extension, treat cardiovascular disease. Statins constitute the largest family of me-too drugs: Lipitor from Pfizer, Crestor from AstraZeneca, Lescol from Novartis, and others. While each medication is promoted as the ultimate solution for lowering cholesterol, active ingredients in each drug remain essentially identical: only the pill colors and shapes vary. When tested at higher intakes (to ensure "effectiveness") these drugs are shown to outperform placebos, but at such dosages the risk of harsh side effects increases dramatically. By the late 1990s, with heart problems in the United States sharply on the rise, the Pharma objective was to have statins prescribed to at least 36 million Americans, which could amount to sales of nearly $40 billion yearly. Known to increase prospects of brain and nerve damage, statins were aggressively pushed not only in medical journals but on TV and across the entire media spectrum, often directly to consumers, as *long-term* drugs. Pill consumption not only became a magical panacea, but the chemical short-cut more frequently served to deflect attention from crucial dietary and lifestyle changes needed to deal with the causes of heart problems . Meanwhile, as Big Pharma profits from statins skyrocketed, new studies revealed their limits for treating heart problems at a time when such problems were aggravated by MacDonaldization of the American diet— powerfully illustrated by the award-winning 2004 documentary *Supersize Me!*

Several heart-disease studies cited by Abramson conclude that five of six cardiovascular problems stem from unhealthy lifestyles that typically involve obesity. Drugs are not prescribed to help people reverse the underlying causes of health problems, which ultimately demand *contextual* solutions. Thus, while millions of people have sought cures and remedies through statins and kindred medications, the costs can be prohibitive: $2,000 on average yearly, not counting what is spent to ameliorate possible harmful reactions. As Big Pharma tries to make drug solutions ever more fashionable, factors producing high cholesterol and heart disease remain stubbornly obvious: Americans consume far more calories and fats than needed for good health, a situation worsened by sedentary lifestyles. Not only do people eat a daily excess of 500 calories on average, these calories are mostly made up of animal products, fast foods, and sugar. Some 440,000 deaths yearly are related to obesity, which usually develops from such conditions as poor nutrition, lack of exercise, poverty, and personal stress—none of which, however, are particularly amenable to drug therapy. Yet fully 95 percent of health care resources spent in the United States are devoted to biomedical interventions, with drugs and surgeries at the top of the list.

The blessings of American "free enterprise" are ritually invoked by politicians, economists, corporate executives, and the media when referring to the U.S. model of production, consumption, and resource allocation—blessings trumpeted even louder when it comes to the medical establishment. Throughout 2009 the public was treated to a long series of full-scale, though fraudulent, right-wing attacks on the perils of "big government" and "socialist takeover" of medicine destroying everything that Americans hold sacred if significant health care reform (meaning a widely accessible public option) were to be passed by Congress. A free market involves an open flow of goods, services, resources, and communication, an exchange system based upon self-regulating mechanisms of supply and demand. By such indicators, however, the U.S. economy operates, today more than ever, to *subvert* free-market principles. It is a system best described as a state-integrated, corporate-dominated, profit-driven oligopoly in which market relations exist within only tiny enclaves of activity. Economic and governmental power is more concentrated than ever in the hands of a small, insulated elite stratum, that controls the flow of resources, goods, services, and labor—a phenomenon discussed more fully in chapter 3. The medical establishment fully conforms to this pattern.

In the specific case of pharmaceuticals, the picture becomes even more sharply focused: fewer than a dozen corporations (some foreign, mostly American) dominate the market landscape, an ensemble powerful enough to shape terms of manufacturing, sales, trade, and pricing. These include Pfizer, Merck, Johnson & Johnson, Roche, AstraZeneca, Bristol-Myers-Squibb, and Novartis—all virtually identical in their operations, all fixated on the lucrative American market where demand for drugs has long been off charts. They depend on government patents for exclusive marketing rights and public sector absorption of R&D costs, along with legislation protecting against competition and price fluctuation. With its remarkable wealth and power Big Pharma casts its influence over Congress, state legislatures, the medical profession, government agencies, political campaigns, and academia, the company is usually able to push through its agendas.[22] There is nothing in standard political science interest-group literature that captures this imposing reality, which has exploded since the early 1980s. A giant corporate apparatus beginning with the Rockefeller takeover, U.S. medicine evolved into a freewheeling Wall Street operation. Bartlett and Steele, who devote many pages to this transformation, show how a mounting wave of mergers, acquisitions, hostile takeovers, consolidations, and bankruptcies has bolstered an empire built on technocratic medicine, deregulation, stock-market maneuvers, and superprofits. The result has been program cutbacks, layoffs, deskilling of the work force, lowered wages, and shocking decline in the quality of health care for the average consumer.

In late 2009 Merck was hoping to acquire rival giant Schering-Plough Corp. in a staggering cash/stock transaction worth more than $41 billion—a move aided by taxpayers' stimulus payments leading to the possible elimination of 35,000 jobs with downsizing. These two behemoths combined for drug sales of $47 billion in 2008. Such mergers and acquisitions have turned the American medical system into a cartel of sprawling, bureaucratic, unaccountable corporations whose managers persist in the myths of "free enterprise" and "personal choice." As the corporate system grows bigger, richer, and stronger, it becomes less vulnerable to challenge and reform from outside, including legislative bodies.

Recurrent promises of "miracle cures" for chronic diseases like cancer—a staple of media culture—help drive the fortunes of Wall Street medicine and, with it, Big Pharma. In early 2005 the NIH reported exciting new clinical tests for the cancer drug Avastin, designed mainly to treat metastatic lung cancer, as one researcher boasted: "This is very exciting. In the not-too-distant future patients will have a new treatment option."[23] Such options have, unfortunately, been proclaimed at regular intervals in the media, yet the stubborn fact is that death rates from cancer have not fallen despite the celebrated progress. In the case of Avastin, reports of life-threatening side-effects such as fatal internal bleeding were buried deep within the press accounts. So too was mention of the exorbitant costs: $18,000 a *month* for enough medication to be "effective." What seemed most salient from this epic "breakthrough" was the upgraded financial status of Genentech, producer of Avastin, as it stocks soared from $10.95 to $55 a share (in March 2005), reviving the world's second largest biotech company. Not only was Avastin embraced as "an important driver of Genentech's growth," but its reported trial success boosted *overall* stocks with the Nasdaq composite index rising by nearly ten points in one day. Launched in February 2004 as a drug to treat colon cancer, Avastin quickly set a record for first-year sales of an oncology drug, posting returns of nearly $700 million over its first 12 months. In the first quarter of 2005 Genentech's net income had soared 61 percent.

With worldwide sales (in 2010) of more than $500 billion, Big Pharma has enough motivation and clout to tear down political obstacles to its marketing ambitions. In the early 1980s Congress passed a series of laws designed to open up the profit-making terrain for the drug industry. Legislation allowed for tax-supported basic research to be speedily translated into new products. The Bayh-Dole Act enabled universities to patent discoveries from NIH-sponsored testing—the NIH being the main distributor of tax dollars for medical R&D—and then grant exclusive licenses to pharmaceutical companies. This ensured not only market exclusivity but huge federal subsidies for required testing procedures, meaning higher profit margins (and less "free-market" credibility). Bayh-Dole transformed the very trajectory of health care in the United States, freeing corporate giants from public regulation while mobilizing crucial sectors (hospitals, HMOs, insurance companies, doctors, government, academia) around the interests of Big Pharma, all in the name of a mythical free enterprise. Such machinations unfolded almost entirely outside the sphere of public debate and intervention.

Owing to its vast stores of capital and its army of lawyers, lobbyists, and public relations operatives, the drug industry has tightened its stranglehold over American medicine with each passing year. Pharmaceuticals easily and routinely stretch out monopoly rights for brand name medications over many years—patent claims with little basis in creative research, innovation, or fair economic competition. When patents run out, the corporations often simply refine the product and extend sales for purposes quite different from what the FDA originally approved. Thus Lilly altered its marketing of Prozac from treatment of depression to another familiar target—obesity. Such practices illustrate a crucial fact: Big Pharma spends three times as much on advertising, public relations, legal activity, and lobbying than on basic R&D (its main justification for price-gouging). The firms not only routinely overcharge for products but make false and misleading advertising claims, offer kickbacks and "free samples" to doctors, collude to keep generic drugs off the market, and spend tens of billions of dollars to propagandize consumers about the lifesaving role of drugs in American life.[24]

The pretense that Big Pharma carries out innovative and medically vital research does not hold up to close scrutiny: of 78 drugs approved by the FDA in 2002, for example, only 17 had new active ingredients, the remainder recycled as me-too substances falsely advertised as improvements. In the decade spanning 1992 to 2002, some 415 "new" drugs were introduced but only 14 percent of these were useful discoveries in any sense. Consumers targeted according to specific health disorders find a wide array of "choices," yet behind different labels and pill colors they end up buying the same products. (For example, in 2005 there were *seven* identical drugs, each aggressively marketed, for high blood pressure.) At the same time, Big Pharma increasingly manufactures its drugs abroad where labor and other costs are much lower: Pfizer, for example, has 62 plants in 32 countries. Further, since these companies depend on the public sector and small biotech companies for the bulk of R&D, they can more easily socialize the costs of production. Angell shows how Big Pharma routinely conceals its huge marketing and administrative costs under an accounting umbrella that grossly overstates research and testing expenses.[25]

The most popular cancer drug in history, Taxol, offers a prime example of how the drug industry operates—how it manipulates the public sector for its own profit-driven interests and violates its own purported free-market ideology. Active ingredients of this drug were derived from Pacific yew tree bark in the early 1960s, then researched by the National Cancer Institute for 30 years at a cost of $183 million in public funds. In 1992, after the FDA approved Taxol for treatment of ovary cancer, Britol-Meyers-Squibb was handed five years of exclusive marketing rights. Because the yew bark was so scarce, NIH-funded scientists at Florida State University developed a method for synthesizing the medication, leaving the corporation the simple task of producing and marketing what would become an extremely lucrative drug—all profits, of course, going to BMSq. By 2000 worldwide use of Taxol was generating up to $2 billion annually, for a product the company neither discovered nor developed. In 2005 a one-year supply of Taxol cost up to $20,000 (affordable to only the wealthiest cancer patients), which, according to Angell, represents a 20-fold markup over production costs.[26] With its monopoly rights extended another three years, BMSq had (by 2003) sold more than $9 billion of Taxol. Typical of Big Pharma, the absence of price controls and competition along with generous federal subsidies entitled the corporation to profit margins unheard of in other sectors.

Megacorporations Rule

Big Pharma and the rest of the medical-industrial complex can push through their interests because, as is generally true of American political life, megacorporations have effectively colonized the public sphere, including electoral campaigns, federal and state legislation, the operation of government agencies like the FDA and NIH, court decisions related to the medical system, and popular media. No sector of the American economy is as powerful as the medical industry, which works tirelessly to maintain and legitimate a profit-driven, technocratic health care system.

In recent years nearly every member of the U.S. Congress and every White House administration, both Democratic and Republican, has enjoyed a cozy relationship with Big Pharma. The trade association PhRMA is by the largest interest group in Washington D.C., and the drug industry (as of 2010) deployed nearly 150 lobbying firms with 675 high-paid operatives working on a yearly budget of $475 million that far surpasses money spent by banking interests ($133 million) and the Pentagon ($211 million). Drug lobbyists include 26 former members of Congress. In the period 1999–2000 Big Pharma gave out $20 million in campaign donations along with $65 million in soft money, 80 percent of it going to Republicans—though by 2008 the figure had dropped to roughly 60 percent. Drug industry executives gave generously to the Bush campaign in 2000 and again in 2004. A number of front groups like Citizens for Better Medicare, masquerading as grassroots organizations, were set up to facilitate Big Pharma concerns such as fighting price controls and imports. Within the second Bush administration pharmaceuticals enjoyed unique political access and clout, all under cover of free-market propaganda.

The all-consuming goals of Big Pharma—no price controls, strict patent enforcement, deregulation, import restrictions—have largely been met with help from the supposed enemy of free enterprise, big government. Megacorporations continue to enjoy market exclusivity despite their oligopolistic status. They receive such huge tax breaks that the most larcenous firms in the world pay just a tiny fraction of revenues to the very government that ensures their superprofits. They win legislation to stop American consumers from buying cheaper drugs from abroad. The 1997 FDA Modernization Act relaxed standards and timetables for new drugs brought to market. Doctors retain the legal power to prescribe medications for whatever condition they choose. In 2003 the United States was the lone holdout among 143 countries in opposing World Trade Organization efforts to relax patent controls—a move that would have lowered drug prices worldwide. The 2003 Medicare Reform Act, passed overwhelmingly by Congress, paved the way toward even richer pharmaceutical bonanzas by, among other things, prohibiting Medicare from using its purchasing power to get lower prices for seniors, triggering a sharp rise in pharmaceutical stock prices. What was good news on Wall Street, however, turned out to be bad news for millions of Medicare recipients whose health care costs were destined to skyrocket.

The jagged legacy of the FDA, set up to monitor the drug industry, furnishes a perfect illustration of how government agencies can be easily taken over by corporate interests. The FDA has been transformed into an adjunct of Big Pharma, a development solidified by the Bayh-Dole Act and later Congressional actions. For example, in 1992 Congress enacted the Prescription Drug User Fee Act, authorizing drug companies to pay "user fees" to the FDA for testing. Such fees were intended to expedite drug approvals, but at $310,000 per application this soon amounted to *half* the entire FDA evaluation center budget, resulting in agency dependency on the very industry it was assigned to regulate. For Big Pharma these "user fees" amount to small change and, as Angell observes, they are readily offset by added income from sending products to market with fewer delays and obstacles.[27] Of course, the faster the approval process the more likely that tests will be unreliable, allowing more potentially harmful drugs to reach consumers. In fact since the user-fee format was introduced a record 13 prescription drugs were taken off the market after causing hundreds and possibly thousands of deaths. Moreover, as drugs reach consumers quicker the understaffed FDA has an increasingly difficult task performing its other functions—monitoring drug safety, ensuring manufacturing standards, and regulating advertisers. One major disaster involved the GlaxoSmithKline drug Paxil, an antidepressant blockbuster that grossed more than $3 billion dollars in 2003. In June 2004 the New York Attorney General sued Glaxo after tests showed Paxil to be ineffective while sharply increasing risks of depression and suicide in children. The case was settled in August 2004, when Glaxo was forced to pay a meager $2.5 million as fine while its executives never faced criminal charges or even disciplinary penalties. Meanwhile, the European Union included Paxil on its most dangerous list of drugs, followed by a British government warning that the medication (along with other U.S. blockbusters like Zoloft and Effexor) should be used with extreme caution.

Equally troublesome, FDA vulnerability to Big Pharma influence further increased given how its 18 standing advisory committees on drug approvals function. Comprised of medical specialists, these committees review new drug applications and make recommendations to the agency, which are routinely accepted. The problem is that committee members have often had financial ties to corporations with drugs under review. While conflict-of-interest rules prohibit bias, the rules are frequently ignored on grounds that expert advice is indispensable. "Consulting fees" granted by Big Pharma to medical experts are usually lucrative. A 2000 survey conducted by USA Today found that 92 percent of FDA meetings were attended by at least one member with such financial ties, while at 55 percent of meetings more than half the members had some conflict-of-interest. At the same time, since FDA commissioners are so often connected to the drug industry, and since bureaucratic inertia runs deep, any unethical modus operandi is typically difficult to overturn. Wolfe and his associates reported in 2005 that in their 33 years of monitoring the U.S. drug business "the current pro-industry attitude at the FDA is as bad and dangerous as it has ever been. In addition to record numbers of approvals for questionable drugs, the FDA enforcement over advertising has all but disappeared."[28] Thus, from a peak number of 157 enforcement actions to stop illegal prescription drug ads that understate risks and/or overstate benefits in 1998, the number decreased to 24 in 2003 at a time when advertising volume had dramatically increased. The FDA section that oversees Big Pharma advertising has feeble resources but the real problem, according to Wolfe and his colleagues, is that "it has also been thwarted by marching orders from higher up in the agency to, effectively, go easy on prescription drug advertising."[29] The authors stress that Congress has enacted legislation greatly weakening FDA capacity to protect the public, with millions of harmful drug reactions yearly speaking loudly to the success of "higher up" power brokers.

One of the most well-known cases of Big Pharma malfeasance involved Vioxx, a painkiller manufactured by Merck and prescribed mostly for arthritis. After the FDA approved the drug in 1998 large numbers of deaths from heart attacks were reported among Vioxx users, matched by test findings showing high risks for cardiovascular problems—findings both the FDA and Merck were later accused of covering up. Vioxx was finally pulled from the market in September 2004 after Congressional testimony by Dr. David Graham, the agency scientist in charge of drug safety. Graham said the Vioxx disaster was symptomatic of FDA failure to exercise its watchdog role because of its intimate ties with the drug industry. For his courageous whistle-blowing, Graham, a 20-year veteran of the agency, was accused by FDA leadership of "scientific misconduct" and reassigned to administrative duties. The Vioxx article was eventually published in *Lancet*, which reported the medication led to possibly 140,000 cases of heart disease including some 56,000 deaths from heart attacks and strokes. Low doses were shown to increase risk of heart attack by 50 percent, with higher doses pushing the incidence to a staggering 358 percent. Merck had sought to conceal this information in order to protect its blockbuster profits.[30]

In *Worst Pills, Best Pills,* Vioxx (rofecoxib) was listed in the "do not use" category since its adverse reactions more than offset any purported short-term benefits. Referring to Vioxx, the authors wrote: "This is another heavily promoted, overpriced nonsteroidal anti-inflammatory drug that now carries a new warning…about heart disease."[31] Citing a VIGOR study pointing to severe heart attack risks, they mention a host of additional side effects including severe abdominal or stomach pain, cramping, severe and continuous nausea, indigestion, bloody stools, and vomiting of blood. The same report mentioned that people suffering from arthritis could eliminate these risks by choosing the over-the-counter painkiller naproxen or even aspirin, but of course such information was embarrassing to Merck, which charged $100 to $134 monthly for Vioxx (while naproxen sold for only $18). Abramson devotes a long section of his book to the Vioxx disaster, detailing how both Merck and the FDA manipulated test findings to conceal worrisome data.[32] In 2004 Vioxx remained among the top-ten selling drugs in the United States, but once the drug was taken off the market Merck's stock plummeted from $45 to $27 a share. In February 2005 an FDA advisory panel voted to lift the ban on Vioxx, directing Merck to sharpen its warnings. Meanwhile, the *New York Times* reported that ten panel members involved in the Vioxx decision (and that of another dangerous painkiller, Celebrex) had worked as consultants for pharmaceutical companies with stakes in the outcome.[33] At the time Senator Charles Grassley (R-Iowa) accused the FDA of subjugating itself to Big Pharma agendas in full violation of basic professional and ethical standards.[34]

The Cancer-Industrial Complex

A leading example of how corporate-technocratic medicine exerts a destructive impact on American society is what Ralph Moss calls the "cancer industry," referring to the phony drug-centered "war" on the disease, the power of big business to set and control health agendas, the corrosive legacy of distorted science, the corruption of professional work, and, above all, failure of medical intervention to curb what has become a growing epidemic. Since President Nixon announced the "war on cancer" in 1971 the situation has only steadily worsened, despite recurrent promises of new "cures" and "remedies" within orthodox medical research, accounting for more than 500,000 deaths yearly in the United States. After being fired from the Sloan-Kettering Institute in 1974 for refusing to accept falsified data about nonconventional cancer treatments, Moss wrote *The Cancer Syndrome* (1980), exposing the pernicious influence of corporations and their lobbies on cancer research and treatment—a book that went through six editions. This was followed by *The Cancer Industry* (last published in 1996), which extended and refined the same argument.[35] Moss was able to show in some detail how behemoths like Mobil, IBM, Exxon, and Union Carbide—along with agribusiness, the food industry, financial interests, and Big Pharma—had colonized the medical sector, including Sloan-Kettering, the Mayo Clinic, that National Institutes of Health, the Food and Drug Administration, and the American Cancer Society. The medical-scientific complex was so permeated by corporate influence that it could never transcend the orthodoxy (surgery, drugs, and other chemicals) or take into account prevention, dietary factors, the environmental context, and alternative medicine. As the incidence of most types of cancer spread despite tens of billions of dollars spent on this "war," the entire research and treatment regimen grew into an institutionalized, high-profit sector insulated from public accountability. For Moss and later critics like Devra Davis, John Robbins, John McDougall, Colin Campbell, and Samuel Epstein, the major hospitals, clinics, institutes, and agencies set up to fight the cancer battle ended up serving business interests rather than the needs of health consumers often faced with life-and-death situations.

After many years at the American Cancer Society, Davis wrote *The Secret History of the War on Cancer* (2007), a lengthy insider's attack on an industry she argues has done more to block than advance scientific-medical efforts to understand the real causes of cancer. Following Moss, she focused on corporate influence—dishonest advertising, expensive lobbying, colonization of government agencies, scientific spin, and strong-arm political tactics—that has steadily narrowed the medical outlook on cancer to symptoms rather than causes, technical intervention rather than natural prevention, drugs and surgery rather than holistic strategies jettisoned from view despite independent research findings that show the limits of orthodoxy and promise of certain alternatives. The problem with prevention and natural approaches, of course, is that little revenue is generated for profit-hungry corporations. As Davis points out, the ACS—itself riddled with business interests—spends less than 10 percent of its budget on independent studies, fearful that revenue-generating products and services might be undermined through the "wrong" findings. At centers like Sloan Kettering as well as ACS, cancer is uniformly assumed to be the result of an invading agent rather than a long-term *process* of health deterioration rooted in diet, lifestyle, and other contextual factors. It is often simply conceded by medical experts to be "the price of modern life."[36] Thus, while the media often tout new innovations or cures in the "war on cancer," this killer health condition is paradoxically viewed as a natural occurrence of American daily life. The "war" has burdened taxpayers at a level of tens of billions while celebrated "remedies" are perpetually elusive—hardly surprising given the prevalence of a diet saturated with fast foods, animal products, and sugar. Business deregulation introduced during the Reagan years and continuing to the present gave corporations almost carte blanche to dictate priorities in cancer treatment, with predictable outcomes.

None of the major centers established to fight cancer—ACS, Sloan-Kettering, National Cancer Institute, many universities—focus on prevention, nutrition, or the larger social and environmental *context* of disease formation. No attention has been devoted to the fast-food diet, shown by dozens of studies to be strongly implicated in most types of cancers. In 1997 the American Institute for Cancer Research, along with the World Cancer Research Fund, issued a report on the basis of 4,500 studies on behalf of the World Health Organization, concluding that up to 70 percent of all cancers are related to lifestyle issues—above all to vast consumption of animal products. Such findings were strongly reinforced by Campbell's seminal volume, *The China Study* (2006), based on extensive comparative analysis of diets and related factors, but the U.S. medical-scientific establishment moved full-speed ahead with its own agendas as if the study had never appeared.[37] Other independent research demonstrated that vegetarians suffer far less than half the cancer episodes of meat-eaters. Meanwhile, in 1998, the NCI announced triumphantly that a breakthrough in cancer treatment had arrived in the form of a potent drug used for chemotherapy, Tamoxifen, which was supposed to help millions of Americans survive many years after cancer diagnosis. While unambiguously endorsed by the FDA and NCI, the drug ultimately failed to deliver on its heady promise but did cause adverse reactions (including new cancers) in large numbers of users. Sold by AstraZeneca, the drug—like other chemical panaceas—had at best only temporary success insofar as it never confronted the basic causes of cancer. The drug maker's parent company, Imperial Chemical Industries, is one of the world's largest producers of pesticides. Yet, despite weak evidence of remedial properties and abundant data showing adverse reactions, Tomixifen became the biggest-selling anticancer drug in the world—a heavily marketed substance that did nothing to reverse the mounting incidence of cancer. As John Robbins notes in his exploration of diet and cancer in *The Food Revolution* (2005), the price paid by the American public for the systematic corporate distortion of cancer research—exemplified by the stonewalling of that crucial 1997 report—can probably be calculated in the millions of deaths.[38] Long before the Campbell study, science had shown an undeniable connection between meat/dairy consumption and cancer, yet the vast majority of Americans, thanks to the power of high-level corporate lobbying and influence, remains ignorant and therefore disempowered.

Campbell's *The China Study* reveals this linkage more systematically than any previous work, on the basis of far-reaching comparative evidence gathered in China and elsewhere. He concludes that nutritional factors explain different cancer rates even where environmental and other conditions that might be implicated, given that such conditions are activated in the human body only where consumption of protein and fats from animal products is high.[39] Obstacles to both understanding and treatment are erected by corporate interests—food, agribusiness, medical, pharmaceutical—that have been able to block or distort the findings of independent research, often working through biased government and private organizations generally viewed by the public as objective and trustworthy. Campbell calls attention to the fact that the seminal 1980s McGovern Report of the U.S. Congress, already warning of the hazards of meat consumption, was quickly dismissed by the political and media establishments that moved to squelch debate over the explosive data and its implications. McGovern Report's dietary goals—less meat, more plant-based foods—were ferociously attacked by the National Academy of Sciences, an institute dominated by meat and dairy interests that had always extolled the virtues of a high-protein, high-fat diet.[40] The same was true of the prestigious American Council on Science and Health (ACSH), promoted as a consumer-interest group yet dependent on animal-food producers for nearly 80 percent of its funding. The ACSH champions the meat and dairy industries while denouncing critics as a bunch of conspiracy theorists and quacks. At the American Institute for Cancer Research (AICR), moreover, nutritional issues received no attention within an organization ostensibly dedicated to uncovering the causes of cancer, as this line of research conflicts with the interests of major funding sources at the drug, medical, and food conglomerates. Scientists' attempts to broaden work in the field are routinely met with intimidation, personal smears, and lies of the sort both Moss and Davis report after spending years at the heart of the cancer establishment.[41] More than that, the very *idea* of cancer prevention is blindly opposed at AICR as well as ACSH and ACS. Notes Campbell: "In the world of nutrition and health, scientists are not free to pursue their research wherever it leads. Coming to the 'wrong conclusions,' even through first-rate science, can damage your career."[42] Following Moss, Campbell refers to this deterioration of medical work as the "science of industry." The American food, medical, and drug corporations remain today among the most powerful and profitable in the world—and thus stand to lose the most with any shift in cancer treatment in the direction of plant-based diets, prevention, and holistic medicine.

The giant corporations, their lobbies, marketing operations, and public relations firms—not to mention various government agencies they dominate—work indefatigably to monitor and control all health-related research, efforts financed by tens of billions yearly. The food, drug, and medical companies exercise influence over a wide range of university work, including conferences, journals, symposia, workshops, videos, and med school curricula. Rarely in any of these venues does linkage between lifestyle and cancer receive much attention. The Federal Nutrition Board welcomes to its governing circles representatives of such firms as Burger King, Dannon, Taco Bell, Coca Cola, Nestle, Pfizer, and Roche, all fiercely resistant to new directions in research and treatment; the "conclusions" of such agencies usually go no further than financial entanglements will allow.[43] As for the all-important National Institutes of Health (NIH), comprised of some 27 institutes and centers, nowhere does its work extend toward the social, nutritional, and environmental dimensions of health, and no funding for alternative research has been made available regardless of the scientific or medical standing of prospective investigators.

Within this corporate-technocratic behemoth, American scientists, doctors and other health care practitioners remain trapped in a medical-industrial complex where "private" and "public," business and government realms converge to render citizens, consumers, and employees largely disempowered. Challenges to the dominant paradigm where cancer and other diseases are framed and treated are easily marginalized, witness the deafening silence accorded the McGovern Report and *China Study*. After exasperating decades of working in health research, Campbell writes: "I have come to the conclusion that when it comes to health, government is not for the people; it is for the food industry and the pharmaceutical industry at the expense of the people."[44] As mounting evidence reveals the professional bankruptcy and ideological rigidity of conventional regimens, the medical apparatus continues its merry way along the same counterproductive path. Meanwhile, by the early twenty-first century the wealthiest country in the world—the one also with the most expensive health care—remains by far the most afflicted by high rates of cancer and such other chronic diseases as diabetes, arthritis, and heart conditions, symptoms of a society rapidly deteriorating in both its medical and political health.

Institutional Paralysis

After many difficult years within the medical establishment, Marcia Angell said she wrote her book to "show how the [drug] industry, corrupted by easy profits and greed, has deceived and exploited the American people."[45] Like Abramson and Bartlett/Steele, whose book won a 2004 Pulitzer Prize, Angell laid out careful arguments illustrating the bankruptcy of capitalist health care and fictions of "free-market" medicine.

Although these critics failed to explore the full economic and polit-ical ramifications of their harsh attacks, they do construct a narrative as to how the early 1980s witnessed a shift toward unfettered corpo-rate profit-making enhanced by deregulation, privatization, and gen-eral freeing up of capital mobility. Matters have only worsened across the intervening years. Behind the ideological façade of market rela-tions, the corporate structure has become steadily more globalized, expansionist, and oligarchic, coinciding with a gradual stripping away of Keynesian public agendas and social contract inherited from the New Deal and Great Society. By 2010 it seemed that most everything had become commodified—government, public services, politics, culture, social life—supposedly in opposition to "big government"—with expanded drug marketing and the shift toward expensive high-tech medicine one outcome of this tendency. Gorging on superprofits and fueled by a culture of "medical necessity" and quick fixes, the pharmaceutical industry has been able to influence vast expanses of American society owing to its financial power and institutional sta-tus; government, the media, medical profession, and academia have all felt the imprint of Big Pharma. To maintain this hegemony, the industry built a public relations, advertising, and marketing empire second to none, spinning grand myths about the curative powers of the hundreds of potent but often harmful drugs it sells.

The corporate-medical structure has corrupted and subverted the public sphere to a degree beyond that of any other sector, revealing a steady trend toward institutional paralysis and disabling politics, indicated by the dismal level of discourse informing the ill-fated 2009 health care "debates." Prospects for desperately needed reforms of crisis-ridden American medicine—the only developed nation in the world without universal coverage—seemed problematic from the outset. President Obama's proposal for far-reaching overhaul of American health care seemed progressive enough on the surface, but the obstacles were daunting: powerful lobbies implacably wed-ded to the status quo, a media fully complicit with corporate agen-das, legislators dependent on medical sector funding to get elected, Obama's own indebtedness to corporate backing during his run to the White House. Big Pharma and the insurance giants had invested tens of millions of dollars to protect their profit-making machines. Within months of Obama's ascension to the presidency, as modest health care proposals began to surface, a predictable battle was engaged to defeat anything but the most watered-down legislation. The specter of even minimal "pubic option" coverage came under savage attack in Washington, the media, and a series of town-hall meetings during the summer of 2009. The campaign moved along four tiers—special-interest lobbying, grassroots mobilization, a talk-radio blitz, and fierce Congressional opposition from both Republicans and "blue dog" Democrats opposed to government "takeover" of health care.

The Obama administration itself had already begun to work closely with Big Pharma and the insurance companies to solicit corporate backing for the reforms, meaning that any legislation would likely produce few benefits for tens of millions of health consumers either denied insurance or saddled with expensive coverage. While Obama the candidate had blasted the drug and medical lobbies, as president, he quickly changed course and established rapport with PhRMA and its agents, including chief lobbyist Billy Tauzin, a frequent White House visitor during the spring and summer of 2009. Working with Tauzin and leading CEOs from Merck, Abbott, Pfizer, and other drug giants, Obama worked out arrangements that ensured blockage of cheap imports, guarantees against price caps, and continued government subsidies in return for Big Pharma endorsement of "reform" that would minimize public sector involvement in health care. These deals, combined with tens of millions of dollars earmarked for campaign funding, set the broad contours of debate and policy-making, decisively shaping the final outcome.. As James Lowe, a spokesperson for global nonprofit health,care interests, remarked: "Since Obama came into office, the drug industry has received everything it wants, domestic and foreign."[46] Drug corporations spent $110 million lobbying Congress in 2009, ensuring that Democrats and Republicans alike would cater to an industry that pulled in more than $40 billion in profits for 2008—at a time when prices for brand-name drugs rose at a record 9.3 percent even as the country was beset with the most severe economic downturn since the Great Depression.[47] Meanwhile, the White House was extending its hospitality to representatives from health insurance companies like WellPoint, Inc. and HealthNet, Inc., and to lobbyists such as Karen Ignani, president of America's Health Insurance Plans and Dr. James Rohack, American Medical Association (AMA) president, all hoping to shape the outcome of pending legislation before it could be debated in Congress.[48] Obama's refusal to take the offensive on this issue, not to mention his tepid response to howling critics, can be understood as "cooptation" by such high-powered lobbying at both the White House and Congress, but in fact these interests were deeply embedded in the process well before Obama's agenda was formulated. It should have been no surprise, therefore, when Obama conceded in September 2009 that the favored "public option" was no longer central to successful health care reform. The end result was predictable enough –a legislative package comprised of a few important reform measures (for example, ending lifetime caps on insurance coverage), but which promised to be a great boondoggle for private companies handed government subsidies for tens of millions of new customers.

Such intense corporate maneuvering at the summit of power, abetted by media distortions and myths about the supposed horrors of "government medicine," was accompanied by a wave of popular outbursts in August 2009 calculated to short-circuit even these limited reforms before they could be seriously considered. Town-hall meetings were besieged by right-wing fanatics denouncing Obama's "socialist" (or "fascist") agenda for turning over the country to "totalitarianism." There was screaming over Obama "death panels," dictatorial government bureaucrats, privacy violations, the end of free choice, illegal immigrants getting subsidized health care, and similar fictions. There were mock local uprisings, threats, violent confrontations, tea parties, and general mayhem fueled by righteous anger that echoed across the talk-radio circuit. Some meetings degenerated into chaos. Many protesters likened Obama's proposals to Nazi agendas, including the "final solution." Media coverage was extensive and largely favorable. Based loosely on the Karl Rove playbook designed to spread public fear and confusion, this crusade was well-organized by right-wing groups manipulating public concerns over taxes, big government, privacy, immigration, and abortion. Organizations like Americans for Fair Play and Freedom Works, financed by the medical lobbies, mobilized thousands of people, arranged bus transportation, and supplied an "August Recess Action Kit" behind a campaign to disrupt and obfuscate. Evidence shows, moreover, that upper-echelon Congressional Republicans fully collaborated with these "rebellions."[49] The strategy underlying such "grassroots" activism as the Tea-Party and town-hall uprisings was geared to assemblies of militant protesters sidetracking or, better, shutting down genuine public debate—thus ruling out significant reforms and, ironically, denying prospects for cheaper, more accessible health care for many of those same protesters. This debacle further dramatized the bankruptcy of American politics, where the needs and aspirations of ordinary people stand directly opposed to megacorporate interests that, however, manage to generate widespread popular support.

In the end, of course, the medical-industrial complex was able to triumph, as its supporters in Congress were able to shepherd through reforms bereft of any real public option, constraints on Big Pharma, binding insurance regulations, and secure health coverage for all individuals. Passed by Congress in 2010, the reforms were still considered by some as Obama's crowning achievement of an otherwise tumultuous first two years in office. Many liberals and progressives referred to these measures, costing roughly a trillion dollars, as the most sweeping changes since the 1960s. As mentioned, medical coverage was extended (indeed mandated) to more than 30 million uninsured Americans, much of it subsidized for low-income citizens. The reforms included a long-overdue patients' Bill of Rights, extension of Medicare solvency by 12 years, new drug benefits for seniors, and, crucially, statutes denying insurance companies' ability to reject coverage for people with preexisting health conditions or to set caps on benefit payments. Despite such progressive measures, however, the legislation (most of it to be implemented in 2014) amounted to a huge financial boon to insurers, now guaranteed millions of new customers. More significantly, with no public option (something taken for granted around the world) Americans were still left at the mercy of price-gouging corporations always ready to find loopholes and exemptions to circumvent new statutes. As mentioned, the Obama administration had bargained away much of its leverage through backroom deals with insurance and pharmaceutical industries even before the proposals were set in motion.

Even these modest reforms, however, proved to be more than the corporate establishment could tolerate. For the 2010 midterm elections, its hundreds of lobbies mobilized to block key elements of what was derisively called "Obamacare," many candidates (fueled by the Tea Party) even promising to repeal changes deemed "unconstitutional." Such insurers as Aetna, Cigna, Humana, WellPoint, and UnitedHealth poured tens of millions of dollars into electoral campaigns, hoping Republicans could mount a fierce counterattack against the reforms, though many in the industry were perfectly happy as beneficiaries of state subsidies for new customers. The insurers were totally opposed to removing caps on coverage (whether annual or lifetime), and to laws mandating care for those with preexisting conditions as well as sick children. All the giant firms were united in affirming their "right" to cancel policies once people become ill. Some threatened to stop selling policies altogether rather than comply with a mandate to insure sick children.[50] All were opposed to federal oversights or regulations, hoping for maximum freedom to gouge citizens with high rates along with plans limited by huge deductibles and co-pays.

In 2010, several years before most of the reforms were expected to take effect, some major insurers moved to "cut costs"—that is, reduce coverage by making policies more expensive while increasing the level of deductibles and co-pays. To sustain profits, the huge carriers were driven to cut services, meaning that millions of Americans would be without badly needed medical care. Meanwhile, the three largest corporations reported massive profits for 2009 and parts of 2010, with Aetna leading the way at nearly $500 million for 2009 (a jump of 53 percent), followed closely by WellPoint and HealthNet.[51] Aetna was given a strong boost through its policy-rate increases of some 20 percent, which actually fell short of the 29 percent hikes at HealthNet and Anthem Blue Cross (all in California). As insurance corporations reaped more profits by denying a larger number of claims, Americans were paying 47 percent more for health care in 2010 than in 2005. Within the mythical "free market," bureaucrats situated in remote, sprawling corporate empires were posed to deny people coverage. Even where coverage is granted, the insured are typically forced to make repeated calls before winning approval. As Ron Pollack, head of Families USA, put it: "The most effective cost management for insurers is to decline services. And when there is a dispute, it is often very difficult to get a satisfactory result from an insurance company."[52] As private insurance companies solidified their power, coverage for doctors' visits, treatments, hospital stays, and drugs continued to skyrocket, further depriving consumers of leverage. As policies became more expensive, with deductibles and co-pays higher, tens of millions of insured were forced to make difficult choice, often between medical treatment and rent. People chose increasingly to forgo preventive measures, including tests, while opting for less-expensive premiums that offered plenty of exceptions and poor coverage. Many employers, at the same time, forced workers into higher-deductible plans. The result is that Americans in larger numbers were forgoing (often urgently needed) medical treatment they could not afford, at a time when even minor visits to the health care system could run into the thousands, or tens of thousands, of dollars.

While profits for major health insurers soared, ratepayers were typically hit with double-digit premium increases—falsely justified by improved patient coverage and services. At the same time, leading executives at five corporations (Cigna, Humana, UnitedHealth, WellPoint, and Aetna) pulled down roughly $200 million in compensation, bonuses, and stock options. As ordinary American families struggled with the economic downturn, UnitedHealth CEO Stephen Hensley received $100 million in 2009 stock options, while H. Edward Hanway walked away from Cigna with a $111 million retirement package.[53] These were the very same business chieftains who fiercely resisted even modest health care reforms on grounds of free choice, quality care, and, of course, "free markets." Indeed rightwing and Tea Party efforts in late 2010 were mounting toward nullification of the Obama reforms, hoping to either repeal or totally erase what Congress had passed. Koch Industries, the Cato Institute, and Americans for Prosperity joined the Chamber of Commerce and related corporate lobbies to fight the legislation as a violation of "health-care freedoms," earmarking tens of millions of dollars to the cause. At the same time, a lengthy California state investigation revealed that several insurers—Cigna, Blue Shield, HealthNet, and Kaiser among them—had failed to pay medical claims to thousands of doctors and hospitals throughout 2009 and 2010. The report further indicated that insurance plans at these companies typically lacked adequate procedures for handling grievances and disputes. Meanwhile, tens of millions of Americans remain fully disenfranchised within a draconian medical empire, a state of affairs that "Obamacare" is unlikely to reverse.

At the end of 2010 this authoritarian and disabling system continued to produce commodified and technocratic health care with sickness and its apparent corollary (and short-term fix), pill consumption, becoming the norm. Expensive pill therapy marketed for hundreds of health ailments—real and constructed—had turned into one of the most destructive legacies of American corporate power: the more sicknesses and disorders to treat, and for the longest periods of time, the more advantageous for those who own and manage the system. As the truncated health care overtures of 2009 reflect, the American medical system is dysfunctional, remote, bureaucratic, and politically stifling. Three decades ago Ivan Illich wrote that this system had become a "disabling profession" ruled by technocratic experts and corporate managers driven by power, money, and status, with arrogant claims to a specialized knowledge that conferred license to dominate.[54] Today it remains among the most undemocratic realms of American public life. A self-proclaimed repository of truth and wisdom, the medical industry denies every progressive, community-based alternative before it while reproducing harshly unequal social and authority relations across a wide spectrum of activity. Rooted in familiar American traditions of profit-maximization, managerialism, and technological fixes, the medical system is geared to fighting costly "wars" against cancer and other diseases mainly through surgery and drugs while success in these "wars" remain more elusive than ever, as political solutions fade into oblivion.

6

An American Fascism?

At a moment when the Barack Obama presidency has raised popular hopes for democratic renewal and social change in the United States, it might be worth consulting deeper historical trends that point toward more sober assessments. Looking at the ever-growing concentration of government, corporate, military, and media power in American society—the focus of previous chapters—a pressing question arises: can *any* political leadership or social force, however noble its intentions, provide a counterweight to the immense variety of anti-democratic trends at work? Put differently, are conditions favoring an authoritarian outcome now so daunting as to be irreversible, at least within parameters of the existing system? In a political order shaped by thriving democratic participation, such questions would seem meaningless since popular mandates for change would presumably be taken seriously. But in a far less vibrant and open system, with citizen involvement episodic and generally limited, these concerns take on a sense of immediacy, all the more so in the wake of Obama's historic rise to the White House. If so, then time-honored assumptions at the center of American public discourse—beginning with "democracy" and "free markets"—ought to be critically engaged, as I have done in this book.

In his classic film *The Grand Illusion* (1937), the great French director Jean Renoir brilliantly dramatized myths that justified the unspeakable carnage of World War I. Politicians, citizens, and soldiers on all sides of the conflict were quickly swept into a bloody, protracted war serving no rationally defined end, everyone disarmed by chauvinistic propaganda that, when fully scrutinized, made little moral or political sense. As the cinematic narrative unfolds, two distinct messages surface—first, that the Great War was a bloody illusion having no purpose beyond death and destruction for millions of people, and second, that *all* warfare ultimately follows the same barbaric logic. The crucial problem for Renoir, of course, was that all such illusions die hard, particularly those embedded in the taken-for-granted flow of everyday life. Today, when warfare seems as futile as ever, other "grand illusions" persist—in the United States, perhaps none more so than mythical beliefs that help solidify an increasingly authoritarian and imperialistic order. In this context, the hubris and fictions that pervade American political culture impose enormous roadblocks to understanding. As Americans cling to outmoded beliefs about the special goodness of their history and destiny—about the world's greatest democracy, home of a classless meritocracy, perfect Constitution, free markets, and citadel of the "free world"—how could talk of a downward spiral, much less drift toward fascism, be taken seriously? After all, is it not a matter of common knowledge that the great evils of militarism, war, dictatorship, and political violence emanate from *elsewhere,* from strange lands and even stranger leaders? While the banality of American politics and media culture permits such empty indulgences, however, historical forces move apace, creating new realities beneath the comfortable façade of grand illusions. The question here is: could some kind of fascist shift occur within the parameters of a liberal-capitalism that Americans persist in seeing as the sine qua non of freedom and democracy? Answers to this and related questions inevitably take us far beyond the dominant categories of political discourse.

Right-wing Ascendancy

Thomas Frank is one writer who has charted the steady deterioration of a political system colonized by Washington-based ultraconservatives whose single-minded purpose has been to subvert public institutions while giving carte blanche to freewheeling corporate interests. Best known for *What's The Matter with Kansas?* (2005), a treatise on the Republican genius for mobilizing workers and the poor around traditional values to the detriment of material interests, Frank shifts attention in *The Wrecking Crew* (2008), to the role of lobbies and kindred elite groups at the summit of power.[1] In both cases we have a fundamental assault on the capacity of American government to serve popular needs or respond to democratic inputs. Democracy shrinks before the massive and intensifying power of corporations, while the political system departs irreversibly away from its Constitutional origins.

The ascendancy of Washington right wingers, spurred by the so-called Reagan Revolution, has depended on a *philosophy* of government (beyond simple electoral tactics) that views the liberal state as a perversion of social values and the "market" a true expression of human potential. In *The Wrecking Crew,* the market penetrates and transforms government, as big business arrogates to itself more and more state functions, enabling us to see with greater clarity how continuous misrule, incompetence, and corruption are less marks of leadership malfeasance than of well-planned right-wing agendas. According to Frank, a frenzied but well-planned "winger" assault on liberal government and the New Deal legacy that kept it alive is the most salient expression of the "wrecking crew in action."[2] For libertarians weaned on reputed laissez-faire principles, the market entails all that is organic and natural while the state, however constituted, is innately coercive and oppressive, the enemy of freedom, democracy, and prosperity. As Frank argues, however, this archaic ideology amounts to little more than a shameless cover for unregulated corporate power, the authoritarian and plutocratic elements of which are never acknowledged. Its pseudolibertarianism is simply faux populism, cynically pedaled not only in the D.C. corridors of power but in the Midwestern hinterlands, that serves to justify diminished citizen participation, while the wingers' market pretenses allow them to "pass off a patently pro-business political agenda as a noble bid for human freedom."[3] As the second Bush administration was drawing to a close, beset with severe economic crisis, the striking reality was that this arrogant and unprincipled "wrecking crew" was able to make inroads into American domestic and foreign policy to the extent that "Washington has truly become a winger wonderland."[4] Whether the wingers' strong presence in the corridors of power could survive an Obama presidency itself riddled with Wall Street and other corporate interests, had not been answered definitively by early 2010.

In *What's the Matter with Kansas?* Frank poses crucial questions that address the American political conundrum, raising the specter of a modern right-wing authoritarian trajectory with its own mass psychology—manipulated, to be sure, by those with special attachment to the status quo. It turns out that Republicans have frequently won elections by appealing to the poorest constituencies in the society—workers, lower classes, marginalized—on a basis of shared social or "moral" concerns: gun ownership, abortion, gay rights, death penalty, "family values," etc. People angry over such concerns and feeling insignificant are often drawn to a shrill talk-radio-style conservatism pitting ordinary folks against "arrogant elites" typified by highly educated, liberal, secular urban professionals. The problem is that disenfranchised people, faced with change and uncertainty, often tend to prefer candidates like George Bush who, once elected, embrace policies and pass legislation serving the rich, Wall Street, and corporations while laying waste to public services and social programs beneficial to those same ordinary folks. Frank refers to this reactionary populism as a "species of derangement" produced by the Great Backlash against left politics, social movements, and counterculture of the 1960s and later.[5] Since the early 1980s the Republican genius has been the capacity—at least until the Obama breakthrough—to manipulate and capitalize on public outrage over this progressive attack on old-fashioned values.

Reactionary populism turns out to be high-level duplicity, for "values" in question are rarely translated into concrete policy while campaign references to "free market," prosperity, and "family values" amount to so much cynical rhetoric. As Frank points out, "Old-fashioned values may count when conservatives appear on the stump, but once conservatives are in office the only old-fashioned situation they care to revive is an economic regimen of low wages and lax regulations."[6] Republicans who stand with the interests of a small plutocratic stratum cannot hope to get elected without broadening their appeals well beyond the rich and privileged, and this is done—as is has been throughout history—by focusing on nonclass social issues while minimizing or suppressing economic concerns. In his book, Frank stresses "moral" appeals connected to family life and sexuality, but he could have called equal or even greater attention to the seductions of patriotism that, especially in the post-9/11 milieu, have served the right admirably as a trans-class ideological pole of attraction. In any event, Backlash politics explored by Frank help give the poor, weak, and disenfranchised a (false) sense of empowerment at the very moment greater power and wealth is being accrued by the rich—assuming, of course, that conservatives succeed in this stratagem. The result, as Frank notes, is a "working-class movement that has done incalculable, historic harm to working-class people."[7] Most remarkably, it has satisfied its aims in a context where policy "failure" seems likely; whatever the actual outcome, the "values" illusion always survives intact. Since the Reagan presidency, for example, the Backlash mantra has been to "get government off our backs," yet big government and federal spending has only grown steadily and sharply under Republican aegis. What Frank depicts as a world of "madness and delusion" is one in which privileged elites have become effective champions of the poor and downtrodden—as partisans of Nascar, the beer taverns, hunting, and country music.

Yet such populism is hardly novel within the American experience: southern Democrats and their kindred partners perfected this strategy more than a century ago, and it has since entered the playbook of both Democrats and Republicans anxious to deflect peoples' attention from pressing material concerns such as poverty, unemployment, and declining public services. Politicians like Huey Long in Louisiana and George Wallace in Alabama cultivated a man-of-the-people image well before Ronald Reagan's faux populism brought millions of poor and workers into the Republican camp. More significantly, the parallels between modern Backlash politics and earlier fascism are quite striking, reactionary populism being central to the power ambitions of Mussolini, Hitler, Franco, Peron, and other right-wing authoritarian leaders whose appeals were rooted in a mix of traditional and patriotic "values." Historical fascism gained popular strength and won state power as a distinctly *oppositional* force doing battle against liberal, socialist, and communist obstacles to national unity and traditional cohesion. They were in some ways "revolutionaries," though once in power chose to operate in the service of modernizing elites tied to corporations, the state, and military. This grand duplicity was, then as now, key to the historic achievements of right-wing groups desperate to isolate or neutralize progressive challenges. Frank writes that "the hallmark of Backlash conservatism is that it approaches politics not as a defender of the existing order or as a genteel aristocrat but as an average working person offended by the arrogant impositions of the (liberal) upper class."[8] Class anger is turned on its head. In fact this use of populist imagery in the service of conservative goals is probably as old as human history, resonating for example in the politics of Cato the Elder at the time of the Roman Empire—"Catonism" emerging as an ideology of moral regeneration through glorification of "the people," with the idea of reinforcing the status quo and ruling interests. Long before Mussolini and Hitler—or the modern Backlash architects—the poor and disempowered were being mobilized behind an antimodern populism in support of ultra-nationalism and militarism.[9]

Frank's work in these two books thus follows a pair of interrelated motifs: the notion that the governing institutions have been thoroughly colonized by corporate interests combined with the thesis of a resurgent conservative populism working to Republicans' electoral advantage. Taken together, and even if slightly exaggerated, these narratives suggest an ever-increasing consolidation of right-wing authoritarian politics in American society. An immediate question arises: could these epic tendencies anticipate a more developed fascist system—or at least some fascist equivalent?

This question ultimately turns on the unfolding relationship between corporate, military, and state power. As for those infamous "free-market" operatives discussed in *The Wrecking Crew,* there is the problem of whether they are really the dedicated assassins of big government Frank claims they are. Evidence suggests that, on the contrary, the wingers have wanted nothing more than to manipulate government toward their own ends, hoping to perpetuate corporate business-as-usual. Of course lobbying in its myriad forms is as old as American capitalism itself, an indelible force that assumed a larger role when the federal government started expanding in the 1930s. Nowadays federal and state agencies are routinely infiltrated or dominated by "private" interests—a practice that rarely elicits much controversy. Frank's "wrecking crew" is best understood in the context of an historic integration of government and corporations that marked the rise of state capitalism in the United States. Although the "wrecking crew" notion dwells on the supposed revival of "free-market" ideology, the earlier trajectory of state capitalism (extended to the military) was already brilliantly analyzed by C. Wright Mills in *The Power Elite* during the 1950s.[10] As discussed in chapter 3, Mills described an oligarchical power structure ruled by an ensemble of corporate, government, and military elites, their roles interchangeable and largely detached from citizen participation. Writing after the war economy had become a "permanent" fixture, Mills observed: "As the institutional means of power and the means of communication that tie them together have become steadily more efficient, those now in command of them have come into command of instruments of rule quite unsurpassed in the history of mankind."[11] For Mills, anticipating an even more concentrated power structure in the decades ahead, the thrust of militarized state capitalism would inevitably clash with the requirements of democracy and free markets, yielding to an irrepressible authoritarian logic. The American behemoth was mainly a product of World War II, when "the merger of the corporate economy and the military bureaucracy came into its present-day significance,"[12] deepening the convergence of "private" and "public" interests. The

resulting erosion of democratic citizenship and institutional accountability was, for Mills, endemic to this system. It is a great tribute to
Mills that, attuned to the war economy and security state, he could
already write that " . . . the structural clue to the power elite today lies
in the enlarged and military state" where "virtually all political and
economic actions are now judged in terms of military definitions of
reality."[13] At the same time, Mills could not have foreseen the extent
to which reactionary populism would become a force in American
politics, endowing the state-capitalist system with broader legitimacy
than it enjoyed in the 1950s.

In a period of expanded state capitalism, Mills surely would have
found the idea of autonomous, unfettered government functions
laughable. And Mills was right, then as now: it is hard to conceive
of state power operating "independent of vested interests."[14] It is also
true that elites at the summit of power tend to share a common outlook, one reason why systemic integration has proceeded over the
years with only minor disruptions. Lobbies, though surely less a factor in the 1950s, were generally taken for granted, with tales of the
"public interest" spun largely to rationalize elite privilege combined
with widespread powerlessness. And such powerlessness above all
extended, then as now, to the realm of foreign and military policy,
considered the domain of white male "experts."

The power structure that Mills probed in the 1950s has grown
more authoritarian in the midst of several wars, a consolidated war
economy and security state, corporate media hegemony, and neoliberal globalization. Backlash politics since the 1980s has surely reinforced this development. Well before the year 2010 it had become
obvious that the famous "military-industrial complex," denounced
by President Eisenhower in 1961, constituted a linchpin of the most
powerful state system ever built. Whether "liberal" or "conservative," statism is now a constituent element of the political culture, just
as patriotism (far more than the familiar "moral" beliefs) remains
the crucial legitimating ideology of empire, cutting across class divisions. Government spending has skyrocketed since the 1940s, regardless of what party controlled the presidency or Congress. During the
Reagan era, when Republicans screamed loudest about the evils of
big government, federal expenditures grew roughly 40 percent, from
$678 billion in 1981 to nearly $1.2 trillion in 1989. While Reagan
declared at his Inaugural Address in 1981 that freedom demands limited government, he presided over record-level budgetary increases,
never troubled by an orgy of federal spending on the Pentagon, Star

Wars, law enforcement, prisons, intelligence, and global surveillance. It was Reagan who imposed protectionist barriers against Japanese goods, authored massive Savings and Loan bailouts, and channeled taxpayer revenue into the gigantic space program. Again, when Republicans controlled both the presidency and Congress from 2001 to 2006—when "free marketers" were once more on the march— federal expenditures increased more than 10 percent, the bulk of it consumed by the military economy and wars. President Bush's projected military budget for 2009 was $805 billion (more than a trillion dollars when veterans' benefits are included), a staggering increase from $358 billion in 2000 when "big-spending liberals" occupied the White House. U.S. military expenditures in 2009 equaled those of the next eight largest nations combined. The total 2009 projected federal outlays, authorized by a "free market" president, stood at more than $3 trillion while the national debt soared past $106 trillion. Tens of billions have been poured into the failed war on drugs. In late 2008, as the American economy descended into severe crisis, the "small government," free-enterprise champion Bush earmarked more hundreds of billions of dollars to bail out Wall Street, banks, insurance companies, and the auto industry—initiatives carried forward and indeed accelerated under Obama. The reality is that Republicans no less than Democrats, "free-marketeers" no less than "tax-and-spend liberals," have worked faithfully to maintain a gargantuan state apparatus because it fully serves their drive for power and wealth.

It follows that the "libertarian" approach to state power turns out to be a far more selective (and indeed deceitful) set of beliefs than is generally assumed. It is sometimes forgotten that government performs a wide range of functions: regulation, law enforcement, ownership, education and research, social programs, bailouts, and military. A closer look at actual political behavior shows that "free marketers" level their sights against just *three* of these functions (regulations, ownership, and social programs) while supporting the often far more generous funding for others—with military and law enforcement (including intelligence and surveillance) especially privileged for the United States. Even more than Democrats, Republicans stand as world champions of big government, not to mention big corporations, big military, big superpower, big surveillance—and, lest we forget, big bailouts. Can the free-marketeers even take their own antistatist rhetoric seriously? In fact, American conservatives have long been Keynesians so long as it met their own interests, and they have always been prepared to embrace concentrated economic and state power.

Despite appearances to the contrary, with just a few exceptions this generalization applies to the recent Tea Party insurgency.

The Power Structure Expands

Naomi Wolf is yet another critic who believes the American political system has deteriorated to the point that it is now just a distant replica of democracy. The second Bush administration, she argues in *The End of America,* set in motion forces threatening to destroy hallowed principles bequeathed by Founders of the Republic. Wolf even suggests that fascist dictatorship is imminent unless these anti-democratic forces are soon reversed—a difficult prospect given the shrewd methods that devious authoritarian leaders employ to advance their own bloated power needs. Such methods could eventually "close down democracy" and lay the groundwork for a menacing "fascist shift"[15] characterized by growing state power, government violence, suspension of civil liberties, enhanced surveillance, incarceration of prisoners without "due cause," and attacks on the "free press."[16] Wolf was particularly alarmed by such moves as Bush's establishment of military tribunals to prosecute terrorist suspects at Guantanamo and elsewhere. The Bush White House, as is well known, resorted to shameful propaganda built on cynical lies and myths to facilitate a bogus war on terrorism and justify the war against Iraq. The rule of law, honored as mere formality, has been routinely and flagrantly subverted both in the United States and abroad through warrantless surveillance, coercive interrogations, and other schemes. Wolf's short book, widely praised when published in 2006, was advertised as a "warning" to American citizens understood as being naively unaware of the coming political catastrophe. In the course of her polemic, Wolf draws facile parallels between the Nazi conquest of power in Germany and practices adopted by the Bush administration. The fascist specter she puts forth runs counter to every ideal held by the Founding Fathers, whose worst fears are said to have revolved around the menace of tyranny. Wolf depicts the Founders as exemplars of freedom, democracy, and limited government, of a system designed to empower ordinary people and create "radical equality." Hoping to escape the authoritarian rule and political violence that pervaded the European experience, the Founders set out to impose restraints on centralized executive rule, leading to a democratic system that flourished across many generations until, within a few short years, Bush and his neocon cronies—motivated by little beyond power and greed—managed to overturn just about everything the Founders represented. Wolf ends her treatise by imploring Americans to revisit their venerable national traditions grounded in a "stewardship of the Founders' vision," before it is too late.

Wolf's view that American politics has entered a new phase of authoritarian decline—much of it thanks to Bush and his crowd—seems uncontroversial today even in the aftermath of Obama's remarkable campaign. The problem, common to liberals, lies in an overly mechanistic analysis focusing on leadership machinations while confining the "big picture" of potential catastrophe to events spanning less than a decade. Does it make sense to lay the major trends at Bush's doorstep, tempting as that might be? Are only Republicans to blame? Could a "fascist shift" (along Nazi lines, no less) gain momentum within an established liberal-democratic system in the span of a few years? Are the forces at work in American society so momentary and episodic as to belie any deeper historical origins? Modest reflection suggests the probability that such epic transformations could occur virtually overnight is the stuff of nothing but nightmares, though Wolf is surely anxious to have others share her nightmare. What makes this apocalyptic imagery even more bizarre is the realization that most of the supposed Nazi-like "methods" identified by Wolf have long been part of American politics, often in more extreme forms. Growth of an imperial presidency? Widespread use of state violence? Government surveillance run amok? Propaganda in support of military ventures? Abrogation of civil liberties? These and other "warning signs" laid out by Wolf have characterized U.S. history for so long their origins have been forgotten and the practices taken for granted. Zinn's *Peoples' History of the United States* is replete with such examples. And Mills, as we have seen, charted the historic merger of corporate, government, and military power already in the 1950s. In fact the Bush presidency, ruinous as it was, introduced nothing especially novel; its "methods" were mostly taken from the past. To select one example, the outrageous stratagem of "preemptive war" in 2003 had plenty of precursors: Polk in Mexico, McKinley in the Philippines, Wilson in Mexico and Central America, the Truman Doctrine, Kennedy in Cuba, Nixon in Indochina, Bush-I in Panama, and Clinton in the Balkans to identify the most noteworthy. None of these presidents cared much about Constitutional restraints nor about the sovereignty of other nations. Military tribunals were created by FDR during World War II. Intelligence and surveillance functions were broadened during the Truman and Eisenhower years, continuing into the present. As for state violence, the United States has been involved in warfare and various modes of domestic violence from the earliest years of the republic, with no sign it is about to end. Bush and the neocons simply inherited (while at times also embellishing) practices that, in any event, are best understood as integral to historical *processes* rather than a congeries of "methods" designed by manipulative leaders. Further, if something akin to a "fascist shift" is actually at work in the United States, both experience and logic dictate that it we are dealing with far more than a handful of bad leaders and bad decisions.

Strangely, Wolf never pursues her thesis in directions that could strengthen her case. Left out of her "big picture" is the steady growth of U.S. imperialism and militarism across the postwar years—a phenomenon, with its strong antidemocratic consequences, that should be difficult to overlook. What of the permanent war economy and national-security state? Repeated and costly military interventions? Development of a satellite-based intelligence and surveillance network geared to maintaining U.S. global supremacy? Corporate-driven globalization that the United States strives to manage for its own imperial ambitions? An oligopolistic media system that serves as a daily conduit of government and corporate propaganda? On these questions Wolf is oddly silent, her attention diverted to questionable White House agendas like military tribunals and the USA Patriot Act. Her silence, however, is hardly surprising, for *The End of America* if glaringly devoid of historical analysis needed to explain and contextualize any possible "fascist" or "Nazi" shift. Mechanistic from start to finish, her book has little to say about deep-seated social and political forces at work over many decades. One example: her section laying out "attacks on the press" focuses entirely on Bush's ambitious manipulation of news and information to support domestic and global agendas. But White House shenanigans of this sort have been recurrent throughout history—one need go back no further than scandalous episodes that rocked the Nixon, Reagan, and Clinton presidencies. Media manipulation is endemic to the American political terrain. Wolf's major flaw lies in her failure to see the larger panorama: a much larger threat to democracy, ignored in the book, is the rampant growth of transnational corporate media empires and their stranglehold over American political and cultural life abetted by grossly undemocratic maneuvers like the Telecommunications Act of 1996.

If an American fascism is actually on the horizon, analysis of conditions favorable to its success would seem in order, but Wolf offers nothing of the sort. The extreme Nazi model is useless for the task, but there is a deeper problem: can fascism, then or now, plausibly be conceived as a mere set of leadership "techniques" used to steal power and hoodwink the masses? Could Bush, Cheney, and the neocons—or their heirs—hope to engineer a fascist takeover by emulating the path of Hitler and Goebbels? The question contains its own answer—any "fascist shift" in a highly industrialized society like the United States (or indeed *any* society) is unthinkable apart from a rather lengthy *process* of historical transformation. This was emphatically true for classical fascism, which mostly defied the "revolutionary upsurge" scenario preferred by so many scholars. In such diverse settings as Germany, Italy, Japan, and Spain, fascism came to power through a coalition of social forces, typically including big business and the military, allied with traditional interests such as landholders, the church, and monarchy, winning popular support through sophisticated multiclass appeals to patriotism and preindustrial values. The social forces, political alliances, and historical conditions crucial to the ascendancy of such regimes never appeared suddenly or unexpectedly—the very narrative Wolf appears to have in mind for the United States. References to vaguely universal political realities like state violence, propaganda, and elite maneuvering scarcely help matters.

Wolf is outraged that Bush and his lieutenants have broken with principles of the Founders and the Constitution. In her overly generous view, the American colonists were dedicated apostles of freedom, democracy, limited government, rights, and equality. Yet, as we have seen, a closer reading of early U.S. history reveals something quite different: the small nucleus of white European men who drew up the constitution embraced such ideals, if at all, in only the most partial and limited form. Possessers of enormous wealth and property, most owned slaves, wanted a strong federal government, and viewed suffrage as restricted to white male property owners—their central ambition being to maintain the wealth and power they accumulated once independence from Britain had been won. As mentioned in chapter 1, the colonial settlers looked to centralized power to maintain social order, destroy Indian resistance, maintain slavery, wage military combat, and (eventually) facilitate conquest of the frontier. In this setting the merger of government, large commercial interests, and military power (though limited) had in fact already come to fruition by the early nineteenth century, those cherished Founding "principles" invoked by Wolf falling into the category of another grand illusion.

In *Democracy, Inc.,* which similarly points toward a harsh authoritarian turn in American politics, Sheldon Wolin harbors no such illusions about the Founders or about U.S. history: the constitution, (lower case?) he argues, laid the groundwork for centralized government and elite rule, a document that evoked contempt for the democratic capacities of ordinary people—the artifact of a predemocratic era in which all forms of domination, later contested, were thoroughly taken for granted. Nor does he entertain any comparable myths about later American development. Taking his investigation of power relations well beyond that of Frank, Wolf, and other critics preoccupied with the Bush presidency, Wolin relies on deeper historical and theoretical accounts to demolish myths supportive of a political system that from the outset barely concealed its darker legacy under the cloak of God-ordained national destiny. He questions whether democracy—even the minimalist kind—has much future in an era of expanding corporate, state, and bureaucratic power enlarged by the drive toward globalization and empire. The political outlook hardly merits optimism. Wolin reluctantly concludes that "One cannot point to any national institutions that [today] can be accurately described as democratic..."[17] Congress, the presidency, court system, parties, bureaucracies, corporate workplaces, schools and universities—all these arenas of public life are hierarchical, lacking much in the way of citizen participation. Power has become so concentrated across the landscape that few commentators nowadays even pause to take notice.

A key historical turning point for Wolin was an expanded "power imaginary" that took hold after World War II. War mobilization, a superpower agenda, the security state, and growth of a war economy all served to extend the boundaries of power, make a shambles of Constitutional restraints, and fuel statist and corporate authoritarianism. The classical liberalism of free markets, small government, and local autonomy had with the start of the Cold War lost whatever efficacy it possessed, even as opinion leaders continued to celebrate its virtues. The new "power imaginary" meant the rise of large-scale management, global expansion, ideological consensus, and cohesive elite culture. As Wolin notes, however, the truly novel aspect of this shift was its *scope,* for the United States had from its founding been a colonial, interventionist nation driven by the ethos of Manifest Destiny. Thus "Virtually from the beginning of the nation the making of the American citizen was influenced, even shaped by, the making of an American imperium."[18] An enlarged "power imaginary" built on this legacy from the late 1940s onward. As mentioned, this was also the focus of Mills' seminal work, but in *Democracy, Inc.* Wolin fixes his attention on a behemoth far more awesome and frightening than anything envisioned by Mills.

Wolin's critical dissection of the power structure is most illuminating when he explores the dialectic between superpower politics and domestic authoritarianism. He sees a "managed democracy" in which popular governance has steadily shrunk in the face of corporate, military, and bureaucratic power—a shrinkage more visible in the post-9/11 milieu where the war on terrorism further legitimates the war economy and security state. In this setting, "terror is both a response to empire and the provocation that allows for empire to cease to be ashamed of its identity."[19] Constraints on power easily vanish in such a spatially and temporally limitless struggle. A global assault on terrorism enables the imperial state to cloak its power in the wounded innocence of avenging victim—a claim, however, that could fade for Bush's successors in the absence of new attacks. The specter of a vengeful superpower facing off against barbaric enemies on a world scale once again suggests a Hobbesian universe in which the threat of anarchy is countered by an order-giving Leviathan. After all, the very logic of imperial power dictates continuous military interventions, political subterfuge, global surveillance, elite flexibility, and "bipartisan" consensus—all signposts of an authoritarian state, where the scope of democratic citizenship increasingly narrows.

Wolin describes a political culture congruent with this Hobbesian dialectic. As defining elements of the liberal state atrophy, the system gradually and almost imperceptibly acquires a new identity in the form of "inverted totalitarianism," a system requiring no fundamental break with the past, no revolutionary upsurge, but just a continuation of existing trends. Yet, as the expanded "power imaginary" engulfs the political landscape, the familiar grand illusions take on greater urgency at the very moment references to democracy, free market, limited government, and humanitarian foreign intervention more frequent such illusions grow more disconnected from reality. Organized on a foundation of corporate interests and priorities, the new system requires elite agreement on the "big issues" (economy, foreign policy); dissent is marginalized, ruled off limits, or channeled into debates over peripheral concerns of the sort discussed by Frank. Thus: "The fact that government rarely challenges corporate power allows capital to define the political terrain to fit its own needs."[20]

Fixation on a narrowing of political discourse echoes Herbert Marcuse's thesis of "one-dimensionality," though the problem for Marcuse was located mainly in the workings of technological rationality.[21] Advanced industrial society, in Marcuse's view, had become totally administered behind a liberal-democratic façade, where the power structure replicates itself through one-dimensional ideology that subverts critical thought and oppositional politics. Thus: "By virtue of the way it has organized its technological base, contemporary industrial society tends to be totalitarian. For 'totalitarian' is not only a terroristic political coordination of society, but also a non-terroristic economic-technical coordination which operates through the manipulation of needs by vested interests. It thus precludes the emergence of an effective opposition against the whole."[22] Here "one-dimensional thought is systematically promoted by the makers of politics and their purveyors of mass information. Their universe of discourse is populated by self-validating hypotheses which, incessantly and monopolistically repeated, become hypnotic definitions of freedom."[23] At this point Marcuse's near-Orwellian interpretation of American society would seem to pose the question of fascist politics, though Marcuse himself never explicitly takes up the issue. Elsewhere, however, Marcuse argued that fascism could evolve out of a "highly-organized capitalism" (state-capitalism) as it lays the structural and ideological conditions of a rationalized new order, presumably akin to the "totalitarianism" of one-dimensional society. He suggested that "the idea of dictatorship and of authoritarian direction of the state is not at all foreign to liberalism."[24] In the case of historical fascism, despite its overt hostility to liberalism, we know that everywhere the regimes built on the capitalist economic order.

In Wolin's understanding, to the degree formal attributes of liberal democracy remain—elections, party competition, legislatures, interest groups, etc.—they have diminished relevance in an ideological milieu where "opposition has not been liquidated but rendered feckless," where "extreme views" (outside the mainstream) are ritually filtered out and neutralized.[25] Alternatives to "inverted totalitarianism" are nullified more by well-managed ideological consensus than by state coercion or heavy-handed propaganda. In this system, Rupert Murdoch is far more potent than Josef Goebbels could ever hope to be. Debates circumvent larger issues tied to distribution of power, wealth, and resources, especially in the main corridors of government. Thus, with the war economy a durable and unquestioned feature of American life, real debates over Pentagon spending are rendered taboo, in both the political system and media. Wolin observes that "...military spending is nearly four times greater than the expenditures on social programs; yet neither party would dream of proposing an amendment specifically limiting or controlling military spending—only one prohibiting same-sex marriage."[26] Given the vast scale of the war economy, those state intrusions so justifiably feared by Wolf—press controls, military tribunals, abrogation of rights, etc.—are better viewed as subordinate to the general modus operandi of an imperial juggernaut that pursues world domination and in the process undermines democracy at home and abroad. Here Wolin sees "managed democracy" as a form of "controlled politics that tolerates dissent but is unresponsive to protests and proposals from below."[27]

A system of "inverted totalitarianism" derives its totalizing impulses mostly from the corporate sector rather than government; economics comes to dominate politics. Wolin distinguishes this phenomenon from earlier totalitarian models said to have sought a full break with the past. Earlier fascist and Communist regimes looked to centralized state power sustained by mass mobilization and harsh party/government controls including random violence, political jailings, banning of opposition, and Orwellian propaganda. As mentioned, the architects of classical fascism despised liberalism as weak and useless, even as they embraced capitalism. For "inverted totalitarianism," on the other hand, the older crude mechanisms of domination wind up superfluous since the system retains outer features of liberalism, preserves continuity, and favors mass political *disengagement* rather than mobilization. "Private" media carries out the functions, ever more efficiently, of propaganda, giving elites greater room to maneuver within an officially "free" and pluralistic communications system. In classic totalitarianism, the general population is excluded from governance at the very instant it is mobilized, whereas the genius of the American new order is that it effectively depoliticizes and *demobilizes* citizens while simultaneously celebrating images of participation, diversity, and change.

Democracy, Inc. extends and reinvigorates the great legacy of Mills at a time when the imperial system, even when hobbled by economic crisis, shows no signs of democratizing or shrinking. Like Mills, Wolin theorizes the complex integration of state, corporate, and military power, and like Mills he explores how mass political inertia is thoroughly interwoven with superpower politics and post-war U.S. global ambitions. As we have seen, however, Wolin goes beyond Mills in his emphasis on ideological factors within the legitimation process, naturally more vital at times of sharpening crisis when the received wisdom loses much of it hold. Wolin expertly dismantles political myths—including a few grand illusions—that have become more detached from the social reality they officially define with each passing year. A question remains, however, as to whether Wolin's categories of "managed democracy" and "inverted totalitarianism" furnish enough conceptual lucidity to do justice to his overall richly textured critique of the power structure.

Fascism of a New Type?

The task of making conceptual sense of the American power structure is more imposing than ever, possibly a major reason the challenge is taken up by surprisingly few scholars. Many observers remain trapped in civics textbook–style discourse, as "democracy" becomes part of a ritualized vocabulary extending across the political spectrum. Meanwhile, familiar references to "power elite," "state monopoly capitalism," "welfare-state capitalism," and the like provide few novel insights at the start of the twenty-first century, while the multiple prefixes to "democracy"—elitist, pluralist, capitalist, polyarchic, and so forth—similarly fall short, for reasons mentioned above. Some labels fail to rise above a lazy sloganeering: thus both "oligarchy" and "plutocracy" capture an abundant kernel of truth about the American system, but say little about ideology, politics, and foreign policy. Wolin selected categories meant to cover the entire system of rule, but these categories too appear somehow rooted in the past, resonant of a Cold War dichotomy that once saw "democracy" and "totalitarianism," West and East, as polar opposites. To be sure, Wolin's discourse never sinks to such a crude bipolarity, yet these labels fail the requisites of a complex radical analysis necessitating a fresher conceptual framework. Can the mature authoritarian system Wolin so painstakingly deconstructs be fairly understood as "democratic," whatever its modifier? Is the very notion of "managed democracy" contradictory on its face, as Wolin himself concedes at one point? At the other extreme, how fruitful today is a totalitarian model historically associated with massive state terrorism, gulags, rampant imperialism, holocausts, and monolithic single-party rule? (Parallels between the two systems might be more suggestive than most Americans might ever want to entertain, but deep contrasts must be kept in mind.)

The problem is that *both* categories impede the critical task at hand, for insofar as the American behemoth is neither "democratic" nor "totalitarian" in any meaningful sense of these terms—or indeed in any way consistent with Wolin's own interpretation—both categories are destined to fall short. The main criteria of democracy—citizen participation, collective decision-making, open public discourse, a well-informed public, institutional accessibility—are effectively lacking, as Wolin shows, leaving more dynamic elements of the political culture to atrophy. Could any semblance of democracy coexist with its opposite, "totalitarianism"? If, as Wolin argues, corporate power represents the new "totalizing force," surely that reality shares little in common with even a minimalist conception of democracy. (Wolin's reference to the "specter" of totalitarianism suggests a future order where democracy might be superseded—but there is little clarity on this point.) At the other extreme, the "totalitarian" model first elaborated by Hannah Arendt in the early 1950s has always exaggerated the totalizing or monolithic element of these societies, obscuring what scholars eventually revealed was a far more complex and plural social reality. It is worth noting, moreover, that none of these regimes managed to sweep away residues of the past—even where they tried—as Wolin and others argue was central to earlier totalitarianism. The interwar regimes fell considerably short of all-encompassing power structures than Arendt and her cohorts writing in the Cold War tradition assumed. Wolin's effort to resuscitate an already problematic concept by "inverting" it, by linking it directly to *corporate* domination, thus seems highly questionable. If the American political system remains grounded in strong manifestations of liberalism and pluralism, as Wolin recognizes, then it is difficult to grasp what is gained by invoking such a time-worn ideal-type.

Efforts to theorize power relations in the United States become all the more challenging when the very uniqueness of American development is fully taken into account. The ensemble of relations appears sui generis, without precedent, as Wolin's superb work affirms. We have the wealthiest, most economically, politically, and militarily powerful behemoth in world history, its ruling elite in possession of the largest war economy ever and fueled by a morally righteous legacy of Manifest Destiny, its superpower ambitions sustained by widespread patriotic legitimacy. This is a nation, driven by superpower agendas, that has routinely and bloodily intervened in other lands around the world. Yet the United States is also a nation that for two centuries has embraced norms of liberal democracy, however partial and incomplete—norms ultimately compromised by colonialism, poverty, racism, minority disenfranchisement, and a grossly unequal class structure. In this context we are entitled to question whether the American political system in all its unvarnished reality could today be adequately described as either "democratic" or "totalitarian," whatever the qualifiers? Or do we need entirely different conceptual guideposts?

Some observers entertain prospects of a U.S. fascist trajectory rooted in well-entrenched traditions—imperialism, militarism, the corporate state, a popular ideology steeped in religious values and hyperpatriotism. Could a postwar militarized state capitalism ultimately evolve into something akin to historical fascism without the same hated symbols of the Hitler and Mussolini era? Wolin himself discusses the specter of a "fascist equivalent" for the United States. Could a modern right-wing authoritarian order be the outcome of a gradual, evolutionary process—a trajectory Wolin takes seriously—in contrast to a full-scale revolutionary break with existing social forces and political institutions? No doubt the system described by Wolin in many ways closely resembles classical fascism, though more ideologically than structurally, but it never pretends to dismantle or "smash" liberal democracy and never upholds a cult of the great leader. Mills must have anticipated such a likelihood in *The Power Elite,* without ever relying on concepts like "totalitarianism" and "fascism." If Wolin indeed believes a fascist shift is on the horizon—and his conclusions do point toward such an eventuality—then a reference to "totalitarianism" probably obscures more than it illuminates.

What, then, of a possible fascist trajectory in a nation that today possesses so many classical fascist indicators but departs from so many others? If democratic structures and practices have been largely reduced to a façade, a pressing question arises as to what institutional and ideological barriers might stand in the way of a more full-blown authoritarian system, or "fascist equivalent." Is the United States, with the largest imperial presence and war machine in history, on the path to a qualitatively new kind of fascism—one conceivably unfolding within the established forms of liberal democracy? Chris Hedges for one seems convinced that ideological tenets of historical fascism have for some time shaped the American public sphere, especially at the level of everyday life. In *American Fascists* he charts the rise of a pervasive Christian fundamentalism he believes could prefigure a more developed theocratic order—an order presumably congruent with some kind of "fascist equivalent." At the time of writing (2006), according to Hedges, there were roughly 70 million "evangelicals" in the United States belonging to some 200,000 churches as well as such large organizations as the Christian Coalition, Eagle Forum, and Focus on the Family, not to mention a far-reaching media presence. Evangelicals count among 40 percent of Americans who reportedly take the Bible as literal truth, a large number of its believers filled with rage and intolerance, anxious to cleanse the world of infidels and enemies through violence and warfare where necessary. Hedges shows how right-wing Christianity has merged with rabid patriotism in support of U.S. military power in a political culture where "war is the final aesthetic of the movement."[28] Possessed of an unshakeable sense of moral supremacy, the evangelicals sometimes "call for the destruction of whole cultures, nations, and religions, [above all] those they have defined as the enemies of God."[29] This loosely structured Christian movement has given rise to a "warrior culture" dominated by white men, its followers ever prepared to do battle with omni-present forces of evil and darkness—forces since 9/11 increasingly defined as Arabs and Muslims. Violence, though fiercely condemned as evil "terrorism" when practiced by others, becomes something of a sacred force, a cleansing tonic sanctioned by God, when used by Americans.

What Hedges scorns as a "callous, hateful, ruthless ideology" is clearly the stuff of historical fascism, reinforced by a deep mood of victimism (the Vietnam syndrome, 9/11) and quest for revenge. The pressing question here is: could this ideology, with its broadened mass appeal, help generate (and legitimate) a more institutionally mature American fascism? Hedges explores some frightening tendencies in the political culture he sees possibly moving toward a new state religion, a "Christo-fascism," its gains readily visible throughout the society and within the ranks of the Republican Party. The great outpouring for Republican vice-presidential candidate Sarah Palin, a dedicated evangelical—not to mention former President Bush's own attachment to right-wing Christianity—testifies to the resonance of this outlook, though also in some ways to its futility. To the degree fundamentalism reinforces popular support for a God-given U.S. right to dominate the planet, it can help reinforce consensus behind endless wars for superpower hegemony. Could this augur the kind of fascistic assault on American political traditions that Hedges (and, in different ways, Wolf) has in mind? Perhaps, but Hedges seems to be widely off the mark in framing right-wing Christianity as some kind of novel break with the past: is this outlook not an extension of traditional, homespun, God-fearing Protestantism that historically intersected with racist, colonial, and exceptionalist currents of Manifest Destiny? Was not slavery, along with every step toward extermination of Native Americans, justified and even celebrated as part of God's will? Did not President McKinley, as the U.S. military was preparing for war in the Philippines that would slaughter hundreds of thousands of civilians, inform Americans that this was a Christian duty? Across U.S. history, of course, institutional and ideological obstacles set limits to this fundamentalism while, moreover, the United States was never able to achieve genuine superpower status until after World War II. The main question today revolves around whether the present historical conjuncture might be more favorable to a *systemic* fascist outcome bringing the reactionary populism described by Hedges into a coherent power structure.

While one's view of this outcome depends in great measure on the chosen definition of fascism—and there are many—the very entry of the prospect into American public discourse is revealing. If the persistence of liberal democracy, however emaciated, clouds the issue, one might still concede that certain *ideological* parallels between historical fascism and the present conjuncture are much too evident to ignore. Thus the "palingenetic" elements linking ultranationalism, imperialism, and militarism that Roger Griffin defines as the linchpin of historical fascism, when viewed in the context of expanding corporate power, recall much (though surely not all) of interwar fascist ideology.[30]

Griffin's penetrating analysis of interwar fascism—centered appropriately on the Italian model—seems particularly relevant to the American setting, whatever the historical differences. Concentrating on the "palingenetic form of populist ultranationalism" that swept Europe in the years after World War I, he locates a "fascist minimum" extending across diverse geographical contexts in which these regimes appeared.[31] This ideological matrix, most explosive at moments of crisis, promised national regeneration, a "new start" in a world filled with corruption, decay, evil, and external threats. For Griffin, fascism tapped into ultranationalism as the powerful and unifying of all ideologies—all the more so when combined with shared religious values—with national rebirth pointing toward an epic turning point in history where the masses feel empowered, part of a special mission energized by "higher" goals of an exceptional community. Fascist leaders were able to manipulate the popular yearning for grand achievements that only a hallowed (charismatic) leadership stratum could deliver; as Mussolini, Hitler, and Franco implored their tens of millions of followers to achieve great deeds, despair, futility, and defeat could be transformed into wondrous rebirth fueled by populist ultranationalism. Typified by Mussolini's Italy, where a new Roman Empire was placed on the political agenda, fascism signified a cultural superiority that the reborn nation could exert over peoples regarded as backward and inferior.[32] To achieve its rightful place in history, fascism required large-scale political engineering: state planning, a powerful military apparatus, armed ventures, and ideological mobilization. Following the classical pattern, therefore, the most fascist equivalent would likely consolidate power through existing societal tendencies associated with the militarized state capitalism analyzed by Mills and Wolin. The palingenetic motifs identified by Griffin have been part of the American landscape for several decades: national exceptionalism, militarism, imperialism, corporatism, religious messianism. As for palingenetic ultranationalism, the post-9/11 ideological milieu with its "war on terrorism" has been congenial to its emergence. If these ideological trends appear rather compatible with the liberal tradition and pluralist norms, it is worth mentioning this was at least partially true of historical fascism, where the degree of "totalitarian" controls has been generally exaggerated. One striking difference today is that an overt attack on liberalism, as with Mussolini, is superfluous insofar as the liberalism of a militarized state capitalism is now entirely compatible with the palingenetic ethos.

In contrast to the views advanced by Frank, Wolf, and Hedges, therefore, the idea of an "assault on democracy" in the United States appears misplaced—in part because it exaggerates the American democratic legacy, in part because any fascist shift will, as in the past, be an expression more of historical forces at work than of diabolical elite schemes or total break with the past. As Bertram Gross presciently argued long ago, an American fascism is destined to be of a more "friendly" variety, without major social disruptions, systematic terrorism, paramilitary actions, Mussolini-style demagoguery, and even outright attacks on the Constitution.[33] If none of these classical fascistic initiatives is ever likely to prevail within the parameters of American political culture, neither would any of them likely be *necessary*.

An American fascism (or its modern "equivalent") would depart radically from the historical experience, itself extraordinarily diverse with the Nazi model (contrary to myth) more exceptional than typical. While Hedges dwells on popular beliefs as fascist ideology, recalling the classic *Authoritarian Personality* studies organized by Theodor Adorno, he never connects those beliefs to changes (actual or potential) at the summit of power. Other contemporary writers on this topic—Michael Mann, Walter Laqueur, and Robert Paxson among them—have a more jaundiced attitude regarding prospects for any modern-day fascism.[34] According to Mann, the ideology was always largely European, one long ago "defeated, dead, and buried."[35] With its overwhelmingly negative stigma, fascism today appeals to just a few crackpots and thugs. The institutionalization of liberal democracy in Europe and North America, moreover, has neutralized the totalizing (and also partly pre-modern) thrust of fascist ideology. Laqueur agrees, stressing that fascism cannot coexist with modernity given its outmoded single-party monopoly, reliance on terrorism, virulent nationalism, and compromise with the old (now vanquished) social order. Laqueur would argue that the right-wing authoritarianism so feared by Hedges is not only harmless but nowadays could never be translated into a durable movement or power structure; it is destined to remain localized, dispersed, and mired in futility.[36] The bulk of mainstream thinking, often derailed by the Nazi model (the only one marked by sustained wars of aggression, concentration camps, and holocaust) has followed this same logic. As mentioned, however, facile comparisons between historical fascism and present-day American conditions are essentially misguided. Structural divergences can obscure striking ideological parallels, as we have seen. As Gross was the first to point out, moreover, right-wing authoritarian elites today are far less likely to embrace Freikorps-style militias, the *Fuhrerprinzip*, and death camps, perforce choosing instead to pursue fascistic agendas beneath the comfortable façade of liberal democracy.

The very expanse of American power today—global, military, corporate, bureaucratic—ought to pose the question of a potential "fascist equivalent" in the modern setting. Despite economic crisis, this behemoth exhibits no signs of retreating. While Mann is correct to emphasize the firm grounding of liberal-democracy in the United States, he forgets that this is also a system marked by such high levels of institutionalization and ideological consensus that electoral politics has diminished impact within a power structure even more concentrated and oligarchic than the one described by Mills. A fascist equivalent would necessarily be less "totalitarian" than interwar fascist states that, in any event, always depended on traditional pillars of support (church, monarchy, aristocracy) enjoying some degree of social and political autonomy. Elements of liberalism and right-wing authoritarian can easily coexist, as they have historically, in countries like Japan, Mexico, Russia, and South Korea. The very notion of a classical fascist "revolution," forcing a total break with the past, turns out to be yet another of the time-honored myths.

That Mann believes fascism will never come to the United States is hardly surprising given a restrictive definition tied to the historical moment when "fascism is the pursuit of transcendent and cleansing nation-statism through paramilitarism."[37] Fixation on paramilitary action linked to rampaging local militias as in the famous but largely fictional "march on Rome" was overdrawn even for best-case Italy. In fact powerful elite coalitions dictated the nature of fascist ascendancy, and most paramilitaries were either weak or absent; mass political activity occurred within a transmission belt that worked from top to bottom. As Laqueur points out, "True, the masses were 'mobilized', not in order to participate actively in politics, not to fight in the streets, but to march in occasional mass demonstrations and parades, to listen from time to time to lectures, and to attend similar functions."[38] For Japanese fascism, Barrington Moore arrived at the same conclusion: the regime was based on an alliance of big business and traditional interests, where elites rallied the masses around nationalism and militarism as they orchestrated everything from above.[39] The Japanese model, though rarely discussed, was closer to the general norm than was Nazi Germany. It follows that a depoliticized public sphere would pose no great obstacle to fascist prospects in the United States, where corporate and imperial power seeks maximum freedom of movement, surely preferring something along lines of Wolin's "managed democracy." For modern authoritarian rule, popular insurgency no doubt ends up more disruptive than system-sustaining.

Predictions of a fully developed fascist order in the United States now seem entirely premature, even crazy, especially where the definition of fascism clings to the classical experience. Whether Constitutional and other liberal modalities are today durable enough to prevent such an outcome in the face of ongoing corporate, imperial, and military expansion, however, seems increasingly doubtful. Counterforces do, of course exist, including social movements and grassroots activism that have pervaded U.S. history. Explosive "demotic moments"—strong but momentary expressions of citizen engagement or protest—that Wolin discusses at some length could be decisive at future critical junctures. The twentieth century witnessed a steady expansion of popular suffrage along with a spirited defense of civil and legal rights, even as the political system itself became more closed and less participatory under the weight of corporate power, the war economy, bureaucratization, media concentration, and "bipartisan" ideological conformity. Indicators of citizen involvement—voter turnout, issue knowledge and awareness, sense of efficacy, etc.—have declined sharply in recent decades, only to be slightly (and no doubt temporarily) revived during Obama's run to the presidency.[40] Leftist and progressive movements capable of posing effective alternatives to an increasingly bankrupt political order scarcely exist. Democratic upsurges cited by Wolin have been most visible at times of social crisis, as during the 1930s and 1960s, but elections as such have rarely produced far-reaching change. In Wolin's view, "demotic moments" can effectively pose short-term challenges to the "arts of management," but their episodic character means their capacity to effectively challenge power or class relations under present circumstances will be limited. Thus, while an Obama presidency offered the American public much-needed imagery of hope and change, it should be remembered that Democrats are beholden to the same corporate and military interests—and subscribe to the same broad political outlook—as Republicans. And these voracious interests exhibit no readiness to abandon their vast network of privilege and power, nor relinquish the "grand illusions" vital to perpetuating their hegemony.

Conclusion

If the preceding chapters paint an excessively dark picture of American politics, the objective has been to frame the contemporary predicament in its starkest reality, devoid of its celebratory fictions and myths against the backdrop of a long history. At present "democracy" constitutes more legitimating symbol than operating mechanism of a system dominated by globalized corporate, state, and military power. The overwhelming evidence reveals a social order that is increasingly oligarchic and inegalitarian, best understood as a complex ensemble of political and economic, institutional and ideological, domestic and global forces at work. The contribution this system has made to the mounting global crisis—simultaneously economic, military, and ecological in its dimensions—makes it central to the unfolding historical drama. Equally central to the American experience is the paucity of democratic politics, placing severe limits on the capacity of human beings to face the challenge and reverse the out-of-control trajectory leading toward planetary catastrophe.

The future prospects of democratization, in the United States as elsewhere, will require a thoroughgoing process of countersystemic change in the long-established patterns of corporate predation, unfettered economic growth, privatized consumption, and harsh social relations that shape the entire terrain of public life, meaning full-scale renewal of a political culture historically imbued with habits of passivity and deference to hierarchical authority. Sheldon Wolin writes: "Put starkly, the crucial political issue or our times concerns the incompatibility between the culture of everyday reality to which political democracy should be attuned and the culture of virtual reality on which corporate capitalism thrives."[1] In other words, fundamental change, including democratization, cannot succeed without a conscious reorientation of the ideological consensus underlying the institutional framework of the public sphere. Wolin adds: "The

persisting conflict between democratic egalitarianism and an economic system that has rapidly evolved into another inegalitarian
regime is a reminder that capitalism is not solely a matter of production, exchange, and reward. It is a regime in which culture, politics,
and economy tend toward a seamless whole, a totality."[2] This essentially Gramscian sensibility—the idea that radical change is unthinkable without reshaping mass beliefs and attitudes—is at the core of
any future democratic renewal. Far removed from the liberal ethos
of business-as-usual, such a process will have to depart from deeply
ingrained norms and rules, opening space for a more insurgent politics: disruptive protests, dynamic popular movements, a vibrant community life, deep citizenship that empowers the great mass of people.

Could the kind of social democracy highlighted at the end of the
introduction—a signpost of "actually-existing democracy"—provide
an initial stepping-stone along the route to a more radical process of
social transformation? Could something akin to the Swedish model
be achieved by simply forcing existing institutions and policies left-
ward? Perhaps, but there is the prior question as to whether a deeply
entrenched corporate-military state, with the mass media as its propaganda arm, could be weakened to the point where its bastions of
structural and ideological strength might be thusly challenged. At present elite hegemony appears solid if not monolithic, virtually impervious to even moderate changes widely accepted in Europe. Hysterical
elite (and popular) opposition to basic health care reforms—to the
sort of national system taken for granted elsewhere—reveals massive
obstacles standing in the way of programs that the power elite views
as even minimally harmful to its interests.

History has bequeathed four distinct roads to fundamental social
change—the evolutionary strategy of social democracy, grassroots
insurgency built around local forms typical of anarchism, Jacobin-
style conquest of state power by a vanguard elite, and broad-based
cultural transformation resulting in a power shift from below. A fifth
model articulated within more recent Green tendencies seeks to com-
bine elements of the first, second, and fourth models. The Swedish
alternative surely represents a marked advance beyond the American
corporate state and war economy—a qualitative step toward democratization—but, as mentioned, political resistance in the United States
would be ferocious. Equally problematic, the growing urgency that
emanates from the global ecological crisis suggests a gradual and limited strategy could be too little and too late to save the planet from
likely cataclysm. Local insurgency, always seductive in its promise

of total freedom and democracy, has a long and tortured history of political futility—often vanishing from the scene owing to its own dispersed spontaneity, often crushed by larger centers of threatened power, other times assimilated into established parties, unions, or governmental structures. Jacobinism, for its part, has an impressive record of political success as the guiding strategy for twentieth-century communist revolutions, but its ultimate fate has been either bureaucratic centralism (the USSR) or state-capitalism (China). Neither of these outcomes is compatible, needless to say, with prospects for democratization, rendering the model useless as a present-day alternative to the corporate state. What remains, virtually by default, is the Green variant of change associated with the initial trajectory of European parties merging electoral politics, cultural transformation, and local insurgency within a new paradigm of radical politics. While the larger Green parties, as in West Germany, eventually fell into the social-democratic orbit, marked by the triumph of "Realos" over "Fundis," the original strategy did champion a project of democratization that was simultaneously anticapitalist, antihierarchical, ecological, and community-based. By focusing on the environmental imperative, moreover, Green politics embraced a degree of radical urgency lacking in all but the elite-driven Jacobin strategy.

For contemporary America, mired in a reactionary impasse, the outlook would seem rather dystopic, hopeless. Radical change requires a dismantling of corporate power, the war economy, security state, and indeed the entire U.S. imperial structure. It further calls for an ambitious reshaping of the mass media, along with a familiar litany of reforms: proportional representation, public campaign financing, progressive taxation, freeing of politics from corporate largesse, local empowerment through revitalized social programs, to name a few. It demands a profound shift toward public investment and social egalitarianism, anathema to the ruling interests. None of these changes—regarded as normal in many industrialized countries—seems even dimly on the American horizon. Whether the Swedish example could serve as a transitional phase in revitalizing American democracy could thus, unfortunately, turn out to be a moot point. The question then turns on whether the global crisis, with its rapidly intensifying contradictions, could in some way force imminent, drastic political solutions in a society so immobilized by oligarchic power relations and ideological conservatism. Historically, as is well known, crisis tendencies generally gave rise to reactionary, indeed often fascist, outcomes as anxious populations gravitated toward strong leaders, ultrapatriotism, traditional values, and established centers of power in the midst of Hobbesian chaos. The rational hope is that new anti-system forces will seize hold of the contradictions, explode upon the political scene, and generate strongly progressive (yet democratic) outcomes at a time when the global crisis threatens the very survival of humanity.

Postscript: Politics in the Nuclear Age

The dawn of atomic warfare at the end of World War II transformed not only the military but social, scientific, and above all political landscape for all time. Bringing a legacy of nearly total destruction and unimaginable death, Hiroshima and Nagasaki—first salvos of the epic Manhattan Project—continue to shadow the global scene in ways unimaginable in 1945. The Bomb ignited a new era of unlimited warfare, checkmating standard defensive responses and countermeasures while eviscerating boundaries separating civilian and military targets, rendering thinkable the mass extermination of human populations as a "rational" calculus of military action. Invention of the Superbomb in 1951, result of the nascent arms race between the United States and Soviet Union, altered this horrifying specter ever more dramatically. Over time the new doomsday weapons spread around the world and became normalized within the military culture of several nations, none more so than the United States. The mass-psychological numbing and general cultural denial that accompanied these weapons has, over the decades, become far too obvious to require further commentary. For American politics, the Bomb signified a great historical watershed, feeding powerfully into the Cold War and postwar national security state and permanent war economy that were so integral to rising superpower ambitions. As the Bomb grew into a fixture of Pentagon strategic doctrine fueled by the U.S. drive toward global military supremacy, it would have long-lasting consequences for virtually every realm of American public life.

On July 25, 1945, when President Truman signed the order to drop the atomic bomb on Japan, there were no doubts among U.S. leaders concerning the efficacy or morality of using this fearsome weapon against densely populated cities. Whether such attacks were necessary seemed highly questionable as the Japanese had already made repeated overtures toward peace; indeed a postwar U.S. bombing survey revealed beyond all doubt that surrender could easily have been achieved without resorting to atomic warfare in early August 1945. The reality was that American leaders in the know were wildly excited about the amazing fruits of the Manhattan Project and, with few exceptions, envisioned the Bomb as a spectacle empowering Washington to dictate the postwar global order to fit its own geopolitical interests. The terror weapon was understood by government and military elites closest to the program as a creative instrument of peace and democracy, a discovery further likely to undercut Soviet postwar leverage. When Truman learned of the successful Hiroshima attack on August 6 while returning to Washington aboard the *U.S.S. Augusta,* he reportedly said "this is the greatest thing in history!" Aside from a small grouping of skeptical scientists, this very sentiment was uniformly shared by the upper circles in Washington. The historical record shows that all of Truman advisers were fully in agreement. As for Japan in the summer of 1945, it was starved, crippled, and defenseless, most of its cities burned to the ground, so defense of the atomic bombardments on strictly military grounds was especially weak. (Japanese leaders wanted only to retain the emperor, which the United States eventually allowed.) The guiding motives resided elsewhere: revenge, racial hatred, and postwar geopolitical maneuvering. Sentiments of outright militaristic sadism cannot be discounted. At the time, as John Dower observed, American political and military discourse was filled with exterminationist rhetoric.[1] Indeed it appears the war was prolonged exactly so that U.S. bombers could extend their missions and reduce Japan to ruins—a project that started months before Hiroshima and Nagasaki with the saturation attacks on 66 cities, leading to loss of hundreds of thousands of civilian lives. In the words of Admiral William Leahy in 1942, "in fighting with Japanese savages all previously accepted rules of warfare must be abandoned."[2]

If the national security state was a product of the Cold War, it was fueled by the Manhattan Project, the bomb, and rise of the nuclear-scientific-industrial complex. From the outset, this system was based on a climate of ideological righteousness, to the extent that virtually anything—any form of barbarism—was thinkable. It was, after all, the nationalist fanaticism of World War II, with its powerful racist connotations, that permitted, indeed encouraged, the saturation bombing of civilian populations in Germany and Japan—the very crimes for which the Allies charged the fascist nations. And it was this same fanaticism that fed into President Truman's decision to drop atomic bombs on Hiroshima and Nagasaki. Howard Zinn writes, in

The Bomb, that "the American people were prepared, psychologi-
cally, to accept and even applaud the bombing of Hiroshima and
Nagasaki [causing at least 250,000 civilian deaths]. One reason was
that although some mysterious new science was involved, it seemed
like a continuation of the massive bombing of European cities that
had already taken place."[3] In fact, Zinn continues, with the later
development of the security state "mass killing of ordinary civilians
by carpet-bombing was now an important strategy of the [warfare],
even as nations were dutifully signing on to the U.N. Charter pledg-
ing to end 'the scourge of war'. It would become American policy in
Korea, in Vietnam, Iraq, and Afghanistan. In short, terrorism, condemned by governments when conducted by nationalist or religious
extremists, was now being adopted as official policy".[4] Such brutal
(and illegal) dimensions of U.S. foreign policy have never elicited
regrets or apologies from American leaders. Nor, indeed, have such
practiced ever entered the public sphere as a matter of discussion or
debate. Zinn sadly concludes: "Down to the present day, the massive
bombing of civilians in justified by intellectuals putting into respectable words the crude and brutish argument: 'Sure we committed mass
murder. But they started it. Our conscience is clear.'"[5]

From this standpoint, it was hardly astonishing that American
decision-makers, already inured to the repercussions of aerial terrorism in Germany and Japan, would view the Bomb as a great triumph
of U.S. technological and military genius, a massive step forward in
the progress of humanity. Through doomsday weaponry Americans
had achieved a supreme status befitting their historical exceptionalism and interests in building a new postwar world order. As pursuit
of continued atomic supremacy became something of an obsession in
Washington, the ruling elites became increasingly arrogant in their
dealings with the USSR and others. As the United States continued
producing and stockpiling nukes, the system quickly evolved into an
insular, secret, bureaucratic security state that, combined with an
expanding war economy, would develop through the coming decades
into a fixture of the militarized society. The nuclear weapons labs
at Los Alamos and Livermore—critical to the Manhattan Project—
would flourish, though largely concealed from the public. U.S. leaders
now saw the nation as impervious to military attack—a confidence
shattered by Soviet discovery of the bomb in late 1949, which accelerated work on the Superbomb and other Washington advances in the
arms race. Having left Japan in ashes, the American military was
plowing full-speed ahead into an era of total warfare that, but its

very nature, was geared to the mass killing of civilians. Amplified by the security state and war economy, the nightmare of atomic horrors visited on Hiroshima and Nagasaki would be carried forward and embedded in the popular consciousness. The very notion of postwar military demobilization was unthinkable, as was public access to and knowledge of a militarized bureaucracy increasingly dependent on intelligence, surveillance, and espionage.

Garry Wills argues that the inevitable secrecy surrounding the Manhattan Project—its work spread across some 80 sites—provided the model for later secret and covert governmental operations, for the rise of an imperial presidency that Truman (and his successors) was only too happy to embrace as a badge of formidable state power.[6] Wills exaggerates somewhat as the imperial executive actually goes back to nineteenth-century presidents such as Jackson, Polk, Lincoln, and McKinley, but the bomb politics did clearly feed into growth of a security apparatus that gathered renewed strength not only from the CIA and NSA but the nuclear project. The executive branch would have nearly unchallenged control over nuclear research, production, stockpiling, and deployment. Keeping Congress, the public, and media in the dark would be easy enough in a crisis-filled world where demonic enemies constantly lurked—a task facilitated once the USSR built its own nuclear arsenal. As Wills notes: "World War II faded into the Cold War, and the Cold War into the war on terror, giving us over two-thirds of a century of war in peace, with growing security measures, increased governmental secrecy, classification of information... "[7] To sustain and legitimate such a costly, authoritarian system American leaders would have to popularize images of a Hobbesian world shaped by chaos and threats—meaning, of course, the Soviet and worldwide Communist menace.

Postwar imperial expansion seemed to gain momentum of its own, celebrated by every U.S. president since Truman. By 1948 the United States had already established worldwide bases and deployed ubiquitous weapons that could readily deliver mass destruction to the Soviet Union, with 70 cities and tens of millions of people targeted. Total warfare was now on the Pentagon agenda, though details and potential consequences were rigorously kept from the American people and the world. At Geneva in 1949 the United States and Britain pushed through a clause exempting civilian protections from nuclear attack, meaning that noncombatants would forever be regarded as strategic targets of annihilation. Meanwhile, Washington was moving enthusiastically toward bigger atomic stockpiles with more sophisticated weapons and delivery systems, relying heavily on Nazi scientists recruited for the task. In 1956 General Curtis LeMay, key architect of aerial terrorism against Japan, proudly announced that a U.S. H-bomb attack would condemn the Soviet Union to a primitive agrarian existence for generations to come. By 1960, the United States had more than 10,000 nuclear devices (reaching a peak of 31,000 in 1967), roughly ten times what the Soviets had at their disposal—even as John F. Kennedy campaigned on a false "missile gap" argument to defeat Richard Nixon. Emboldened by the Strategic Air Command (SAC) and its round-the-clock preparedness to strike the Soviet Union, once in office JFK moved to further reinforce American supremacy at a time the U.S. arsenal could already destroy the world several times over. At this time American popular culture (in literature, TV, movies) was saturated with images and narratives of doomsday fantasies auguring the end of human civilization.

While many scientists and others came to reject the bomb as an inherently genocidal weapon, the nuclear state continued to deploy its planes, subs, and land-based missile launchers aimed at the USSR, China, and other targets. Nukes were regarded in Washington as the ultimate instruments of the "free world," supported by a widening stratum of cheerleading politicians, military leaders, and the media. Those opposed to the Cold War arms buildup, like Robert Oppenheimer and Linus Pauling, were denounced as traitors or Communists. The government-military-corporate system became more concentrated and secretive by the year, anchored in a permanent state of emergency. Wills observes that "the nature of the presidency was irreversibly altered by this grant of unique [secretive, emergency] power. The president's permanent alert meant our permanent submission."[8] The American presidency took on a new mystique as sacred commander-in-chief. It was the president, after all, as "leader of the free world," who would lead the struggle for "democracy" against "totalitarianism" anywhere on the globe. This was the essence of the famous Truman Doctrine in 1947, with its economic, political, and military vigilance in the fight against communism wherever American interests were seen as threatened—a prelude to the notion of "preemptive war." Indeed Truman's declaration, preceding the Korean War by three years, emerged as the first salvo of the Cold War. On the basis of a fearsome Soviet and communist menace to the United States, the watershed National Security Act was enacted in 1947. Contending the USSR was seeking absolute "world domination", U.S. leaders called for a vigorous "worldwide counter-offensive," laying the strategic groundwork for virtually everything that followed.

It would require an entire book to catalogue the endless antidemocratic maneuvers of the postwar security state, with their simultaneous domestic and global reverberations. We know that the decades-long U.S. nuclear program was itself marked by repeated first-moves in the arms race, engineered by a few elites at the summit. Postwar CIA, NSA, and other intelligence operations took place mostly outside the public view, beneath even media scrutiny. Truman's presidency, from beginning to end, was marked by constant machination of the imperial executive—nuclear initiatives, Soviet encounters, interventions in Greece and Turkey, and the Korean War (where Truman reportedly considered atomic warfare to break the military impasse). Eisenhower's activities on behalf of the French in Indochina and his efforts to overthrow governments in Guatemala and Iran—all done secretly—are too well known to require further comment. As for that liberal icon John Kennedy, he initiated the Vietnam catastrophe, ordered the failed "Bay of Pigs" invasion of Cuba, and sponsored the illegal Operation Mongoose targeting Fidel Castro—without consulting anyone outside his inner circle. It was JFK, moreover, who brought the world close to nuclear conflagration during the Cuban Missile Crisis, when only last-minute Soviet retreat saved the world from JFK's anticommunist brinkmanship. Security state maneuvers such as Lyndon Johnson's famous Gulf of Tonkin resolution and Richard Nixon's "secret" bombing of Cambodia and Laos, all shrouded in a trail of lies, myths, and obfuscations, and all without the approval of Congress or any international body. The implicit (sometimes explicit) threat of nuclear warfare hovered over most postwar U.S. military ventures.

A pattern of continuous military interventions, covert actions, and proxy wars has unfolded in the shadow of the security state and war economy, with few breaks up to the present. Changes in White House occupancy, Democrat or Republican, have mattered little in the face of overpowering institutional and ideological pressures. President Reagan, claiming new dimensions of executive power in the 1980s while chattering about "reduced government," utilized that power to organize Islamic jihadists in Afghanistan, sponsor death squads in Central America, and allow for the notorious (and illegal) Iran-Contra shenanigans that ignored Congressional resolutions. The elder George Bush could invade Panama without so much as a warning, then later unilaterally setting in motion an Iraq catastrophe (military attacks, deadly sanctions) that even in 2010 seemed to have no end in sight. President Clinton not only amplified the 1990s military and economic assault on Iraq, but also he waged a nearly three-month war against Yugoslavia in the absence of either Congressional or UN endorsement. Both the first Bush and Clinton, moreover, approved the Pentagon's ample use of toxic depleted uranium (DU) in Iraq and Yugoslavia, one of the largely forgotten products of the nuclear state. As for the younger George Bush, his record of security state abominations—illegal wars against Iraq and Afghanistan based on fraudulent claims, illegal surveillance, sponsorship of torture, suspension of Constitutional rights—has been thoroughly detailed in earlier chapters. Here it might simply be mentioned that Bush's 2002 nuclear posture review not only laid out four contingencies for first-use of nuclear weapons but called for a modernized arsenal including a new cycle of "mini-nukes" (later rescinded by Obama) while threatening other countries over their *potential* WMD.

Steady warfare-state expansion was always congruent with U.S. designs on world supremacy. Despite Constitutional provisions giving Congress special leverage over matters of war and peace, the reality has been one of unchallenged executive power in the realm of foreign policy. As Wills notes: "The whole history of American since World War II caused an inertial rolling of power toward the executive branch."[9] Yet the warfare state would encompass far more than the presidency, encompassing the famous military-industrial complex that Eisenhower so presciently warned about in his 1961 farewell address. In the end, the fateful institutionalization of the security state and war economy was fed not only by Bomb politics but by a more all-consuming imperial agenda that in 2010 would devour nearly $1 trillion of the federal budget.

Possession of doomsday weapons has long been a centerpiece of what Robert J. Lifton calls the "superpower syndrome" that, in fact, has deep origins in pre–World War II American history.[10] From the onset of the Manhattan Project and the atomic bombings of Hiroshima and Nagasaki, Washington elites embraced the Bomb as something noble and life-enhancing, part of God's purpose consistent with the familiar doctrine of American exceptionalism. Warfare against civilians was not only tolerated but in some instances celebrated, as it had already been carried out during the strategic bombing attacks on German and Japanese cities. The idea of mass murder from the skies glibly shifted from the moral to the technical plane once the bomb entered the picture, as it signified new arenas of national superiority.

With doomsday scenarios ordained by God Almighty, the very idea of total destruction was welcomed and legitimated within an increasingly aggressive imperial outlook. As Lifton points out, "For nuclear weapons are inherently apocalyptic, and with them America took over a form of ownership of death, believing it could now be operated in the service of good."[11] With its unrivaled military force, the United States. was mobilizing the vast technological potential of modernity behind awesome destructive force that inevitably terrorized civilian populations. This was indeed the essence of nuclearism, a virulent ideology embedded in postwar U.S. military strategy that would shape crucial elements of American identity. Nuclearism would eventually enter into the political and popular culture.[12]

The great fear set loose by the bomb scarcely prevented the United States from turning atomic warfare into a keystone of its foreign and military policy; aerial terrorism morphed into a rational strategy articulated and refined by "theorists" like Herman Kahn, Edward Teller, and Henry Kissinger. As such terror weapons became normalized, they fueled a deeply chauvinistic ideology that shaped intellectual work in the nuclear labs (mentioned in chapter four). Scientific, government, and military elites found in nuclearism such Strangelovian conceits as "massive retaliation" and "mutually-assured destruction" (MAD) while they dared think about the "unthinkable." In this heady milieu, the massive deployment of nukes amounted not only to real weapons but to symbols of American power, as tools of blackmail, as threats that could be used repeatedly. Such unfettered nuclearism meant that architects and promoters of the Bomb politics never had to concede ambivalence over resorting to total warfare, especially while the evil Soviets were supposedly preparing to attack. As for the scientists, technicians, and academics involved in this insular nuclear subculture, theirs was a scientific ethos that dismissed broader questions of political ethics, wrapped in a techno-strategic discourse in which such academic fetishes as game theory obscured the human consequences of their deadly work.

In the late 1960s the Nuclear Non-Proliferation Treaty (NPT) was drafted with the purpose of controlling—and ultimately abolishing—nuclear weapons from the face of the earth. The NPT came into legal force in March 1970, signed by 189 states including the United States and the four other nuclear states at the time. While U.S. leaders embraced this landmark agreement, beneath the surface it has often been met with ambivalence and even (in some quarters) hostility as the NPT was explicitly designed to restrain WMD development for *all* nations. After all, the United States was the only nation to have dropped the bomb and, as mentioned, nuclear strategy (including first-use doctrine) remained central to its postwar military outlook. That Washington had also resorted to other weapons of mass destruction—biological in Korea, chemical in Vietnam—was likely to make the Pentagon reluctant to dismantle its WMD arsenals much less embrace disarmament, as the NPT urged. Above all, the Pentagon was never prepared to relinquish its quest for global American military supremacy, even if that meant retaining and possibly using weapons designed to annihilate large numbers of civilians. By its own definition, the U.S. military construed WMD as "weapons that are capable of a high order of destruction and/or being used in such a manner as to destroy large numbers of people." Not surprisingly, U.S. rhetorical opposition to WMD and their proliferation hardly extended to its own policies or its approach to the NPT.

The NPT stipulated that nuclear weapons states would fight proliferation and move toward disarmament, with all signatories allowed peaceful atomic programs under international monitoring. Thus Article I said that nuclear states agree not to assist non-nuclear countries in building weapons projects, while Article IV affirmed the right of all NPT members to develop nuclear energy and Article VI crucially obliged nuclear states (five at the time) to begin dismantling nukes in "good faith." By the early twenty-first century, however, nine countries had nuclear arsenals with prospects that many others would follow: no less than 70 nations had research facilities and reactors for processing enriched uranium. Several countries had the technical capability and resources to achieve nuclear weapons status, including Japan, Brazil, Australia, Iran, Argentina, Turkey, and South Africa. Three states outside the NPT framework—Israel, Pakistan, and India—possessed sizeable nuclear arsenals. Meanwhile, the United States and some other nuclear states appeared indifferent to Article VI as they moved to modernize their own weaponry, even while lecturing and threatening others about proliferation. Alone among nations, the United States held to its long-standing first-use doctrine while maintaining a global nuclear presence across land, sea, and air, reinforced by its ambitious missile-defense system. Washington had also secretly deployed dozens of tactical nukes to such NATO countries as Germany, Belgium, Italy, Holland, and Turkey, in clear violation of the NPT. In opposition to Article I, moreover, the United States agreed with non-NPT member India to transfer atomic resources and technology to the New Delhi government, with its already developed weapons program, as a move to counter China. With this assistance and the work of 1,100 U.S.-trained scientists, India has built a stockpile of 65 warheads or more in the absence of external monitoring. As for Israel, its contempt for the NPT and international rules has given permission to amass a nuclear arsenal of perhaps 200 warheads, all under diplomatic umbrella provided by Washington, which shares the Israeli pretense of "ambiguity."

By the time President Bush laid out the 2002 Nuclear Posture Review identifying four contingencies for American resort to nuclear weapons, Washington had long before taken the lead in shredding the NPT as a binding international document, though the Russians and others must share blame. The security state had established its own powerful logic that triumphed over global arrangements and kept it insulated from general political inputs. While the United States preached against proliferation, assailing Iran and North Korea for their nuclear programs, it spent hundreds of billions of dollars to upgrade its state-of-the-art capabilities and extended assistance to allies like Israel and India—a set of double standards destined to reduce the NPT (and watchdog IAEA) to utter impotence. In the absence of any tangible strategy of disarmament consistent with Article VI, no viable answer to proliferation could be forthcoming; non-nuclear states were effectively pressured into joining the club, all the more so in the case of targeted states like Iran. Egyptian president Gamal Abdul Nasser anticipated this in the early 1970s when he lamented that the nuclear powers "basically did whatever they wanted to do before the introduction of NPT and then devised it to prevent others from doing what they themselves had been doing before." With Bush's 2002 Nuclear Posture Review the United States pushed this one-sided and dysfunctional agenda to new extremes at the very moment it was preparing to invade Iraq over its supposed possession of WMD. Genuine UN and other initiatives for disarmament or nuclear-free zones were routinely dismissed by Washington, which chose to enter into bilateral agreements with Russia to reduce its arsenal to 1500 by 2017 without, however, much reducing total U.S. firepower. Nukes remained a cornerstone of U.S. military strategy, ensuring continued American supremacy and NPT impotence.

As suggested in earlier chapters, the key to understanding such U.S. outlawry is heightened institutionalization of the security state and war economy linked to the American drive toward imperial hegemony. The United States stands in perpetual violation of NPT Article VI because of its infinite "security" requirements in the face of an anarchic world. While negotiations leading to international monitoring, inspections, binding treaties, and nuclear-free zones might be the demanded norm for others, as exceptional superpower the United States chooses to follow its own set of rules. Meanwhile, a new global nuclear order has arisen in which the nine nuclear states appear largely impervious to the NPT while the atomic have-nots (many with enhanced capabilities) are expected to refrain from weapons projects at a time when the shift from peaceful to military nuclear energy faces reduced technological obstacles.

The authoritarian irrationality of American nuclear politics is revealed nowhere more clearly than in the Middle East, where escalating threats against NPT-member Iran are matched by protections for NPT-outlaw Israel—one lacking weapons capabilities (as of 2010), the other possessing a huge WMD arsenal. Here the familiar double standards abound throughout both the political system and media: Iran has followed NPT guidelines, cooperated with the IAEA, and possesses no nuclear weapons but is branded a renegade and threat, while Israel owns dozens of warheads, maintains total secrecy, and rejects all international cooperation but is treated with benevolent understanding. In targeting Iran alone for its undocumented nuclear outlawry, the United States and Israel have played on a mixture of ignorance, fear, paranoia, and hypocrisy in a manner that guarantees future confrontation. The United States took the lead in accusing Iran of erecting a weapons program, backed by threats of economic sanctions and military attacks that could augur still another regime change strategem. A close look at IAEA reports, however, indicated a far less threatening actuality leading into the 2010 NPT review. In February 2010 the agency, while calling on Iran to be more forthcoming on some issues, stated: "The information available to the Agency in connection with these outstanding issues is extensive and has been collected from a variety of sources over time. It is also broadly consistent and credible in terms of technical detail, the time frame in which the activities were conducted, and the people and organizations involved." While looking for more data, the IAEA concluded that, while an enrichment process was in full swing, evidence supporting of a weapons program was lacking. Iranian "defiance," therefore, was less a matter of going along with outside inspections than of resisting (illegal, unreasonable) U.S. and Israeli demands for total nuclear shutdown.

As former inspector Scott Ritter points out in *Target Iran* (2006), the Iranians were never offered positive incentives or security guarantees by nuclear states to constrain their enrichment program—only threats that ensured mounting hostility.[13] Veiled warnings of future military action, itself a violation of the UN Charter, were a familiar refrain in U.S. and Israeli elite discourse after 2003, producing heightened Iranian fears and likelihood that the Tehran regime would indeed look to atomic weaponry as a protective shield. President Bush and the neocons seemed ready for war even though (as in the case of Iraq) evidence of a WMD project was nowhere to be found. The idea, moreover, that the Iranians constituted an imminent threat to the United States or even neighboring countries was preposterous on its face. Iran never posed such a threat: it has never invaded any country, has indeed never threatened military attack, and has no motive for doing so. (An Iranian attack on Israel would be suicidal given the latter's massive nuclear arsenal.) On the contrary, the United States—in partnership with Israel—has for years militarily surrounded Iran, threatened both economic and military warfare, and clearly aspired to destroy this center of power in the Middle East. The United States has a long history of interventions in Iran, having overthrown the Mossadegh government in 1953 followed by decades of abundant support for the Shah's brutal dictatorship, for which the United States helped build a nuclear program in the 1970s, in violation of NPT statutes. Both the United States and Israel have vast nuclear deployments in the region, which Iran, Egypt, and the UN earlier proposed turning into a nuclear-free zone, a move naturally rejected out of hand by Washington and its partner Israel. The question then is: who is threatening whom? The correct answer obviously departs from the propaganda churned out by the American media and politicians. If Iranians actually plan to shift from civilian to military uses of nuclear energy, under the circumstances it would be a rational decision, essentially forced by U.S.-Israeli hostility, encirclement, and threats.

While Israel amasses its atomic stockpile behind a veil of "nuclear ambiguity," rejects the NPT, and refuses to allow international monitoring, it hypocritically leads the charge against proliferation fixated on Iran. No U.S. or European pressure has ever challenged this hypocritical outlawry. In September 2009 the General Conference of the IAEA called on Israel to open its nuclear facilities for inspection—the same regimen agreed to by Iran—but the chief Israeli delegate flatly and arrogantly refused. Earlier, the 2005 NPT Review Conference famously broke down because the United States wanted to isolate Iran while protecting Israel at a time world consensus favored a move toward nuclear disarmament in the original spirit of the NPT. American efforts to label Iran as a "defiant" rogue state were met with cynical disbelief by most delegates to the conference. It was at this very moment, in fact, that Washington was preparing a treaty to further assist India's own nuclear outlawry. Meanwhile, arguing that weapons of mass destruction are banned under the Koran, Iranian supreme leader Ayatollah Khamenei not only proposed (in April 2010) that Israel join Iran within the NPT but referred to the United States as an "atomic criminal" for its duplicity, calling for its suspension from the IAEA. After all, for several years, the Bush administration seemed ready to attack Iran as the military option continuously remained "on the table." This was the same Bush who was expanding the U.S. nuke program to include a new cycle of bunker-busting tactical weapons to be targeted precisely on such countries as Iran. And the same Bush who in June 2002 withdrew from the Anti-Ballistic Missile Treaty that the United States had earlier signed with Russia. In summer 2002 the U.S. Congress overwhelmingly passed a resolution (illegally) calling for Iran to cease nuclear enrichment or face severe sanctions, a measure amounting to a virtual declaration of war. Once in office, Obama continued the pattern of U.S. economic and military threats. In the end, the specter of (illegal, aggressive) war embraced by American and Israeli elites promised nothing so much as an endless chain of international horrors.

Such nuclear swagger reflects the degree to which the national-security state has transcended checks and restraints on its power as the White House assumed virtually unlimited authority to conduct foreign and military policy, with Congress reduced to something of a consulting body. The perpetual war on terrorism only enhances this authority, reducing the Constitution to a scrap of paper. As Wills observes, "The whole history of America since World War II caused an inertial rolling of power toward the executive branch."[14] In the case of the Bush administration, this meant a litany of autocratic, unlawful actions: launching illegal wars, scrapping treaties, violating the Geneva Conventions on torture, warrantless wiretapping, setting up military commissions that could sidestep Constitutional rights. Of course Bush was simply building on the expanded power accumulated by his predecessors, who routinely covered up foreign adventures with secrecy, lies, distortions, and cover-ups.

The transition from Bush to Obama in the realm of atomic politics, as elsewhere, seemed to promise new departures. And change did seem to produce something of a renovated nuclear zeitgeist filled with hopes for more enlightened policies. In April 2009, speaking in Prague, Obama affirmed his dedication to a world without nuclear

weapons—a goal earlier championed by such former American statesmen as Robert McNamara, Henry Kissinger, and George Schultz.
Many establishment figures had concluded that nuclear weaponry
was now strategically counterproductive and should yield to a more
flexible conventional approach in which the weapons were, after all,
more eminently *usable*. In fact Bush's plan for mini-nukes had been
essentially junked. Fears of proliferation were rife in Washington,
as the scientific knowledge required to develop nukes was rapidly
spreading well beyond the nine nuclear states to possibly include terrorist groups. The new global atomic order was destined to eviscer-
ate the NPT, already in a fragile state. An even more salient concern
for U.S. military strategists was the obvious absurdity of deploying
thousands of nuclear warheads that could serve no meaningful foreign policy objectives, as the arsenal was deemed not only costly but
essentially useless. Such thinking likely prompted Obama's dramatic
call for nuclear reductions, leading to new global initiatives and a
renovated Nuclear Posture Review for 2010.

Exactly one year after his Prague speech Obama agreed to a new
Strategic Arms Reduction Treaty (START) with Russia, setting a limit
of 1,550 warheads for both countries by 2017, a 30 percent reduction
from the 2002 Moscow Treaty (also with Russia). The new START
allows for on-site inspections, data exchanges, and sophisticated
methods of monitoring, but allows for mutual flexibility and places
no restrictions on testing, production, and deployment of current or
planned missile programs. According to the Nuclear Posture Review,
however, Washington has renounced testing and development of new
weapons as well as refinement of existing weapons. (Yet there is no
hint that the weapons labs will be dismantled or even downsized.)
In any event, the Obama administration had decided that existing
nuclear stockpiles and deployments had no conceivable political or
military purpose, especially since just a few hundred nukes would
be enough to deter any foreign threat. While START appears to justify renewed grounds for optimism that the United States is finally
prepared to take its NPT obligations seriously, the overall strategic
picture—reflected above all in the Nuclear Posture Review and actual
military behavior—suggests cause for deep skepticism.

Although START calls for significant arms reductions, both the
Nuclear Posture Review and the 2010 Quadrennial Defense Review
loudly reaffirm the long-standing American commitment to world
military supremacy that includes further nuclear development.
The NPR states: "The U.S. will modernize the nuclear weapons

infrastructure, sustain the science, technology, and engineering base, invest in human capital, and ensure senior leadership focus." Atomic vigilance remains an obsession: the NPR does not renounce conventional first-use doctrine, nor does it shrink from implicit threats of nuclear attacks on other nations deemed in violation of the NPT. Indeed nukes remained a "core mission" of Pentagon global strategy. Moreover, START is confined to the two leading nuclear states, excluding the larger community of nations (within and outside the atomic club) that must eventually participate in any full-scale move toward nonproliferation and disarmament.

The problems with Obama's overtures go far beyond such limitations. As mentioned, the United States retains some 200 tactical nuclear weapons spread across Europe—mostly targeting Russia—with no indication of change even as several nations press for removal of nukes from the continent. Second, and more troubling, the NPR continues to specify contingencies under which the United States feels it can justifiably launch a first nuclear attack—in this case those said to be in violation of the NPT. Leaving aside the hypocrisy involved in such a posture (as the United States itself has consistently violated the treaty), threats are bound to encourage proliferation because targeted nations (like Iran) are sure to scramble for means of deterrence. Contained within what looks to be a call for arms reduction, therefore, concrete American initiatives present a much different picture. This message is hardly lost on the leaders of designated "rogue states," who perceive in Obama's disarmament pretenses a form of nuclear bullying. Third, the United States continues to extend generous nuclear assistance to other states—not only India, as mentioned, but such countries as Japan that Bush earlier included within a Global Nuclear Energy Partnership that would bring new breeder reactors and other technology to a lucrative world market. This deal (extended by Obama) would involve sale of massive amounts of nuclear fuel to Japan and other states. As the gap between peaceful and military uses of atomic power narrows, such moves clearly jeopardize any genuine nonproliferation agenda.

There is also the thorny question of space weaponization, with its broad implications for earthly nuclear as well as conventional warfare. Since the days of Reagan's famous Strategic Defense Initiative (1983), the Pentagon has kept most of its space designs hidden behind a veil of secrecy. It is well known that space satellites already perform crucial military functions in the area of surveillance, global positioning, intelligence, and weapons guidance. Thus, while the United States has disavowed any intention of space weaponization (much less nuclear-ization), the main elements of such a program are already in place.[15] In 2009 the Pentagon earmarked $520 million for space weapons research, which occupies a central place in ongoing missile-defense projects that are closely linked to future nuclear potential. Programs for space militarization, like the Eschelon System, have long been on the drawing boards. In 2008, both Russia and China drafted an agreement at the UN Conference on Disarmament that would ban outer space weaponization and avoid a space-based arms race, but this overture was quickly rejected by Washington, which stringently opposed any treaty imposing limits on U.S. "access to space." Russian foreign minister Sergei Lavrov responded predictably: "Weapons deployment in space by one state will inevitably result in a chain reaction. And this in turn is fraught with a new spiral in the arms race, both in space and on the earth."[16] Obama has done nothing to reverse this outlook.

Also largely hidden from view has been widespread American use of depleted uranium (DU), a form of low-level nuclear warfare attached to missiles and other projectiles, deployed in Iraq, Afghanistan, and Yugoslavia, with no reservations or apologies. Since the early 1990s the Pentagon has fired off millions of weapons tipped with DU, the long-term health consequences of which are bound to be catastrophic for the targeted regions. Made of nuclear waste materials, DU weapons spread deadly radioactive dust far and wide upon explosive impact, leaving in their wake untold cases of leukemia, cancer, and birth defects. Plutonium is the most carcinogenic substance known, yet its waste products have been used indiscriminately by the U.S. military, which says that only "small traces" of DU materials are left on the battlefield. Whether strictly "legal" or not, DU weaponry introduces a form of toxic warfare that can arguably be said to constitute wanton destruction of civilian populations.

There is, finally, the crucial issue of nuclear missile defense that fig-ured so centrally in U.S. strategic thinking in the wake of SDI, which, though always technically flawed, gave rise to American fantasies of a fail-proof defensive shield against foreign nukes. Bush held to these fantasies as he forged ahead with an NMD project oriented not only toward China and Russia but such smaller nations as Iran. This scheme entailed deployment of ground-based interceptors in Poland supported by radar stations in the Czech Republic as the first phase in a sophisticated NMD shield. In September 2009, however, Obama moved to scrap the NMD shield, in part owing to intense Russian pressure. But appearances were deceiving: still convinced Iran posed a menace to Europe and Israel, the United States simply repositioned NMD to ship-based programs like the Aegis Ballistic Missile Defense System deployed on Navy vessels in the Mediterranean and Atlantic. In 2009 several Navy ships were fitted with SM-3 missiles, complements to the Patriot system, with the aim of fitting 21 ships by the end of 2010, 24 in 2012, and 27 in 2013. Meanwhile, several airborne NMD schemes were being explored by the Pentagon. Given that both sea-based and airborne NMD systems are far more mobile than ground-based shields, it is hard to resist the conclusion that Obama's missile-defense plan is a vast improvement over Bush's more provocative strategy tied to Eastern European land deployments. As of 2010, therefore, the much-maligned NMD project remained very much a centerpiece of American nuclear policy.

Obama's continuation of previous U.S. nuclear agendas reflects not so much his own personal hawkishness as the overriding logic of an institutionalized national security state grounded in imperial ambitions. Nuclear politics bolsters this system insofar as its great obsession—threats of proliferation, fears of terrorist attacks, perpetual needs to modernize—depends on a Hobbesian universe of chaos and anarchy that must be tamed or fought. Atomic proliferation means, more than anything, new deterrence capabilities for "rogue states" (like Iran) labeled actual or potential enemies. Bureaucratic rigidity perfectly fits the modus operandi of the nuclear state, reinforced by elite attitudes of paranoia, fear, and arrogance fueled by national exceptionalism. Further, the entire nuclear project from the outset has been shrouded in secrecy, with crucial questions of deployment, missile defense, space weaponization, budgetary allocations, and even treaty negotiations partially or fully outside public deliberation. General knowledge of these issues in the United States is virtually nonexistent beyond the inner circles of government and military leaders. There is, however, broad sentiment in the United States and around the world that nuclear states should be more transparent in their activities and should move toward disarmament. In a 2010 Angus Reid Public Opinion survey, more than two-thirds of American respondents said they would prefer the United States to pursue extensive reduction of nuclear weapons if not their total elimination.[17] An earlier (2008) poll conducted by the University of Maryland showed that in 20 of 21 countries surveyed large majorities ranging from 62 to 93 percent favored universal abolition of nukes within a specific timetable, by numbers of 77 percent in the United

States, 83 percent in China, 86 percent in France, and 81 percent in Great Britain. The average for all countries surveyed was a telling 76 percent.[18] Unfortunately, none of the major nuclear states has taken such popular consensus into account. In the United States, the venerable security apparatus, confident of its superior knowledge and sensibilities in these matters, moves according to its own momentum. As the warfare system consolidates its reach in the wake of perpetual wars—and more threats of war—growth of authoritarian power inevitably builds. The security state has witnessed the steady expansion of Washington bureaucracies that possess a monopoly of either secret or forbidden knowledge, since "national security" concerns are regarded as far too sensitive for public involvement. Such knowledge is the unique possession of high-tech civilian and military experts whose opinions and agendas cannot easily be monitored within the broader political arena.

In June 2006 Hans Blix, former chief UN weapons inspector, presented a report to the UN titled "Weapons of Terror," authored by the Commission on Weapons of Mass Destruction, with the aim of ultimately freeing the world of nuclear, chemical, and biological warfare.[19] The report asked nations of the world to address this vital issue before it is too late—before, that is, a cataclysmic military event occurs. It calls on nations to take international laws and treaties more seriously than they have, implicitly (and often explicitly) urging the United States to cease blocking arms control, disarmament, and moves toward curtailing proliferation. Point 2 of the report states: "All parties to the [NPT] should implement the decision on principles and objectives for nonproliferation and disarmament, the decision on strengthening the [NPT] review process and the resolution of the Middle East as a zone free of nuclear and all other weapons of mass destruction."[20] The latter idea had been proposed by Egypt, Iran, and others but predictably opposed by the United States and Israel, which together deploy hundreds of warheads in the region. Point 7 urges nuclear states to provide security assurances to non-nuclear states, since clearly the only way to counter proliferation is for leading WMD nations to extend such assurances to smaller and weaker nations that rightly fear being attacked in the absence of a WMD deterrence, but neither the United States nor Israel has offered any such assurances. Point 15 urges "all states possessing nuclear weapons [to] declare a categorical policy of no first-use of such weapons. They should specify that this covers both preemptive and preventive action, as well as retaliation for attacks involving chemical, biological, or conventional weapons."[21] Point 16 calls for nuclear states to abolish triads—sub-based, ground-based, and air-based weaponry—as this strategy reinforces atomic redundancy and the arms race.[22] Neither possibility has ever been taken seriously by American leaders, still committed to the nuclear status quo and to the full array of strategic options seen as indispensable to national security.

Washington has long regarded nuclear supremacy—and its freedom of action—as a matter of entitlement, not subject to negotiation or concessions. Here the WMD Commission emphasized (point 22) that "every state that possesses nuclear weapons should make a commitment not to deploy any nuclear weapons of any type, on foreign soil." This injunction ought to be self-evident, but for decades the United States has felt privileged enough to deploy nukes in Europe, Korea, and elsewhere, and is the only nation with such a global military presence. Suggestions by disarmament advocates that the United States should cease this policy, which clearly encourages proliferation, have been rejected out of hand. As for the NPT strictures, point 30 states: "All states possessing nuclear weapons should begin planning for security without nuclear weapons. They should start preparing for the outlawing of nuclear weapons through joint practical and incremental measures that include definitions, benchmarks, and transparency requirements for nuclear disarmament."[23] As we have seen, Obama's initiatives fell considerably short of fulfilling this imperative. In its nuclear posture reviews, quadrennial defense reviews, and global behavior Washington has shown that nuclear weapons remain central to its military doctrine, as it retains thousands of warheads, adheres to a first-use policy, lays out a multitude of nuclear options, deploys warheads around the world, and moves forward with its secret atomic labs. Here even the mainstream *Defense Monitor* is chastened to add: "At a time when the United States is...alarmed about other countries establishing military nuclear programs, it is hard to justify why Washington not only thinks it needs thousands of nuclear weapons, but is fighting to retain its gargantuan complex of nuclear weapons labs."[24] This point is amplified by Jonathan Schell in *The Nation* (April 19, 2010), in which he stresses that the only viable nonproliferation agenda is one leading to complete abolition, to be achieved through a global nuclear-weapons convention.[25]

Despite rhetorical nods toward disarmament, in 2010 the United States remained firmly on the path of nuclear modernization as key to retaining world military supremacy. There are some indications, however, that many Pentagon strategists would prefer added reliance on conventional weapons, which are more flexible and carry far less moral stigma. New generations of conventional bombs and missiles, moreover, can reach nearly atomic levels of destruction. Meanwhile, the powerful nuclear labs—supporting think tanks like the Hoover Institution—still lobby intensively for a more highly developed nuclear-armed U.S. empire. Investments in science, technology, engineering, and logistics are moving full-speed ahead even while arms control discourse is being marketed to domestic and global publics. The nuclear establishment has its sight focused on a new plutonium bomb core production facility at Los Alamos, identified as the Chemical and Metallurgy Research Replacement (CMRR), with costs already running more than $2 billion. The bomb core project would be the centerpiece of a new cycle of warheads vital to nuclear modernization even as Washington promises atomic demobilization and negotiates with Russia to reduce its general stockpile. In its 2011 federal budget, the Obama administration called for a "surge" in nuclear spending, with some of the increment likely earmarked for the CMRR project. High-level officials in Washington, including the undersecretary of arms control and international security, Ellen Tauscher, were aggressively urging a more vigorous nuclear program that could pass the START agreement. Such moves call into question Obama's highly publicized initiatives on nonproliferation and disarmament.

In his book analyzing the WMD Commission recommendations, Blix sees a disastrous road ahead in a context where the major nuclear states continue to violate crucial NPT strictures. The United States is repeatedly singled out for its particularly flagrant brand of outlawry. A crucial question keeps surfacing: how can dangerous proliferation be averted while nuclear outlaw states (Israel, India, Pakistan) are supported at every level by the United States, itself a leading outlaw state? As Blix observes, "The [NPT] is under strain today because non-nuclear weapon states have over the years become increasingly dissatisfied that the nuclear-weapon state parties are not moving seriously toward disarmament. Moreover, the ambition to induce India, Pakistan, and Israel to adhere has been abandoned."[26] He adds: "that convincing states that they do not need weapons of mass destruction would be significantly easier if all U.N. members practiced genuine respect for the existing [U.N.] restraints on the threat and use of force."[27] What this means—especially in view of the Iranian predicament—is that *all* states must follow NPT statutes if the treaty is to be enforceable. "It is not a treaty that appoints the nuclear-weapon states individually or jointly to police non-nuclear weapon states and to threaten them with punishment. It is a contract in which all parties commit themselves to the goal of a nuclear weapon-free world."[28] The urgent need here is for globalization of security requirements and processes that, in the end, would demand a full reconstitution of the American security state apparatus.

Through every presidency since the Manhattan Project, nuclear weaponry has occupied a central place in the national-security state, never more so than in the contemporary period. The Manhattan Project unleashed a wave of technological fanaticism linked to militarism that fitted perfectly into security state agendas. Of course, U.S. leaders pretend to favor nonproliferation and even disarmament, but their actual foreign policy speaks loudly against such priorities. President Obama's visionary embrace of a nonnuclear world was therefore unlikely to have any practical consequences: nuclear spending for 2010 increased by $8 billion, significantly greater than Bush's final budgetary hike. Anticipating a massive nuclear investment of $175 billion over the next two decades, the Pentagon was set to modernize the vast American arsenal of missiles, bombers, subs, and communications networks—along with an already sophisticated missile defense system—all part of a nuclear strategy designed to *augment* global destructive capacity and flexibility. Obama's START goal of reducing the U.S. arsenal from roughly 5,000 to 3,500 warheads by 2021 was accordingly misleading, with fewer nukes intended to have far greater military potential in a world that elites see filled with endless national and subnational threats. Meanwhile, as the April 2010 Nuclear Posture Review makes clear, the United States had still not abandoned its notorious first-use policy as various scenarios for nuclear warfare remain integral to Pentagon planning. Not only do such policies reinforce the well-justified fears of other nations, fueling proliferation and militarism, they further exacerbate trends toward secrecy, intrigue, and centralized power within the security state.

Where such trends are well advanced, the preoccupation with intelligence and surveillance operations is inescapable: Washington revealed that, for the year 2009, intelligence expenditures had reached a staggering $80 billion—more than any other country spends on its entire military forces. Indeed Obama's spending actually *doubled* what the Bush administration had allocated for all U.S. espionage agencies in 2001. The Homeland Security budget amounted to yet another $53 billion at a time when Republicans were screaming about big government and onerous taxes while ignoring these especially outlandish revenue outlays.

By 2010 both nuclear weaponry and the intelligence apparatus had become so integral to the security state—and to the imperial presidency—that it typically passed without much notice, invisible within the media and political arenas. Superpower ideology, after all, essentially dictates that executive power should operate above domestic and international law, beyond effective constitutional or democratic constraints. Within this trajectory not only the mass media but Congress and even the Supreme Court have been largely compliant. The aftermath of 9/11, above all the "war on terror," served to bolster authoritarian and statist tendencies of the imperial presidency. Erwin Chemerinsky has argued persuasively that American society, from the Richard Nixon administration onward, has witnessed a sustained conservative assault on the Constitution, as shown by a long series of Supreme Court decisions favoring governmental power over individual rights.[29] Behind much libertarian fanfare, the right wing—with the court leading the way—slowly whittled away at the power of consumers, labor, community groups, and trial defendants, meanwhile endowing the White House with unsurpassed flexibility. In its famous 2000 decision handing over the presidency to George W. Bush, the court even went against its time-honored defense of states' rights. With the national security state firmly entrenched in American society, there was unfortunately no end in sight to this authoritarian trajectory, as the legacy of global warfare, surveillance, espionage, secrecy, proxy wars, and outright violation of international law assumes its own logic.

Notes

Introduction

1. Sheldon S. Wolin, *Democracy, Inc.* (Princeton, NJ: Princeton University Press, 2008), pp. 260–61.
2. Ibid., p. 196.
3. Kevin Phillips, *Wealth and Democracy* (New York: Broadway Books, 2002), p. xv.
4. C. Wright Mills, *The Power Elite* (New York: Oxford University Press, 1956).
5. The argument that the U.S. Constitution has been hijacked, notably by the George W. Bush administration, is strenuously put forth by Naomi Wolf, in *The End of America* (White River Junction, VT: Chelsea Green, 2007).
6. See Ron Takaki, *In a Different Mirror* (New York: Little, Brown, and Co., 1993).
7. Alexis DeTocqueville, *Democracy in America* (New York: Harper and Row, 1969), p. 50.
8. Ibid., p. 58.
9. Ibid., p. 60.
10. Ibid., p. 237.
11. Ibid., p. 241.
12. Barrington Moore, Jr., *Social Origins of Dictatorship and Democracy* (Boston, MA: Beacon Press, 1966), p. 112.
13. C.B. Macpherson, *The Life and Times of Liberal Democracy* (New York: Oxford University Press, 1977), p. 42.
14. See Macpherson's concept of "equilibrium democracy" in ibid., ch. IV.
15. Takaki, *In a Different Mirror,* p. 88.
16. Ibid., p. 24.
17. Michael Rogin, *Ronald Reagan the Movie* (Berkeley: University of California Press, 1987), p. 153.
18. Ibid., p. 155.
19. Ibid., p. 154.
20. See Ward Churchill, *A Little Matter of Genocide* (San Francisco: City Lights, 1997, p. 4.

21. Howard Zinn, *A Peoples' History of the United States* (New York: The New Press, 2003), p. 100.
22. Churchill, *A Little Matter of Genocide,* p. 7.
23. Zinn, *Peoples' History,* p. 146.
24. Moore, *Social Origins,* p. 124.
25. Chalmers Johnson, *Nemesis* (New York: Henry Holt and Co., 2006), pp. 88–89.
26. Rich Shenkman, *Just How Stupid Are We?* (New York: Basic Books, 2008), p. 16.
27. Ibid., pp. 32–33.
28. Susan Jacoby, *The Age of American Unreason* (New York: Vintage Books, 2009), p. xviii.
29. Sheldon Wolin, *Democracy, Inc.* (Princeton, NJ: Princeton University Press, 2008), ch. 12.
30. See Zinn's introduction to the volume *Voices of a Peoples' History of the United States,* edited by Howard Zinn and Anthony Arnove (New York: Seven Stories, 2004).
31. Wolin, *Democracy, Inc.,* p. 260.
32. Ibid., p. 258.
33. Noteworthy treatments of radical democracy include: Michael Albert, *Parecon* (London: Verso, 2003); Murray Bookchin, *Remaking Society* (Montreal: Black Rose Books, 1989); Cornelius Castoriadis, *Political and Social Writings,* translated and edited by David James Curtis (Minneapolis: University of Minnesota Press, 1988), two volumes; Takis Fotopoulos, *Inclusive Democracy* (London: Cassell, 1997); and C. Douglas Lummis, *Radical Democracy* (Ithaca, NY: Cornell University Press, 1996). See also Paul Barry Clarke, *Deep Citizenship* (London: Pluto, 1996).
34. On the concept of social ecology, see Bookchin, *Remaking Society,* pp. 19–40.
35. See Lummis, *Radical Democracy,* pp. 22–24.
36. Henry Milner, *Sweden: Social Democracy in Practice* (New York: Oxford University Press, 1989), p. 69.
37. Ibid., pp. 200–1.
38. Kent Asp and Peter Esaison, "The Modernization of Swedish Campaigns", in David L. Swanson, ed., *Politics, Media, and Modern Democracy* (New York: Greenwood Press, 2007), pp. 872–83.

I   From Manifest Destiny to Empire

1. Howard Zinn, *Howard Zinn on War* (New York: Seven Stories Press, 2001), p. 153.
2. Howard Zinn, *A People's History of the United States* (New York: The New Press, 2003), p. 74.
3. Robert A. Dahl, *How Democratic is the American Constitution?* (New Haven, CT: Yale University Press, 2003), p. 2.

4. Sheldon S. Wolin, *Democracy, Inc.* (Princeton, NJ: Princeton University Press, 2008), p. 228.
5. Wolin, p. 181.
6. Richard Hofstadter, *The American Political Tradition* (New York: Vintage Books, 1973), p. 13.
7. Kevin Phillips, *Wealth and Democracy* (New York: Broadway Books, 2002), p. 11.
8. Phillips, p. 42.
9. Mary Elizabeth Lease, "Wall Street Owns the Country," in Howard Zinn and Anthony Arnove, eds., *Voices of a People's History of the United States* (New York: Seven Stories, 2004), p. 226.
10. Howard Zinn, *A People's History of the United States*, p. 23.
11. Michael Rogin, *Ronald Reagan the Movie* (Berkeley: University of California Press, 1987), pp. 135–38.
12. Cited in Rogin, p. 155.
13. Ward Churchill, *Fantasies of the Master Race* (San Francisco: City Lights Books, 1998), pp. 167–224.
14. Ronald Takaki, *A Different Mirror: A History of Multiculturalism in America* (Boston: Little, Brown, 1993), p. 10.
15. Cited in Takaki, p. 85.
16. Cited in Takaki, p. 88.
17. Quoted in Zinn, *People's History*, p. 228.
18. Zinn, *People's History*, p. 229.
19. Quoted in Zinn, *People's History*, p. 268.
20. Smedley D. Butler, *War is a Racket* (Los Angeles, CA: Feral House, 2003), p. 35.
21. See Michael Slackman, *Target Pearl Harbor* (Honolulu: University of Hawaii Press, 1990), p. 8.
22. Robert B. Stinnett, *Day of Deceit* (New York: The Free Press, 2000), Chapter 1.
23. John Dower, *War Without Mercy* (New York: Pantheon Books, 1986), p. 33.
24. Dower, p. 37.
25. Dower, p. 53.
26. Stinnett, *Day of Deceit*, p. xiv.
27. Stephen Endicott and Edward Hagerman, *The United States and Biological Warfare* (Bloomington: University of Indiana Press, 1998), p. 198.
28. Cited in Endicott and Hagerman, pp. 98–99.
29. Endicott and Hagerman, p. 97.
30. H. Bruce Franklin, *Vietnam and Other American Fantasies* (Amherst: University of Massachusetts Press, 2000), p. 26.
31. James William Gibson, *The Perfect War* (New York: Atlantic Monthly Press, 1986), pp. 461–76.
32. See Robert McNamara, *In Retrospect: the Tragedy and Lessons of Vietnam* (New York: Vintage Books, 1998).
33. Gibson, *The Perfect War*, p. 462.

34. Quoted in Bruce Miroff, *Pragmatic Illusions* (New York: David McKay Co., 1976), p. 55.
35. Miroff, p. 143.
36. See Andrew J. Bacevich, *The Limits of Power* (New York: Henry Holt, 2009).
37. See Andrew Kohut and Bruce Stokes, *America against the World* (New York: Henry Holt, 2006), pp. 101–3.
38. Rob Woodward, *Bush at War* (New York: Simon and Shuster, 2002), pp. 145–46. Woodward quotes Bush as saying: "I'm the commander—see I don't need to explain—I do not need to explain why I say things. That's the interesting thing about being president. Maybe somebody needs to explain to me why they say something but I don't feel I owe anybody an explanation." (p. 20)
39. Robert Jay Lifton, *The Superpower Syndrome* (New York: Nation Books, 2003), p. 41.
40. Fred Cook, *The Warfare State* (New York: Collier Books, 1962), p. 50.
41. Nafeez Mosaddeq Ahmed, *The War on Truth* (Northampton, MA.: Olive Branch Press, 2005), p. 33.
42. See Diana Johnstone, *Fool's Crusade* (New York: Monthly Review, 2002), pp. 60–62.

2   The Imperial Labyrinth

1. See Bruce Cumings, Ervand Abrahamian, and Moshe Ma'oz, *Inventing the Axis of Evil* (New York: The New Press, 2004), pp. 9–27.
2. Gary Dorrien, *The Neoconservative Mind* (Philadelphia: Temple University Press, 1993), p. 8.
3. Michael Ledeen, *The War against the Terror Masters* (New York: St. Martin's Press, 2005).
4. *Los Angeles Times* (September 19, 2009).
5. Cited in Dorrien, *The Neoconservative Mind,* p. 327.
6. Dorrien, p. 328.
7. Cited in Dorrien, p. 337.
8. See Samuel Huntington, *The Clash of Civilizations and the Remaking of World Order* (New York: Simon and Shuster, 1996), pp. 301–18.
9. Huntington, pp. 20–21, 184.
10. David Brock, *The Republican Noise Machine* (New York: Crown Publishers, 2004), pp. 48–52.
11. Robert Kagan, *Of Paradise and Power* (New York: Alfred A. Knopf, 2003).
12. Kagan, p. 4.
13. Kagan, p. 27.
14. Kagan, p. 76.
15. Kagan, p. 87.
16. Kagan, p. 90.
17. Robert D. Kaplan, *Warrior Politics* (New York: Vintage Books, 2003), p. 55.
18. Kaplan, p. 77.

19. Kaplan, p. 108.
20. Kaplan, p. 118.
21. Kaplan, pp. 119–20.
22. Kaplan, pp. 146–47.
23. Robert D. Kaplan, *Imperial Grunts* (New York: Vintage Books, 2005), p. 3.
24. Kaplan, p. 6.
25. Kaplan, p. 12.
26. Kaplan, p. 364.
27. Kaplan, p. 366.
28. Smedley D. Butler, *War is a Racket* (Los Angeles: Feral House, 1935), pp. 23–37.
29. Ledeen, p. 10.
30. Ledeen, p. 232.
31. Ledeen, p. 221.
32. Kaplan, *Warrior Politics*, p. 118.
33. In the immediate period after 9/11, several endorsements of the U.S. practice of terror under certain circumstances surfaced among American scholars. The most well-known and influential was John Yoo's *Memorandum to President Bush* submitted on January 9, 2002. See also Alan Dershowitz, *Why Terrorism Works* (New Haven, CT: Yale University Press, 2002).
34. Philippe Sands, *Lawless World* (New York: Viking Press, 2005), p. 48.
35. Jack Goldsmith and Eric Posner, *The Limits of International Law* (New York: Oxford University Press, 2005), pp. 225–26.
36. David Frum and Richard Perle, *An End to Evil* (New York: Random House, 2003), p. 267.
37. Frum and Perle, pp. 271–72.
38. Frum and Perle, p. 273.
39. Douglas Murray, *Neoconservatism* (New York: Encounter Books, 2006), p. 203.
40. Murray, p. 199.
41. See, for example, "Bolton vs. World", *American Prospect* (November 2006).
42. Peter Steinfels, *The Neo-Conservatives* (New York: Simon and Schuster, 1979), p. 12.
43. See Chalmers Johnson, *Blowback* (New York: Henry Holt, 2000), ch. 1.
44. *Los Angeles Times* (September 11, 2009).
45. *Los Angeles Times* (September 11, 2009).
46. *Los Angeles Times* (September 11, 2009).
47. Frum and Perle, *An End to Evil*, p. 33.
48. Frum and Perle, p. 213.
49. Frum and Perle, p. 267.
50. Christopher Hitchens, *A Long Short War* (New York: Plume Books, 2003), p. 99.
51. Hitchens, p. 102.
52. Hitchens, p. 83.
53. Hitchens, p. 11.

54. Murray, *Neoconservatism,* p. 161.
55. Murray, p. 90.
56. Murray, pp. 133–34.
57. Murray, p. 141.
58. Murray, p. 153.
59. Murray, pp. 148–49.
60. Murray, p. 217.
61. Johns Hopkins School of Public Health Report, in *Lancet* (October 2006).
62. *Los Angeles Times* (October 9, 2009).
63. *Los Angeles Times* (September 29, 2009).
64. *Los Angeles Times* (September 26, 2009).
65. *Los Angeles Times* (October 15, 2009).
66. Tom Hayden, *The Nation* (September 24, 2007).

3 The Power Elite Today

1. Andrew J. Bacevich, *The Limits of Power: The End of American Exceptionalism* (New York: Henry Holt and Co., 2008), p. 15.
2. Jean Bethke Elshtain, *Just War against Terror* (New York: Basic Books, 2003), p. 167.
3. Elshtain, p. 168.
4. Elshtain, p. 169.
5. Chalmers Johnson, *Nemesis: The Last Days of the American Republic* (New York: Henry Holt and Co., 2007), p. 17.
6. Chris Hedges, in www.CommonDreams.org (February 2, 2009).
7. Karl Marx, "Manifesto of the Communist Party", in Robert C. Tucker, ed., *The Marx-Engels Reader* (New York: W.W. Norton, 1978), pp. 476–77.
8. Marx, op.cit., p. 476.
9. C. Wright Mills, *The Power Elite* (New York: Vintage Books, 1956), p. 23.
10. Mills, p. 12.
11. See Michael Parenti, *Land of Idols* (New York: St. Martin's, 1994), pp. 94–95.
12. Mills, p. 23.
13. Mills, p. 212.
14. Mills, p. 275.
15. Kevin Phillips, *Wealth and Democracy* (New York: Broadway Books, 2002), pp. 141–48.
16. Phillips, p. 415.
17. G. William Domhoff, *Who Rules America?* (New York: McGraw-Hill, 2006), ch. 2.
18. Domhoff, p. xiv.
19. Domhoff, p. 200.
20. Naomi Klein interview of Michael Moore, in *The Nation* (October 12, 2009).

21. Domhoff, *Who Rules America?*, p. 25.
22. Nelson Lichtenstein, *The Retail Revolution* (New York: Henry Holt and Co., 2009).
23. See Harold Meyerson, "The Shipping Point", *The American Prospect* (July/August 2009).
24. Jamie Court, *Corporateering* (New York: Tarcher/Penguin, 2003), pp. 53–54.
25. Chris Hedges, *Death of the Liberal Class* (New York: Nation Books, 2010), p. 17.
26. Smedley D. Butler, *War is a Racket* (Los Angeles: Feral House, 2003), pp. 23–24.
27. Seymour Melman, *The Demilitarized Society* (Montreal: Harvest House, 1988), p. 9.
28. Mills, *The Power Elite*, p. 275.
29. Sheldon Wolin, *Democracy, Inc.* (Princeton, NJ: Princeton University Press, 2008), ch. 2.
30. James M. Cypher, "From Military Keynesianism to Global Neoliberal Militarism", *Monthly Review* (June 2007), p. 38.
31. Mills, p. 219.
32. Mills, p. 223.
33. Fred J. Cook, *The Warfare State* (New York: Collier, 1962), p. 100.
34. Cook, p. 189.
35. See Seymour Melman, *The Permanent War Economy* (New York: Simon and Schuster, 1974), and *Profits without Production* (New York: Knopf, 1983).
36. Cook, *Warfare State*, p. 354.
37. Helen Caldicott, *The New Nuclear Danger* (New York: New Press, 2002), p. 20.
38. Ken Silverstein, *Private Warriors* (London: Verso, 2000), p. ix.
39. See Sourcewatch.org/index (2010).
40. Cook, *Warfare State*, p. 189.
41. See Carl Boggs and Tom Pollard, *The Hollywood War Machine* (Boulder, CO: Paradigm, 2007), introduction.
42. See Chris Hedges, *War is a Force that Gives Us Meaning* (New York: Public Affairs, 2002), p. 3.
43. Nick Turse, *The Complex: How the Military Invades our Everyday Lives* (New York: Henry Holt and Co., 2008), pp. 33–40.
44. Turse, pp. 244–70.
45. *Los Angeles Times* (January 19, 2010).
46. *Los Angeles Times* (January 19, 2010).
47. Catherine Lutz, *Homefront* (Boston: Beacon Press, 2001), p. 3.
48. Lutz, p. 4.
49. Mary Edwards Wertsch, *Military Brats* (New York: Ballantine, 1991), p. 1.
50. Wertsch, p. 33.
51. Wertsch, p. 16.
52. Wertsch, p. 15.

286   Notes

53. Richard Falk, "Slouching Toward a Fascist World Order," in David Ray Griffin, et al., eds, *The American Empire and the Commonwealth of God* (Louisville: Westminster John Knox Press, 2006), pp. 59–63.
54. Falk, in Griffin, p. 57.
55. Falk, in Griffin, p. 62.
56. Tom Lantos, quoted in *Los Angeles Times* (October 9, 2002).
57. Robert Byrd, quoted in *Los Angeles Times* (October 11, 2002).
58. James Bamford, in *Rolling Stone* (December 1, 2005), p. 61.
59. Bamford, in *Rolling Stone,* pp. 61–63.
60. Dilip Hiro, *Iraq: in the Eye of the Storm* (New York: Nation Books, 2002), Chapters 5 and 6.
61. Hiro, pp. 78–84.
62. Lawrence Davidson, *Foreign Policy, Inc.* (Lexington: University Press of Kentucky, 2009).
63. Davidson, pp. 93–95.
64. See John J. Mearsheimer and Stephen M. Walt, *The Israel Lobby and U.S. Foreign Policy* (New York: Farrar, Stauss, and Giroux, 2007).
65. See Jeremy Scahill, "The Secret U.S. War in Pakistan", *The Nation* (December 21–28, 2009).
66. Andrew J. Bacevich, *Washington Rules* (New York: Henry Holt and Co., 2010), p. 27.
67. Murray Bookchin, *The Ecology of Freedom* (Palo Alto: Cheshire Books, 1982), p. 127.
68. Herbert Marcuse, *Counter-Revolution and Revolt* (Boston: Beacon Press, 1972), p. 25.
69. Peter Irons, *War Powers* (New York: Henry Holt and Co., 2005), p. 272.
70. Irons, p. 2.
71. Charlie Savage, *Takeover: the Return of the Imperial Presidency* (New York: Little, Brown, and Co., 2007), p. 47.
72. Savage, p. 75.
73. Savage, p. 329.
74. Nancy Chang, *Silencing Political Dissent* (New York: Seven Stories, 2002), p. 119.
75. Hannah Holleman, et. al., "Penal State in The Age of Crisis", *Monthly Review* (June 2009, p. 8.
76. James Bamford, *The Shadow Factory* (New York: Doubleday, 2008), p. 304.
77. Bamford, p. 13.
78. Bamford, p. 110.
79. Quoted in Bamford, pp. 190–91.
80. Gaetano Mosca, *The Ruling Class* (New York: McGraw-Hill, 1939), pp. 70–71.
81. Robert Michels, *Political Parties* (New Brunswick: Transaction Publishes, 1999), p. 369.
82. Antonio Gramsci, "Revolutionaries and the Elections", in *Selections from Political Writings 1910–1920* (New York: International Publishers, 1977), p. 128.

83. Bertram Gross, *Friendly Fascism* (Boston: South End Press, 1980), p. 240.
84. Domhoff, *Who Rules America?*, pp. 154–55.
85. www.OpenSecrets.com.
86. Ibid.
87. Ibid.
88. Matt Taibbi, "Obama's Big Sellout," *Rolling Stone* (December 10, 2009), p. 45.
89. Taibbi, p. 47.
90. *Los Angeles Times* (November 4, 2010).
91. On this point, see Matt Taibbi, "Tea and Crackers," *Rolling Stone* (October 14, 2010).
92. Robert Michels, *Political Parties* (New Brunswick, NJ: Transaction Publishers, 1999), p. 336.
93. Chris Hedges, *Death of the Liberal Class* (New York: Nation Books, 2010), pp. 9–10.
94. Ibid., p. 12.
95. Tariq Ali, *The Obama Syndrome* (London: Verso, 2010), p. 76.
96. Ibid., p. 33.
97. Cornell West, *Democracy Matters* (New York: Penguin Books, 2005), p. 8.
98. Zygmunt Bauman, *In Search of Politics* (Stanford, CA: Stanford University Press, 1999), pp. 120–22.

4   The Many Faces of Corporate Power

1. Robert McChesney, *Rich Media, Poor Democracy*, p. 281.
2. Ben Bagdikian's contribution is *The Media Monopoly* (Boston, MA: Beacon, 1992).
3. David Brock, *The Republican Noise Machine* (New York: Crown Books, 2004), p. 50.
4. Ibid., p. 28.
5. See Peter Phillips and Mickey Huff, eds., *Censored 2010*.
6. Edward Said, "America's Last Taboo", *New Left Review* (November-December 2000).
7. See Douglas Kellner's excellent treatment of the connection between technowar, superpatriotism, and media spectacle, in *The Persian Gulf TV War* (Boulder, CO: Westview, 1992), pp. 200–24.
8. Norman Solomon, *War Made Easy* (Hoboken, NJ: John Wiley and Sons, 2005), pp. 110–11.
9. See *Censored 2010*, p. 123.
10. Ibid., p. 125.
11. Ibid., pp. 88–91.
12. See Mickey Huff and Frances A. Capell, "Infotainment Society: Junk Food News and News Abuse," in *Censored 2010*, pp. 147–74.
13. Sut Jhally, "Advertising at the Edge of the Apocalypse," in Paula Rothenberg, ed., *Race, Class, and Gender in the United States* (New York: Worth, 2010), p. 621.

14. Ibid., p. 627.
15. Michael Lowy, "Advertising is a Serious Threat to the Environment," *Monthly Review* (January 2010), p. 21.
16. McChesney, *The Problem of the Media* (New York: Monthly Review, 2004), p. 138.
17. Ibid., p. 167.
18. Sheldon Wolin, *Democracy, Inc.*, p. 160.
19. G. William Domhoff, *Who Rules America?*, p. 119.
20. Ibid., p. 114.
21. See John Nichols and Robert McChesney, "The Money and Media Election Complex", *The Nation* (November 29, 2010).
22. Ibid., pp. 12, 14.
23. Arianna Huffington, *Third World America* (New York: Crown Publishers, 2010), p. 149.
24. On the "liberal-labor coalition", see Domhoff, pp. 158–60.
25. Thomas Frank, *The Wrecking Crew* (New York: Henry Holt and Co., 2008), p. 8.
26. Ibid., p. 115.
27. Ibid., p. 95.
28. Ibid., p. 274.
29. Philip Selznick, *TVA and the Grassroots* (Berkeley: University of California Press, 1949).
30. Ibid., p. 14.
31. Ibid., p. 251.
32. Ibid., pp. v, vi.
33. See Kelly Hearn, "Tennessee Spill," *The Nation* (May 25, 2009).
34. Ibid., p. 26.
35. Robert F. Kennedy, Jr., *Crimes Against Nature* (New York: Harper/Collins, 2004), p. 24.
36. Ibid., p. 24.
37. Ibid., p. 34.
38. Ibid., p. 39.
39. Ibid., p. 99.
40. See Robert S. Devine, *Bush versus the Environment* (New York: Anchor Books, 2004), ch. 4.
41. Helen Caldicott, *The New Nuclear Danger* (New York: New Press, 2002), p. 26.
42. Ibid., p. 28.
43. Smedley D. Butler, *War is a Racket* (Los Angeles: Feral House, 2003), pp. 23–24.
44. *Los Angeles Times* (March 9, 2010).
45. Ibid.
46. C. Wright Mills, *The Power Elite*, pp. 260–97.
47. Ibid., p. 275.
48. Quoted in Peter H. Stone, *Casino Jack* (Brooklyn: Melville House, 2010), p. 179.

49. Quoted in Stone, op. cit., pp. 180–81.
50. See John Hari, "The Wrong Kind of Green," *The Nation* (March 22, 2010).
51. See Matt Taibbi, "Wall Street's Bailout Hustle," *Rolling Stone* (March 4, 2010).
52. Ibid., p. 54.
53. *Los Angeles Times* (February 16, 2010).
54. Ibid.
55. Kevin Drum, "Capital City," *Mother Jones* (January–February, 2010), p. 43.
56. Ibid., p. 50.
57. William Greider, "Blue-Dog Democrats," *The Nation* (November 30, 2009), p. 23.
58. Robert Auerbach, *Deception and Abuse at the Fed* (Austin: University of Texas Press, 2009).
59. *Time* magazine (December 30, 2009), p. 48.
60. Ibid., p. 48.
61. Ibid., p. 49.
62. Ibid., p. 47.
63. Robert Scheer, *The Great American Stickup* (New York: Nation Books, 2010).
64. See Antonio Gramsci, "Americanism and Fordism," in Geoffrey Nowell Smith and Quintin Hoare, eds., *Selections from the Prison Notebooks of Antonio Gramsci* (New York: International Publishers, 171), p. 317.
65. Richard Edwards, *The Contested Terrain* (New York: Basic Books, 1979), ch. 7.
66. Ibid., p. 131.
67. Ibid., p. 132.
68. Ibid., p. 145.
69. Ibid., p. 148.
70. See John Tomaney, "A New Paradigm of Work Organization and Technology?", in Samir Amin, ed., *Post-Fordism: A Reader* (Oxford: Blackwell, 1994).
71. Ibid., p. 176.
72. Barbara Ehrenreich, *Nickel and Dimed* (New York: Henry Holt and Co., 2001), pp. 158, 181.
73. Harold Meyerson, "The Shipping Point," *The American Prospect* (July–August, 2009).
74. Eric Schlosser, *Fast-Food Nation* (Boston: Houghton-Mifflin, 2001), p. 8.
75. Ibid., p. 172.
76. Ibid., p. 164.
77. George Ritzer, *The McDonaldization of Society* (Thousand Oaks, CA: Pine Forge Press, 2000), p. 16.
78. See John Van Maanen, "The Smile Factory: Work at Disneyland", in David M. Newman, ed., *Sociology* (Thousand Oaks, CA: Pine Forge Press, 1997).
79. Ibid., p. 208.

290 Notes

80. Mary Edwards Wertsch, *Military Brats* (New York: Fawcett/Columbine, 1991), p. 16.
81. Ibid., p. 19.
82. Ibid., p. 34.
83. See Catherine Lutz, *The Homefront* (Boston, MA: Beacon Press, 2001), pp. 2-6.
84. Frank, *The Wrecking Crew*, p. 214.
85. Ibid., p. 223.
86. Ibid., p. 229.
87. Clark Kerr, "Selections from *The Uses of the University*," in Seymour Martin Lipset and Sheldon Wolin, eds., *The Berkeley Student Revolt* (New York: Anchor Books, 1965).
88. Ibid., p. 49.
89. Lawrence C. Solely, *Leasing the Ivory Tower* (Boston, MA: South End, 1995), p. 109.
90. Ibid., pp. 152–53.
91. Helen Caldicott, *The New Nuclear Danger*, pp. 15–17.
92. Upton Sinclair's classic work in this area is *The Goose Step: A Study of American Education* (Whitefish, MT: Kessinger Publishing, 2004). This book was first published in 1923.
93. On the Norman Finkelstein case, see Bill Martin, "Postmodern Fascism and the Long Arm of Israel: Reflections on the Finkelstein Case", in Anthony Nocella, et al., eds, *Academic Repression* (Oakland: AK Press, 2010), pp. 216–26.
94. David Noble, *Digital Diploma Mills* (New York: Monthly Review, 2001), Chapter 2.
95. Ibid., p. 21.
96. For a classic statement on the closing universe of political thought, see Herbert Marcuse, *One-Dimensional Man* (Boston, MA: Beacon Press, 1964), pp. 84-122.
97. See Jeff Lustig, "The FSM and the Vision of a New Left", in Robert Cohen and Reginald Zelnick, eds., *The Free Speech Movement* (Berkeley, CA: University of California Press, 2002).
98. www.ucdemocracy.org.

5 Medical Tyranny

1. On U.S. health spending, see section on National Health Expenditures, Centers for Medicare and Medicaid Services (2008). For U.S. health data, see www.who,int/whois/whostat/2009/en/index.html (2009).
2. *Los Angeles Times* (April 6, 2005).
3. See Centers for Medicare and Medicaid Services (2008), and www.AmericanCancer Society (2009).
4. Centers for Medicare and Medicaid Services (2008).
5. John Abramson, *Overdosed America: The Broken Promise of American Medicine* (New York: HarperCollins, 2004).

6. See Ivan Illich, *Medical Nemesis* (New York: Vintage, 1978), and John Robbins, *The Food Revolution* (Berkeley, CA: Conari Press, 2001).
7. Abramson, p. xiii.
8. Marcia Angell, *The Truth about the Drug Companies* (New York: Random House, 2004), and Donald L. Bartlett and James B. Steele, *Critical Condition: How Health Care in America Became Big Business and Bad Medicine* (New York: Doubleday, 2004).
9. E. Richard Brown, *Rockefeller Medicine Men* (Berkeley: University of California Press, 1979), p. 8.
10. Ibid., p. 52.
11. Ibid., p. 14.
12. Angell, p. 169.
13. See Angell, pp. 10–11.
14. See the account by Matt Taibbi in *Rolling Stone* (February 24, 2005).
15. Sidney M. Wolfe and associates, *Worst Pills, Best Pills* (New York: Pocket Books, 2005), p. 10.
16. According to DrugWarFacts (2010), for the year 2009 death rates from various substances were as follows: tobacco, 435,000; alcohol, 85,000; prescription drugs, 40,000; illicit drugs, 17,000; marijuana, none. Illicit drugs include not only heroin and cocaine but hallucinigens, methamphetamine, and many others. See DrugWarFacts.org (2010). As mentioned, Wolfe and associates report a death toll of roughly 100,000 yearly from prescription drugs, along with 1.5 million people hospitalized from adverse drug reactions. See *Worst Pills, Best Pills*, p. xxii.
17. Mike Gray, *Drug Crazy* (New York: Random House, 1998), p. 187.
18. *Los Angeles Times* (February 7, 2005).
19. Wolfe, p. xxiv.
20. Ibid., p. xxiii.
21. Abramson, p. 97.
22. On Big Pharma lobbying, see Angell, Chapter 11.
23. *Los Angeles Times* (March 16, 2005).
24. See Angell, Chapter 7.
25. Ibid., p. 43.
26. Ibid., p. 66.
27. Ibid., pp. 210–11.
28. Wolfe, p. 6.
29. Ibid.
30. On the Vioxx research and scandal, see Abramson, pp. 33–38.
31. Wolfe, p. 302.
32. Abramson, pp. 25–37.
33. *New York Times* (February 22, 2005).
34. *Los Angeles Times* (February 26, 2005).
35. Ralph W. Moss, *The Cancer Industry* (New York: Equinox Press, 1996).
36. Devra Davis, *The Secret History of the War on Cancer* (New York: Basic Books, 2007), p. 4.
37. T. Colin Campbell, *The China Study* (Dallas: BenBella Books, 2006).
38. On the cancer disaster, see Robbins, pp. 37–38.

39. See Campbell, Chapter 7.
40. Ibid., p. 258.
41. Ibid., pp. 261–64.
42. Ibid., p. 265.
43. Ibid., p. 312.
44. Ibid., p. 318.
45. Angell, p. 237.
46. *Los Angeles Times* (August 4, 2009).
47. *Los Angeles Times* (November 17, 2009).
48. *Los Angeles Times* (July 23, 2009).
49. Tim Dickinson, "The Lie Machine," *Rolling Stone* (October 1, 2009).
50. *Los Angeles Times* (October 5, 2010).
51. *Los Angeles Times* (November 9, 2010).
52. Ibid.
53. *Los Angeles Times* (August 11, 2010).
54. Ivan Illich, et al., *Disabling Professions* (New York: Marion Boyars, 1987), pp. 14, 17.

6   An American Fascism?

1. Thomas Frank, *What's the Matter With Kansas?* (New York: Henry Holt and Co., 2005), and *The Wrecking Crew: How Conservatives Rule* (New York: Henry Holt and Co., 2008).
2. Frank, *The Wrecking Crew*, p. 8.
3. Ibid., p. 115.
4. Ibid., p. 95.
5. Frank, *What's the Matter with Kansas?*, p. 5.
6. Ibid., p. 6.
7. Ibid.
8. Ibid., p. 254.
9. See Barrington Moore, Jr., *Social Origins of Dictatorship and Democracy* (Boston, MA: Beacon Press, 1967), pp. 495–96.
10. C. Wright Mills, *The Power Elite* (New York: Oxford University Press, 1956).
11. Mills, p. 23.
12. Mills, p. 212.
13. Mills, p. 275.
14. Mills, p. 276.
15. Naomi Wolf, *The End of America: Letter of Warning to a Young Patriot* (White River Juncton, VT: Chelsea Green, 2006), p. 14.
16. Wolf, p. 14.
17. Sheldon Wolin, *Democracy, Inc.: Managed Democracy and the Specter of Inverted Totalitarianism* (Princeton, NJ: Princeton University Press, 2008), p. 105.
18. Wolin, p. 181.
19. Wolin, p. 70.

20. Wolin, p. 144.
21. Herbert Marcuse, *One-Dimensional Man* (Boston, MA: Beacon Press, 1964).
22. Marcuse, p. 3.
23. Marcuse, p. 14.
24. Herbert Marcuse, *Negations* (Boston, MA: Beacon Press, 1968), p. 9.
25. Wolin, *Democracy, Inc.*, p. 141.
26. Wolin, p. 157.
27. Wolin, p. 196.
28. Chris Hedges, *American Fascists: the Christian Right and the War on America* (New York; Free Press, 2006), p. 29.
29. Hedges, p. 27.
30. Roger Griffin, *The Nature of Fascism* (London: Routledge, 1991), ch. 1.
31. Griffin, p. 38.
32. Griffin, p. 42.
33. Bertram Gross, *Friendly Fascism* (Boston, MA: South End Press, 1982).
34. See Michael Mann, *Fascists* (New York: Cambridge University Press, 2004); Walter Laqueur, *Fascism Past, Present, Future* (New York: Oxford University Press, 1996); Robert O. Paxson, *The Anatomy of Fascism* (New York: Alfred A. Knopf, 2004).
35. Mann, *Fascists*, p. 370.
36. Laqueur, *Fascism*, pp. 224–25.
37. Mann, *Fascists*, p. 13.
38. Laqueur, *Facism*, p. 36.
39. Moore, *Social Origins*, p. 385.
40. On the decline of democratic participation in American politics, see E.J. Dionne, Jr., *Why Americans Hate Politics* (New York: Simon and Schuster, 1991); Carl Boggs, *The End of Politics: Corporate Power and Decline of the Public Sphere* (New York: Guilford, 2000); and Wolin, *Democracy, Inc.*

Conclusion

1. Wolin, *Democracy, Incorporated*, p. 268.
2. Ibid., p. 269.

Postscript: Politics in the Nuclear Age

1. See John Dower, *War Without Mercy*, p. 37.
2. Cited in Dower, pp. 141–42.
3. Howard Zinn, *The Bomb* (San Francisco, CA: City Lights Books, 2010), p. 37.
4. Ibid., pp. 38–39.
5. Ibid., p. 61.
6. Garry Wills, *Bomb Power: The Modern Presidency and the National Security State* (New York: Penguin, 2010).

7. Ibid., p. 2.
8. Ibid., pp. 46–47.
9. Ibid., p. 237.
10. Robert Jay Lifton, *Superpower Syndrome*. (New York: Nation Books, 2003).
11. Ibid., pp. 42–43.
12. On the connection between Cold War nuclear politics and American popular culture, see Ronnie Lipschutz, *Cold War Fantasies* (Lanham, MD: Rowman and Littlefield, 2001).
13. Scott Ritter, *Target Iran* (New York: Nation Books, 2006), pp. 198–200.
14. Wills, *Bomb Power,* p. 237.
15. On U.S. plans for space weaponization, see Helen Caldicott and Craig Eisendrath, *War in Heaven: The Arms Race in Outer Space* (New York: The New Press, 2007), Chapters 3 and 4. See also Karl Grossman, *Weapons in Space* (New York: Seven Stories, 2001), pp. 9–18.
16. *New York Times* (February 1, 2008).
17. www.visioncritical.com/2010.
18. www.icanw.org/polls.
19. See Hans Blix, *Why Nuclear Disarmament Matters* (Cambridge, MA: MIT Press, 2008).
20. Ibid., p. 76.
21. Ibid., p. 85.
22. Ibid., p. 85.
23. Ibid., p. 95.
24. *The Defense Monitor* (October 2008), p. 13.
25. Jonathan Schell, "Reaching Zero", *The Nation* (April 19, 2010).
26. Blix, *Why Disarmament Matters,* p. 45.
27. Ibid., p. 49.
28. Ibid., p. 55.
29. See Erwin Chemerinsky, *The Conservative Assault on the Constitution* (New York: Simon and Schuster, 2010).

Index

Abbott Laboratories, 222
Abramoff, Jack, 162, 168–69, 186
Abramson, Dr. John, 199, 202, 216, 220
Adorno, Theodor, 89, 249
Aegis Ballistic Missile Defense System, 273
Afghanistan, 54, 109, 122
    And Taliban, 83, 86
Albert, Michael, 20
Ali, Tariq, 143
Allende, Salvador, 53, 54
Al Qaeda, 119
American Cancer Society, 216–17
American Council on Science and Health (ACSH), 219
American Enterprise Institute, 70, 82, 98, 193
American Farm Bureau, 163
American Institute for Cancer Research (AICR), 219
American Medical Association, 136, 222
Americans for Prosperity, 226
Ancien regime, 9
Angell, Dr. Marcia, 200, 202, 212, 220
Angus Reid Public Opinion Survey (2010), 273
Anti-Ballistic Missile Treat (ABM), 269
Arendt, Hannah, 244
AstraZeneca Corp., 207, 209, 218
AT&T Corp., 136
Auerbach, Robert, 175

Bacevich, Andrew, 47, 90, 120
Backlash Politics, 231, 233

Bagdikian, Ben, 147
Balkans, 46, 54, 55, 76
Bamford, James, 117, 130, 131
Bank of America Corp., 171, 189
Bartlett, David, 200, 209
Bayh-Dole Act (1984), 201, 210
Bechtel Corp., 191
Belshe, Kim, 198
Bennett, William, 203
Bernanke, Ben, 175
Big Pharma, 199–211, 213, 215, 220–22
Blackwater (PMC), 119
Blix, Hans, 274–76
Blockbuster Corp., 183
Board of Regents (University of California), 188–89, 196
Bolsheviks, 1
Bolton, John, 74
Bookchin, Murray, 20, 120
Bosnia, 54, 55
Boxer, Barbara, 141
Bristol-Meyers-Squibb Corp., 212
British Petroleum (BP), 169–70, 195
Brock, David, 65, 66, 148, 149, 158
Brown, Richard, 200
Bureaucratic Centralism, 255
Bush, George H. W., 262
Bush, George W., 5, 35, 42, 48, 49, 58, 77–80, 88, 108, 121, 123, 126, 128, 130, 137, 140, 153, 165, 192, 213, 229–30, 234, 246, 263, 266, 269, 272–73, 277–78
    And "Bush Doctrine," 72
Butler, Gen. Smedley, 36, 37, 69, 102, 166

Caldicott, Helen, 107, 165, 166, 192
Cambodia, 262
Campaign for U.C. Democracy, 196
Campbell, Colin, 217–20
Cancer-Industrial Complex, 217
Castoriadis, Cornelius, 20
Cato Institute, 226
"Catonism" (Cato the Elder), 231
Center for Media and Democracy, 158
Center for Science in the Public
    Interest, 206
Central America, 153, 262
Central Intelligence Agency (CIA), 106,
    117–19, 122, 124, 127, 129, 150,
    260
Chamber of Commerce (U.S.), 166–67,
    170, 226
Chang, Nancy, 125
Chemerinsky, Erwin, 278
Chemical and Metallurgy Research
    Replacement (CMRR), 276
Chemical Manufacturers Association,
    165
Chile, 53, 54
China, 182, 255, 261, 266, 272, 274
Chomsky, Noam, 147, 193
Christianity, 247
And Christian Fundamentalism, 247
Churchill, Ward, 11
Citigroup Corp., 171, 177
Civil War (U.S.), 29
Clear Channel Corp., 149
Clinton, William, 75, 125, 128, 263
COINTELPRO, 125
Cold War, 40–44, 59–62, 110, 111,
    122, 124, 239, 257–58, 260
And Cold War Liberalism, 74
Colombia, 153, 204
Commission on WMD, 274–76
Commodities Future Modernization
    Act (2000), 173
Communism, 52, 54, 60, 75, 242,
    260–61
And Soviet Union, 124, 242
ConAgra Corporation, 182–83
Consumer Finance Protection Agency,
    138, 166, 172, 177

Controlled Substance Act (1970), 204
Cook, Fred, 13, 50, 105, 110
Corporate capitalism, 3, 145, 140–47,
    244
Council for Environmental Quality,
    165
Counterinsurgency (U.S. policy), 85,
    86
Court, Jamie, 100
Cuba, 262
Cyber Security, 113
Cypher, James, 104

Dahl, Robert, 26
Davidson, Lawrence, 118
Davis, Devra, 217
Debs, Eugene, 36
Delay, Tom, 162, 186
DeMint, Jim, 139
Democracy, 1, 15, 253
And democratization, 18, 181
"Demotic Moments" (Wolin),
    250–51
Forms of, 243
Jacksonian democracy, 7
Myths of, 3
Department of Energy (DOE), 191
Depleted Uranium (DU), 263, 272
Dershowitz, Alan, 72, 193
de Tocqueville, Alexis, 4, 6, 10, 48
Disney Corporation, 184
Dodd, Christopher, 157, 173
Domhoff, G. William, 97–99
Dorrien, Gary, 60
Dower, John, 37, 38, 258
Drum, Kevin, 173

Eastern Europe, 272–73
Eastman, Dr. Richard, 207
Edwards, Richard, 179–80
Egypt, 266, 268, 274
Ehrenreich, Barbara, 181
Eisenhower, Dwight, 40, 42, 52, 104,
    262
Elshtain, Jean, 90
Emmanuel, Rahm, 138
Enemy of the State, 131

Energy Bioscience Institute, 191
Engels, Friedrich, 131
Environmental Protection Agency
    (FDA), 164, 185
Epstein, Samuel, 217
Eschelon System, 272
Evangelicals, 246
    And Christian Coalition, 246
ExxonMobil Corp., 136, 170

Fascism, 232, 235–39, 244–45, 249–50
    And History, 247–48, 255
    Imperialism, 245, 248
Federal Communications Commission
    (FCC), 164
Federalist Papers, 70
Federal Nutrition Board, 220
Federal Reserve Bank, 170–75
Feith, Douglas, 123
Ferguson, Charles, 87
Finance Services Modernization Act
    (1999), 173
Financial Services Roundtable, 172
Finkelstein, Norman, 193
Food and Drug Agency (FDA), 164,
    202–203, 206–207, 211–12,
    215–16
    And FDA Modernization Act
    (1997), 213
Ford, Henry, 183
Fort Bragg (North Carolina), 114
Fotopoulos, Takis, 20
Founders (of U.S. Constitution), 6, 25,
    26, 56, 69, 134, 236, 238–39
FOX TV Network, 65, 70, 148,
    158–59
France, 274
Franco, Francisco, 52
Frank, Barney, 124
Frank, Thomas, 160–63, 167, 186,
    228–32, 239–40
Frankfurt School (Critical Theory), 89,
    92, 131
Freedom Works, 223
Free Speech Movement (Berkeley),
    188, 196
Froman, Michael, 137

Frum, David, 73, 78, 79
Fukuyama, Francis, 64

Gabler, Neal, 77
Gates, Bill, 96
Gates, Robert, 85
Geithner, Timothy, 137, 138
Genentech Corp., 210
General Electric Corp., 146, 180, 199
General Motors Corp., 180
Geneva Conventions, 269
Germany, 259, 263
Gibson, William, 43
Gillibrand, Kirsten, 173
Glass-Seagall Act (1933), 173
GlaxcoSmithKline Corp., 214
Globalization, 4, 101, 237
Global Nuclear Energy Partnership,
    271
Goldman Sachs Corp., 137, 177
Goldsmith, Jack, 73
Goodman, Paul, 20
Google Corp., 189
Graham, Dr. David, 215
Gramsci, Antonio, 93, 132, 133, 178,
    254
The Grand Illusion, 227
Grassley, Charles, 216
Great Britain, 214, 274
Greece, 262
Greens (European), 255
Greenspan, Alan, 174–75
Greenwald, Robert, 181
Greider, William, 174
Griffin, Roger, 247
Gross, Bertram, 133, 248–49
Guantanamo (Prison), 83, 235
Guatemala, 53
Gulf of Tonkin Resolution (1965), 262
Gulf War (1991), 45, 62, 109, 152

Hague Tribunal, 45
Hamilton Project, 137, 138
Hastert, Dennis, 117
Hayden, Tom, 86
Hedges, Chris, 91, 100, 142, 143,
    245–49

Heritage Foundation, 164
Herman, Edward, 147
Hiro, Dilip, 118
Hiroshima, 38, 40, 257–60, 263
Hitchens, Christopher, 79, 80
Hobbes, Thomas, 67, 70, 240, 260
    And Hobbesian, 273
Hofstadter, Richard, 27
Homeland Security Office, 124, 126,
    129, 277
Hoover Institute, 190, 276
Horkheimer, Max, 89
Horowitz, David, 193
House Finance Services Committee,
    174
Huffington, Arianna, 160
Huntington, Samuel, 64, 65
Hussein, Saddam, 62

Illich, Ivan, 200, 226
India, 265, 276
    And NPT, 265
Indian Removal Act (1830), 11–12
Indonesia, 53
Industrial Workers of the World
    (IWW), 36
International Atomic Energy Agency
    (IAEA), 151, 266–67, 269
International Criminal Court (ICC),
    48, 72
International Law, 73, 153, 278
International Monetary Fund, 150,
    170
Iran, 53, 83–85, 266–69, 271, 274
    And WMD, 151, 265
Iraq War, 68, 76–88, 117, 118,
    262–63, 266
    And Iraq Body Count, 81
    And Iraq Freedom Act, 75
Irons, Peter, 121
Israel, 150–51, 193, 265–66, 268–69,
    274, 276
    Israel-Palestinian Conflict, 150
    And NPT, 265–66
Israel Lobby (U.S.), 82, 84, 118, 119,
    193
Izetbegovic, Alija, 55

Jackson, Andrew, 7, 10, 34
Jacobinism, 254–55
Jacoby, Susan, 16
Japan, 257–59, 263, 271
Japanese (World War II), 38
Jefferson, Thomas, 2, 8, 9
Jhally, Sut, 155
Johnson, Chalmers, 13, 90
Johnson, Lyndon B., 262
Johnson & Johnson Corp., 209
J.P. Morgan Chase Corp., 137, 172,
    177

Kagan, Robert, 66, 67, 72
Kahn, Herman, 264
Kaplan, Robert, 67–69, 72
Kennedy, John F., 40, 44, 60, 62,
    261–62
Kennedy, Robert F., Jr., 165
Kerr, Clark, 187–88, 194–96
    And Multiversity, 187–90, 193
Khalidi, Rashid, 193
Khamenei, Ayatollah, 269
Kissinger, Henry, 264, 269
Koch Brothers, 139–40, 226
Korean War, 41, 42, 52, 53, 60,
    261–62, 265
Kosovo Liberation Army, 45, 55
Krauthammer, Charles, 62
Kristol, Irving, 60, 61
Kropotkin, Prince, 20
Kyoto Accords (1997), 72

Laqueur, Walter, 249–50
Lavrov, Sergei, 272
Leahy, Adm. William, 258
Ledeen, Michael, 70, 71
LeMay, Gen. Curtis, 261
Lenin, V. I., 1
Liberalism, 9, 132, 134, 187, 228, 239,
    242, 244, 247–50
Lichtenstein, Nelson, 99
Lifton, Robert J., 263–64
Lilly Corp., 211
Limbaugh, Rush, 148
Livermore National Laboratory, 191,
    259

Lobbies, 136, 141, 159–64, 228, 233
And Medicine, 219
And Wall Street, 177
Lockheed-Martin Corp., , 130
Los Alamos Facility, 259
Lowe, James, 222
Lowy, Michael, 155
Lukacs, Georg, 92
Lummis, Douglas, 20
Lutz, Catherine, 113, 114, 185

MacArthur, Gen. Douglas, 41
Machiavelli, Nicolo, 67, 70, 71
Macpherson, C. B., 9
Madison, James, 12
Madoff, Bernie, 176
Manhattan Project, 257–60, 263, 277
Manifest Destiny, 13, 15, 25, 31, 33, 39, 42, 57, 71, 77, 119, 239, 244, 247
Mann, Michael, 249–50
Marcuse, Herbert, 89, 121, 194, 241
Marshall Plan, 51
Marx, Karl, 2, 12, 20, 91, 92, 100, 131, 179
Mayo Clinic, 216
McCain, John, 154
McCarthyism, 40, 126, 187, 193, 194
McChesney, Robert, 146–47, 155–59
McConnell, Rich, 136
McDonaldization, 179, 182–83, 185, 208
McDonnell-Douglas Corp., 189
McDougall, Dr. John, 217
McGovern Report, 219–20
McKinley, William, 35, 63, 247
McKinney, Cynthia, 119
McNamara, Robert, 43, 269
Mearsheimer, John, 119
Media Oligarchy, 146–50
Medical-Industrial Complex, 223
Medicare Reform Act (2003), 213
Melman, Seymour, 13, 103, 105
Merck Corp., 209, 215
Mexico, 204
Michels, Robert, 2, 132, 141
Microsoft Corp., 137, 191

Middle East, 274
Military Keynesianism, 2, 106, 108
Military Tribunals, 128
Miller, Judith, 117
Mills, C. Wright, 3, 4, 6, 89, 92–95, 102–105, 133, 141, 144, 167–68, 187, 232–33, 236, 240–45, 248–49
Milner, Henry, 22
Milosevic, Slobodan, 45
Mineral Management Service (MMS), 169
"Mini-nukes," 270
Monroe Doctrine (1823), 31, 35, 58
Moore, Barrington, 11, 250
Moore, Michael, 99, 197
Morgan Stanley Corp., 137
Morris, Errol, 43
Mosca, Gaetano, 2, 131, 132
Moscow Treaty (2002), 270
Moss, Dr. Ralph, 216, 219
Muravchik, Joshua, 61, 62
Murdoch, Rupert, 158, 191, 241
Murray, Douglas, 73, 80
Mussolini's Italy, 248
"Mutually-Assured Destruction" (MAD), 264

Nader, Ralph, 133
Nagasaki, 38, 40, 257–60, 263
Nasser, Gamal Abdul, 266
National Academy of Sciences (NAS), 219
National Cancer Institute (NCI), 217
National Economic Council (NEC), 138
National Institutes of Health (NIH), 202, 210, 212, 220
National Labor Relations Board (NLRB), 185
National Security Act (1947), 261
National Security Agency (NSA), 83, 106, 122, 124, 129, 130, 150, 260
National Security Operations Center (NSOC), 129–30
National Security State (NSS), 120–28, 278

Native Americans, 247
NATO Alliance, 14, 15, 46, 54, 55, 76,
    107, 265
Navy SEALs, 127
Nazis (World War II), 52, 236
    And Nazi Model, 238, 249–50
Neoconservatives, 71–76, 80–84, 238
New Deal, 161, 163, 221, 229
New World Order, 62
Nichols, John, 158–59
9/11 Events, 58, 74, 75
Nixon, Richard, 199, 203, 216,
    261–62, 278
    And War on Cancer, 199
Noble, David, 194
No End in Sight, 87
North Korea, 266
Norton, Gail, 165
Novartis Corp., 207
Nuclearism, 264
Nuclear Non-Proliferation Treaty
    (NPT), 82, 84, 151, 264–68,
    270–71, 274–75
Nuclear Posture Review, 49, 266, 270,
    277
Nuclear Regulatory Commission
    (NRC), 165

Obama, Barack, 77, 78, 82, 84,
    136–37, 139, 142–44, 152, 166,
    169–71, 176, 251, 269–72, 275–77
Occupational Safety and Agency
    (OSHA), 97, 162
Operation Mongoose, 262
Oppenheimer, Robert, 261
Orszag, Peter, 138

Paine, Thomas, 2, 8, 9
Pakistan, 265, 276
    And NPT, 265
Palin, Sarah, 158, 246
Panama, 262
    And U.S. Invasion, 262
Parenti, Michael, 93, 94
Pareto, Vilfredo, 2, 132, 141
Patriot Act (USA), 74, 76, 124–26,
    128, 154, 237

Patriot System (weapons), 273
Pauling, Linus, 261
Paxson, Robert, 249
Pearl Harbor, 38, 39
Pelosi, Nancy, 136–37
Pentagon, 122, 124, 212, 260, 265,
    272, 277
    Contractors, 113
    Propaganda, 112
    R&D, 190–92
    And Spending, 107–10, 142, 154
    Strategy, 257, 271, 275
Perle, Richard, 73, 78, 79
Petraeus, Gen. David, 85
Pfizer Corp., 203, 207, 209, 211, 220,
    222
Philippines, 35
Phillips, Kevin, 3, 96
PhRMA (lobby), 212–13
Pipes, Daniel, 193
Plutocracy, 3
Political Action Committees (PACs),
    15, 136, 141, 148
Polk, James K., 8, 31
Pollack, Ron, 225
Posner, Eric, 72
Posse Comitatus Act (1878), 127
Price-Anderson Act (1957), 166
Private Military Contractors (PMCs),
    109, 110
Progressivism, 28, 29
Project for a New American Century
    (PNAC), 63, 116
Public Citizen, 141

Quadrennial Defense Review (2010),
    270

Radical democracy, 19
Radio Free Europe, 70
Rambo movies, 43, 61
Raytheon Corp., 130
Reagan, Ronald, 35, 75, 127, 142,
    160, 176, 191, 217, 229, 231,
    262, 271
    And Reagan Era, 233–34
Reid, Harry, 136–37, 173

Rendon Group, 117, 157
Renoir, Jean, 227
Revolution in Military Affairs (RMA), 108, 109
Rhee Sygmun, 52
Ridgeway, Gen. Matthew, 41
Ritter, Scott, 267
Ritzer, George, 182–83
Robbins, John, 200, 217–18
Rockefeller Legacy, 197
Rockefeller Medicine Men, 201
Rogin, Michael, 10, 32
Roosevelt, Franklin, 38, 163, 236
Roosevelt, Theodore, 33, 63
Rousseau, J. J., 12, 19
Rove, Karl, 61, 223
    And Crossroads GPS, 139
Rubin, Robert, 137–38, 171
Rumsfeld, Donald, 87, 108
Russia, 266, 269, 270–72, 276

Said, Edward, 150, 193
Sands, Philippe, 72
Savage, Charlie, 123
Scahill, Jeremy, 119
Scheer, Robert, 176
Schell, Jonathan, 275
Schlosser, Eric, 182–83
Schultz, George, 269
Schumer, Charles, 136, 173
Schumpeter, Joseph, 2, 9, 92
Scott, Tony, 131
Second International, 20
Security Exchange Commission (SEC), 173
Selznick, Philip, 163–65
Shell Oil Corp., 170
Shenkman, Rick, 16
Sicko, 197
Sierra Club, 169
Silicon Valley, 185
Silverstein, Ken, 109
Sinclair, Upton, 192
Sloan-Kettering Institute, 216
Social Darwinism, 9, 98, 186
Social Democracy, 254
Solomon, Norman, 152

Somoza, Anastasia, 36
Soviet Union, 255, 257, 259–61, 264
Stack, Admiral Harold, 37
Starbucks Corp., 183
State Capitalism, 102, 131
Steele, James, 200, 209
Stockpile Stewardship Program, 191
Strategic Air Command (SAC), 261
Strategic Arms Reduction Treaty (START), 270–71, 276–77
Strategic Defense Initiative (SDI), 271
Summers, Larry, 138
Superbomb, 257, 259
Supersize Me!, 208
Supreme Court (U.S.), 139–40, 278
Sweden, 21, 22, 254–55
    And Riksdag (parliament), 21
    And social democracy, 23, 24
Sweezy, Paul, 13

Taibbi, Matt, 138, 172
Takaki, Ron, 9, 33
Tauscher, Ellen, 276
Tauzin, Billy, 222
Taylorism (also Fordism), 178–80, 185
Tea Party, 16, 77, 138–45, 158, 177, 223, 226
Telecommunications Act (1996), 147, 237
Teller, Edward, 264
Tennessee Valley Authority (TVA), 163–65
Thompson, Loren, 113
Time-Warner Corp., 146
Totalitarianism, 242–45, 249
Truman, Harry, 41, 106, 121, 122, 130, 257–61
    And Truman Doctrine, 59, 261
Turkey, 153, 262

United Nations, 73, 74, 77, 79, 153, 274, 276
    And U.N. Charter, 153, 259, 268
Universal Declaration of Human Rights, 50

U.S. Constitution, 5, 26, 27, 28, 56,
    115, 121, 134, 236, 239, 248,
    250, 263, 278

Van Maanen, John, 184
Viacom Corp., 146
Vietnam War, 42–44, 116, 262, 265
Vioxx Disaster, 215–16

Wall Street, 135–38, 143, 166, 170–77,
    200, 213, 229
Wal-Mart, 99–100, 181–84
Walt, Stephen, 118
War Economy, 6, 14, 17, 102, 107
Warfare State (Cook), 105
Warner-Lambert Corp., 207
War on Cancer, 199
War Powers Act (1973), 123
Waxman, Henry, 153
Weapons of Mass Destruction (WMD),
    265, 266–68
Weber, Max, 2, 9, 92, 141
Well Point Corp., 225
Wells Fargo Corp., 171
Wertsch, Mary Edwards, 114–15,
    184–85
West, Cornell, 143–44

Whitman, Meg, 141
Wikileaks, 129
Williams, William Appleman, 13
Wills, Garry, 260–61, 263, 269
Wilson, Woodrow, 35, 36, 102
Wolf, Naomi, 235, 238–39,
    242, 246
Wolfe, Sidney, 206, 215
Wolin, Sheldon, 2, 3, 17–19, 27, 104,
    156–57, 239–48, 250–53
World Bank, 170
World Cancer Research Fund, 218
World Health Organization (WHO),
    198, 218
World Trade Organization (WTO),
    170, 213
World War I, 58, 102, 103, 227
World War II, 40, 41, 57, 104, 114,
    115, 232, 236, 239, 257–58, 260,
    263, 269
Wounded Knee, 33

Yoo, John, 72
Yugoslavia, 263, 272

Zinn, Howard, 11, 25, 26, 31, 236,
    258–59

.

9 781349 296767